Geomancy in Theory and Practice

Books on the Western Esoteric Tradition by Stephen Skinner

Agrippa's Fourth Book of Occult Philosophy (edited) – Askin, Ibis
Aleister Crowley's Astrology (edited) – Spearman, Ibis
Aleister Crowley's Four Books of Magick - Watkins
Ars Notoria (with Daniel Clark) – Golden Hoard, Llewellyn
Clavis or Key to the Mysteries of Magic (with Daniel Clark) – Golden Hoard, Llewellyn
Complete Magician's Tables – Golden Hoard, Llewellyn
Cunning Man's Grimoire (with David Rankine) – Golden Hoard
Dr John Dee 's Spiritual Diaries: the fully revised and corrected edition of *A True & Faithful Relation of what passed…between Dr John Dee…* – Golden Hoard
Geomancy in Theory & Practice – Golden Hoard, Llewellyn
Goetia of Dr Rudd: Liber Malorum Spirituum (with David Rankine) – Golden Hoard
Grimoire of Saint Cyprian: Clavis Inferni (with David Rankine) – Golden Hoard
Key to the Latin of Dr John Dee's Spiritual Diaries - Golden Hoard, Llewellyn
Keys to the Gateway of Magic (with David Rankine) – Golden Hoard
Magical Diaries of Aleister Crowley (edited) – Spearman, RedWheel Weiser
Michael Psellus 'On the Operation of Daimones' (edited) - Golden Hoard
Millennium Prophecies: Apocalypse 2000 – Carlton
Nostradamus (with Francis King) – Carlton
Oracle of Geomancy – Warner Destiny, Prism
Practical Angel Magic of Dr. Dee (with David Rankine) – Golden Hoard
Sacred Geometry – Gaia, Hamlyn, Sterling
Search for Abraxas (with Nevill Drury) – Spearman, Salamander, Golden Hoard
Sepher Raziel: Liber Salomonis (with Don Karr) – Golden Hoard, Llewellyn
Splendor Solis (with Rafal Prinke, Joscelyn Godwin & G Hedesan) - Watkins
Techniques of Graeco-Egyptian Magic – Golden Hoard, Llewellyn
Techniques of High Magic (with Francis King) – C. W. Daniels, Golden Hoard
Techniques of Solomonic Magic – Golden Hoard, Llewellyn
Terrestrial Astrology: Divination by Geomancy – Routledge
Veritable Key of Solomon (with David Rankine) – Golden Hoard, Llewellyn

Books on Feng Shui by Stephen Skinner

Advanced Flying Star Feng Shui – Golden Hoard
Feng Shui Before & After - Haldane Mason, Tuttle
Feng Shui History: the Story of Classical Feng Shui in China & the West – Golden Hoard
Feng Shui Style - Periplus
Feng Shui the Traditional Oriental Way - Haldane Mason, Parragon
Feng Shui: the Living Earth Manual - Tuttle
Flying Star Feng Shui - Tuttle
Guide to the Feng Shui Compass – Golden Hoard
K.I.S.S. Guide to Feng Shui (Keep it Simple Series) – Penguin, DK
Key San He Feng Shui Formulae – Golden Hoard
Living Earth Manual of Feng Shui – RKP, Penguin, Arkana
Mountain Dragon – Golden Hoard
Original Eight Mansion Formula – Golden Hoard
Practical Makeovers Using Feng Shui – Haldane Mason, Tuttle
Water Dragon – Golden Hoard

Geomancy

in Theory and Practice

the most complete history of
Western divinatory geomancy in English

by Dr. Stephen Skinner

GOLDEN HOARD PRESS
2020

Published by
Golden Hoard Press
PO Box 1073
Robinson Road PO
Singapore 902123

www.GoldenHoard.com

Third Edition (Paperback)

Expanded from the book previously published by Routledge Kegan Paul entitled *Terrestrial Astrology: Divination by Geomancy*

ISBN 978-1912212-27-9

Printed in Malaysia

"Everlasting glory, continual and abiding prosperity, constant power, supreme peace, perpetual well-being, increasing good fortune, favourable fate, a comfortable manner of life, a long unimpaired life, complete honour, a pure manner of life, sufficient satisfaction, peace of mind, blessing, compassion, support and success."

[The benefits of decisions based on rightly applied geomancy.]

- Arabic inscription on the back of the *raml* machine dating from 1241.[1]

[1] See Plate VIII.

Contents

LIST OF PLATES

LIST OF FIGURES

Acknowledgments

To the memory of Helene Hodge who had the idea of writing an up-to-date manual on geomancy, and who then pestered me till I revised this second edition. My thanks to Beverley Lawton and Christine Galea who originally undertook the task of typing it. My thanks to the staff of the British Library, Museum of Mankind, Warburg Institute and the School of Oriental and African Studies, London University for helping in so many ways. My thanks especially to the late Dr Nicholas Tereshchenko, who assisted with translations from French, the late Dr Donald Laycock for linguistic help, and Abdurahman ben Yahya who helped with Arabic sources. Lastly my thanks to Zoe Low of Johor Bahru who worked on transferring and editing the text from the first edition into its present format.

The author and publishers are grateful for the following permissions originally granted to reproduce illustrations:

Éditions Bordas, Dunod, Gautheir-Villars, Paris, for Figure 5, Figure 8 and Figure 9 (from manuscripts in the Bibliothèque Nationale);

Biblioteca Medicea-Laurenziana, Florence, for Figure 22;

The British Library, London, for Figure 23, Figure 24, Figure 28, Plate I, Plate XI and Plate XIV;

Askin Publishers, London, for Figure 25;

The Bodleian Library, Oxford, for Figure 27;

B.P. Grimaud, Paris, for Figure 34;

The Lowie Museum of Anthropology, University of California, Berkeley, for Plates II - IV, from William Bascom, *Ifa Divination* (Indiana University Press, 1969);

Presses Universitaires de France for Plate V, from Andre Caquot and Marcel Leibovici, *La Divination* (1968);

Colin Washington, a present day Babalawo, for Plate VI and Plate VII;

The British Museum for Plate VIII & IX (and for Plate X, from Savage-Smith, *Islamic Geomancy and a 13th Century Divinatory Device,* 1980) all photographs of a thirteenth century Islamic geomancy machine;

Biblioteka Jagiellonska, for Plate XV and Plate XVI as reproduced in Benedek Láng, *Unlocked Books*, Pennsylvania: PSU, 2008;

Les Enluminures for Plate XII and Plate XIII from MS 396 previously from the Montefiore Library; and Jamie Barras for Plate VIII.

Author's Note on the Word 'Geomancy'

The word 'geomancy' covers three completely distinct subject areas.

1. The original use of the word, was solely for divinatory geomancy, a technique which used sixteen binary figures composed of dots to foretell the future. These figures were derived from ninth century Islamic sand divination.

2. In 1880s 'geomancy' was used by a missionary in China as a translation for the completely different and unrelated subject of *feng shui* (which concerns the interrelation of man, his buildings and tombs with the life force, or *ch'i*, which flows through his environment). Feng shui is a Chinese practice that dates back more than two thousand years to before the Chin (Qin) Dynasty, and has nothing to do with divinatory geomancy.

3. In the last few decades of the twentieth century 'geomancy' was also applied to the study of megalithic alignments and ley lines in the UK and Europe, and was often used to describe the application of sacred geometry to these structures. This third usage is a recent imposition of the term.

These three applications of the word have been applied to completely unrelated practices, which spring from completely different cultures, with *no* historical linkages. The sole exception to this lies on the island of Madagascar where Chinese 'geomancy' was mixed with the Islamic geomancy brought down to that island by Arab traders. Despite New Age attempts to link them, their only connection is the use and misuse of the term 'geomancy.'

This book is concerned *solely* with the original geomancy, Islamic, African and European divinatory geomancy. See the page facing the title page for other works by the present author on both feng shui and sacred geometry, in which these other 'geomancies' are adequately explained.

Introduction to the Second Edition

The year 2008 was a most significant year for geomancy, because, after a long period of being almost totally ignored by the academic community, that year saw the simultaneous publication of three volumes which significantly moved forward the study of geomancy. One of these books was the present volume, which for the first time tied together the history of geomancy and its spread from the Islamic world to tropical Africa, and both Greek and Latin speaking Europe. Although a number of studies had been done on separate areas, like Madagascar or Medieval Europe, no one study had actually tied it all together. The second significant advance was the research done by Thérèse Charmasson on documenting the Medieval Latin manuscripts of geomancy.[1] I realise in retrospect that we were probably both sitting in the same libraries, reading the same manuscripts, at the same time, but were not aware of each other. The third significant contribution was that of Emilie Savage-Smith and Marion Smith who published their *Islamic Geomancy and a Thirteenth-Century Divinatory Device* also in 1980. Although they were studying a device, its date of 1241/2 pre-dates that of almost all Arabic manuscript sources, and it is therefore most significant for the study of the source of Islamic geomancy.

Apart from those advances there has been a popular resurgence of interest in the subject in the last three decades which has resulted in a number of books which concentrate on practice rather than the history. The best of these is by John Michael Greer.[2] Sadly there have been a lot of 'cut and paste' books on geomancy produced in the last two decades, in English, French and Spanish, and some of which contain some amazing confusions, with feng shui being dragged in as a relative of, or even as the 'source' of geomancy: something that is patently not true.

I feel I can say with some degree of authority, and total certainty, that geomancy and feng shui are totally unrelated, because I have spent 35 years researching both, and have also practicing feng shui in Asia, resulting in the publication of what (in any European language) is the most comprehensive documentation of feng shui's history and the structure of its primary

[1] Charmasson, *Recherches sur une Technique Divinatoire: la Géomancy dans L'Occident Médiéval,* Droz, Geneve, 1980.
[2] Greer (2009).

instrument, the *lo p'an*.[1] Because of this, I feel sure that I would have noticed any connections between these two subjects, if there was any.

My greatest regret about the first edition of this book was allowing the publisher to entitle it *Terrestrial Astrology*. Not only was that a misnomer, but a whole generation of readers overlooked it when searching for a book on geomancy. The publisher was of the opinion that nobody had heard of geomancy, and that by using that title, rather than my original title *Divinatory Geomancy*, he would capture a wider range of readers. In the even he was sadly wrong, for anyone looking for a book on geomancy would have overlooked it, and anyone picking up this book in the hope of learning astrology would have been woefully disappointed. Now re-titled and considerably expanded, it has finally been republished under a title that actually reflects its subject.

More recently it has come to my notice that the *Ifa* divination chains, which rely upon the figure of geomancy for their interpretation, were in use in ancient Egypt. The discovery of The Egyptian origin of the *Ifa* chain in a girdle of Princess Sithathor of Egypt, Middle kingdom 12th dynasty (1887-1813 BC) puts the invention of geomancy back from the 9th century to 4000 years ago. The archaeologist who discovered it assumed it was a girl's belt, although it didn't have a clasp. But with 8 gold cowries connected by a chain it has got to be the forefather of the *Ifa* chain (see Plate III).

- Stephen Skinner
Singapore,
September 2020

[1] Skinner, *Guide to the Feng Shui Compass: a Compendium of Classical Feng Shui,* Golden Hoard Press, Singapore, 2008.

Plate I: A Royal geomancy on vellum, showing the figures of Populus (top) and Via (bottom), with their astrological correspondences in tabular form to the right: *Presentum geomancie libellum,* one of the astrological geomancies compiled for King Richard II in March 1391.[1]

[1] British Library Royal MS 12.C.v, f. 23v. See also Figure 23.

Plate IIa: The divining tray being used to mark a figure. The sixteen palm nuts are in the left hand of the diviner and the tray is covered with wood termite dust.

Plate IIb: A typical round wooden Yoruba *Ifa* divining tray.

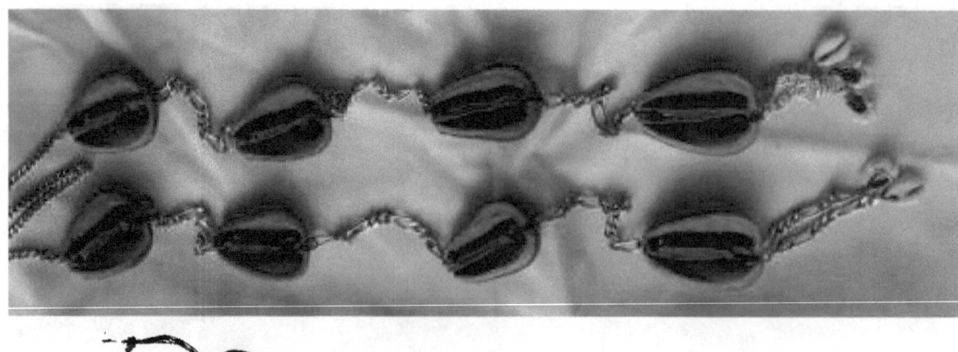

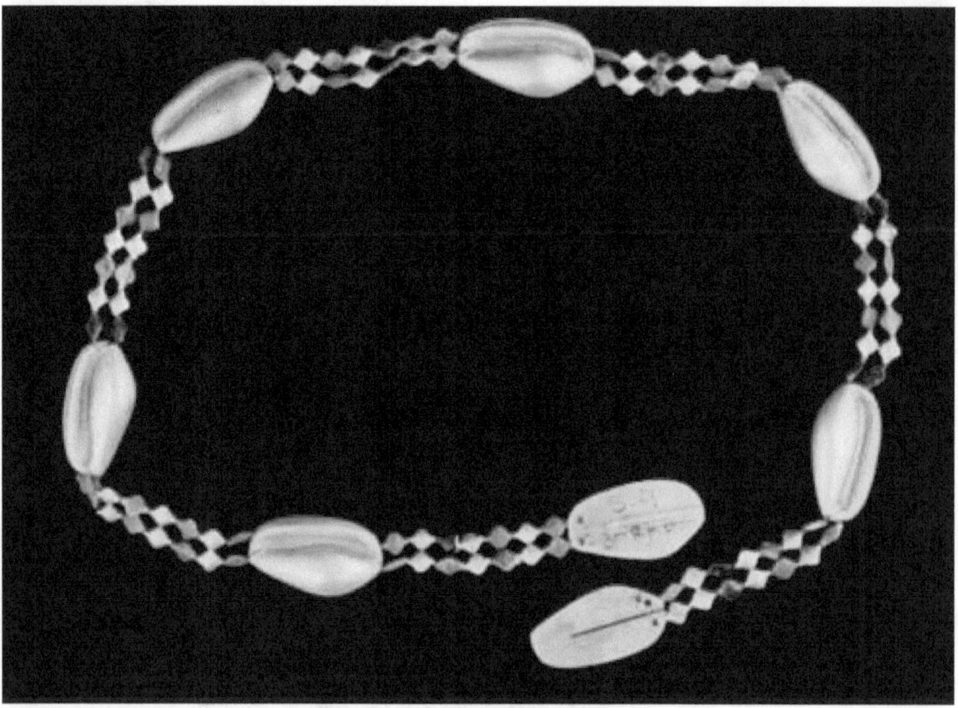

Plate III: *Ifa* divining chains and their ancient Egyptian origin. Top: Two *Ifa* divining chain made of *ọpẹlẹ* pods and brass chain with cowries showing the geomantic figure Ọṣẹ-Ofun. Bottom: The Egyptian origin of the *Ifa* chain: a girdle of Princess Sithathor of Egypt, Middle kingdom 12th dynasty (1887-1813 BC).

Plate IV: An *ifa* divining tray with the face of Eshu at the top (right), and a set of sixteen palm nuts ready for divination.

Plate V: The figure *adabara* (Fortuna Major) obtained by sikidy and carved on a stone roadside marker to enhance the prosperity of a village in Madagascar.

Plate VI: A modern Lukumi Awo Babalawo, Colin Washington, manipulating the *ọpẹlẹ* chain and performing *ifa* divination.

Plate VII: Modern *ọpẹlẹ* chains. The *ọpẹlẹ* are the Babalawo's divining chain. The right one is made of traditional seeds that have been passed through the digestive tract of an elephant. The one on the left is a Cuban variety which has had the concave sides painted white. In Sierra Leone these were often made of stones taken from the stomach of an alligator.

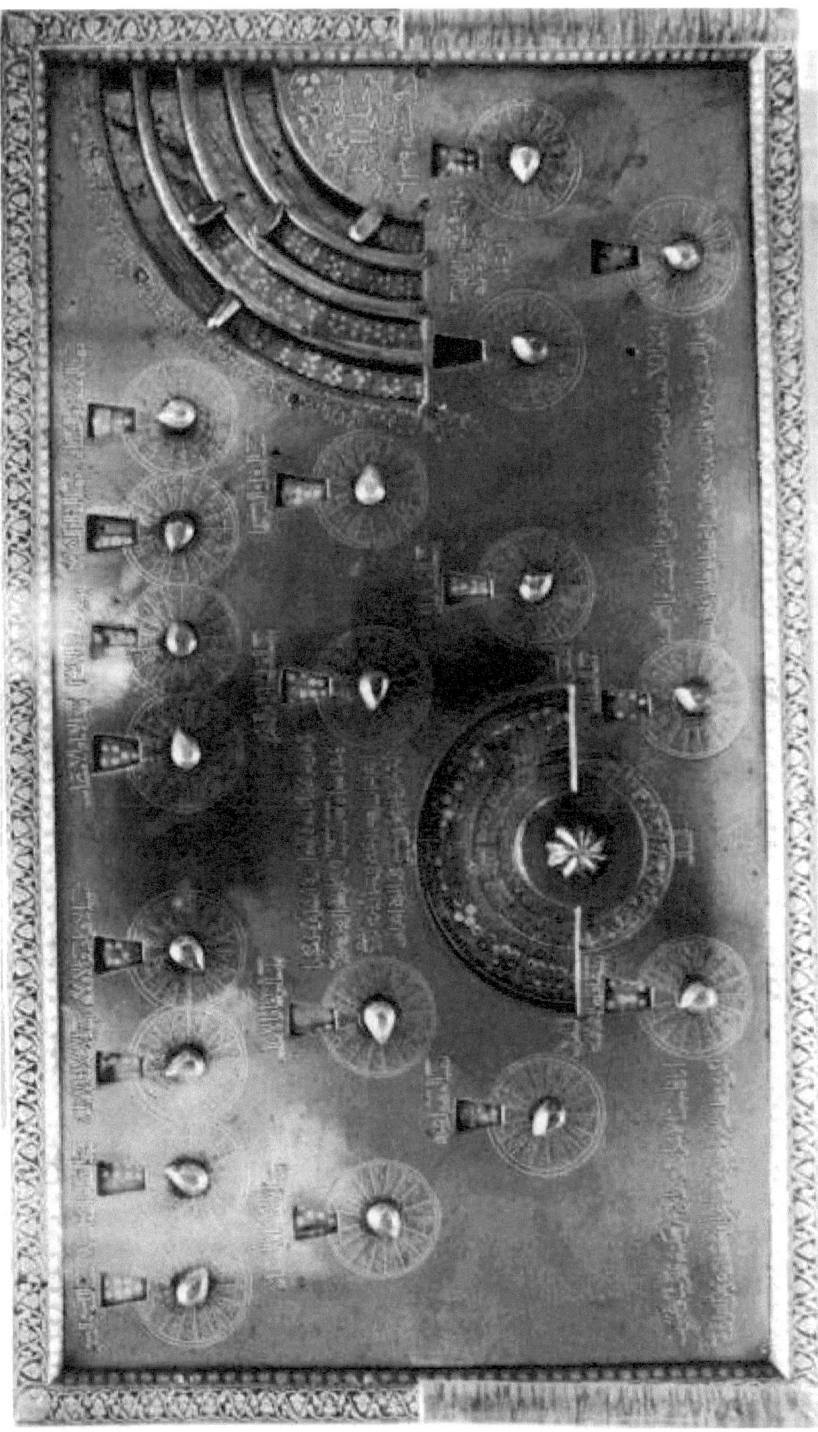

Plate VIII: An Islamic geomancy *raml*/geomancy machine manufactured in 1241-2 in Egypt (or Mosul or Damascus), by Muhammad ibn Khutlukh al Mawsuli.

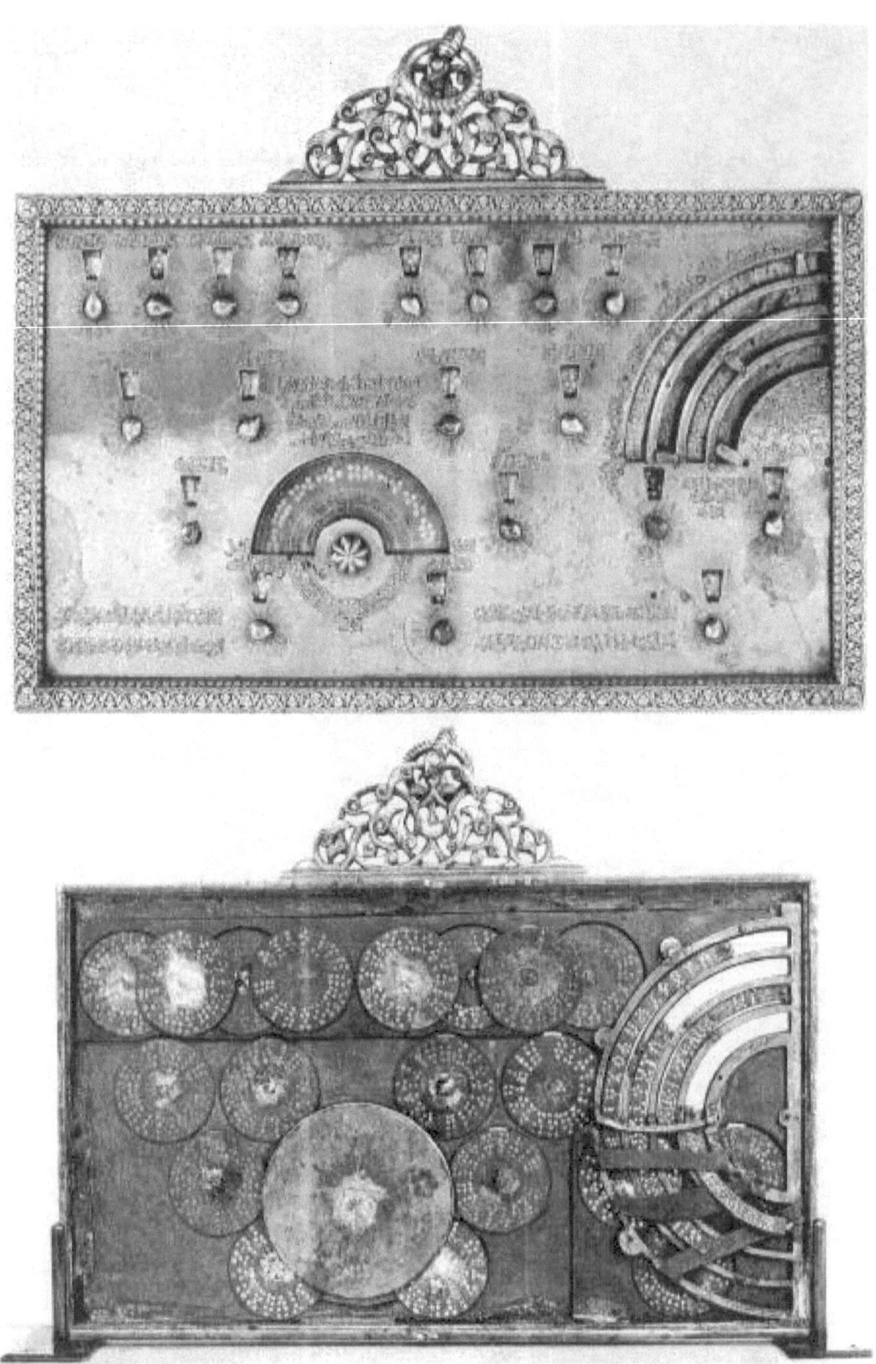

Plate IX: Inner workings of the Islamic geomancy *raml* machine, from its back (picture left-right reversed so that its inner workings can be related to its front). On the right are the arc slides used to generate the 4 Mothers. The 19 small discs show geomantic figures through apertures on the front (16 parts of the spread, plus three calculator discs. The large disk shows the seasonal and lunar Mansion data.

Plate X: Enlargement of the right side of the dial of the Islamic geomancy machine. The four arc-shaped 'windows' are finger slides which are used to generate the 4 Mothers (*unnahāt*). Each slide has all the geomantic figures marked on in the order of a particular *taskin*. In this enlargement, seven and a half of the 19 small dials show. Each dial has a window showing one figure, and simultaneously points to the name of the figure in Kufic script, using standard Arabic names as shown in Appendix V, column G7. At the top left are two and half Mothers, below which are one Nephew, and the right Witness. Beneath the 4 arc slides are three 'calculator dials.'

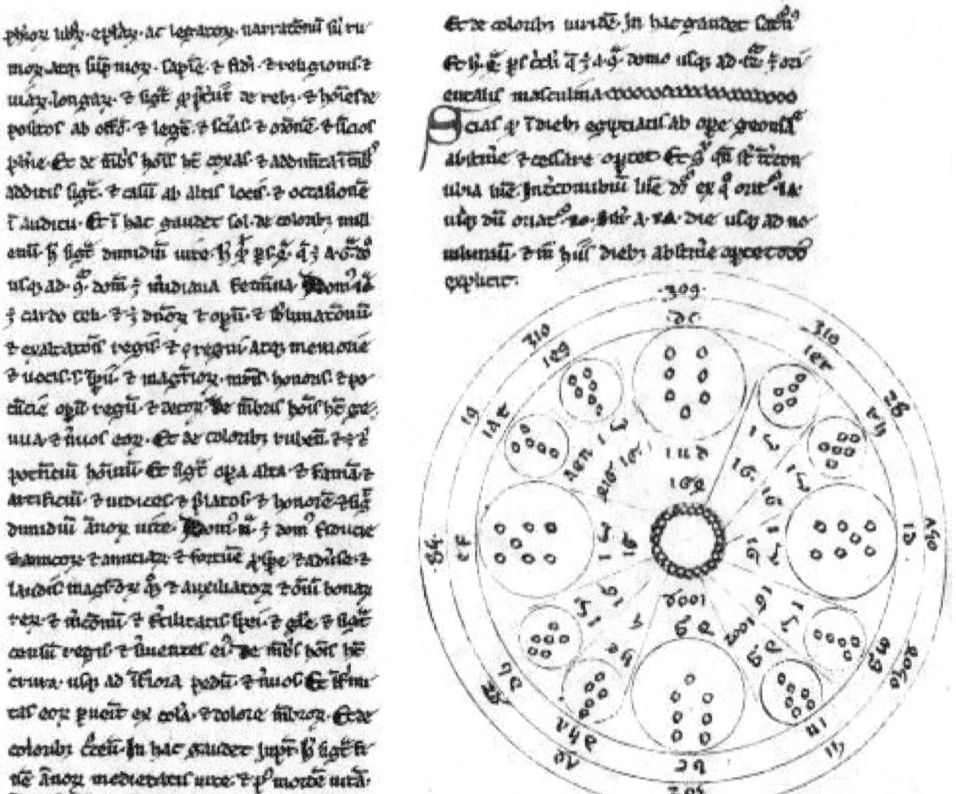

Plate XI: Hugh of Santalla's *Ars Geomantia,* probably the first Latin geomancy.[1]

[1] Florence Laurentiana MS Plut. 30.c.29, f.xxv.

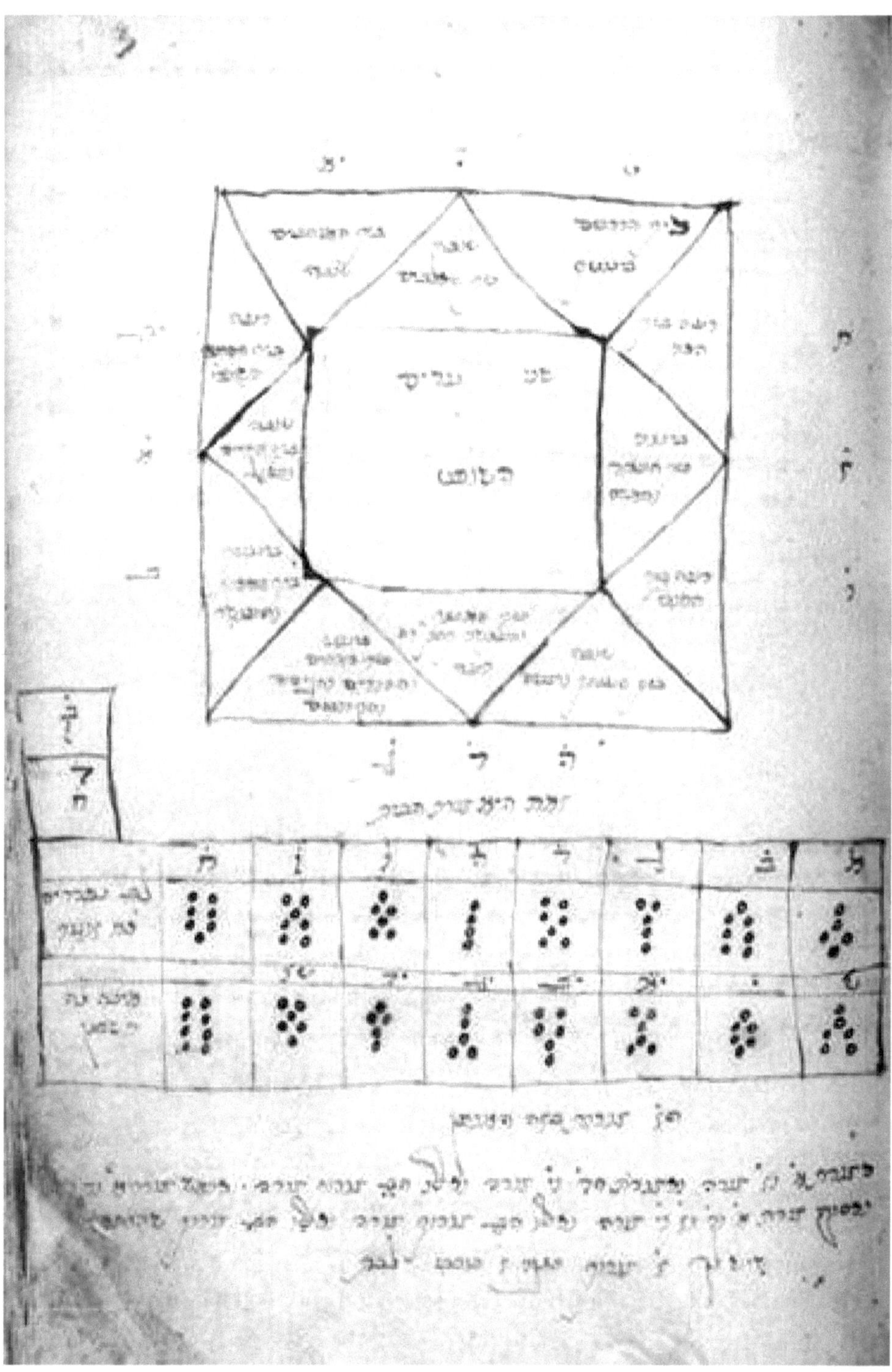

Plate XII: Abraham ibn Ezra's cursive Hebrew geomancy, showing the sixteen geomantic figures, with each pair related to a Hebrew letter, plus a horoscope, f. 3.

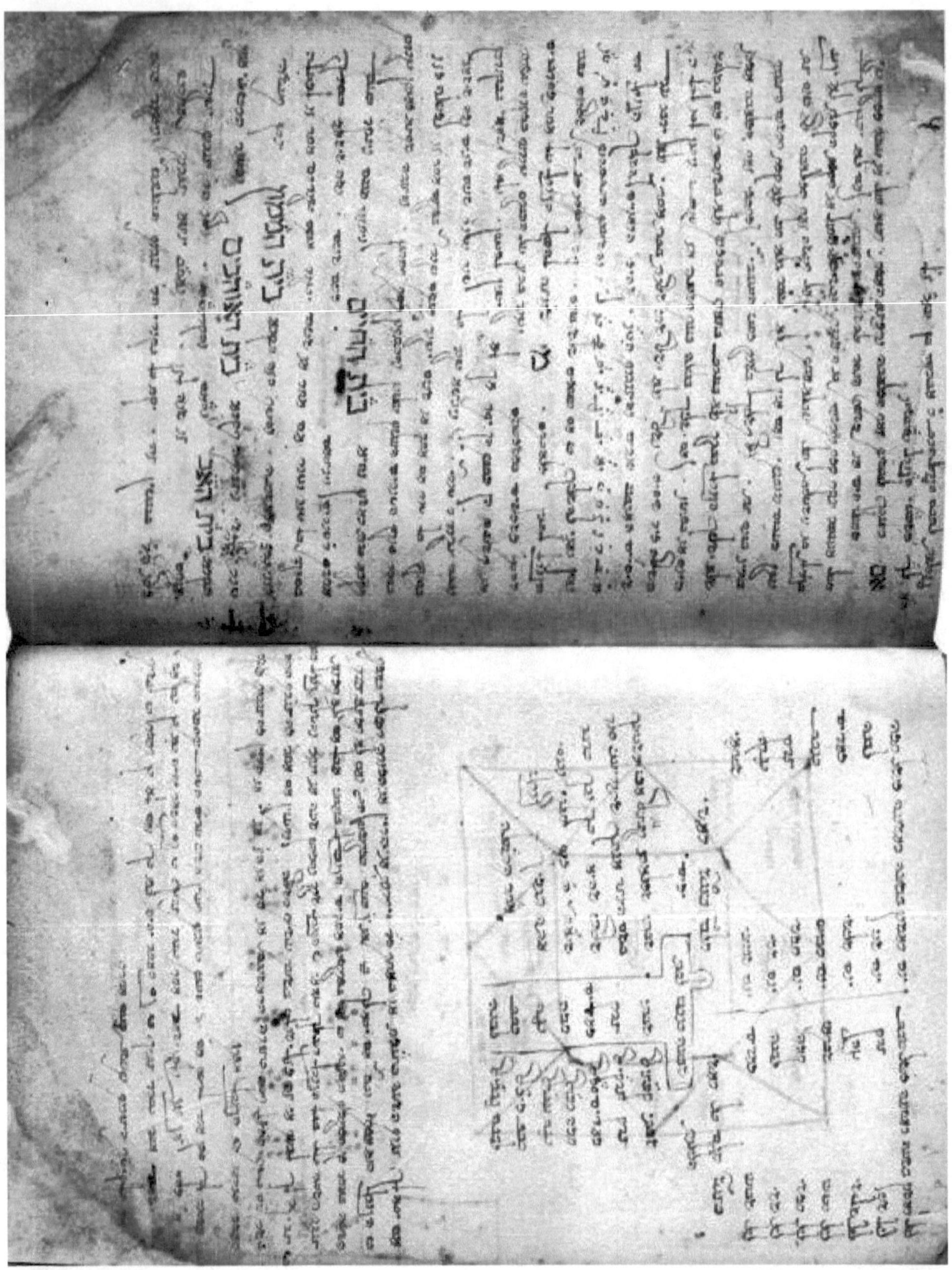

Plate XIII: Geomancy of Abraham ibn Ezra (1089-1164) showing the geomantic House names, like 'Beit ha-Chiim' (House of Life) and 'Beit ha-Avhkim,' on f. 4.

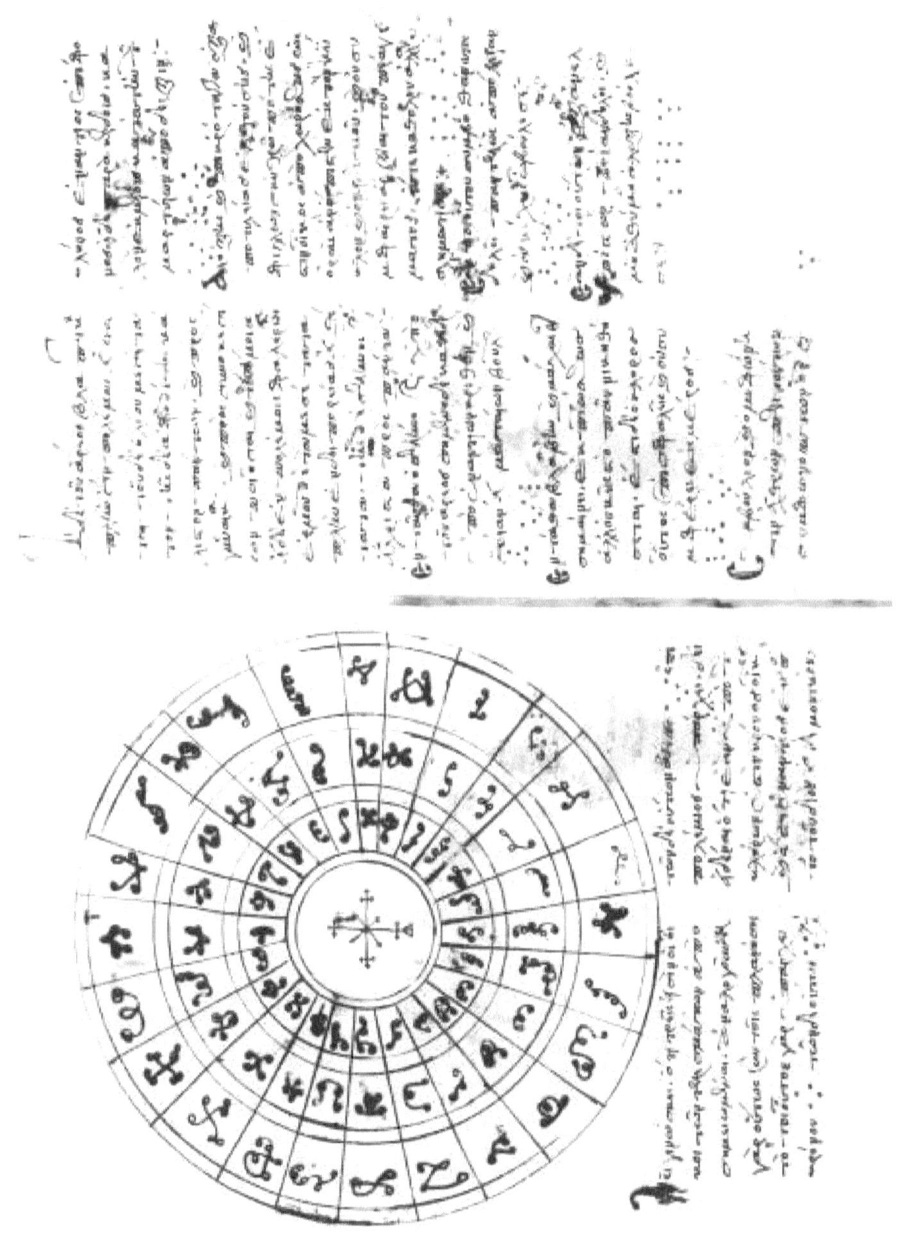

Plate XIV: A 15th century Greek geomancy containing geomantic sigils. This manuscript also contains one of the most complete copies of the *Magical Treatise of Solomon* or *Hygromanteia.*[1]

[1] Harley MS 5596, f. 3v-4. See Ioannis Marathakis, *The Magical Treatise of Solomon or Hygromanteia,* Golden Hoard Press, Singapore, 2011, for more detail of this manuscript.

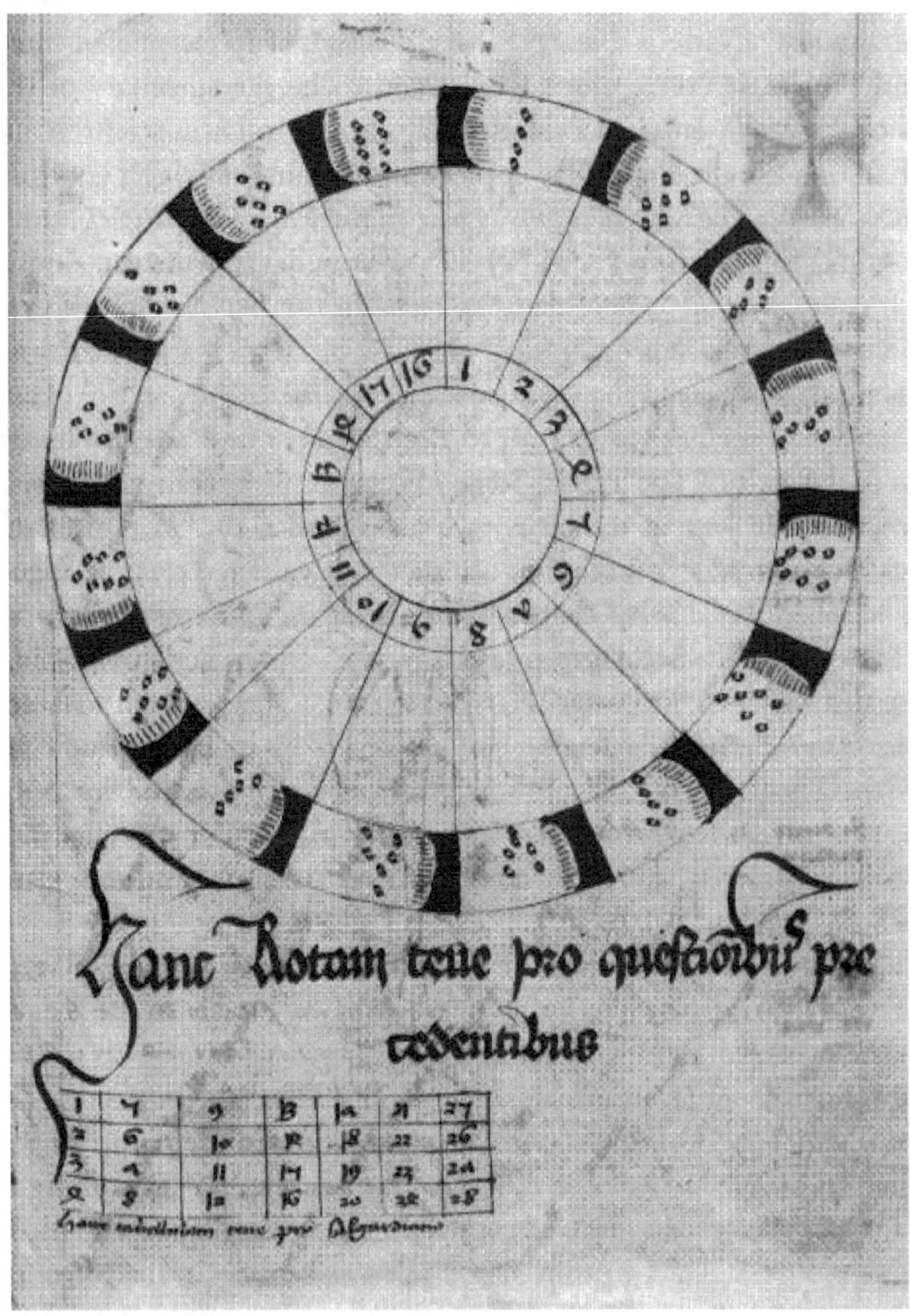

Plate XV: Geomancy wheel (*rotam*) for answering previously prepared questions, with a table of the 28 Mansions of the Moon below, from Socrates Basileus' *Prognostica*, which is primarily a 'lot book' rather than a geomancy.[1]

[1] MS Kracow BJ 793, f. 67.

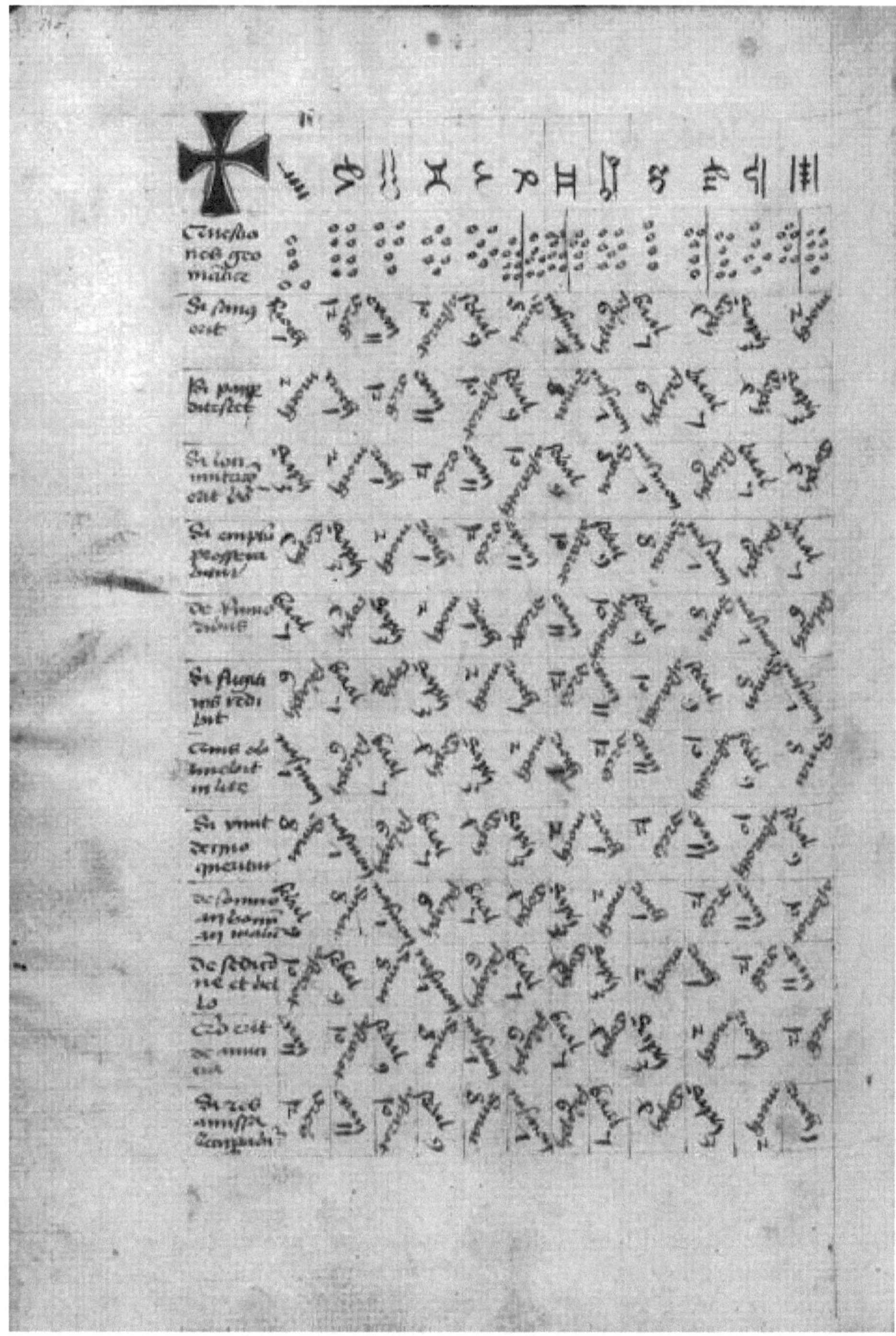

Plate XVI: Table showing the attribution of the geomantic figures to the zodiacal Signs (across the top, from Sagittarius to Scorpio) and the corresponding answers (shown diagonally) from Socrates Basileus' *Prognostica,* MS Kracow BJ 793, f. 71v.

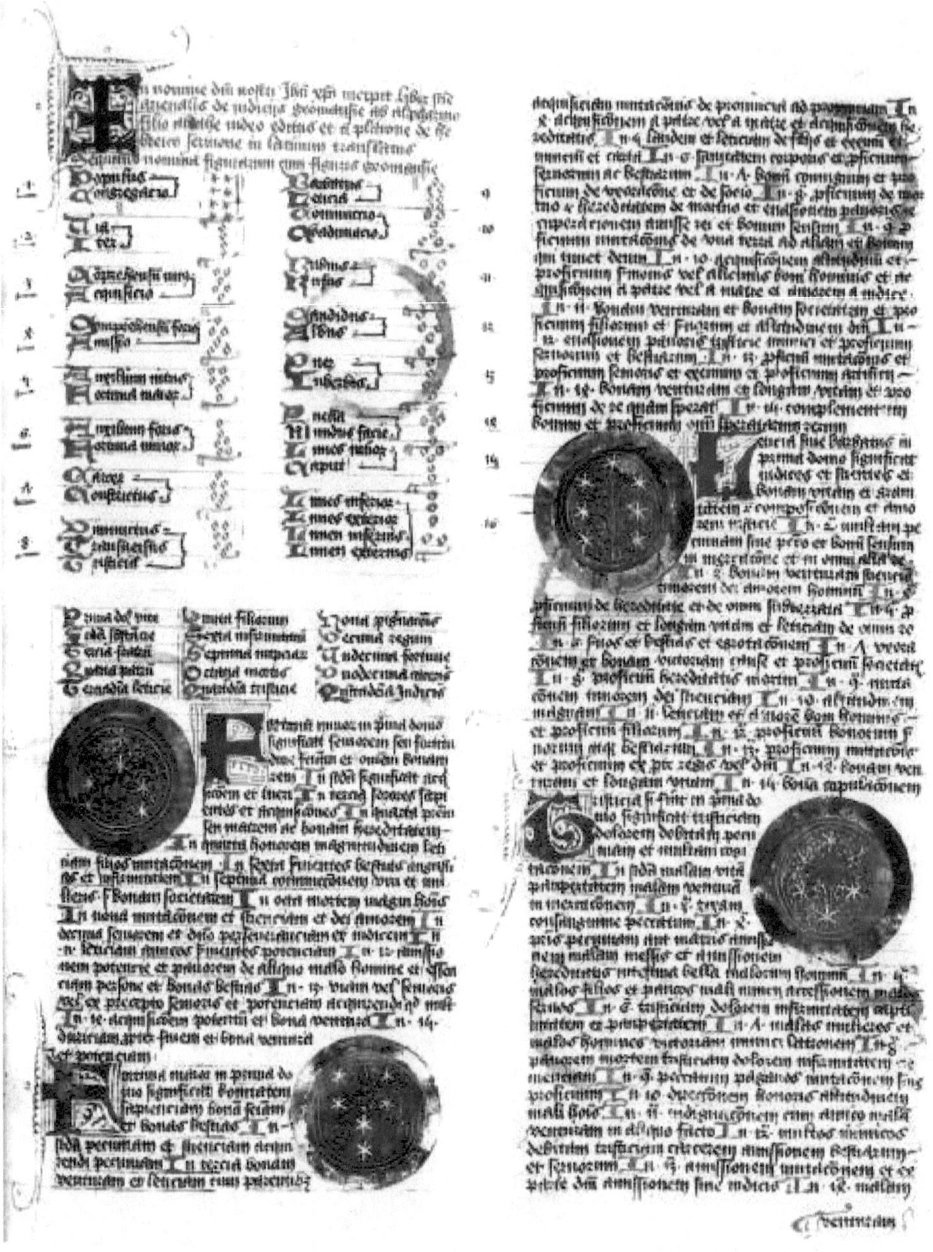

Plate XVII: Illuminated Latin vellum geomancy by Plato of Tivoli from 14th-15th century. Note the panel with 16 geomantic figures clearly listed (upper left) and the four roundels bearing the geomantic figures Fortuna Minor, Fortuna Major (left), Laetitia and Carcer (right) but using the earlier Latin names such as are shown in Table G34 in Appendix V.[1]

[1] British Library Arundel MS 66, f. 269.

Introduction

This book is about divination by earth: it is a book of the art of geo-mancy. The *New English Dictionary* defines geomancy as 'divination by means of lines, figures or dots on the earth or on paper, or by particles of earth cast on the ground.' The word is derived from two Greek words, γαια or γη *(gaia* or *gé)* meaning the earth, and μαντεια *(manteia)* meaning divination.

The techniques of geomancy are many and varied. Although in popular accounts these include the inspection of random configurations made by scattered pebbles, or the manipulation of handfuls of earth (rather like tea-leaf reading), in practice geomancy is a lot more structured. The casting of palm nuts or seeds, the use of divining chains, or the making of marks apparently haphazardly in the ground with a stick, all relay upon a precise binary arithmetic. Divination by marking the earth in due course developed into the interpretation of lines or dots made more or less haphazardly on paper with a pen or pencil.

Divinatory geomancy has its roots in Arabic sand divination, which spread also in various guises as African divinatory systems along with the spread of Islam. On the West Coast it manifested as *ifa* and *fa,* and in Madagascar as *sikidy.* It also moved north into Europe, and across the Atlantic to North and Central America. The first chapter considers this history in outline, while the subsequent chapters consider the varying techniques of interpretation as they manifested in each area in detail.

Geomancy has come to be one of the three or four great European methods of divination, like the tarot or astrology. It is also the most easily apprehended of the four theoretical elemental modes of divination: pyromancy (divination by fire), hydromancy (by water), aeromancy (by air) and geomancy (by earth).

Geomancy could be defined as the art of obtaining insight into the present or future by observing the combinations of patterns made in the earth or on paper by a diviner allowing his intuition, or 'the spirits of the earth,' to control the movement of his hand or pencil. To become familiar with the basic practice of geomancy let us try a very simple geomantic divination, using paper and pencil.

First formulate a question and write it at the top of the paper. Place the paper at arm's length. Then, with eyes half closed and thinking only of the question, make a line of random dots, making as many dots as you feel inclined in each line. Repeat this procedure four times, so that you generate four lines of dots.

Fortuna Major – great fortune
○ ○
○ ○
○
○

Fortuna Minor – lesser fortune
○
○
○ ○
○ ○

Via – the way
○
○
○
○

Populus – people
○ ○
○ ○
○ ○
○ ○

Acquisitio – acquisition
○ ○
○
○ ○
○

Laetitia – joy
○
○ ○
○ ○
○ ○

Puella – girl
○
○ ○
○
○

Amissio – loss
○
○ ○
○
○ ○

Conjunctio – conjunction
○ ○
○
○
○ ○

Albus – white
○ ○
○ ○
○
○ ○

Puer – boy
○
○
○ ○
○

Rubeus – red
○ ○
○
○ ○
○ ○

Carcer – prison
○
○ ○
○ ○
○

Tristitia – sorrow
○ ○
○ ○
○ ○
○

Caput Draconis – head of the Dragon
○ ○
○
○
○

Cauda Draconis – tail of the Dragon
○
○
○
○ ○

Figure 1: The geomantic figures and their basic meanings.

Next, mark off the dots you have made in each line, a pair at a time. Take each line in turn and you will be left with either one or two dots.

o if there is an odd number of dots.

o o if there is an even number of dots.

Starting with the first line, transcribe the one or two dots remaining. Below this, mark the one or two remaining dots of the second line. Do the same with the third and fourth lines. You have now created a geomantic figure (see Figure 1 for the sixteen possible figures).

Somewhere in the sixteen possible combinations in that Figure will be the geomantic figure you have generated. Look it up and read off the answer to your question.

This simple operation may be extended by producing four such figures which are referred to as Mother figures. From these, by a form of lateral addition, are produced a further dozen figures. The final or Judge figure derived from them by mechanical means, gives the answer. In Part Two this practical technique is explained in detail, together with its astrological amplification. Here it is sufficient to grasp the basic technique so that the historical chapters that follow make sense.

The performance of casting the figures may well remind the reader of the coin and yarrow stalk systems of establishing the hexagram for *I Ching* divination. The mechanics are less complicated, but the system is the same. The binary mathematics which govern both the 64 (2^6) hexagrams of the *I Ching* and the 16 (2^4) figures of geomancy are the basis of the physical work of both divinatory systems. In this century when computers now make many of man's economic, political and commercial forecasts, it is easy to forget that these machines work on the same simple principles of binary mathematics as the infinitely more ancient machines of the *I Ching* and geomancy.

It is interesting to note that Leibniz (1646-1716) who is the father of modern binary mathematics and the algebra of classes, drew some of his inspiration from the Jesuit translations of the *I Ching* which were just beginning to reach Europe in his lifetime, and may well have been familiar with Flacourt's work on *sikidy,* the geomancy of Madagascar, which was published in Paris in 1661.

It might seem as if geomancy provides a very simple set of meanings with which to discover the answer to *any* question, but these are just the beginning, useful for getting quick answers to simple questions. The *modus operandi* described above is a very simplified version of geomantic practice, but adequate to introduce geomancy and its figures.

Having outlined *divinatory* geomancy in its original form, it is worthwhile to consider briefly the more recent applications of the word to *telluric* geomancy. When the Chinese science of divining the presence of the subtle currents in the earth and their effect on man was first investigated by Europeans, the Chinese term *feng-shui* was translated 'geomancy.' Certainly *feng-shui* was concerned with the earth, but the appropriation of a word which applied to a divinatory technique to describe this practice was rather confusing. Around 1870 writers on the then strange art of *feng-shui* began to call it 'geomancy' for want of a better name, falsely connecting it with the system of divination which is completely different from the Chinese practice. 'Topomancy' or even 'geoscopy' might have been a much better translation of *feng-shui,* the art of discovering 'dragon veins,' the subtle telluric currents of *ch'i* which for the Chinese determined the propitiousness of any particular site for building or burying. Stephan Feuchtwang, who has written one of the most comprehensive works on *feng-shui* in English, says:

> 'I draw attention to the fact that Chinese geomancy would be defined more accurately as topomancy. It is not divination by means of an earth or sand tray, which is the most common type of divination to be described as geomancy.'[1]

However, as we have now been stuck with the name for just over a century, 'geomancy' has come to describe both dot-divination and *feng-shui.*

However, once *feng-shui* began to be known more popularly in the West, the hardworked term 'geomancy' was applied to yet another study. Exponents of the ley-line theory, noticing superficial similarities between ley-lines and dragon lines, christened their own work 'geomancy.' There is however a world of difference between Alfred Watkin's old 'straight tracks' connecting sites in England apparently on the same ley-line, and the sinuous coilings of the dragon veins of *feng-shui.* Nevertheless 'geomancy' acquired yet another meaning.[2]

Finally there is a brief mention in Henry Cornelius Agrippa of divination by physical earth movements:

> 'The first, therefore, is Geomancy, which foreshows future things by the motions of the earth, as also the noise, the swelling, the trembling, the chops, the pits, and exhalation, and other impressions thereof, the art of which

[1] Stephan Feuchtwang, *Anthropological Analysis of Chinese Geomancy,* Vithagna, Vientiane, 1974, p. 224.

[2] See Stephen Skinner, *Sacred Geometry*, Gaia Books, London, 2003.

Almadel, the Arabian, sets forth.'[1]

Polydore Virgil ascribes this type of geomancy to the Persian Magi.[2] Livy also wrote at length about the meaning of earthquakes and their effect on the destiny of Rome, referring their cause to the goddesses Ceres and Libera, and the god Liber. This fourth use of the word, despite the observations of Diodorus Siculus or 'Almadel the Arabian,' partakes more of seismography or omenology than geomancy. It is interesting however that this Roman writer attributes geomancy to the Arabs, the actual source of geomancy. By attributing it to 'Almadel' he implicitly associates it with Arab magic.

'Geomancy' has come therefore to have several meanings. We have

i) a system derived from Arabic sand divination, which developed into African systems of divination by earth, nuts and beads, and into mediaeval divination by binary mathematics north of the Arab world;

ii) an independent Chinese method for determining the location of dragon veins in the earth;[3]

iii) ley-line theories coupled with the interpretation of the siting of Megalithic monuments; not to mention

iv) omens derived from seismography.

In this book we will treat only of the first variety, being various systems of *divinatory* geomancy.

The geographical dispersion of belief in both *divinatory* and *telluric* geomancy is shown in Figure 2 to clarify how different are their very origins, provenance and extent. This map will also serve to elucidate the next chapter.

---

[1] *De Occulta Philosophia,* Book I, chapter LVII.

[2] *De invent. rer.,* Book I, chapter XXIII.

[3] See Stephen Skinner, *Flying Star Feng Shui,* Tuttle, Boston, 2003 and Skinner, *Living Earth Manual of Feng Shui,* Penguin/RKP, London, 1977. For a technical treatment and history see Skinner, *Guide to the Feng Shui Compass: a Compendium of Classical Feng Shui,* Golden Hoard, Singapore, 2008.

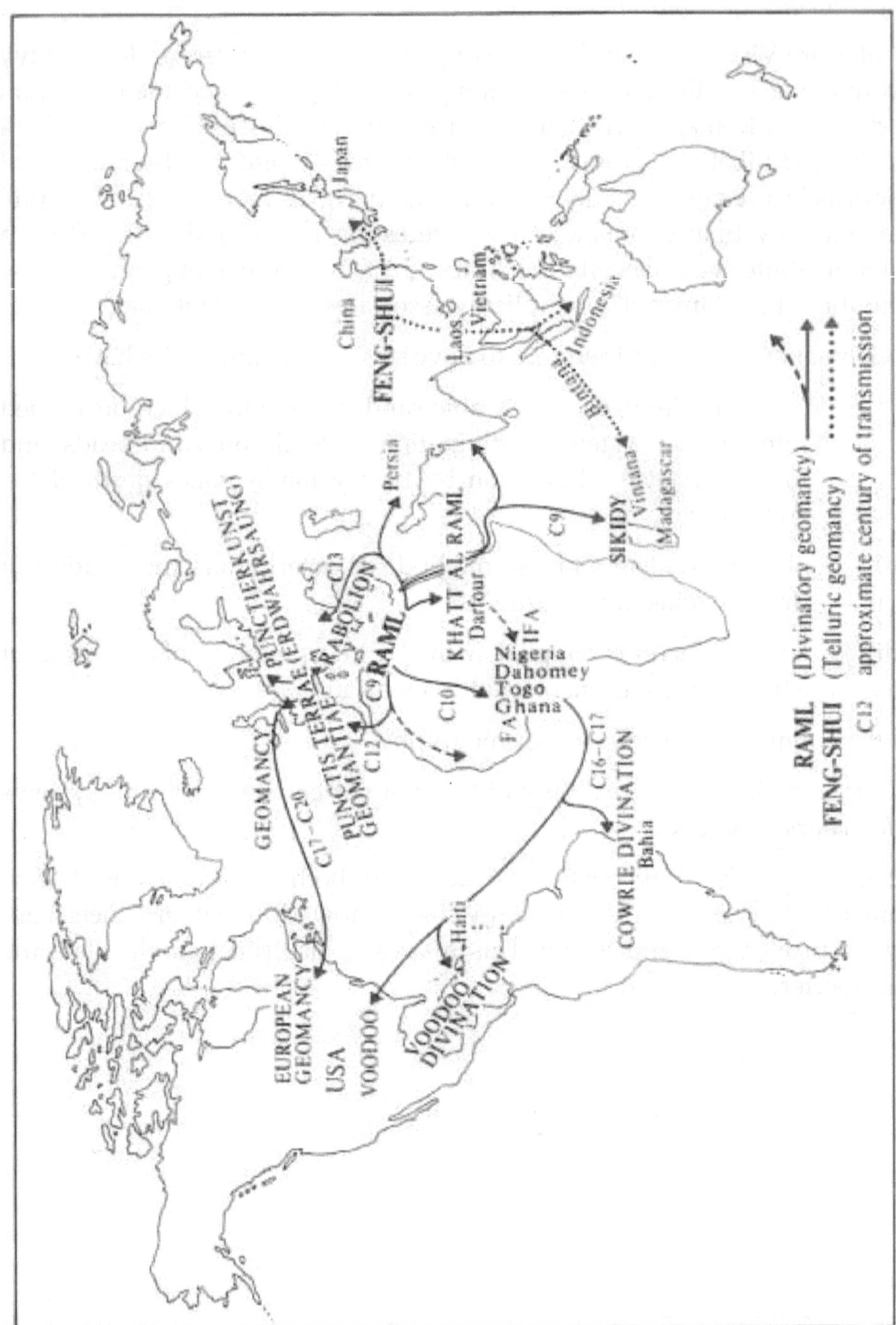

Figure 2: Origins and geographical lines of transmission of geomancy.

PART ONE

History

1. The Roots of Geomancy

One of the difficulties of writing even a short history of geomancy is that to date studies of its emergence in one culture have tended to disregard manifestations of the *same* divinatory technique in other cultures. Even within Africa there are few studies (with one or two exceptions, notably Rene Trautmann, Bernard Maupoil and J. C. Hebert) which even appear to realize that *ifa* and *fa* on the west coast of Africa are exactly parallel with *sikidy* in Madagascar, and that both stem from *raml,* a common Arab origin.

The position gets worse when the question of comparison between African and European manifestations of geomancy arises. A classic example of such lack of cross-cultural information occurs in Lars Dahle's study of *sikidy,* one of the more comprehensive works in English to date.[1] When Dahle comes to assessing the work of Flacourt on geomancy, he fails to follow up the references of his predecessor to 'the authors of Europe.' Flacourt, who was much wider read then Dahle, described the sixteen figures of the *sikidy* by giving each its equivalent Latin name, rather than by drawing the figures in full. Instead of looking up the many works on European geomancy, Dahle criticizes Flacourt for 'merely translating' the Malagasy into Latin, and proceeds to *guess* (wrongly) what figure each Malagasy term applied to. Dahle then satirizes Flacourt:

> "He adds that 'all these figures have the same meaning and power as are attributed to them by the authors of Europe.' As it would almost amount to an insult to my readers to suppose that any of them are ignorant of what 'the authors of Europe' teach with regard to geomancy, I shall of course abstain from commenting upon this very conclusive information!"

He abstains from commenting because he has no idea which authors Flacourt refers to, or even that there was a flourishing European interest in geomancy contemporary with Flacourt's study of its appearance in Madagascar!

There is nothing new in 'authorities' ignoring each other's work, except that in the case of geomancy, many European field-workers have not

[1] 'Sikidy and Vintana,' in *The Antananarivo Annual and Madagascar Magazine,* Antananarivo, 1886-8, pp. 222-4.

realized that geomancy was just as much a part of the undergrowth of *European* magical beliefs as it is of the North African Arabs, Malagasy of Madagascar, tribes of Benin (Dahomey), or of the voodoo cult in the Americas. Furthermore, such a lack of historical identification has also led to some false identifications, based on semantic confusion rather than a thorough study of the system concerned, such as that of Chinese *feng-shui.*

Because so many geomantic works are anonymous, and because it has become fashionable among scholars to doubt geomancies attributed to famous men (sometimes on no better grounds than "so-and-so would not have written a geomancy"), in examining the written sources of this art I have for the most part attributed works according to the title pages of their first printed version, or manuscript incipit and catalogue entry. In doing so, some will be falsely ascribed works, but this is a preferable course of action to listing unlimited anonymous texts of uncertain date. Besides, in many cases of disputed authorship, the critics can suggest no more likely an author than the one they dispute.

Finally, geomancy was *not* looked upon during the Middle Ages as the poor relation of the divinatory sciences, as it has come to be, an attitude which has biased many scholars to the point where they look upon the subject, which was important in its own time, as below the notice of the great men of the period under study - a situation rather similar to doubting that Newton was interested in alchemy, when in terms of written output it far exceeded his interest in physics.

THEORIES OF ORIGIN

Classical references

The earliest mention of the word is made in Archimedes (278-212 BCE), in which he reputedly drew geomantic figures in the sand during the siege of Syracuse to determine the outcome of the situation, but the nature of these signs cannot satisfactorily be established.

Roman divination by augury has sometimes been pointed to as a possible origin for geomancy, but this too is a red herring, for the rules of augury have been carefully preserved for us by writers such as Cicero and bear no resemblance at all to geomancy.

The method of augury consisted chiefly in the augur using a crooked staff *(lituus)* which is free of knots (like a magic wand), to frame an area of sky or land within whose bounds an omen was to appear. He then settled down to watch and wait for a sign. The *lituus,* according to Livy, 'marked off the heavens by a line from east to west, designating as 'right' [*dextrae partes*] the regions to the south, as 'left' [*laeuae partes*] those to the north, and fixing in his mind an [easterly] landmark opposite to him and as far away as the eye could reach.' The augur 'next shifting the crook to his left hand and, laying his right hand' on the head of the person for whom the augury was performed, uttered a prayer to Jupiter. Within the bounds of this *templum* any natural phenomena now would be interpreted by the augur as a message from the gods. This interpretation of the signs was extremely complex and, although some of the detailed rules have now been lost to us, it is known that the meaning of the appearance of specific varieties of birds in particular quarters and in particular numbers was clearly defined. Factors taken into account included the height and manner of flight, perch, tone of call, and the direction from which the bird came. Obviously this description is not of the sixteen figures of geomancy, and so it is that when Marcus Terentius Varro (116-28 BCE) speaks of *geomantia* he also does *not* refer to the present method of divination.[1]

Greece

Normally one would examine the etymology of a word to derive data on its origin. However in the case of geomancy the classical Greek and Roman uses of the word had only a general meaning which persisted throughout the early Middle Ages to mean simply divination by observing patterns or cracks in the earth, just as the three other elementary methods of divination, pyromancy, hydromancy and aeromancy were basically techniques of *divination by inspection* rather than systematized mathematically based practices with specific rules, figures and formulations.

As Paul Tannery, the well-known French historian of science, has pointed out:

> "the Greek words which now refer to this form of divination [geomancy] had in antiquity only a general meaning. In the middle-ages in the West this name was given to an Arabic practice by the translator Hugh of Santalla, who lived in Aragon in the first half of the 12th century. The later Byzantine Greeks did not use the word geomancy in this context, but called the practice by a different name which had been derived from the Arabic *raml* (meaning sand)." [2]

A translation of Paul Tannery's letter dated 15 June 1897 confirms this:

> "Their exist in Greek treatises of geomancy, which are said to be translations from the Persian with the title *῾ράμπλιον rhamplion* or alternatively *῾ράβόλιον rabolion* which seems to indicate a Semitic route from רבל as in Byzantine

[1] This is further confirmed in the etymological work of Isidore of Seville (VIII, 9,13) in which he defines Varro's use of the word.

[2] *Mémoires Scientifiques,* Vol. IV, Paris and Toulouse, 1920.

> Greek, the letters μπ are equivalent in sound to *b*. On the other hand this word seems to be translated into Greek under the form λαξευτήριον *laxeuterion*, which is a Greek word meaning 'the stone cutter's chisel.' The metaphor is perhaps justifiable by the shape of the geomantic lines which will be a point of departure for further combinations.[1] But I have vainly tried to find the Arabic or Persian word transcribed as *rhampliôn* or *rabolion* and translated by the word 'chisel.' Nor have I seen either that geomancy has been designated in Arabic by a similar word, but this has relatively little importance."[2]

To sum up, in such Byzantine Greek manuscripts[3] as that of Georges Midiates (1462), *rabolion* is a Greek transliteration of the Arabic *raml* which means 'sand,' while the word *laxeuterion* probably refers to the *method* of divination, involving the poking of holes in the earth, which is an act which has been compared with chiselling a stone. As *laxeuterion* is simply a figurative word for the divinatory procedure, Tannery instead used the word *rabolion* when speaking about geomancy.

With the exception of two anonymous manuscripts, the word *geomantia* does not appear in any Greek manuscripts on the subject, the word *rabolion* being much more common. Thus the etymological incorrectness of the word 'geomancy' is sufficiently established, and the fact that geomancy passed from the Arab to the Greek world, rather than the other way around.

The fact that portions of the practice of geomancy first appear in a Greek manuscript, translated *from* the Arabic,[4] and not in any classical sources, indicate quite definitely that the practice was of Arab origin rather than Greek.[5] This is contrary to the usual line of cultural transmission (in which many of the Greek sciences passed into Arabic), but nevertheless supported by a number of facts which we will consider later in this chapter, and again in chapter 5.

---

[1] I think it far more likely that the meaning of *laxeuterion* extended to cutting lines in the earth as well as to cutting stones.

[2] Quoted by Baron Carra de Vaux in his introduction 'La Géomancie chez les Arabes' to Vol. IV of Tannery's posthumous *Mémoires Scientifiques,* Paris and Toulouse, 1920.

[3] See Plate XIV.

[4] The Greek text very obviously betrays its Arabic origin, and may be consulted in the printed version in Tannery, *Mémoires Scientifiques,* Vol. IV, 1920, pp. 359-71.

[5] See Plate XIV for an example of a 15th century Greek geomancy.

Persian origins

Other origins have been posited for the practice of geomancy, often motivated by 'romance of the East' thinking rather than historical fact. One such study is the historical appendix written by Dr Alexander Rouhier in Eugene Caslant's *Traite Elementaire De Geomancie.* Dr Rouhier supposes that geomancy was established in Persia at least as early as the eighth or ninth centuries, during that epoch of Iranian culture which flourished at the universities of Gonde-Shapour and Baghdad which attracted the intellectual elite of many countries. However, he does not educe any proof in support of this theory, merely asserting that the Arab and Jewish scholars who attended these universities, and brought various sciences back to their homelands with them, also carried the science of geomancy to the University of Damas[cus], Alexandria, and eventually to Cairo.

The attribution of the origins of geomancy to Persia is shown to be completely false because all of the words connected with geomancy have come originally from Arabic rather than the Greek or Persian. The reason for this is that from the thirteenth century the Greeks were no longer in direct communication with the Arabs, and it is to Persia that they looked, on the other side of the Turkish hordes, for the centre of the civilization and the science of Islam. For the same reason the great authority on geomancy, az-Zanātī is often called a Persian, although he is in fact a north African Arab of the twelfth to thirteenth century. This false nationality lent colour to the hypothesis that Persia was the home of geomancy.

Indian origins

India as a possible origin is however harder to dispose of. The basis for attributing the roots of geomancy to India probably lies in the reputed authority on geomancy called Tum-Tum el-Hindi. The epithet has been thought by many commentators to indicate India as his birthplace, however *'el-Hindi'* was applied to a number of other writers including Apollonius of Persia (who certainly was not an Indian) which in his case at least evidently meant 'the ingenious.' In addition, the word *hindasi* meant a geometer, and *hindi* is more likely to have been an indication of the occupation of the person so designated, rather than his country of origin.

The other half of the name, 'Tum-Tum,' has sometimes been construed by French savants as a corruption of Ptolemy. Whilst this is not proven, it would at least tie in with the tradition concerning the Islamic derivation of geomancy through Idris, Tum-Tum and Hermes Trismegistus. This last mentioned line of adepts will be examined at greater length in chapter 2. Suffice it to say that India is less likely as an origin for geomancy, when the only basis for this ascription rests on the epithet *el-hindi.*

Mediaeval geomancies often claim a connection with India. One condemned at Paris in 1277 began, 'The Indians have believed...,' and several geomancies have been called *Indeana* indicating their supposed origin. Another manuscript in the British Library[1] begins, 'This is the Indyana [i.e. geomancy] of Gremmgi[2] which is called the daughter of astronomy and which one of the sages of India wrote...' However it was almost as common practice to attribute a work of this nature to a fabulous country of origin as to a fabulous author, and although it is *possible,* it seems unlikely that India was the fountainhead of geomancy.

The most convincing argument against India as the source of geomancy is provided by David Pingree, who confirms that geomancy was an Arab import to India because it has retained *raml* as its name when referred to in India in the *ramalashastra.*[3] Furthermore their authorship was ascribed to a *yavana*, or 'foreigner.'

Hebrew origins

Daniel, the Biblical prophet, was in great vogue in the Middle Ages as the reputed author of various books of prediction and dream interpretation. Amongst writing allegedly by Daniel is a manuscript on geomancy written in Turkish now in the British Library[4] Although Daniel remained a popular author-designate for Latin manuscripts from the tenth to the fifteenth century, this particular geomancy is an exception to this rule. The fact that it is written in Turkish puts it in a class of its own, and Seyyed Hossein Nasr, in a letter to the present author in 1977, suggests that:

> "the traditional account that [geomancy] was founded by Prophet Daniel who received it as an inspiration from heaven accords very well with the historical evidence as far as its Semitic origin is concerned."

He goes on to say,

> "of course historical sources cannot either prove or invalidate the traditional doctrine concerning the inspired origin of this discipline. But they have borne out the fact that this [is] closely related to old Semitic practices of divination."

---

[1] Sloane MS 314.

[2] Given the presence of six *minims* (identical vertical scribal strokes used to form the letters i, u, m, n'), a more likely reading would have been 'Gremingi,' especially as '–ing' is a common syllable. However 'Gremmgi' has become the standard reading.

[3] Pingree, D. *Yavanajataka of Sphuji-dhvaja,* Harvard University Press, London, 1978.

[4] BL Additional MS 9702.

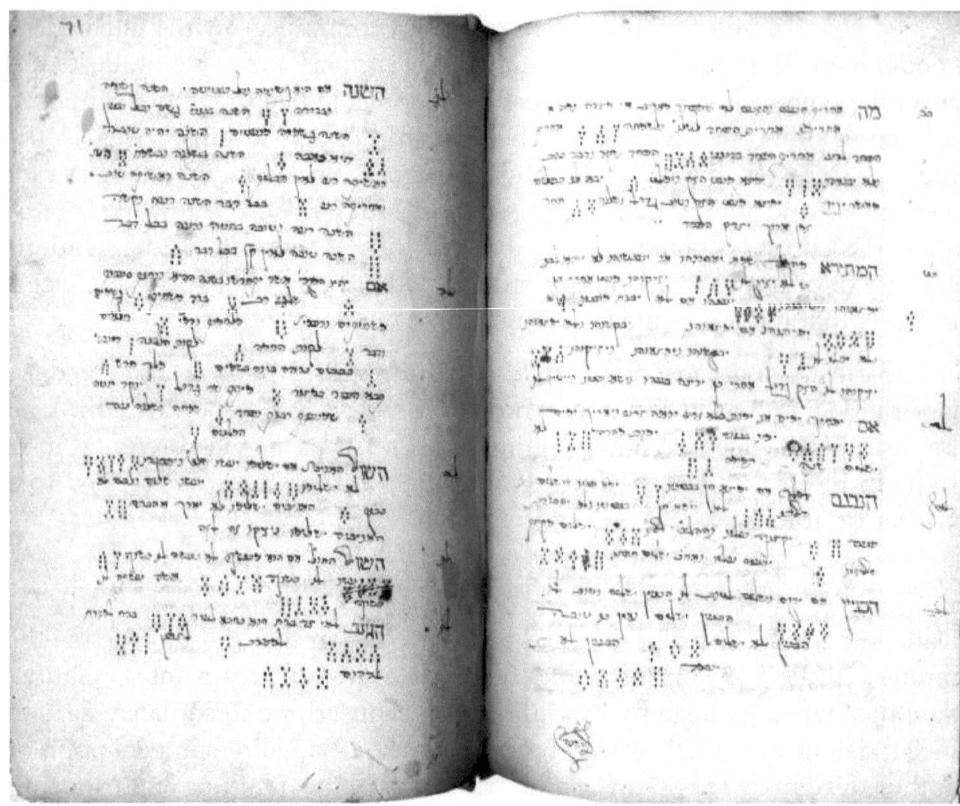

Figure 3: Hebrew Geomantic figures of Abraham ibn Ezra.[1]

Here we have a suggestion of a Semitic origin for geomancy, a birthplace not as far east as Rouhier suggested. A number of authors also parallel geomancy with ancient divinatory practices, such as Sassanian divination techniques; but direct evidence of the existence of specifically *geomantic* techniques in early texts of this period is missing, so we are still on rather shaky ground.

The *Jewish Encyclopedia* places the origins of geomancy in North Africa about the ninth century from where, it maintains, the practice penetrated into Jewish literature. Here we are on much firmer ground for the *one* fact we can be sure of is that the practice was well established in North Africa about the ninth century CE. At this time, geomancy was referred to in Arabic as *raml,* whilst in Hebrew it was called by a number of names, including גורל החול *Goral ha-Hol,* literally 'the lot [divination] by sand' or *Hokmah ha-Nekuddot,* the 'science of points.' Aran ben Joseph refers to diviners who use geomancy as *Yidde 'Oni,* or 'he who casts by means of

[1] Manuscript 396 previously in the Montefiore Library, courtesy of Les Enluminures.

points,' in his commentary on *Deuteronomy* (18: 11).

Although Hebrew may not have been the source of geomancy, it was seminal in spreading it from Muslim Spain up into the rest of Europe. The key figure is Abraham ibn Ezra (1089-1164) who has written well attested works on geomancy, one of which is illustrated in Figure 3, Plate XII and Plate XIII. The manuscript illustrated in these Plates comes from Northern Italy, and dates from around 1550-75. It contains three separate works, and formed part of the collection of Solomon Hayyim Halberstam (1832-1900) before becoming part of Sir Moses Montefiore's collection, as a result of a purchase by Moses Gaster.[1] It was subsequently sold at Sotheby's in 2004. To understand how widespread this work was, it is worth noting that there are upward of 300 known manuscripts of this work. However it was not printed till 1556, and the second printing only appeared in 1701.

Ibn Ezra lived initially in Spain, where he probably came into contact with *raml* from the Muslims living there. After 1140 he travelled extensively throughout Europe, writing copiously on geomancy, and probably assisting in the dispersion of geomantic knowledge through that continent. The other route that geomancy took to Europe was via the translation of an Arabic work of az-Zanātī by the monk Arsenius in Istanbul/Constantinople.

Other well known Hebrew writers who refer specifically to geomancy include Maimonides (1135 -1204) of Cordova in Spain who travelled across most of the Arab world to die finally in Cairo, and Nachmanides who mentioned geomancy in his commentary on the Pentateuch. Maimonides, most famous for his work *Guide for the Perplexed,* refers to geomancy in his commentaries on the *Mishnah.*[2] However these were all Hebrew writers living in a Muslim world, still pointing strongly to an Arab origin as the real genesis of the practice. Following these authoritative writers, came a host of lesser Hebrew commentators. [3] An undergrowth of literature subsequently grew up, mostly anonymous works on geomancy, many of them called *Sepher ha-Goralot,* of which numerous examples will be found in any extensive library of Hebrew literature.[4] The Hebrew literature however was a cul-de-sac in the history of geomancy. Rather it was the Arab *raml*

---

[1] A well known Hebrew scholar who edited the Hebrew book of magic, the *Sword of Moses.*

[2] *'Ab. Zarah,* iv.

[3] Including Nissim ben Moses, who wrote on the subject in *ha-Haluz* (chapter VII, 124), Aran ben Joseph and Joseph Albo who wrote extensively about geomancy in his *Ikkirim* (chapter IV, 4) in which he not only defined it, but referred specifically to the upper and lower points, establishing the existence of a Hebrew geomantic vocabulary.

[4] To name but a few authors of this title: Ahithophel ha-Giloni, Abraham ibn Ezra (whose work enjoyed numerous translations into Latin and other European languages), and a further *Sepher ha-Goralot* by the qabalist Saadia Gaon.

which was most widely disseminated and which had the most influence on the later development of geomancy.

It would seem for this reason fairly safe to attribute the actual origin of the technique to the Muslim area of North Africa.

Africa

A few researchers have suggested sub-Saharan Africa as the source of geomancy, but as we will see in Chapter 3 and 4, all the technical terms used in these forms of divination stem from Arabic, not from any African language. The theory that geomancy originated in Equatorial Africa will be considered, and rejected, in greater detail at the end of Chapter 3. If you look at the map in Figure 12, showing the spread of *raml* across Africa, you can see very clearly that it spread from the north, alongside Islamic incursions into central Equatorial across Africa, rather than from the south.

Egypt

The fact that sophisticated geomancy/*raml* machines such as the one shown in Plate VIII-IX were manufactured in Egypt[1] as long ago as 1241 CE suggests that geomancy/*raml* was well established in Egypt by this date. But this is simply a function of Egypt being an important part of the general spread of Islam. See Plate VIII, Plate IX and Plate X.

Abayomi Cole,[2] suggested *ancient* Egypt as the source of *Ifa,* and hence geomancy, based on the Afro-centric ideas which saw a resurgence in the 1970s, and which viewed Africa not just as the genetic source, but also the source of all Western civilisation.[3] Cole found a sympathetic audience amongst the occult community of 1899 London, but these theories are unlikely to find a sympathetic audience now.

Fanciful and Eccentric Origins

Before passing on to consider the actual Islamic origins of geomancy, I would just like to outline, and dispose of, one of the more eccentric recent contributions to the history of geomancy. Wim van Binsbergen suggested a number of possible scenarios for the origin for geomancy, all based on rather slim evidence, on one page espousing Mesopotamia,[4] on the next the

---

[1] Damascus, Syria is another possible but much less likely origin for that machine.
[2] Cole (1990), p. 14.
[3] See Cheikh Anta Diop, *The African Origin of Civilisation*, Lawrence Hill, New York, for a more extreme version of this (discredited) theory.
[4] Van Binsbergen (1996-2004), p.4.

Ikhwan al-Safa'.[1] Binsbergen's text reads like an impressionistic stream of consciousness[2] in which he bounces from one culture to another as the possible origin of geomancy without providing any reference, rhyme or reason, dodging from Zurvan to Ahriman, the *I Ching* to Osiris, from the Tetragrammaton to Jachin and Boaz, the Talmud to the Great Mother, Iran to India in a manner that would confuse even the most ardent New Age synthesiser, yet taking time out to reprove Nigel Pennick, (who has at least provided a useful and detailed descriptions of *sikidy*), for that very sin.

Binsbergen then suddenly announces that as the Ikhwan al-Safa, or 'Brethren of Purity' had access to all the necessary ingredients of geomancy including access to Chinese trading ships in the Persian gulf, so they must be the origin of geomancy![3] Further, according to him it is "very plausible that specific traces of their presumably vital contribution to the origin of geomancy were effectively concealed or destroyed,[4] leaving absolutely no proof of their involvement,"[5] and therefore leaving him with no burden of proof!

He then turns his attention to just one Greek manuscript Parisinus MS 2419 by Georges Midiates, dated 1462, a rather late date for considering the origins of geomancy.[6] He notices a certain regularity in the meaning of the Greek names of the 16 figures.[7] But rather than simply seeing the natural pairing of the figures which are part of the structure of geomancy, e.g. Puella (girl) with Puer (boy); Laetitia (joy) with Tristitia (sadness); or Amissio (loss) with Acquisitio (gain), or the well accepted astrological correspondences, he attempts to force totally unrelated astrological concepts, which he clearly does not fully understand, on to the 16 figures.

For example, he interprets 'thresholds' and 'lintels' as specific astrological technical terms, which they are not. The original Arabic (*'ataba dākhila* and *'ataba khārija*) very clearly refers to the inner and outer doorstep of the house, and these terms of course simply apply to the arrival and/or departure of fortune. From this he derives some rather strange and often incorrect 'astrological significance.'

---

[1] Ibid, p.26.

[2] Especially Binsbergen (1996-2004), pages 26 to 36.

[3] It is not clear what the Chinese could have contributed to geomancy apart from the idea of the combination of binaries, a concept that must be latent in almost every culture.

[4] Ibid, p. 38.

[5] He derives this idea entirely from a casual reading of Felix Klein-Franke (1973). And a mention in Savage-Smith (1980), p. 4. There is no trace of any Chinese input in either.

[6] See Appendix V, column G12 for the relevant Greek terms and their transliteration.

[7] Binsbergen makes mistakes with the Greek transliteration of both Puer (which he glosses as 'female' despite the fact that 'boy' is obviously male) and Caput Draconis.

Another clear example drawn from his text is the geomantic figure *conjunctio* (which actually means 'conjunction') he leaves with a blank space in his table, whilst applying the description of an astrological conjunction to Rubeus (meaning red, and clearly associated with Mars). Even his description of conjunction so applied, as an "angle between 0 and any other planet less than 12^{0}" has been taken from its context in some other astrological text without any understanding of it.[1]

Binsbergen makes a number of other basic mistakes in his use of astrological technical terms in his article which further detracts from his integrity.[2] For example he defines an astrological House as "a section (usually 1/12) of the zodiak (*sic*) specific to a particular person, place, and moment of time,"[3] when in fact the zodiac is a division of the (moving) ecliptic, whilst the House is a fixed division of the sky into 12 sections relative to a specific place. Worse still he repeats the old chestnut of trying to categorise the *I Ching* as part of the "geomantic family"[4] purely on the basis of its binary arithmetic base. This is on a par with categorising all computer programming as a form of geomancy, based on the same reasoning.

His final, and not very useful, conclusion is that "the question as to which particular nation, ethnic group, language group, religion or sect would have been the system's cradle, turns out to be rather irrelevant."

We will look at the real and relevant Islamic origins of geomancy/*raml* in the next Chapter.

---

[1] What he means is an angle between two planets of less than 12^{0}, rather than between 0 and a planet!

[2] Ironically, he goes on to accuses Klein-Franke of having "little grip on the intricacies of astrology," (Ibid, p. 26) while he simply copies pages from a basic popular internet-derived text on astrology and adds them, without any comment, at the end of his essay.

[3] Ibid, p.11.

[4] Ibid, p. 17-18, a very rough map, which shows neither detail nor accuracy.

2. *Raml* and Islamic Origins

Divination in the world of Islam took many forms. The best summary of these in a European language is Toufic Fahd's *La Divination Arabe.* The main forms of divination include *kihana, djafr, fa'l, ihhtiladj, ta'bir* (oneiromancy or dream interpretation), and of course *raml,* more precisely *al-khatt bi-raml,* the original name for Arab geomancy. Of course, *ta'bir* has always been the most popular, closely followed by *raml.* There was never any suspicion that *khatt ar-raml* was imported from outside of Islam, indeed the attribution of the Muslim caliphs to the individual Figures confirms that the system was not an alien importation.

> "*khatt ar-raml* was practised by Muslims and was clearly identified both by its practitioners and its clients as being a Muslim form of divination."[1]

Raml, literally 'sand,' is variously spoken of as *derb-al-raml, derb-al-ful, 'ilm al-raml* (the science of sand), *hati ramli* (colloquially) and *khatt al-raml.*[2] In the Islamic era, the term, *raml* (or *'ilm al-raml)* was dominant, but with the growing influence of astrology on the occult sciences, the term *shakl* (plural *ashkal),* 'figure' came into prominence. From *shakl* may be derived the expression to 'squill' or practise divination by sand, and perhaps *sikily* or *sikidy,* the terms used in Madagascar to denote geomancy.

Khatt in Arabic originally meant a straight furrow or line drawn in the sand by a stick or with the finger. In time the word came to mean a line drawn on parchment or paper, or a line of writing, and finally, the art of calligraphy. For our purpose, the earlier meaning is the most interesting because it especially applied to the lines which a diviner *(hazi)* drew in the sand to prognosticate the happy or unlucky outcome of an undertaking or event about which he was consulted.

At first sight, *khatt* is the line which the geomancer traces on the sand

---

[1] Brenner (2000), p. 153.

[2] According to Fahd in his article on *Khatt* in *Encyclopedia of Islam* (new edition): 'Instead of *khatt, darb* began to be used especially in dialect; *darb* is in fact the modern substitute for *tark,* which was used originally to denote lithomancy (or the casting of pebbles on the sand).' Thus a certain confusion has resulted in *khatt* = *tark* = *darb* as Arabic terms for geomancy. We will here use the more correct term, *khatt.*

when, strictly speaking, he is practising psammomancy. This is also the meaning of *raml*. Finally the development from *khatt* to *raml* began with the juxtaposition of the two terms. Indeed, *khatt al-raml* is the term most frequently used to denote geomancy.[1]

For the purpose of divining by *khatt al-raml*, the diviner, accompanied by an assistant or acolyte, drew with the utmost haste a quantity of lines or ripples in the sand, allowing himself to be carried away, so that he did not know how many lines he had drawn. Then he slowly wiped out groups of two ripples at a time, whilst his assistant often recited an incantation in Arabic, such as the words: 'Ye two sons of 'Iyan hasten with the explanation!'

The marks they made were joined by other marks *(khutut)* in order to complete a figure *(shakl)*. When these figures became stylized, a board was used, which was covered with sand or even flour, and the finger was drawn over it at random; the shapes formed in this way were then examined. If in the end two lines were left (i.e. there was an *even* number of lines drawn) then this foretold success. If however only one line remained (an *odd* number of lines drawn) then disappointment was certain. Here can be seen the germ of the later and more complex practice, where each line is reduced to odd (only one left) or even (two remaining). In this, the simple form of *khatt al-raml*, only *one* set of marks were made, leading straight to a lucky or unlucky prediction.

A more modern Arab version of this technique involves the making of lines in the sand. On to these lines, corns of barley or date-stones (or even cubes resembling dice with combinations of one or two marks on each face) are thrown. Where dice are used, the four possible markings on their six faces are:

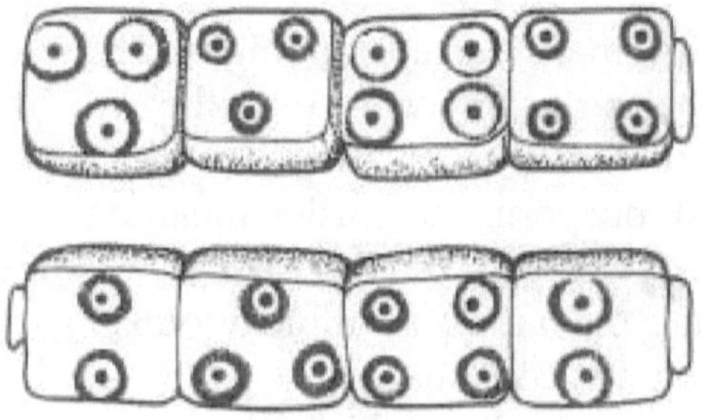

Figure 4: Arab Geomantic dice.

[1] Fahd adds that *'raml* and *khatt* also mean the black or white lines on the hooves of wild cattle or on the flanks and the backs of stags,' a linguistic point which though quite suggestive really does not add much to our comprehension of geomancy.

The resultant patterns provide a more complex prognostication. Examples of such dice are to be found in the Ni'matallahi Khanaqah Library in Tehran.

One interesting sidelight on the origin of *raml* stems from the observation that during a divination the line of generation of the figures (as will be seen in Part Two) is Mothers - Daughters - Nieces.[1] This is a totally *matrilineal* line of descent, and very strange to find amongst the strongly patriarchal societies of the Middle East and North Africa. There are however two matriarchal societies in this area: Jews (as discussed in the previous section) and Tauregs.[2] Given the emphasis on sand, it would seem quite possible that the origin of *raml*, and hence of geomancy was the Tauregs of North Africa. However this is only a tentative hypothesis.

The great magical tome of Ahmed al-Buni (d. 1225 CE), the *Shams al-Ma'arif al-Kubra* ('Sun of the Great Knowledge or Gnosis') is one of the most widely read mediaeval Arabic treatises on talismans, magic squares and sorcery. This book rivals the *Picatrix* in importance, but is sadly currently only available in Arabic and Turkish. Interestingly Ahmad al-Buni's medical works still remain a point of reference among Muslim Yoruba healers in Nigeria, and it is likely that Arab works on divination with sand would also have made their way across to the Gulf of Guinea along the same trading routes. Al-Buni was well known as a Sufi and wrote on the esoteric value of letters, mathematics, the construction of magic squares,[3] *sihr* (magic or sorcery) and geomancy. More acceptable terms for *sihr* (sorcery) amongst Muslims were *Ilm al-Hikmah,* [4] ('Knowledge of the Wisdom'), *Ilm al-Simiyah* ('Study of the Divine Names') or *Ruhaniyat* (spirituality). By whatever name it is called, most of the books on sorcery in the Muslim world are simply excerpts from the *Shams al-ma`ârif*. However, despite claims to the contrary, al-Buni did not include any mention of *raml* in his encyclopedia,[5] and the dot figures in his texts were more relevant to books of 'lots' than to geomancy.[6]

---

[1] The original Arabic is 'niece' rather than the rather more modern 'nephew.' In Spanish these figures are referred to as *sobrinas,* and in French as *nieces.*

[2] Other less likely matrilineal contenders are the Amirites of Yemen, some social classes of the Nabateans of north Arabia, and the Akan (Ashanti) of Ghana.

[3] An interesting line of research might be to compare al-Buni's magic squares with those of Abramelin.

[4] Recognisably similar to the Hebrew *Hokmah*, the second *Sephirah* on the Tree of Life.

[5] See Savage-Smith (1980), p. 39.

[6] Al-Buni's dot figures for the 6th, 17th and 19th lunar Mansions look like geomantic figures, but all the figures for the other 25 Mansions are not, leading to the conclusion that his dot figures probably relate to star patterns rather than geomancy.

Interestingly Al-Buni numbered Plato, Aristotle, Hermes, Alexander the Great, and various obscure Chaldean magicians amongst his sources, which one might expect of someone living in Alexandria.[1]

Geomancy machine

Also from Egypt comes a precision instrument designed to speed up divination by *raml*. See Plates VIII-X. The existence of such a machine means that geomancy/*raml* was established in this area for some considerable time before its date of manufacture. This Islamic geomancy *raml* machine was manufactured in Egypt (or possibly Damascus or Mosul), by Muhammad ibn Khutlukh al Mawsuli.[2] The fact that all the inscription on the machine are all in Arabic, rather than Arabised versions of ancient Egyptian (or even Greek) words, helps to confirm that the origin of *raml* was Islamic rather than ancient Egyptian.

The translation by the British Museum of the inscription on the front of the machine runs as follows:

> "I am the revealer of secrets; in me are marvels of wisdom and strange and hidden things. But I have spread out the surface of my face out of humility, and have prepared it as a substitute for [marking in the] earth. […] From my intricacies there comes about a perception superior to books concerned with the study of this art [of *raml*]."

To use the device, the diviner randomly moves the four arc-shaped slides, to reveal 4 geomantic figures. These form the first four Figures or Mothers. He then transfers these to the first four dials on the top, reading from the right. It would have been nice if the turning of these four dials, automatically calculated the remaining 12 Figures, by virtue of the ingenious interlocking toothed wheels, but sadly each dial has to be set manually using the rules for creating a geomantic spread. Twelve dials are marked with the 12 Houses of astrology enabling the diviner to read off the answer for questions from any particular department of life. The larger semi-circular disk relates the figures to the seasons, Mansions of the Moon and directions, and the client thus receives a detailed answer to his question. The same attribution of the geomantic figures to each of the 4 cardinal directions is also repeated in Figure 5 on the next page.[3]

---

[1] In one of his books, he claimed to have discovered a collection of manuscripts buried under the pyramids, which included Hermetic texts.

[2] 'Al-Mawsuli' indicates that he originally came from Mosul in Iraq, but exactly where in the Islamic world he made this machine is uncertain. An incense burner from Damascus bears his name, but neither are conclusive evidence of the *raml* machine's origin.

[3] South is shown at the top, and East on the left.

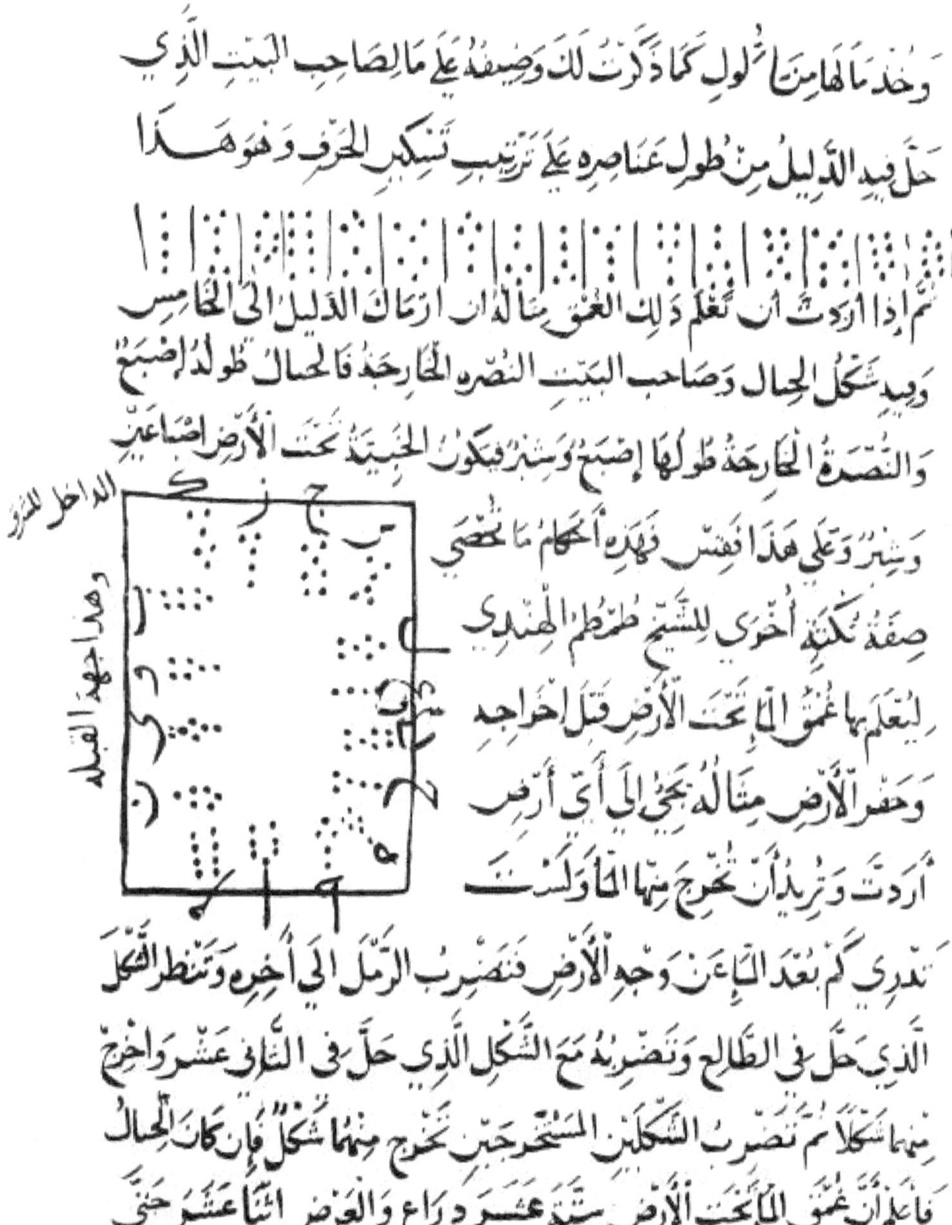

Figure 5: Arabic manuscript attributed to Tum-Tum el-Hindi, showing a geomantic arrangement or *taskin* for finding water.[1]

[1] Bibliothèque Nationale MS Arabe 2697, fol. 16.

Traditional History

Ahmad ben 'Alī Zunbul (who lived circa 1553)[1] outlined the traditional Arab pedigree of geomancy, according to which the angel Gabriel first appeared before Idris (the Arabic name for Hermes Trismegistus) and taught him the art of geomancy. In the usual Hermetic texts, a revelation is bestowed on Hermes who in turn passes it on to his son Tat or to Asklepios. Such texts form part of the vast corpus of 'Hermetic literature,' of which the *Poemanders* is perhaps the best known. These names, real or mythical, all relate to Egypt.

Zunbul describes the meeting of Idris with the angel Gabriel in the following terms:

> "Idris, on the instruction of a spiritual being had travelled extensively. During one of these journeys, Gabriel appeared to him in the shape of a man, drew lines in the sand and said to him: 'You are a prophet; but you hide your gift of prophecy out of fear of your fellow men.' And Idris answered: 'Yes out of love and reverence for you.' Idris was surprised at the [geomantic] knowledge that Gabriel possessed and said to him: 'Dear Brother, I will become your companion and you shall teach me that which is known to you.' And Gabriel answered: 'Out of love and respect for you will I do this.' Thus Idris met Gabriel every day until he had mastered this science. Then Gabriel said unto him:... 'Go to the Indian Tum-Tum and his people and teach them this science.' "

So from Idris/Hermes Trismegistus the chain of tradition passes to the elusive 'Tum-Tum' (see Figure 5). Tum-Tum appears to belong to legend rather than history, although as we have seen his name may be a corruption of an actual personage, and he may not necessarily come from India.[2] For Islam, India had the same aura of mystery as Egypt has had for Europe in more recent years: consequently if it was necessary to give a subject greater authority, an Indian source was invoked by Islamic writers: Tum-Tum also occurs as an authority in other occult writings in Arabic. Zunbul even claims that Tum-Tum's geomancy was written 'in the language of the inhabitants of India.' Moreover, Muslim travellers often made a pilgrimage to India, and 'to be an Indian, wise in the interpretation of secrets' was a common phrase, and one of the ideals of the Brethren of Purity.

Halaf al-Barbari was next in the Arabic chain of traditional descent. He travelled to India to study geomancy, where he copied Tum-Tum's text into Arabic. Abu 'Abdallāh Muhammad az-Zanātī drew on al-Barbari's work in

---

[1] See Klein-Franke (1973), p. 5 for Zunbul's mention of Sultan Sulaiman I.

[2] The Tum Tum people are an ethnic group from the Nuba hills in Sudan, and this might have been the source of this name, and one conveniently close to Egypt.

turn to produce one of the more complete geomancies of his time. Although az-Zanātī's dates are not known, it is suspected that he lived during the twelfth or thirteenth centuries, as he is quoted by Ibn Khaldoun in the following century. Az-Zanātī's works have often been reprinted in Arabic from the thirteenth century to the present day, and he stands as one of the greatest Arabic authorities on geomancy. In turn Ahmad ben 'Alī Zunbul drew his material from az-Zanātī in the sixteenth century (when geomancy in Europe and *raml* in Islam simultaneously reached their peaks), establishing *raml* as an integral part of the world of Islam. Its special features are examined in the next chapter.

By the time the system was fully developed, the 16 Figures had specific names and have a wide range of correspondences, such as

> Males or female, good or bad associations, the four elements of air, earth, fire and water, the cardinal points of the compass, the signs of the Zodiac, days of the week, months of the year, numbers, letters of the [Arabic] alphabet, parts of the body, planets, colours, and finally prophets or Muslim caliphs.[1]

The expansion of geomancy in the Muslim world would seem to have occurred in four directions: firstly, Africa southwest across the Sahara to the Gulf of Guinea; secondly, via the Red Sea and the Indian Ocean to Madagascar and the Kenya coast; thirdly, north through Muslim Spain to the rest of Europe, and finally via the Byzantine Empire to Istanbul, Greece and the rest of Europe. Geomancy migrated finally from both Europe *and* the Gulf of Guinea (in the sixteenth and seventeenth centuries) to the New World of the Americas, by which time it had lost many of its essentially Muslim features.

The migration of nomadic Arabs and the consequent spread of Islam south through the Sahara along the trade routes into the rich Equatorial Africa or present-day Nigeria, Dahomey (Benin), Togo and Ghana, is the first line of migration we shall consider.

Islam first stirred Africa out of its lethargy in the eighth century. The Berbers, who were already masters of the Sahara when the Arabs arrived, accepted Islam, and in about 800 CE drove the Tukulors and the Oulofs as far south as Senegal. In the later part of that century, almost all the black dynasties seem to have been replaced by others of northern Islamic origin, Berbers perhaps, so that in about 850 the Dya-Ogo of Diara (south of Senegal) spread from the Gambia to Aoudaghost; while the Songhai of Dahomey later occupied Gao, and in 990, made it their capital. Likewise the Hausa of the lower Niger, whose king (circa 890) rejoiced in the Arab name, Abu Yazid. The only kingdom which escaped northern domination was the

[1] Brenner (2000), p.153. See also Appendix V.

empire of Ghana, whose creation seems to have dated from much earlier. At the beginning of the ninth century, this empire of the Sahel stretched from Timbuktu to Kayes, and from the upper Niger to Hodh, and at the end of the tenth century the Sarakolle occupied Mauritania, where Muslims were also numerous.

Although Islam was not formally introduced into these regions before the eleventh century, trade was active, and Arab civilization had penetrated deeply. Caravans escorted by Berbers maintained commercial links across the Sahara, and cultural contact was established between black Africa and the Mediterranean, the Arabs taking with them the habit of 'sand-cutting' or *raml*. The introduction of the camel greatly assisted this contact between the seventh and tenth centuries, and clothing, food, customs and textiles spread to lower Senegal. The Sahara traffic directed towards Egypt or Tunisia used the regular tracks from Khumbi, Timbuktu, and Gao in the south, and Tripoli, Tahert and Marrakesh in the north. The salt of the Sahara, the gold of the upper Niger, the copper of Agades and the slaves of Guinea were traded for dates, coral and textiles. Later, Saladin's relations with the Muslim rulers of Bornu and Gao brought the reopening of the caravan routes from Egypt to Lake Chad and the Niger.

Communications with Madagascar via the Red Sea explain how the practice of *raml* made its way down the east coast of Africa to Madagascar, where it was easily adopted by the indigenous Malagasy population, between the ninth and fourteenth centuries, when Arab colonies were set up in the north-west corner of that island.

The history of geomancy at this point closely parallels the history of the expansion of Islam, which made great progress in Negro Africa in the eleventh and twelfth centuries. In the Sudan the three great empires were all Muslim. The empire of Melle on either side of the upper Senegal and the upper Niger was formed from the old kingdom of Ghana. Its ruler from 1255 to 1270 even went on a pilgrimage to Mecca; and its architecture, in cobwork and fired brick, was influenced by the style of the Maghreb. From Egypt and Morocco also came a large number of merchants. The Mellistine empire stretched from Senegal to the south Algerian oases, and the River Niger. This was the great period of Timbuktu, a flourishing intellectual centre from which the customs of Islam spread southwards. This empire reached its highest point at the end of the fifteenth century.

At the same time several Hausa states had come into existence in the central Sudan, between the Niger and Lake Chad, the most important of them being the one centred on Kano. One of its rulers, Yeji (1349-1385), was visited by Muslims from Melle and converted to Islam.

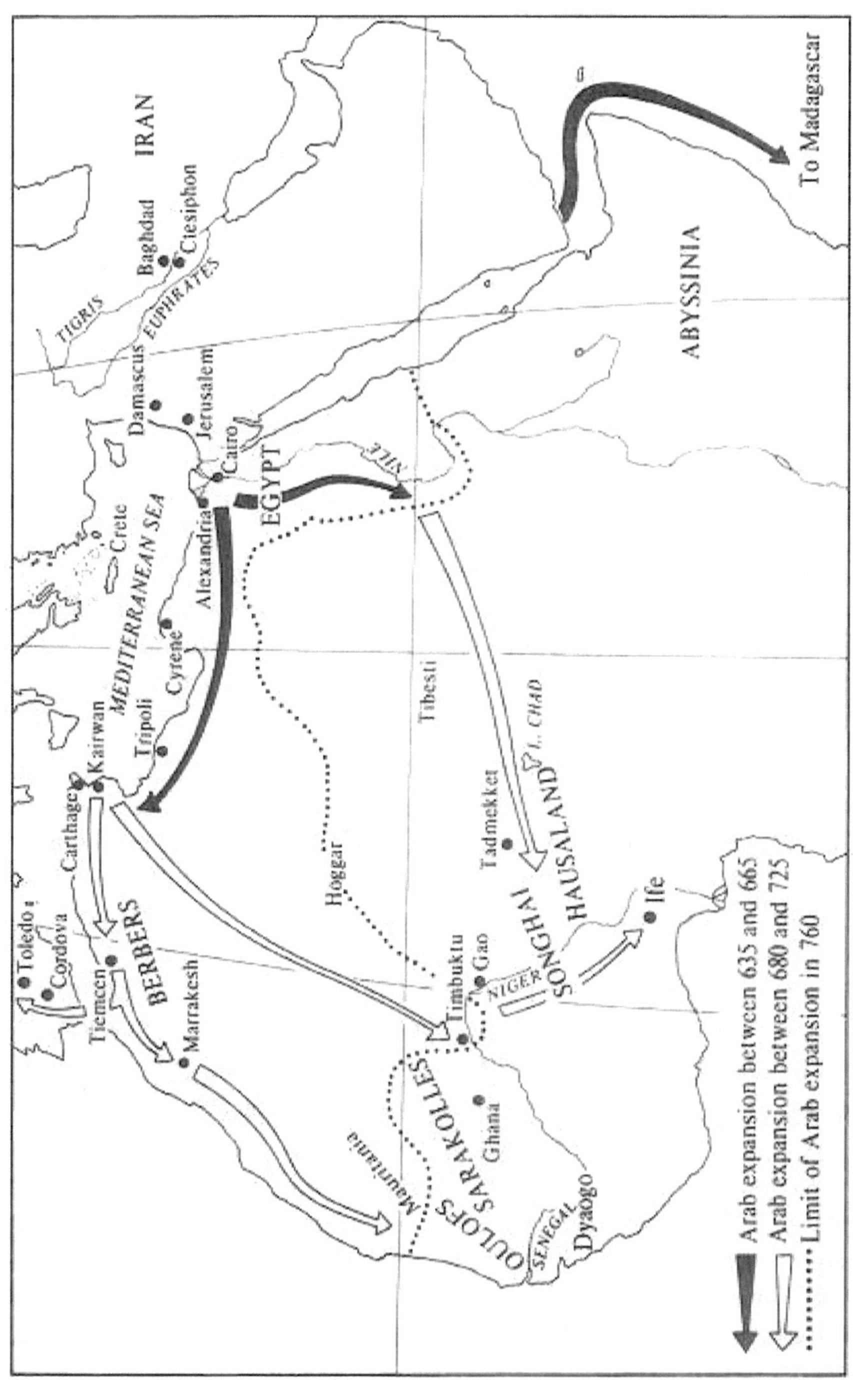

Figure 6: The initial expansion of Islam and spread of *raml* 635-760 CE.[1]

[1] *Raml* also later penetrated other parts of Africa, by routes shown in Figure 12.

Islam thus penetrated to the heart of Africa, so far in fact that even the Maghreb scholars of the fifteenth century did not hesitate to go to Timbuktu to consult with African scholars. It must be added, however, that only the sovereigns and upper social levels adhered to Islam; the masses remained loyal to the beliefs of their ancestors, adapting the Islamic practice of *raml* to their own style of worship.

In its simplest form, *raml* was called 'sand-cutting,' which consisted in making a random number of marks in the sand or dust, cancelling them off two by two until only one or two marks are left, and from this drawing a single or double line. Repeated four times, this procedure yields one of the basic sixteen geomantic figures of *raml*. Sand-cutting was and is a widespread form of geomancy practised by many Islamic groups in both west and north Africa: its similarities to the Dahomean divinatory system of *fa,* and the Yoruba *ifa* , were first noted by Fischer in 1929, and later elaborated on by Monteil, Trautmann, Schilde, and most importantly, Bernard Maupoil in 1943, who also drew attention to the similarities with Madagascan *sikidy* divination. Steinschneider (1877) made the highly significant point that *sikidy* comes from the Arabic word for 'figure,' *shikl,* confirming its Arabic origin.

However, as early as 1864, the well-travelled and well-read Sir Richard Burton noted similarities between the Dahomean *fa* and the 'geomancy of the Greeks, much cultivated by the Arabs under the name of *al-raml*.' Here he erred in attributing the ultimate origin to the Greeks, but he was in some ways even better read than his successors, because he drew yet a further parallel with Napoleon's *Book of Fate* which he described as 'a notable specimen of European and modern [geomantic] vulgarisation,' [1] thus leaping centuries of the development of geomantic divination to that forgery of the 1820s (see chapter 7).

A chapter of *Voyage au Darfour* (Paris, 1845) written by Sheikh Muhammad ibn Omar al Tounsi and translated by Dr Perron, contains a study of geomancy as it was practised in Darfour (a country annexed by Egypt in 1874), with the Arab names and meanings of the figures, description of the operations of *khatt al-raml* (literally calligraphy traced in the sand) and of *dharb* (or *derb) al-raml* ('the art of marking the sand') by the sand diviners. These are obviously a 'halfway house' between *raml* and the west-coast African divinatory systems.

Further suggestive evidence of the direct connexion between *raml* and the divinatory systems of the Yoruba comes from the presence among the

---

[1] R. F. Burton, *A Mission to Gelele, King of Dahome,* London, 1864, pp. 334-5.

Yoruba of a form of sand-cutting, called by them *iyanrin tite,* which is practised by Muslim diviners known as *alufa* who often referred to the technique as *hati ramli* (or *atimi* for short). The names of the sixteen basic figures (Al Káusẹji, Aláhika, Utúba dahila, etc.) clearly differ from those of *ifa* but correspond to those given by az-Zanātī. The order in which these figures were recently given by an *alufa,* a native of Zaria, is identical with that in which they are listed by az-Zanātī. Although this system of the *alufa* may be a recent introduction of Islamic geomancy, the local parallels in practice between it and *ifa* help to confirm the Muslim origin of the latter.

The practitioners of *ifa* divination rely upon extensive verses which are memorized and recited in response to the generation of a particular geomantic figure: traces of such verses exist in Islamic *raml,* but not the propitiatory sacrifices which are of such central importance to *ifa.* On the positive side, sand-cutting is sometimes used rather than the throwing of seeds to generate a figure in both *ifa* and *raml,* and the whole mathematics of addition of odds and evens, the shapes of the figures, and some meanings are identical.

Burton and Maupoil[1] both came to the conclusion that *ifa, fa* divination and *sikidy* (in Madagascar) are all derived from Islamic geomancy. Considering the trade routes and general expansion of Islam, together with the incredible internal similarity, this thesis seems to be inescapable. A final piece of evidence is produced by Ellis (1894) who says of the divination board used by the *ifa* diviners that it is 'exactly similar to those used by children in Muslim schools in lieu of slates, about two feet long and eight or nine inches broad...,' thus reinforcing the evidence for the Islamic origin of *ifa.*[2] It could even be conjectured that Muslim practitioners demonstrated *raml* on school boards whilst teaching the Yoruba other subjects. The Yoruba then might easily have assumed that the board was a necessary part of the impedimenta of divination rather than merely a convenient writing surface.

Farrow also specifically refers to the divining board as 'an engraved circular board, or a rectangular one, with a handle, similar to a Mohammedan writing tablet....'[3] Although the reference to the use of a Muslim type of slate as a divining tray may possibly stem from a misinterpretation of Burton's account of 1893, it seems a fairly likely cultural transition. Accordingly, in chapter 3 we investigate the techniques used by the Yoruba for their Ifa related divination, and by their

[1] Ibid. See also Bernard Maupoil, *La Geomancie a l'ancienne Cote des Esclaves*, Paris, 1943.

[2] Burton, *op. cit.* 15.

[3] Stephen Farrow, *Faith, Fancies and Fetish or Yoruba Paganism*, London, 1926, pp. 38-9.

neighbouring Dahomean Fa diviners.

With the introduction of slavery in the sixteenth century, many of the slaves taken to the New World took with them the religion of their ancestors, the cults of Şango, Eshu, Fa and Ifa, together with the divination techniques associated with these gods. Consequently, to this day the islands in the Caribbean, particularly Haiti, have inherited these ancestral divination systems which still bear an uncanny resemblance to Arabic *raml.* Slaves sent to Bahia, who integrated much of their religion with Christianity, have also preserved an elaborate ritual divination based on the sixteen figures of Ifa, derived from *raml,* which are generated by the manipulation of cowrie shells, a traditional form of African currency from the Gulf of Guinea.

In Recife and Bahia the shell is so altered that there is an artificial opening opposite the natural opening. When the shells are thrown on a flat surface, either the artificial opening or the natural opening remains uppermost, and it is the different proportions of open to closed which provide the odd and even components of the figures. The traditional deities associated with the verses and divinatory meaning are still part of the technique of divination. Unfortunately, in the last couple of decades, specialists in these techniques of divination in these areas seem to have mostly disappeared.

Returning to the world of Islam in North Africa, we can trace the trade routes down the Red Sea round the Horn of Arabia past the Yemen and along the coast of Africa down to Madagascar where the tradition of *sikidy,* which is examined in detail in chapter 4, has been brought almost intact, with its original Arabic names for the various figures. The arrival of Arab traders bearing with them this technique of divination is well documented, and it has blended successfully with the traditional beliefs of the native Malagasy. In fact it held such a sway over the imagination of the population before the coming of Christianity, that the missionaries responsible for the latter found it harder to conquer than the ritual religious practices of a non-divinatory kind!

In chapter 5 we move north from the world of the Prophet to the great school of translators at Toledo in Spain, who were responsible for transmitting so much of the best of Arab civilization and science into the comparatively backward Europe of the Dark Ages.

We have already examined the almost mythical roots of geomancy deriving the doctrine from the Archangel Gabriel through Idris to the possibly mythical Tum-Tum. From here we are on firmer ground with the copying of Tum-Tum's work into Arabic by Halaf al-Barbari. Unfortunately it is difficult to determine from what language it may have been copied into Arabic, and whether this throws doubt upon Arabic being the ultimate origin of the practice, or whether it is merely a distancing device designed to give the practice more authority.

AZ-ZANĀTĪ

Much more is known about al-Barbari's successor Abu 'Abdallāh Muhammad az-Zanātī who lived in the twelfth or early thirteenth century, and who founded a school of geomancy: his followers are to this day called al-Zanātīyya. Not only has his work been reprinted many times from the thirteenth century to the present day, but a number of manuscripts are still extant purporting to be from his pen.

The work on geomancy which is attributed to him bears different titles, one printed version of which was issued in Cairo in 1863 under the title *Kitab al-Fasl fi usul 'ilm al-raml,* and again in 1908 under the title *al-Akwal al-mardiyya fi'l-ahkam al-ramliyya.*

Az-Zanātī was also responsible for some of the earliest transmissions of geomancy in to Greek, because his classic work was translated from Persian into Greek verse by the monk Arsenius in 1266.

IBN MAHFUF

Next in order of fame comes 'Abdallah ibn Mahfūf al-Munadjdjim ('the astrologer') who died before 1265 CE leaving a work entitled *Muthallathat Ibn Mahfuf fi'-l-raml.*[1] (and sometimes called *Risalat raml).*[2] A manuscript of this work bearing Berber glosses has found its way to the Berlin Library,[3] and it is from this manuscript that the Berber equivalent of each of the geomantic figures comes.[4] Connected with the treatise by 'Abdallah ibn Mahfūf may be the Latin translation *Astrologia Terrestris* attributed to Ali ben 'Umar which was translated from Arabic into Italian and German.[5]

---

[1] Rağip Paşa MS 964, copy made by Ahmad 'Isā.

[2] Esat Ef. MS 1988, copy made by Ahmad 'Iyād at the al-madrasa al-Zāhiriyya.

[3] Berlin MS 4200 (2), ff. 12-67, according to Fahd.

[4] These were originally included in Appendix V of the 1st edition of the present book, but have been omitted in this edition, as these names were shown to be corrupt Arabic, not Berber. See Savage-Smith (1980).

[5] Steinschneider, *Europ. Ubersetz.* II, 1, No. 125.

THE ASSASSINS

The Assassins of Alamut were a group of Persian Isma'ilis founded by Hasan ibn-al-Sabbah (also known as the Old Man of the Mountain). His followers were given hashish as a reward to induce absolute obedience and disregard of their own safety; hence the name Assassin, 'one who takes hashish.' Later, in the twelfth century, the Assassins spread to Syria where the Crusaders first came into contact with them. The tales which the Crusaders spread to Europe of the exploits of the Assassins were coloured with not a little envy; envy of the Assassins' ruthless murder of their opponents, their sense of brotherhood imitated by later chivalric orders such as the Templars, their belief in Muhammad and his daughter Fatima (faintly reflected in the later obedience supposed to have been given by the Templars to Baphomet). Lastly, their 'paradise' to which were escorted the flower of their guerrilla force, to spend a few days in the arms of both *houris* and hashish before leaving Alamut on their missions.

It seems likely that one of the recensions of az-Zanātī's work, or possibly that of ibn Mahfuf may have made its way into the library of the Assassins, who had a mystical and cultural impact on their period wider than the merely political ramifications of their religious zeal. Some of their books may even have reached Europe via the Templars. From Alamut they carried out raids on adjoining areas not only assassinating political opponents, but sometimes kidnapping scholars and others whom they thought might be of use to them.

AL-TUSI

One of the greatest mathematicians and scientists of the thirteenth century, Nasir Al-Din Al-Tusi (1201-74), was one such victim. Persian by birth, Al-Tusi was also a philosopher, astronomer and physician, who wrote in both Arabic and his native language. His devotion to systematic scientific inquiry led to him being dubbed 'al-Muhaqqiq,' the investigator. Born in Savah, or in Tus, Khurasan, he was kidnapped at an early age by the Isma'ili governor of Quhistan, and sent to Alamut, where he remained, if not a prisoner at least an unwilling guest, until its capture by the Mongols in 1256. It may have been here that Al-Tusi first became interested in geomancy, for the Isma'ili doctrines contained much of an esoteric nature.

Al-Tusi was however responsible for the destruction of this community, for it was on his advice that the then Grand Master of the Assassins, Rukn al-din Khurshah, gave himself up peaceably to the besieging Mongol horde who had surrounded Alamut, thereby ending the reign of the Assassins.

This apparently extremely subtle betrayal of his captors has never been adequately explained, for when the Assassins quietly handed over their stronghold, Al-Tusi entered the service of the grateful Mongol chief, taking with him much of the library and knowledge of the Assassins. He later founded the observatory at Maragha.

He remained in Mongol service, becoming a *wazir* and obtaining increasing influence over the Mongol chief Hulagu Khan by his astrological knowledge. Soon Hulagu did not dare to undertake anything without his astrologer's advice, and Al-Tusi was finally appointed administrator of the property revenues which he may have used to help build and endow the observatory and library of Maragha, where he resided from 1259 until almost the end of his life in 1274.

A large number of writings (at least fifty-six) on many subjects are ascribed to him. These mainly included astrological and astronomical works concerned directly with such questions as the trajectory, size and distance from earth of specific planets, as well as their more arcane influence on people and politics. His knowledge was largely derived from Greek sources of which he had made a deep study, probably in the library of the Assassins. He knew the main Greek mathematicians through Arabic translations and commentaries, wrote commentaries on al-Kindi, Qusta ibn Luqa, and other famous Arab astrologers and astronomers, and compiled works on the calendar. Amongst all this activity, both political and scholarly, he found time to write his *Kitab al-wafi fi 'ilm al-raml* ('The Perfect Treatise on the Science of Sand,' i.e., geomancy), also entitled *Al-risala al-sultaniya fi khatt al-raml* ('The Royal Epistle on the Sand Figure'), which figured as a classic of geomancy for many centuries.

IBN KHALDOUN

During the fourteenth century, the celebrated Ibn Khaldoun (who died in Cairo in 1406) devoted a chapter of his *Prolegomena,* or *Muqaddimah,* to the art of geomancy.[1] Ibn Khaldoun assumed that geomancy was developed by the sand diviners

> "because they found it difficult to establish the attitude of the stars by means of instruments, and to find the adjusted [position of the] stars by means of calculations. Therefore, they invented their combinations of figures."

After a description of the sixteen geomantic figures, each named and classified into favourable and unfavourable, Ibn Khaldoun explains this classification in terms of the astral influences which are brought to bear by

[1] Ibn Khaldoun, *The Muqaddimah,* London, 1958, Vol. 1, pp. 226 ff., Vol. 2, p. 201.

each of them. The sixteen figures are then set under the domination of the twelve Signs of the Zodiac and of the four Cardinal Points.

Geomancers are called by him *munadjdjdimun* or 'astrologers,' thereby connecting the derived meanings of the geomantic figures with astrological speculations. There is, however, never any doubt that Ibn Khaldoun is talking about geomancy and not astrology.

Ibn Khaldoun objected to geomancers because they used 'artificial' geomantic figures rather than observing the real and natural astrological phenomena of the various stars in the sky. Here the rationalist Arab philosopher makes the error of confusing geomancy, which works by the chance formation of patterns, with the precise calculations of man's location in time and space which gives his relationship with the universe, as expressed in astrology. Geomancy is however not a debased form of astrology as Ibn Khaldoun would have us believe, but a valid divination system in its own right.

Even more aberrant, Ibn Khaldoun thinks, is the pretension of certain geomancers to succeed in perceiving the unknown by applying their minds to the geomantic figures, then abstracting from them a complete understanding of the human sphere and the spiritual realm. He parallels this with the manner of the soothsayers and particularly those who practised omoplatoscopy, hydromancy and lecanomancy. Ibn Khaldoun concludes:

> "the truth that you must present to the mind is that the supernatural cannot be revealed by any technique; it cannot be perceived by an elite class of men naturally predisposed to pass from the conscious world into the spiritual."

Ibn Khaldoun did however concede that the better types of geomancers 'attempt to remove [the veil of sense perception] by occupying their senses with the study of combinations of figures' by which they 'may attain intuitive supernatural revelation *(kashf)* through complete freedom from sense perception,' thereby exchanging bodily perceptions for spiritual ones. For Ibn Khaldoun, the ability to 'soothsay' was god-given, and it did not matter at all if the soothsayer used bones, sand, pebbles, water or anything else as an aid to stimulate his ability. However, anyone who used sand divining, without this natural ability was, according to Ibn Khaldoun, 'merely trying to spread the falsehoods to which they are committed.'

The *modus operandi* outlined in the *Muqaddimah* is much as it occurs in mediaeval European works on geomancy, having sixteen figures which are produced by rows of dots made on paper, sand or flour, which are made at random whilst asking the question. Each row is then marked off, a pair of dots at a time, until only one or two dots are left. These are transcribed and form the first four figures. From these (Mother figures) the remaining twelve figures are generated by juxtaposition and addition, the details of which are set out later in this book. In applying these geomantic figures to the Houses of Heaven the Arab geomancers, according to Ibn Khaldoun, limited themselves to using only the sextile (60°) aspect rather than the whole range of possible astrological aspects from conjunction (0°) to opposition (180°).[1]

Arab diviners assumed the existence of sixteen Houses in all: twelve corresponding to the Signs of the Zodiac (the ordinary Houses) and four to the *cardines.* The practitioners of *khatt-al-raml* thus invented 'a discipline which runs parallel to astrology and the system of astrological judgements.'[2]

Ibn Khaldoun thought that horary questions put to astrology

> "do not come within the influence of the stars or the positions of the spheres, nor do (the stars and the positions of the spheres) give any indications with regard to them. This branch of [horary] questions has indeed been accepted in astrology as a way of making deductions [concerning a particular query] from the stars and positions of the spheres. However, it is used where it is not natural for it to be used." [3]

How much less legitimate then is geomancy in Ibn Khaldoun's view, as geomantic figures 'are based upon arbitrary conventions and wishing thinking. Nothing about them is proven.'

In accord with the tradition, Ibn Khaldoun ascribes the origin of the art of geomancy to the prophets of old, frequently to the Biblical Daniel or the Koranic Idris.

AHMAD BEN 'ALĪ ZUNBUL

Ibn Khaldoun, together with az-Zanātī's classic work on geomancy, provided the basis for the later works of Ahmad ben 'Alī Zunbul. Zunbul's dates are not certain, but as he mentions the Sultan Sulaiman the First (1520-66), and also that one of his sons died in 1553, it can be assumed that Zunbul flourished circa 1550. Between the time of Ibn Khaldoun in the fourteenth century and Zunbul in the sixteenth century there is little mention of *raml.* Zunbul's key works were the *Kitāb lamm aš-šaml fī 'ilm al-raml,* and the more important *Kitāb al-māqālat fī hall al-muškilāt* ('Treatise on

---

[1] Modern geomantic practice also takes cognizance of the square and opposition.

[2] The usual resolution of the numerical difference between 16 geomantic Figures and 12 Houses is that 16 Figures = 12 Houses + 2 Witnesses + Judge + Reconciler. This statement will make much more sense after reading Part Two.

[3] *The Muqaddimah,* Vol. 1, p. 204.

the Solution of Problems') by Ahmad ben 'Alī Zunbul al-Mahalli al-Munaggim, which occurs in manuscript versions in the library of the Greek Patriarchate in Jerusalem, in Cairo, and in Istanbul. However, the Jerusalem manuscript is not contemporary with its author, and dates from the year 1721.

Apart from az-Zanātī, Zunbul's sources probably number amongst them works by the literary circle of the Isma'iliyya, such as the *Rasa'il ikhwan as-safa'* or *Epistles of the Brethren of Purity* (written in the second half of the tenth century, but an Arabic edition of which was last published in Cairo in 1928). Other sources cited by Zunbul include at-Tarabulusi, Muhammad al-Kantawi, Ahmad al-Kurdi, al-Hamdani, at-Ta'labi and Abu-I-Hasan 'Ali ben Yunus al-Misri (author of an astronomical table), Ptolemy's *Tetrabiblos,* and 'Antiquus' who is often cited in the *Astrology* of the ubiquitous Masa'allah, and perhaps some of these will provide fruitful avenues of exploration.

Zunbul's longest work, the *Kitāb al-māqālat fi hall al-muškilāt,* is designed to be a very practical manual of geomancy. It is the largest of Zunbul's books and is divided into thirty-one chapters. After outlining the history of geomancy in his preface, Zunbul (in the guise of Hermes Trismegistus or Idris) explains that the sixteen figures of geomancy *(ashkal)* are allocated to the sixteen Houses or Mansions *(buyut).* Zunbul then outlines the sixteen different figures explaining that the primary figure is Via, or in Arabic *Tariq* (the path or way). This is the primary figure because it contains one dot on each of its four layers: these layers corresponding with the four Elements, so that reading downwards we have:

o Fire *(Nar)*

o Air *(Hawa')*

o Water *(Ma')*

o Earth *(Turab)*

From this basic figure of Via *(Tariq),* Zunbul states that all the other figures are derived, and are less perfect than this prime figure. Here geomancy, like alchemy, utilized a method of mixing the Elements, to form the various figures. Thus if the bottom dot (corresponding to Earth) is removed, and replaced instead by two dots (or by a line, in the manuscript) we get the figure *el 'ataba el kharga:*

•
•
•
• •

which is Cauda Draconis. Cauda Draconis therefore symbolically consists of Fire, Air, Water, but not Earth. Likewise for *nusra el-kharga* or Fortuna Minor:

•
•
• •
• •

which consists of Fire and Air but not Water or Earth The other figures listed by Zunbul are tabulated in Appendix V.

The first four geomantic figures are cast in the usual manner and the remainder worked out by addition till you have a series of sixteen figures to place in the Houses or Mansions. This configuration, or *taskin,* is then interpreted on the basis of the astrological relationships between figures, and with reference to their Elemental constitution. This division of individual geomantic figures into Elements is almost unique to the Arab tradition as expressed in Zunbul's manuscript, and does not seem to have been carried through into later European developments of geomancy, although of course *whole* individual figures have always had specific Elemental attributions.

In interpretation the most powerful figure is again *Tariq,* or Via, because it includes all of the four Elements. This is quite the reverse of later geomantic interpretations when Via was attributed to the fluctuating Moon, and became one of the less powerful figures. Perhaps the nomadic element in Arab life, and the importance of the Moon in Islam, has contributed to the importance of *Tariq.*

Further qualities are denoted by the position of the dots of the figure, so that, from the geomancy of the 'Indian' Tum-Tum, the first dot equates with minerals, the second with living creatures, the third with plants, and the fourth with inorganic bodies. Time sequences can also be determined from figures by attributing certain numbers of years, months, weeks or days to each figure, so that the length of a life, of a journey, of a dynasty, or of an appointment can be determined by geomantic manipulation.

So much for Zunbul's preface. The first chapter explains in detail the sixteen Houses: the twelve usually known to astrology, and the further four which are derived from them by addition. Some of the Houses are considered to be fortunate (numbers 1, 2, 3, 7, 9, 11, 13, 15), whilst some are less favourable (4, 10). The most unfortunate Houses are the 6th, 8th, 12th, 14th and 16th. This division of Houses into fortunate and unfortunate assists in the later interpretation by examining the figures which fall into one or other category of House.

The second chapter considers the result of discovering anyone of the sixteen geomantic figures in anyone of the sixteen Houses. Thus some figures are more propitious in some Houses than in others, giving flesh to the skeletal interpretation. This theory of combination falls under sixteen times sixteen (or 256) different headings.

The third chapter considers specific questions, such as the fate of a ship *(taskin al-markab),* in which case examination of each House in turn determines events happening at every stage of the voyage. Other special combinations of figures reveal whether the travellers are Muslims, Christians or Jews, what their business is, and whether it will be profitable or not.

Further specialized configurations or *taskins* are outlined together with mnemonics for remembering their order. Gematria, or the art of interpreting words in terms of the total of the numerical equivalents of each of their letters, is introduced at this point. Using the mnemonic of a particular *taskin* such as *bzdh,* Zunbul explains that the letters represent the four Elements, in descending order of grossness. Each letter also represents a number in Arabic, thus:

b - 2 – Fire
z - 7 – Air
d - 4 – Water
h - 8 - Earth

This mnemonic therefore indicates House number 2 for Fire, House number 7 (Air), House number 4 (Water), and House number 8 (Earth). For each of the Houses indicated in this *taskin,* we see that the second is most compatible with Fire, the seventh with Air, and so on. Therefore, if the geomantic figure *Laetitia* (or in Arabic *Hayyan),* which is solely Fire, occurs in the second House, this would be a favourable omen. Likewise, the occurrence of *Rubeus* (or *Humra),* which is solely Air, in the seventh House would also be extremely auspicious. Further chapters are devoted to even more complicated combinations of the basic figures, and to labyrinthine rules for everything from marriage to medicine. Diagnosis by *raml* even became a lay rival of the latter, and tables were educed of the relationship between specific parts of the body and the geomantic figures.

For example, a particularly beautiful Arabic manuscript of the 18th century[1] attributed to the prophet Idris, deals with the medical application of geomantic theory. It contains diagrams correlating the various parts of the body and diseases with the sixteen geomantic figures including the stylized figure of a man drawn in red and black ink with the following attributions:

Head	Laetitia
Throat	Rubeus
Right Shoulder	Puella
Left Shoulder	Puer
Chest (heart?)	Carcer
Right Side of ribcage	Conjunctio
Left Side of ribcage	Populus
Solar Plexus	Albus
Stomach	Via
Right Hand	Amissio
Left Hand	Acquisitio
Right Thigh	Fortuna Major
Left Thigh	Fortuna Minor
Genitals	Tristitia
Right Foot	Cauda Draconis
Left Foot	Caput Draconis

The figure (in Figure 9) faces outwards from the page, so left and right have been designated from the point of view of the figure rather than the manuscript page. This arrangement of figures, or *taskin,* is designed to diagnose diseases of various parts of the body. Other *taskins* such as that shown in Figure 10 are for the uncovering of hidden treasure. The square in which the sixteen geomantic figures are arranged is much more than just a talisman, for it gives the correct cardinal direction in which to look or dig. Such techniques have persisted into European geomancy of the seventeenth century, where geomancy was used to locate hidden treasure.

With the advent of Zunbul's book came a deluge of lesser treatises and a general upsurge of interest in *raml* in the Muslim world. Indeed geomancy was second only to oneiromancy (dream interpretation) in the prestige it enjoyed in the lands under Muslim domination. The practice of geomancy was also supported by Sura XLVI, 4 of the *Koran* which has been interpreted by some as alluding to geomancy.[2]

However, its most formal claim to fame lies in the saying attributed to

---

[1] Bibliothèque Nationale, MS 2631, f. 64v. See Figure 9.

[2] See Tabari, *Tafsir*, xxvi, 3, 1. 3 ff.

Muhammad: "among the prophets there was one who practised *khatt;* whoever succeeds in doing it according to his example will know what that prophet knew."[1] As a result of this passage, some licence was given to the art of geomancy and it was allowed to experience an amazing expansion across the Islamic world.[2] Like that other popular form of Arab divination, oneiromancy, *raml* or Arab geomancy has extended beyond the frontiers of the Muslim empire both to the coast of India, the coasts of Byzantium (as explored in chapters 1 and 5), south through black Africa (chapter 3), Madagascar (chapter 4) and finally to the Latin west (chapters 5-8) then across the Atlantic to the New World.

In modern times such usage has continued, with an absence of scholarly interest in *raml* till 1980, but a wide dissemination of material pitched at a popular level. Although the rules as outlined by Zunbul still hold sway throughout the Muslim world, there are many regional variations in the system of interpretation of the basic figures. Davies, in *Sudan Notes,*[3] describes in some detail a system of sand divination which was practised early this century by Mahamid and Ta'aisha Arabs, but which was common in northern and central Kordofan and the northern Sudan. Locally it retained its traditional name of *khatt al-raml.* It is representative of *raml* as it is practised today in such village communities.

A smooth patch of sand is prepared by the practitioner or *khattat* at a specific hour of the day, according to the nature of the question. The querent places the tip of the middle finger of his right hand on the sand whilst at the same time concentrating on his question, which he usually does not tell the *khattat.* At the same time the *khattat* makes in the sand four lines or jabs of random length with his fingers. These are then marked off, a pair at a time, until either one or two are left over. This process is repeated four times, generating a geomantic figure made up of four levels containing either one or two marks in the sand. A further three figures are made in the same way. These four figures are the 'Mother' figures and, placed in order from right to left, and they 'breed' the rest of the *khatt,* or geomantic spread.

The technique for deriving the remaining eleven figures is detailed in chapters 9-15. However, briefly it is as follows: figure V is the figure formed by taking in order the top components or heads of figures I, II, III and IV. The four components next below these (or necks) give figure VI; those

[1] Wensinck *et al., Concordance,* i, 40. Noted by 'Atā' ben Yasar.

[2] This expansion has led to a great number of manuals and treatises, examples of which can be found in almost all the Arab collections in the East and the West, and details of which may be found in the *Encyclopedia of Islam* (new edition).

[3] R. Davies, 'A System of Sand Divination,' in *Moslem World,* Vol. XVII, New York, 1927, pp. 123-9.

components next below (or bodies) give figure VII; those at the bottom (or feet) give figure VIII.

Figure IX is bred from figures I and II by a different process. The top two components are combined to form the new top component, which is a single mark if the combined components amount to an odd number of marks, and a double mark when they amount to an even number.

Similarly the remaining components of figure IX are derived by combining in pairs the remaining components of I and II. In exactly the same way, figures III and IV breed X; V and VI breed XI; VII and VIII breed XII; IX and X breed XIII; XI and XII breed XIV; XIII and XIV breed XV, the Judge.

The fifteen figures shown in a 'shield' formation now look like Figure 8. The fifteenth figure is the Judge and final determinant of the entire *khatt.* These fifteen figures formed by the above process are now interpreted according to the position in which they fall.

The Houses on the right of the central line are relevant to the querent, together with the Seventh House, whilst those on the left are concerned with his enemies, or the object of his question. Additionally the Eighth House is 'double-faced,' and rather mercurially neutral. If the same figure as that occurring in House 8 also occurs in Houses 1-4, the figure in House 8 allies itself with the Houses of the querent.

The fifteen positions or Houses into which anyone of the figures may fall are designated as follows. This rule may also help determine where some lost item is presently located. At this point a wide range of very specific interpretative rules come into play, some of which are still contained in European geomancy, and some of which are purely unique to the Arab system. Basically they indicate the effects of a specific geomantic figure in a specific House position.

For example, a *Rasn* (Fortuna Major) in House 1 would indicate a journey on the part of the querent. If it were combined with a *Jebbar* (Fortuna Minor) in House 9, the inference would be that the journey would be delayed by some powerful person, rather than a fortunate journey, because in the Arab system *Jebbar* represents a powerful sheikh or notable.

House number (Position)	House name	Interpretation of figure falling in that House
1	*Beit al niya*	the House of the object of the quest
2	*Teni al beit*	the repetition of 1
3, 4	*Buyut al jiran*	the neighbour's Houses
5	*El beit al muqabila*	the House opposite
6	*Beit al zulm*	the House of wrong
7	*Sabi' al buyut*	the seventh House
8	*Al shatteir*	the double-faced
9, 10, 11, 12	*Watid*	a 'peg'
13, 14	*Farash*	a bed
15	*Al khatima* or *Majma' al khatt*	the seal or sum total of the whole *khatt*

Figure 7: One possible interpretive layout.

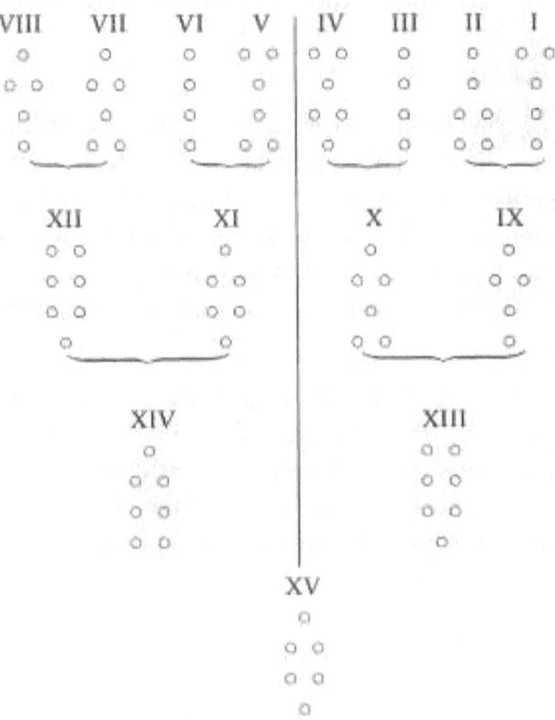

Figure 8: The traditional 'shield' layout.

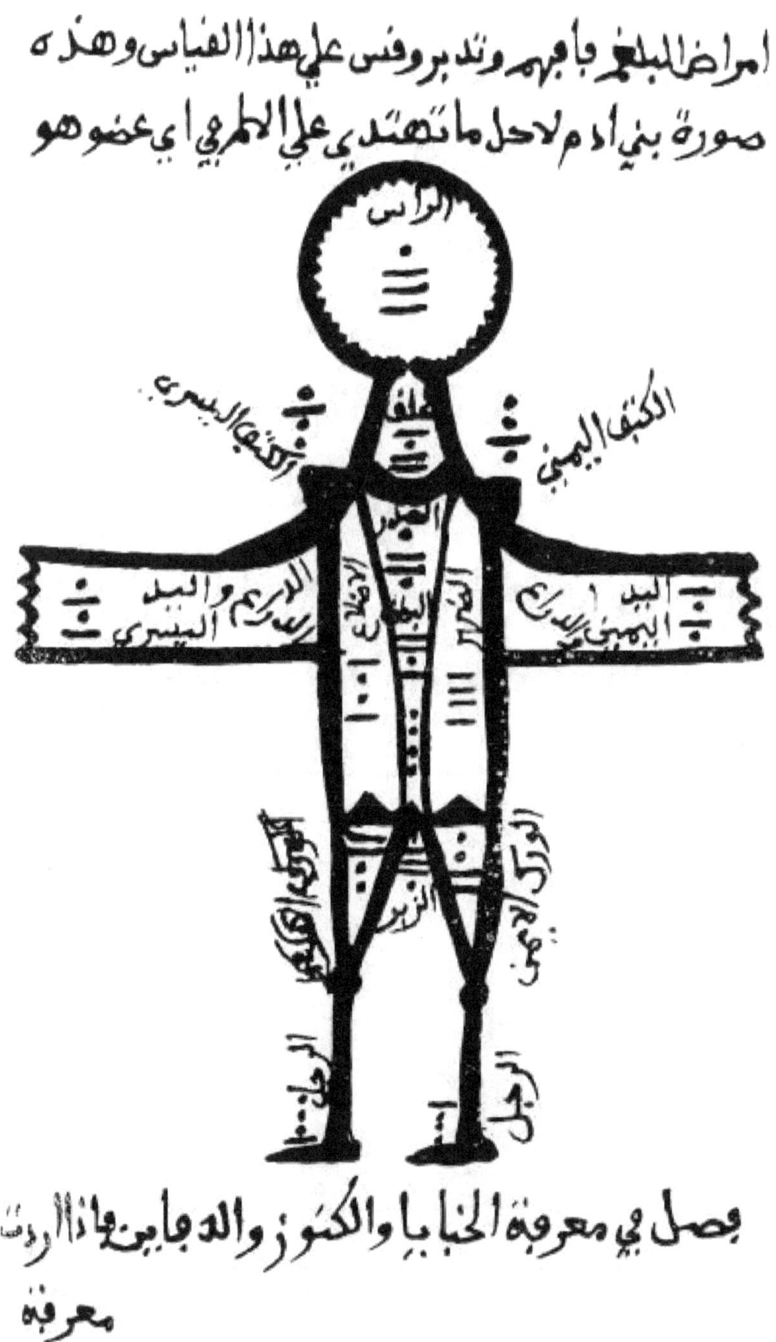

Figure 9: Geomantic *taskin* for dealing with diseases of various parts of the body, from an eighteenth-century Arab manuscript attributed to Idris.[1]

[1] Bibliothèque Nationale MS Arabe 2631, fol. 64v.

معرفة ذلك فاضرب الرمل على تلك النية وانظر الى البيت
الرابع فان وجدت فيه احد هذه الاشكال الثلاثة وهم
هولاي فاعلم ان الموضع فيه شي من الاجلا
وان ردت الحق من الكذب كالفارغ والملبان فاضرب
شكل البيت الرابع مع الشكل السادس فان تولد منهم
شكلا داخلا ففي ذلك الموضع دفين والا فلا وان
كان الشكل منقلبا سعيدا فيكون الدفين شي يسير واذا
علمت في ذلك الموضع شي فاقسم الموضع على هذه الصورة

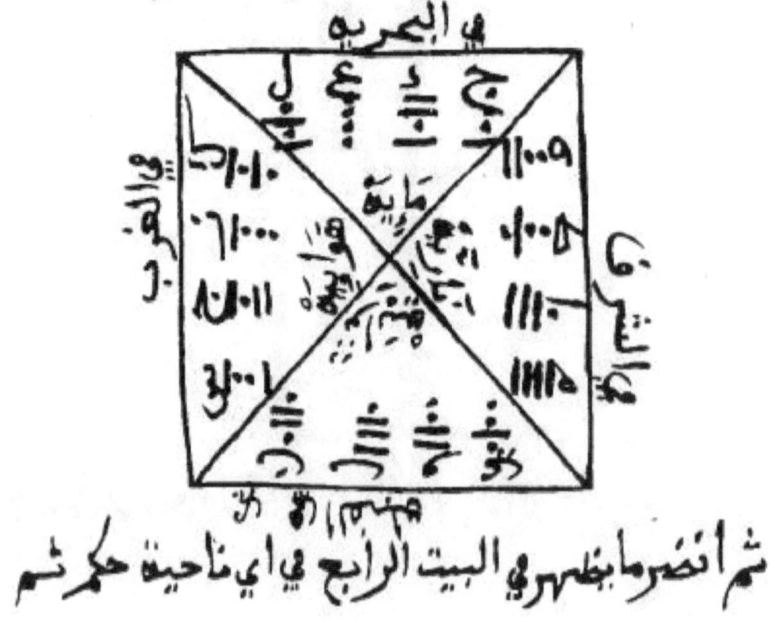

ثم انظر ما يظهر في البيت الرابع في اي ناحية حكم ثم

Figure 10: Geomantic *taskin* for uncovering hidden treasure, showing the attribution of the 16 geomantic figures to the 4 compass points.[1]

[1] MS Arabe 2631, fol. 65r, Bibliothèque Nationale.

Before the specific rules are applied, the *khattat,* or diviner, would generally examine the fifteenth or 'Judge' figure which was the 'sum total of the *khatt'* and which would indicate the general trend of the answer. If, for example, the fifteenth figure was a *Qabid* (Acquisitio) then the diviner would be absolutely sure that the querent was going to get what he was seeking. One *khattat* made his name by 'throwing' the *khatt* for some police who came at night to his village looking for an escaped prisoner. Seeing a *Qabid* as the 'seal' of the *khatt,* he prophesied immediate success to a search of the village, and the prisoner was duly caught in one of the houses. Conversely, a *Qabid* in House 5 or 6 would have indicated that the thief was most unlikely to be caught. Conversely, a *Kharij* (Amissio) in the same position would be the worst possible omen, unless of course the querent was trying to sell or rid himself of something.

The *khattat* then proceeds to examine each of the Houses in turn so that, for example, if identical figures are found in both the First and Second Houses, the *khatt* is infallibly interpreted as a bad omen. If the question concerned the fate of a sick man, the appearance of a *Jihin* (Laetitia) in both of these positions would indicate almost certain death. If the question concerned a business venture, then its outcome looks very bleak indeed. However, as a precaution against a complete dashing of hopes, the querent has the right to try the *khatt* three times, if a preliminary inspection of the first two tries should show the omens to be unfavourable. However, two figures of the same kind in the first *four* Houses would 'bring over' a third figure of the same kind from the left or 'enemy side,' to the aid of the searcher. Obviously, in this context, the interpretation is very strongly connected with tribal and family life, so that under these circumstances, it would appear that an enemy is to be considerably handicapped, perhaps by losing an ally to the querent's cause or party.

Obviously the combinations are almost unlimited, and the *khattat* needed a prodigious memory. This was however aided by a series of rhymes which indicated the auspicious or inauspicious combinations of figure and House, learned by each diviner during his apprenticeship, but largely lost to the printed literature of the subject. Oddly enough, although Zunbul considered the figure *Tariq* (Via) to be the most powerful of the figures (being the sum total of all four Elements together, and thus the only 'complete' figure of the sixteen), modern Arabs consider it to be the most insignificant of all the figures.

The order of the figures outside of the *khatt* is significant in as much as they are grouped by the Arabs of the Kordofan in complementary pairs[1] so

[1] See Arabic section of Appendix V for the local order of the figures.

that the first and second figures have, if compared at each level, one dot where the other has two, and vice versa. Likewise the third and fourth figures are complementary, the fifth and sixth figures, and so on. This of course is only one way of arranging these figures in order, but interpreted by the Arabs to mean that certain family relationships occur between the different figures. For example:

Jihin (Tristitia) and *Rakiza* (Cauda Draconis) are man and wife
Hurr (Laetitia) and *Raiya* (Caput Draconis) are man and wife
Beyyad (Albus) and *Jodala* (Puer) are man and wife
Muhzum (Puella) and *Humra'* (Rubeus) are man and wife
Damir (Conjunctio) and *Surra* (Carcer) are also man and wife
Jebbar (Fortuna Minor) and *Rasn* (Fortuna Major) are brothers
Qabid (Acquisitio) and *Kharij* (Amissio) are also brothers
Tariq (Via) and *Tiql* (Populus) bear no relationship to each other.

Figures which contain a total number of even points are said to be *Helu,* sweet or a good omen, whilst those which contain odd numbers of total points are *Murr,* bitter, or ill-omened.

Further details of the modern practice of *raml* can be found in *Magie et Religion dans l'Afrique du Nord* by Edmond Doutte, while a more romantic and living description is given by Dr J. C. Mardrus in *Sucre d'Amour,* where the atmosphere and magic accompanying a *raml* consultation are perfectly evoked.

3. Africa: *Fa, Ifa* and Ancient Egypt

On the great trade routes from the Maghreb,[1] across the western end of the Sahara through what is now Algeria and Mali, to the fabulous city of Timbuktu, and along the banks of the Niger River, came the camel trains, the merchants, the missionaries of the Prophet, the slavers and the traders of Islam, to the rich tropical areas south of the Niger, into which territory they thrust at different times both peacefully and with violence.

Travelling down the Niger and across country to the sacred city of Ifẹ and to Benin, they brought with them the *raml* of the desert dweller. Hamilton described the system of divination he observed in the Sahara, which was called *derb al-raml* or *derb al-ful,* according to the medium used to 'project' the initial figures: for the desert dweller it was sand, but in the tropical area beans were used. The latter method is the simplest, but both are in principle the same. Hamilton relates the relatively simplified *modus operandi*:[2]

> "beans are held in the palm of the left hand, which is struck with a smart blow with the right half-closed fist, so that some of the beans jump into the right hand - if an odd number, one is marked; if even, two... This being repeated four times gives the first figure, and the operation is performed until there are obtained four [geomantic] figures, which are placed side by side in a square."

The square defines the various geomantic Houses into which any of the sixteen figures may fall, and the technique of *derb al-raml* goes on to add the four geomantic figures together in the usual way to obtain fresh combinations and interpretations. *Derb al-ful* is a half-way house between Islamic sand-cutting or *raml* in the traditional sense, and the use of beans to produce figures by the diviners of Ifa to the south of the Sahara.

Thus as the practice is carried across the Sahara and into the tropical areas of Dahomey (Benin), Togo and Nigeria, the sand which was previously used to generate the figures becomes the powder on the

---

[1] The Maghreb is the region of North Africa, west of Egypt including Morocco, Algeria, Tunisia, Libya, and Mauritania.

[2] Cited in A. Ellis, *The Yoruba-speaking People*, London, 1894, p. 63.

diviner's board, whilst the figures themselves are generated by manipulations of beans or palm nuts (see plate IV). Together with this adaptation, the unique verbal heritage of the Yoruba contributed material to the complex set of verses designed as a mnemonic to aid the practitioner to memorize the interpretations of the various combinations of geomantic figures passed on to them by the Arab traders.

In trying to ascertain an exact point of contact between Islamic *raml* and the divination system of *ifa,* we can do no better than accept the traditions of the Fọn and the Ewe tribes who acknowledge the Yoruba city of Ifẹ as the centre from which the practice of *ifa* divination has spread. The Yoruba themselves consistently refer back to the early kings of Ifẹ and their diviners from whom the system was said to be derived. It seems therefore that this was the reception and subsequent diffusion point of the Islamic heritage of *raml.*

Ifa is the best known and most respected form of divination used by the Yoruba people of Nigeria, their African neighbours and their descendants in the Americas. *Ifa* is both the method and the deity of divination. The diviners that work the *ifa,* known in the Yoruba language as *babalawo*[1] (literally 'father that has secrets'), are devotees of the god Ifa.[2]

The divination technique is based on the sixteen figures or *odu,* and their 256 (i.e. 16 x 16) derivatives. These are formed by either the throwing down of a divining chain *(ọpẹlẹ)* which has eight half seed shells strung on it (see Plate III and Plate VII), or by the manipulation of sixteen palm *(ikin).*

The divining chain is quicker than the sixteen palm nuts, but the latter are considered more reliable, perhaps because they were more traditional, while the chain is a more recent 'short-cut method.' Ifa, the oracle god, is supposed to have been the god who directed creation. Ifa took the materials of the universe from a snail shell in a 'bag' suspended between the thighs of an older god,[3] and used them to form the universe, scattering 'soil' to form the earth. Ifa later descended to earth in human form to help with child-bearing, teach medicine and give information on secret and hidden matters. Like the Roman Mercury, or the Greek Hermes, Ifa brings messages from the gods and is patron of divination and medicine. Also like Mercury, he is multi-lingual, and the god of language. Rather than attributing *ifa* divination to the Arab traders, the Yoruba people say that Ifa taught his method of divination to them directly whilst he was on earth.

---

[1] The words *baba* meaning 'father' and *alawo* meaning 'secrets' come originally from Arabic, a clear indication of the origin of these practices.

[2] See Plate VI for a picture of a modern day Babalawo, and Plate VII for his divining chains.

[3] Very suggestive of the scrotum.

A similar system of divination is practised in near-by Dahomey, and dedicated to the god Fa, who was said to have presented the tribes with some special palm nuts brought down from heaven. The diviner in both systems is supposed to throw the nuts from one hand to another, and, depending on whether the remaining nuts were odd or even, mark down either one or two marks on the powder scattered on a divining board. It is this pattern traced on the board which provides the data for the interpretation of the oracle.

It is obvious, with but little examination, that these two systems of divination, which have remarkably similar names, have a common source. Although we will concentrate on the *ifa* divination of the Yoruba, it is useful first to survey briefly the myths connected with *fa* divination.

Fa was said to have sixteen eyes, made of the sixteen nuts of divination which enabled him to see everything in the world: a parable suggesting that the sixteen figures of geomantic divination enable the diviner to discover everything going on in the world. Fa lived on a palm tree in the sky, from where he could see the world; it was also said that the mischievous god Legba had the duty every morning of opening Fa's eyes. Legba, who lived on the earth had to climb the palm tree to open Fa's eyes. As Fa did not wish to speak to Legba unless he was uttering an oracle, he put palm nuts into Legba's hands to indicate how many eyes he wanted opened. However, as Legba was such a mischievous god, and delighted in doing exactly the opposite of that which the other gods wanted him to do, Fa used to put one palm nut in Legba's hand if he wanted two eyes opened, but two nuts if he wanted only one eye opened. To this day, one palm nut thrown by the diviner means two marks on the divining board, whilst two nuts means one mark, because of the deceitfulness of Legba.

Each of the sixteen possible 'figures' that may arise are associated with sacred verses, and as many myths, which can then be applied in various combinations to the question in hand; the *babalawo,* or diviner, using the elements of the verses to build up a story-like reading.

The *babalawo* is both a focal point in the traditional Yoruba religion, arbitrating in the matter of sacrifices and ritual acts, as well as a professional diviner who is consulted by the worshippers of many of the Yoruba deities and also by Muslim and Christian converts. Rather like the practitioners of *sikidy* (chapter 4), he is involved in prescribing means of avoiding the fates which he predicts, as well as the more straightforward prescription of medicines. The many thousands of verses which he has to commit to memory to perform his function as a diviner even resulted in the establishment of a church in Lagos in 1934 which takes these verses as its

'Bible.' It has always been meritorious amongst the worshippers of Ifa, to know his verses by heart.

Apart from a prodigious memory, the *babalawo* must naturally have or acquire during his three initiations a reasonable degree of clairvoyance, as it is standard practice for the querent to whisper his question to the palm nuts, rather than asking the *babalawo* directly. It is even commonly said that it is wrong for the diviner to know the nature of the problem, because this would tempt him to lie to satisfy the client, either by faking a verse or manipulating the figures accordingly.

Because of the similarity between the divinatory systems associated with Ifa and Fa, and their obvious historical connexion, we will simply consider the *ifa* system in detail, drawing occasional parallels with that of *fa* where necessary. Considering for the moment the distribution of *ifa* divination, we find that in recent literature there is no mention of it west of Togo or east of Nigeria, but early references have mentioned it as far west as the Ivory Coast (at Assinie) and in coastal Ghana, north of the River Niger (the Nupe people) and almost as far east as the Cameroons.

The principal tribes practising *ifa* divination are the Yoruba and Benin Edo of Nigeria. In Dahomey the Fọn practice *fa,* and the Ewe of Togo call it *afa.* The Gbari or Gwari of Niger province practise the Islamic form of sand-cutting *as well as* using the palm nuts which would be accounted for by their northerly position, and geographical proximity to the strongly Islamic influenced town of Kano.

What may be the earliest report of *ifa* divination comes from the coast of what is now Ghana in a description given by Bosman, who served as factor (agent) for the Dutch at Elmina and Axim. Bosman, who was in Ghana by 1690 says:

> "the second way of consulting their Idols, is by a sort of wild Nuts, which they pretend to take up by guess and let fall again: after which they tell them, and form their Predictions from the number falling even or odd."[1]

Another early account comes from Assinie in the south-eastern corner of the Ivory Coast, still farther to the west. Loyer in about 1700 describes a method in which palm nuts are taken from a wooden or copper cup, and marks are made with the finger in wood dust on a board (a foot long and half a foot wide) as a result of this operation. [2]

Allowing for occasional misinterpretations by early travellers and missionaries, the system of divination has not changed much since the late

---

[1] W. Bosman, *A New and Accurate Description of the Coast of Guinea*, London, 1705, p. 152.
[2] G. Loyer, *Relation du Voyage... en Afrique,* Paris, 1714, pp. 248-9.

seventeenth century, and has been passed down from *babalawo* to *babalawo* for the last three hundred years. If we ignore, for the moment, the persistence of some forms of sand-cutting in this area, we find that the initial figures are generated either by palm nuts or by the (possibly more modern) use of a 'divining chain.'

THE AWAKENING OF IFA

In divining with either the palm nuts or the divining chain, the diviner is first seated on a mat, with a carved wooden divining tray placed in front of him (see Plate IIa, IIb and Plate VI).

A description by Irving of the significance of the god Ifa in the divining process, portrays well the dependence upon the indwelling god to assure the accuracy of the divination, a far cry from the attitude of Islamic diviners to their art:[1]

> "Ifá, the god of palm-nuts, or the god of divination, is said to be superior to all the rest. He is consulted on every undertaking - on going on a journey, entering into a speculation, going to war, or on a kidnapping expedition, in sickness, and, in short, wherever there is a doubt of the future. To him are dedicated palm-nuts, as by these the oracle is consulted. Various acts of adoration and prostration, touching the nuts with forehead &c., initiate the performance."

After the preliminaries, the *babalawo* spreads wood dust on the tray, and places the divining cup in the centre of it. An assortment of miscellaneous objects is placed on the right side of the tray and two bags of cowrie shells (one containing eighteen palm nuts) in front of the tray. The diviner first takes the palm nuts out of the bag, separating two nuts from the rest, which are then sometimes returned to the bag.

PRELIMINARY INVOCATION

Before the first divination of the day, and while the apparatus is being arranged, invocations are made to both Ifa and Eshu. Blowing spit on the palm nut, the *babalawo* says:

> "Ifa awake, oh Ọrunmila [a synonym for Ifa]. If you are going to the farm, you should come home, oh. If you are going to the river, you should come home, oh. If you are going to hunt, you should come home, oh."

He then places the divining cup on the ground to the left of the divining

[1] Dr Irving, 'The Yoruba Mission,' in *Church Missionary Intelligencer*, Vol. IV, p. 233.

tray, saying:

> "I take your foot and press the ground thus. I take your foot and press the top of the mat thus. I carry you to sit on the mat, so you can carry me to sit on the mat forever."

He replaces the cup on the divining tray:

> "I carry you to sit on Ifa's tray, so that you can carry me to sit on Ifa's tray forever."

Prayers for longevity, fertility, children and money follow, as he draws a line clockwise in the wood dust around the base of the divining cup:

> "I build a house around you, so you can build a house around me: so you can let children surround me, so you can let money surround me."

The line is wiped out with his cow-tail switch and taking some of the wood dust from the tray he places it on the ground, paying homage to the earth. He sets the divining cup aside again and marks a line away from him in the divining powder at the centre of the tray, saying:

> "I open a straight road for you, so you can open a straight road for me."

After a nod in the direction of various other gods including Eshu (the messenger of Ifa), Ọṣun, Ṣango and Ọrunmila,[1] the *babalawo* removes the palm nuts from the cup and handles them according to the prescribed form, whilst reciting protective formulae. See Plate IV.

Having established the preliminaries, the *babalawo* now generates the two geomantic figures from which the meanings of the oracle are derived. There are two pieces of equipment designed for this purpose: either the sixteen palm nuts already referred to or a divining chain. As the divining chain is probably a modern short cut, we will consider the method of the sixteen palm nuts first.

GENERATING THE FIGURES WITH PALM NUTS

The sixteen nuts, or *ikin,* are picked up with the right hand. As sixteen nuts form a large handful (and as they are heavily polished through use) some usually remain in the diviner's left hand. If one or two nuts remain in the left hand then corresponding marks are drawn on a divining tray: if two nuts remain, a single mark, but if one nut remains, a double mark. This apparently arbitrary reversal is justified in Dahomey in terms by the

---

[1] Due to setting limitations, some diacritic marks were not available, so note that occasionally a right turning diacritic mark will be used under some letters (ọ), when ideally all such marks in this chapter should be left turning (ẹ).

deceitfulness of the god Legba in conveying the oracle to the diviner. If no nuts, or more than two nuts, are left in the left hand the operation is repeated until the desired binary number of nuts is left.

The operation is repeated a total of eight times, giving two geomantic figures (each line of which will either have one or two marks). These are drawn in the dust of the divining board side by side. An example of such a set of marks forming *Irẹtẹ* the geomantic figure, or Puer (on the left) and *Ọkanran* or Tristitia (on the right) is shown below: this figure is called *Ọkanran Irẹtẹ*.

Unlike the more northerly variations of geomancy, where four Mother figures are necessary, Ifa makes do with two figures. These are stylized as below, so that consecutive single marks or consecutive double marks will be drawn in a stylized manner in the dust with the fingers like continuous lines; the same figures now become:

However we will not concern ourselves with the actual stylized marking down of the figures. Instead we will use the first version in which the figures are recognizably like the familiar geomantic figures, which we have already encountered.

Obviously each one of the pair of figures could be any one of the sixteen basic geomantic figures. Hence as a combination, there are a total of sixteen multiplied by sixteen possibilities, or 256 derivative figures. In forming these pair of figures, the marking order is slightly eccentric passing from one figure to another and back again rather than concentrating on generating one figure first, then the other, as shown in the scheme below:

2 ← 1
↘
4 ← 3
↘
6 ← 5
↘
8 ← 7

Like the yarrow stalks of the *I Ching,* where one extra stalk is removed from the bundle before divining with the rest, so it is with *ifa.* Only sixteen palm nuts are manipulated in divining, but in Ifẹ; the diviner has a seventeenth or eighteenth nut that he places opposite him beyond the divining tray, on a ring of cowries known as 'the money of Ifa.' The nuts themselves are from the oil palm, *Elaeis guineensis,* and are about an inch long, ovoid with hard, black shells marked with lengthwise grooves. Inside are white kernels from which the Yoruba extract palm kernel oil for soap-making and for export. Alternatively one of the 256 *odu* of Ifa can be obtained by a single cast of the divining chain, which is a considerably faster method for generating the *odu* than the eight passes made with the nuts.

THE DIVINING CHAIN

The most common divining chain is made from the seed pod known as *ọpẹlẹ* from which the chain takes its name. It comes from the *ọpẹlẹ* tree, *Schrebera golungensis.* This seed pod has a distinctive pear shape and naturally splits open at the base, with the two halves splaying out from the top, where they are joined. On the concave inner surface of each half is a marked ridge. See Plate III and Plate VII.

Other items which have at one time or another been used to make divining chains include:

1) Seed shells from the oro tree, the African mango *(Irvingia gabonensis* or *Irvingia barteri),* egbere shells (widely used in Nigeria and often found in elephant dung), seeds of *Mangitera gabonensis, Mangitera indica* (the mango) and seeds of the apuraga fruit;

2) Metal markers in the shape of *ọpẹlẹ* pods or seeds decorated with simple geometric patterns and cast in brass, copper and a light white metal (perhaps aluminium), and less usually in silver, lead and iron (although the last three metals are used for the chain in preference to the markers);

3) It is probable that cowrie shells were used in the past in place of seed shells;

4) Pieces of calabash strung together with cord are popular amongst

apprentice *babalawos* in Ifẹ;

5) Animal derived markers, including the scales of the pangolin or scaly anteater and the crocodile, head bones of fish (the *abori),* and sea-turtle shell pieces; also items that have passed through animal's digestive system;

6) Wood or ivory.

Altogether a wide range of items, with the common denominator being a concave and a convex side, capable of being interpreted as a double or single mark. The divining chain, which is called *ọpẹlẹ Ifa* by the Yoruba, is about three to four feet long and usually consists of eight halves of seed shells or pods joined by sections of chain three to four inches long. The chain is held in the middle so that there are four shells or seeds hanging on the right and four hanging on the left. The chain is thrown with the right hand, and tossed in such a way that the two lines of shells fall parallel with each other. Each of the eight seeds or shells can then fall with either the concave inner surface or the convex outer surface facing upwards. The ends of the chain have various items attached to them so that the diviner can establish which is the left and which is the right geomantic figure (it being essential to know which is the first and which is the second column, to prevent the reverse figure being read by erroneous juxtaposition of the columns). Half a seed shell falling with the concave surface facing upward is equivalent to a single line on the tray, while a fall in the 'closed' position with the convex outer surface up, is the equivalent of a double mark.

Divination with the chain of seeds, though regarded as inferior, is more rapid, but otherwise the two systems are identical. They employ the same set of figures with the same names and rank order, and the same verses. William Bascom explains:[1]

> "the divining chain is said to 'talk more' than the palm nuts, but it is regarded as an inferior instrument, less reliable than palm nuts for deciding important questions. It is also spoken of as Ifa's servant... a number of Ifẹ diviners employ only the chain, because they dislike using the palm nuts... the divining chain arrives at the same interpretation through the same set of figures and verses more rapidly, and answers more questions than are usually asked when the slower method with palm nuts is employed."

It is interesting to note that other tribes use different variations of this chain, including divination with four strings of four markers each, which is used in the Yoruba system of divination called *agbigba.* Some tribes, for example the Igbira, produce a quadruple figure which instantly generates the four Mother figures familiar to European geomancy. Among the Fọn of

[1] *Ifa Divination,* London, 1969, p. 29.

Dahomey the chain is called the *agummago,* but is used in much the same way as the *ọpẹlẹ.*

The diviners see the fall of the seeds not as a matter of chance but as an act controlled by Ifa, the deity of divination. Any interference with the free fall of the chain by the diviner garbles the message which Ifa wishes the client to receive: hence the ritual of throwing the chain is governed by very precise rules.

THE SIXTEEN FIGURES OF IFA

Whichever method is used, the palm nuts or the *ọpẹlẹ,* two of the sixteen basic figures of Ifa are generated and marked down on the divining tray. Bearing in mind that the concave side of the shell on the divining chain is equivalent to a single mark, and the convex equivalent to a double mark, the sixteen basic figures of Ifa are listed below in the order recognized by the south-western Yoruba, which is the most widespread arrangement in Africa:

1	2	3	4	5	6	7	8
Ogbe	Ọyẹku	Iwori	Edi	Irosun	Ọwọnrin	Ọbara	Ọkanran
○	○ ○	○ ○	○	○	○ ○	○	○ ○
○	○ ○	○	○ ○	○	○ ○	○ ○	○ ○
○	○ ○	○	○ ○	○ ○	○	○ ○	○ ○
○	○ ○	○ ○	○	○ ○	○	○ ○	○

9	10	11	12	13	14	15	16
Ogunda	Ọsa	Ika	Oturupọn	Otura	Irẹtẹ	Ọṣẹ	Ofun
○	○ ○	○ ○	○ ○	○	○	○	○ ○
○	○	○	○ ○	○ ○	○	○ ○	○
○	○	○ ○	○	○	○ ○	○	○ ○
○ ○	○	○ ○	○ ○	○	○	○ ○	○

Figure 11: The 16 figures of Ifa.

The order of the sixteen basic figures of *ifa* is not standardized throughout the areas where *ifa* is practised. However, with some modifications in pronunciation and spelling, there is a consensus between the Fọn of Dahomey, the Ewe of Togo and Ghana, and their descendants in Cuba and Brazil. This ranking of the figures, which is important for answering questions asked in terms of specific alternatives, is said to be based on the seniority of the figures, that is, the order in which 'they were born and came into the world.' Although it is easy to recognize the sixteen geomantic figures of Via through to Acquisitio in the above list, the order of the figures is uniquely African.

The meanings of the names of the geomantic figures of *ifa* are unknown. Various 'authorities' suggest similar words in Yoruba, such as the cock's comb *(ogbe),* camwood *(irosun),* lagoon *(ọsa),* wickedness and finger *(ika),* soap (*ọṣẹ*) and loss *(ofun);* but according to Bascom,[1] all of these have distinctly different pronunciations. Puns on some of these similar words occur in the verses, but these are not serious etymologies, and one draws a similar blank comparing the Yoruba names of the figures with the corresponding Arabic. This is in direct opposition to the very obvious Arabic derivations of the terminology of Madagascan geomancy which we will consider in the next chapter.

THE DOUBLE FIGURES OF IFA: THE *ODU*

From the sixteen basic figures are manufactured 256 double figures or *odu* by taking each figure in turn and combining it with each of the others, giving sixteen times sixteen possible *odu.* These *odu* are also spoken of as the 'roads of Ifa,' and each figure is named and interpreted in terms of its two halves, of which the right is regarded as male and more powerful than the left (female). For this reason the name of the right half precedes that of the left.

The *odu* in our example is *Ọkanran Irẹtẹ,* taking the right geomantic figure first, then the left. The two components of the *odu* are spoken of as feet, sides, arms or hands. The fact that the figures are read right to left was taken by Burton as yet another proof of the Islamic/Arabic origins of the system.

When considering the 256 double *odu,* remember that each half of the figure can be *any one* of the sixteen basic forms shown in the table of the figures of *Ifa.* Although any basic figure can make up the two halves of the *odu,* it sometimes happens that the same basic figure appears twice. This creates a double or *meji odu,* for example:

is *Irẹtẹ,* while two *Irẹtẹ* together form an *Irẹtẹ Meji:*

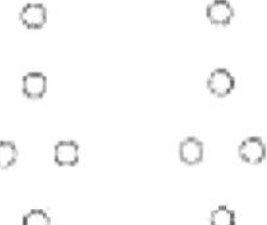

[1] *Ibid.*, p. 43.

Therefore in sixteen of the 256 *odu* the two component figures will be identical, so that one finds *Ogbe Ogbe, Ọyẹku Ọyẹku, Iwori Iwori,* and so on. These paired figures are known as Two *Ogbe* (or *Ogbe Meji),* Two *Ọyẹku* (or *Ọyẹku Meji).* All the double or *meji* figures are very important in divination, and each were thought to generate the fifteen other possible combinations of that figure with all the others, thus for example *Ogbe Meji* was the father of *Ogbe Ọyẹku, Ogbe Iwori,* and all the other combinations beginning with *Ogbe.*

THE ORDER OF THE 256 ODU

The paired figures rank in power from *Ogbe Meji,* which is the strongest, to *Ọṣẹ Meji. Ofun Meji,* the last of the paired figures, is an exception. It has some of the strongest magic associated with it, and when it is generated, it is immediately turned over so as to make a different figure. Although listed sixteenth, *Ofun Meji* is equal in rank with *Ọwọnrin Meji* in the eighth position. This is explained conventionally in terms of the story of a fight between *Ogunda Meji* and *Ofun Meji,* when the figures were historic persons who spent time on earth.

It is interesting that *Ogbe* is considered the most powerful of all the figures and *Ogbe Meji* is spoken of as 'father of all the figures,' as *Ogbe* corresponds to the Arabic figure *Tariq,* originally thought by the Arabs to be the prime figure from which all the others have been generated. In terms of the order of the figures, this points to a closer link between Arab *raml* and *ifa* than between Arab and European geomancy, where the supreme importance of *Tariq* (Via) has been lost.

To summarize, the rank order descends from the double or *meji* pairs which are the most powerful, and so occupy the first sixteen places. After them come the fifteen other variations of *Ogbe,* then the fifteen variations of *Ọyẹku,* and so on down to the variations of *Ofun* , completing the 256 paired *odu.* To return to the *modus operandi,* one of these *odu* will be generated by either the nuts or the chain and then drawn on the divining tray.

THE DIVINING TRAY (ỌPỌN IFA) AND POWDER (IYẸROSUN)[1]

This tray is flat and usually circular, or sometimes rectangular, ranging from about six to eighteen inches in width. The outer edge is carved in a variety of geometric designs or representations of human and animal forms in low relief, and often numbering four or sixteen (obvious key numbers in *ifa* divination). The raised edged of the tray must have at least one stylized

[1] Remember, in each case (Ọ and Ẹ) it is actually an 'O' and 'E' with the diacritical mark turning left, not right.

face representing Eshu (the equivalent of Legba in the Fa divination of Dahomey), which is placed opposite to, and facing the diviner, so that he can address his questions to Eshu, who conveys Ifa's answers. Virtually all trays are made of wood, with the occasional quartz or brass tray being made for special occasions. The figures of Ifa are marked on the tray in a powder *(iyẹrosun)* which is scattered on its surface. This powder probably comes from *Baphia nitida,* the camwood or *irosun* tree, and is actually the dust made by wood termites. When some is needed, the diviner takes a termite infested piece of *irosun* wood, pounds it to knock out the dust, panning it on the divining tray so that larger bits of wood can be removed. Although *iyẹrosun* is preferred, the kind of wood does not matter as much as the fact that the dust is made by termites.

Wyndham and Price[1] refer to the use of sand on the divining tray in Ifẹ instead of termite powder, paralleling closely the sand which is basic to Islamic *raml.* Whatever substance is used, it is not merely considered as a convenient marking device, but part of the magic of Ifa, an assurance of a correct answer. In fact the word for 'dust' in Arabic, *afar,* is probably the origin of the name of the god Ifa.

THE 256 VERSES OF IFA

The real core of *ifa* interpretation lies in the thousands of memorized verses associated with the 256 *odu* of Ifa. The verses form a corpus of myth, folk-tale, incantation, song, proverb and riddle: to the Yoruba their aesthetic merit is secondary to their religious significance. A *babalawo* is expected to know a large number of these verses, as an accepted authority on Yoruba religion. When the *odu* has been produced, the correct verse bearing on the client's problem must be selected from those which the diviner has memorized for this figure. This verse may prescribe a sacrifice to be offered, to modify the outcome of the matter. It is then necessary for the client to offer this sacrifice in the prescribed manner in order to avert the consequences that have been foretold, or to ensure the benefits described. Such offerings may be:

1) a calabash of cold water;
2) two dried fish and two dried rats;
3) food and drink (stew and yam loaves);
4) dry meat, i.e. game caught by the querent;
5) a live animal killed at home.

---

[1] J. Wyndham, 'The Divination of Ifa (A Fragment).' in *Man,* Vol. XIX, 1919, pp. 151-3. W. Price, *Dark Subjects,* London, 1939, p.134.

To the selected offering is added a specific sacrifice to indicate to which god it is made. For Orişa, two snails; for Ifa, kola is added to the cold water; or maize beer is added to the stew and yam loaves, and so on.

Further play is made with the various contents of the *babalawo's* divining bag, a feature which may have caused some confusion with a completely different form of African divination, *Ndembu* divination. *Ndembu* divination actually owes nothing of its theory or mechanics to the *raml* derived divinatory techniques of geomancy and *ifa* divination. However other systems of divination, based on *raml* have made their way as far south as Botswana.[1]

When slavery took root in the Gulf of Guinea early in the sixteenth century, many of the Dahomean and Yoruba slaves took their traditions with them, and their descendants practise divination, sometimes in the name of Ifa, in the USA, Cuba, Brazil, Bahia and Haiti to this day, while remnants of *ifa* divination survive quite strongly in Recife in Brazil. René Ribeiro[2] relates that he was once actually asked by a priestess of a Yoruba-derived Afro-Brazilian cult to 'look Ifa' for her, when he showed her the cards for a Rorschach psychological test!

One of the earliest writers on Ifa was Professor Abayomi Cole.[3] His book was effectively the text of a lecture he gave in London in 1899 before the Astrological Society. The copy donated to what was then the British Museum went missing at an early date, and therefore has not received as much attention as it otherwise would have. I have reason to believe that some members of the Hermetic Order of the Golden Dawn attended that lecture, and they had the opportunity, at this point, to see the commonality between Ifa and geomancy, which they were certainly familiar with.

---

[1] See Van Binsbergen (1996).

[2] Rene Ribeiro, 'Projective Mechanisms and the Structuralization of Perception in Afro-Brazilian Divination,' *Revue Internationale d'Ethnopsychologie Normale et Pathologique* , Vol. I, No.2, 1956, pp. 18-19.

[3] Cole (1898, 1990).

Figure 12: Map showing the pattern of dispersal of *raml* related divination across Africa. From this you can clearly see that *raml* spread to the sub-Saharan Equatorial regions of Africa which were influenced by the Islamic caliphates, plus the east coast Arab dhow trading routes south to Madagascar and Kenya, but nowhere else in Africa. This helps to demonstrate the Islamic origins of *raml*. See Figure 13 for the key.

Map no	Location	Cent-ury[1]	Contemporary mention[2]	20th century Academic study[3]
1	Morocco	13th	az-Zanātī	
2	Tunisia	14th	Ibn Khaldoun (1332-1406)	
3	Egypt and Istanbul[4]	16th	Alī Zunbul (d.1552 or 1574)	Klein-Franke (1973)
7	Dahomey, Nigeria (Yoruba, Ifa)	16th	Burton (1864); Ellis (1894); Cole (1898)	Herskovits (1938); Trautmann (1939); Abimbola (1976); Bascom (1966, 69)
4	Madagascar	17th	Flacourt (1661); Ellis (1838); Dahle (1886-8)	Ferrand (1902-5); du Picq (1930); Berthier (1933); Caquot (1968); Herbert (1961); Beajard[5] (1988) Vérin[6] (1991)
5	Mali (Mande culture)	17th		Kassibo (1983, 92); Sissoko (1936)
8	Dahomey, Benin (Fon)	18th		Maupoil (1943a,b)
9	Borno (NE Nigeria)	18th	Al-Jabarti (1880)	Brenner (1985, 2001)
10	Darfur (Sudan)	18th	Al- Tounsi (1789) in Perron (1851)	-
11	Ivory Coast	19th	Binger (1892)	
6	Sudan (Kordofan)[7]	20th		Davies (1927)

[1] The dates are the recorded dates, not necessarily the date of the first arrival of the practice. Although the table has been sorted by date, these dates do not establish a sequence, but merely indicate when a *raml* related practice was first noticed.

[2] Practitioner, author/translator, early explorer/colonial administrator.

[3] A selection of a few 20th century anthropologists and researchers.

[4] Istanbul/Constantinople was the Eastern route and Spain the western route that Islamic *raml* took to become geomancy in Europe.

[5] Maybe as early as the 14th century in the Antemoro district of SE Madagascar.

[6] & Rajaonarimanana.

[7] I have not mapped Mutapa (Shona) as their four tablet divination does not derive from *raml,* but is from the Persian dice that were often strung together in groups of four, and is therefore not relevant to the present study. I have replaced this with the much more relevant Sudanese practice, which is related to *raml.*

Map no	Location	Cent-ury[1]	Contemporary mention[2]	20th century Academic study[3]
13	Mauritania	20th		Trancart (1938)
16	Niger	20th		Leroux (1948)
17	Sara (Chad)	20th		Jaulin (1957)
14	Lamu (Kenya)	20th		El-Zein (1974)
12	Senegal	20th		Dupire (1998)
15	Yemen	20th		Regourd (1999)

Figure 13: Table showing the historical spread of *raml* related divination across Africa. The first part of the table is sorted by century, but the second part by the dating of modern anthropological studies. The numbers refer to the map in Figure 12. See Figure 21 for similar details of the diffusion of geomancy in Europe.

I also think it is highly likely that Cole met one specific member of the Golden Dawn, Dr. R W Felkin, at that lecture. Felkin had been seriously involved in African studies[1] and Cole specifically referred to him in an affectionate manner in his book.[2] Cole defended Felkin's rather bizarre suggestions for keeping poisonous snakes at bay, suggesting that Felkin was familiar with Africa and its dangers. The presence of references to the Hebrew Kabbalah and Tarot in Cole's 1899 book suggests also that he moved in the same circles as Golden Dawn members. Cole subscribed to the old, but discredited, idea that the Tarot (as well as Ifa divination) derived from ancient Egypt.

Having examined the penetration of *raml* in West Africa north of the Gulf of Guinea, let us look at the other parts of Africa which adopted *raml* derivatives. I have adapted a map (see Figure 12),[3] and table (see figure 13), listing the local manifestations of *raml*, the approximate century of its appearance, and details of the main studies, both colonial and modern anthropological, done on that particular manifestation.

---

[1] Felkin, Dr. R. W. 'Treatise on the Climatology of Africa' written at the request of the Committee of the African Ethnological Congress, which assembled at Chicago in 1893.
[2] Cole (1990), pp. 43-44.
[3] With acknowledgements to Brenner (2000), p. 155.

4. The *sikidy* of Madagascar

In Madagascar, a system of geomancy has grown up partly derived from Arab influence and partly from local tradition and practice. This system of geomancy which is locally called *sikidy* is particularly interesting because it demonstrates that, despite geographical remoteness, it has a close connection with its European cousin, at least in the mechanical manipulation of the geomantic figures.

When Lars Dahle asked a Malagasy practitioner, 'what is *sikidy?*,' the answer was, 'the Bible of our ancestors,' indicating how central the practice was to the beliefs of the pre-Christian Malagasy people. Accordingly, practitioners of *sikidy* were called either *mpisikidy* (one who understands the *sikidy)* or *ny màsina* (the holy or powerful ones) or in the southwest, *ambiàsa* (derived from *anbia,* the Arabic for 'prophet').

The origin of the word *'sikidy'* is not known for sure but it has been conjectured that *sikidy* is derived from Arabic *sichr,* 'incantation' or 'charm'; or from *chikel* meaning 'figure.' However, it is universally believed by the Malagasy people that this divinatory art was supernaturally communicated to their ancestors. They have a tradition that God gave it to Ranakandriana, who passed it on to a line of diviners terminating with one who gave it to the people, declaring:

> "Behold, I give you the *sikidy,* of which you may inquire what offerings you should present in order to obtain blessings; and what expiation you should make so as to avert evils, when any are ill or under apprehension of some future calamity."

Fortunately, the practical details of *sikidy* have been thoroughly documented by various missionaries and colonial governors from the mid-seventeenth century (notably Flacourt) to the late nineteenth century (notably Lars Dahle and William Ellis), and in this century by a number of French anthropologists.

The consciousness of time/space appropriateness which is strongly rooted in Chinese belief also manifests itself in Madagascar, and with it comes the use of common directional terminology. It is called *vintana* but owes its origin to the Malay word *bintana* and the migration of Malay ideas and people to Madagascar in the 5th to 7th century CE, as opposed to the Arab imported *sikidy*. The consequent confusion of these practices with the *divinatory* geomancy of *sikidy* is a conspicuously false trail which is immediately highlighted by conversation with practitioners of either art. Of course, the belief systems of any self-contained culture deserve to be treated as a whole, but to associate aspects of belief merely because they were mistakenly given the same English name, and attempt thereby to draw conclusions is bravely stepping on very shifting ground.

Let us examine *sikidy* in some detail, taking its mechanics step by step.

THE AWAKENING OF THE SIKIDY

Like many systems of divination the practice of *sikidy* was often prefaced by an invocation to the gods or earth spirits, designed to ensure an accurate response. One such formula quoted by Dahle reads: [1]

> "Awake, O God, to awaken the sun! Awake, O sun, to awaken the cock!
>
> Awake, O cock, to awaken mankind! Awake, O mankind, to awaken the *sikidy*, not to tell lies, not to deceive, not to play tricks, not to talk nonsense, not to agree to everything indiscriminately; but to search into the secret; to look into what is beyond the hills and on the other side of the forest, to see what no human eye can see.
>
> Wake up, for thou art from the long-haired Mohammedans from the high mountains, from [Anakandríananàhitra, the almost mythical founder of the art in Madagascar, whose name is followed by those authorities who passed the art on to the people and their present diviners, thereby establishing an historical line of legitimacy]...
>
> Awake! for we have not got thee for nothing, for thou art dear and expensive. We have hired thee in exchange for a fat cow with a large hump, and for money on which there was no dust [i.e. good value]. Awake! for thou art the trust of the sovereign [the ruling house of pre-colonial Madagascar used court diviners literally dozens of times a day to decide the advisability of even the most everyday actions, from matters of state to the timing of matters of personal hygiene] and the judgement of the people. If thou art a *sikidy* that can tell, a *sikidy* that can see, and does not [only] speak about the noise of the people, the hen killed by its owner, the cattle killed in the market, the dust clinging to the feet [i.e. uninteresting commonplaces], awake here on the mat!
>
> But if thou art a *sikidy* that does not see, a *sikidy* that agrees to everything indiscriminately, and makes [false statements, as if] the dead [were] living,

[1] Lars Dahle, 'Sikidy and Vintana' in *The Antananarivo Annual and Madagascar Magazine*, Antananarivo, 1886-8, p. 121.

and the living dead, then do not arise here on the mat."

Of course the invocation varied from practitioner to practitioner, but the message was the same: to constrain the earth spirits to tell the truth. The emphasis is upon the trickiness of the communicating entities, who misled if they could.[1]

Anthropologists certainly rationalise this tendency by explaining it in terms of the psychology of the 'primitive' mind, which has a supposedly infinite capacity for belief, despite any number of disappointments; each time avidly rationalizing the cause of the fault rather than discarding the belief.

Those with practical experience of the system worked by a competent practitioner will be more inclined towards the native explanation that there really *is* a perversity in the agency of divination, be it an external spirit or the diviner's subconscious mind. To counter this trickiness the invocation stresses the power of the *mpisikidy,* which is the only guarantee the querent has that the communicating agent will be constrained to 'deliver the goods.'

THE SIXTEEN FIGURES OF THE SIKIDY

The operator or *mpisikidy* lays out a mat on the ground, and uses a bag of seeds, usually those of the fano tree (a species of acacia, *Piptaenia chrysostachys*), to produce a series of figures necessary for the divination.

Not more than eight, or less than four seeds can be used in any one figure, and all figures must have four lines containing either one or two seeds. This means that in all there are sixteen possible configurations of beans, whose names and forms are listed in Appendix V (Malagasy section).

Most of the Malagasy names for the sixteen figures are of Arabic origin, others are probably modifications of Arabic words. Comparison of the tables in the various columns of Appendix V conclusively point to the Arab origin of *sikidy.* Although Lars Dahle makes a number of mistaken identifications in his article on *sikidy,* owing to his lack of knowledge of the Latin names used by Flacourt, his semantic conclusions, when filled out somewhat, are a clear indication of the Arabic origin of the names of the *sikidy.*

ERECTING THE GROUND PLAN (*TOETRY*) OF THE SIKIDY

Having outlined the sixteen basic figures, let us examine a specific divination, which generates various combinations of these sixteen figures.

[1] A common feature of spirit communication in many cultures.

The fano beans are first laid out by the *mpisikidy* on a grid which determines their meaning and the order of their generation. This grid is called a *toetry* or ground plan, the basic sixteen squares of which are labelled thus:

Figure 14: The *Toetry* of the *Sikidy*.

Each box will contain only one or two beans, while each column of four boxes constitutes one whole geomantic figure. The same figure may of course occur more than once or may not occur at all, according to the laying out of the beans at each particular divination.

The practitioner, having completed his invocation, settles down to the manipulation of the beans, which he refers to as literally 'the raising up of the *sikidy*': the phrase applies equally well to the conjuring of the spirits of earth and the erection of the geomantic figures which take place as follows:

(a) The *mpisikidy* takes a handful of beans at random, and taking two beans at a time out of his hand proceeds until he is left with either one or two beans. The bean or beans left are placed in the top right Talè square of the grid.

This procedure is repeated three more times to fill the other three squares of the Talè column.

(b) The same technique, working down each column in turn, fills the figures of Harèna, Fàhatelo and Vòhitra columns, in that order, For example:

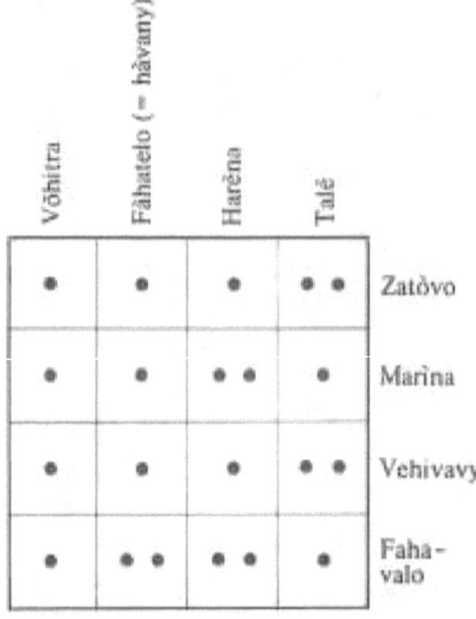

Figure 15: The four Mothers of *Sikidy*.

The four basic geomantic figures thus created now become the Mothers of all the rest. The remaining eight figures are generated from them without further recourse to the above technique.

(c) To do this, two figures are taken at a time, for example:

o	o o
o o	o o
o	o
o o	o

These are examined at each level and added together according to the formula:

o + o o	gives	o	i.e. an odd
o o + o	gives	o	number of beans
o o + o o	gives	o o	i.e. an even
o + o	gives	o o	number of beans

Thus in our example above:

the first line yields	o
the second line yields	o o
the third line yields	o o
and the fourth line yields	o

Thus the two geomantic figures add together to spawn a third.

By combination of the four Mothers, eight more boxes are filled with figures. These boxes are laid out :

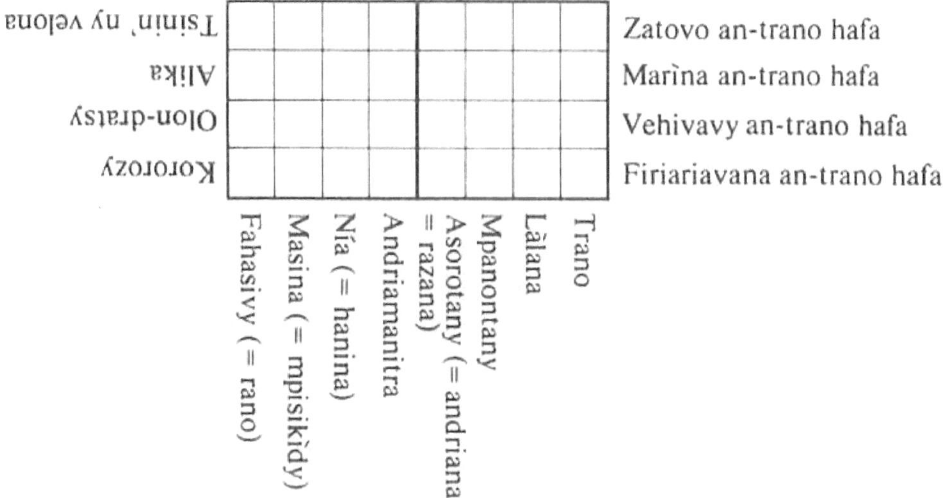

Figure 16: The next stage of *toetry* construction.

Completed, the whole *toetry* or grid with the four Mother figures and the eight newly generated figures looks like Figure 17.

(d) The generation of the lower eight figures from the four Mother figures takes place as follows:

(i) For convenience, the four vertical Mother figures are numbers I to IV.

(ii) The fifth figure is the horizontal row comprising the tops of columns I to IV. The sixth to eighth figures are manifested in the same way.

(iii) The ninth figure (Làlana) is formed by the addition together line by line of figures I and II (i.e. Talè and Harèna). Thus:

o	+	o o	=	o
o o	+	o	=	o
o	+	o o	=	o
o o	+	o	=	o

(iv) Likewise the tenth figure (Asorotany) is formed by the addition of figures III and IV (Fàhatelo and Vòhitra).

(v) The eleventh figure (Nía) from figures V and VI (Zatòvo and Marìna).

(vi) The twelfth figure (Fahasivy) from figures VII and VIII (Vehivavy and Fahavalo).

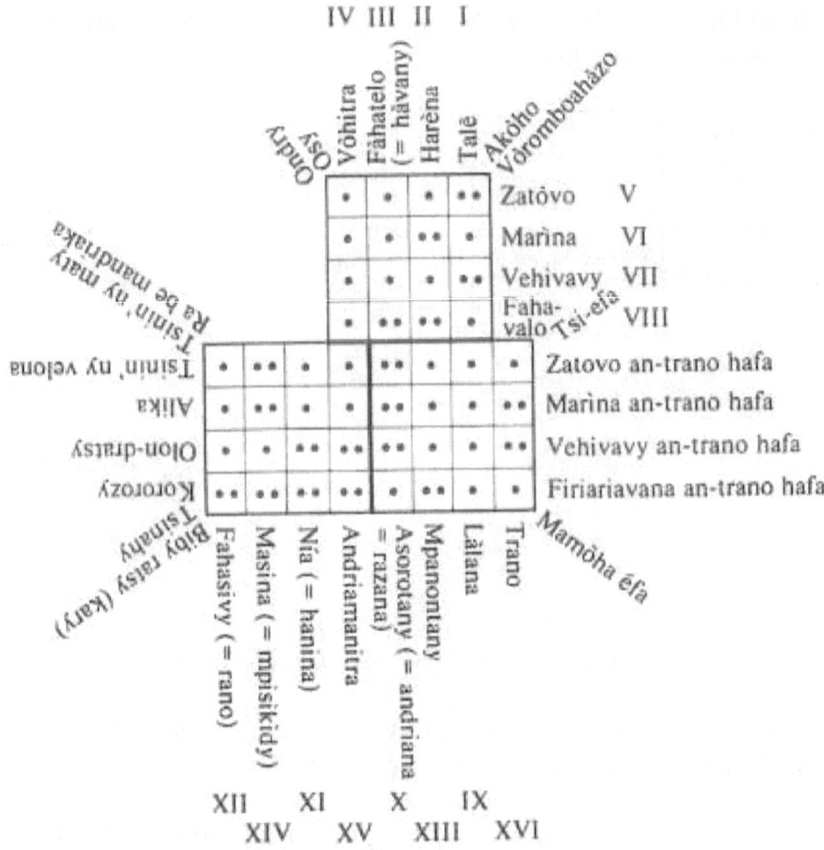

Figure 17: The complete toetry.

(vii) The thirteenth figure (Mpanontany) from figures IX and X (Làlana and Asorotany).

(viii) The fourteenth figure (Masina) from figures XI and XII (Nía and Fahasivy).

(ix) The fifteenth figure (Andriamanitra) from figures XIII and XIV (Mpanontany and Masina). This being the figure for God it stands as a sort of Judge for the whole question, determining amongst other things, the divination's right to survive or be wiped out without interpretation. It is also the central column of the bottom figures *so far formed* with three columns flanking it on either side.

(x) Finally the last and sixteenth figure (Trano) is formed from the first (Talè) and fifteenth (Andriamanitra) figure, thus uniting God and the querent in a last figure which stands to the right of all the others.

The generation could be *summarized* as follows:

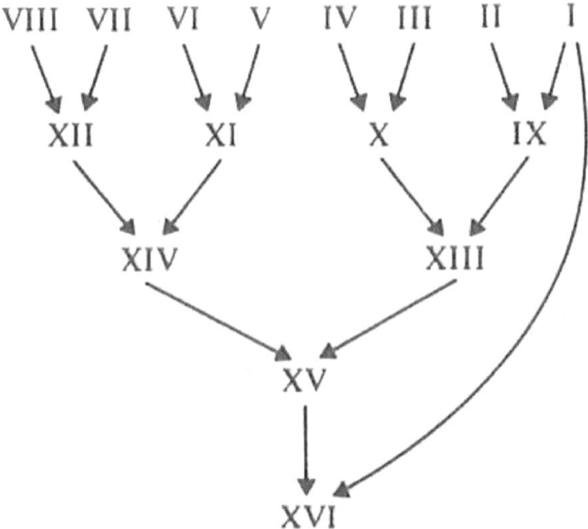

Figure 18: The sequence of generation of the figures.

This matches closely the pattern of generation in European geomancy as outlined in Part Two.

INTERPRETATION OF THE *SIKIDY*

The *toetry* is now filled, and sixteen figures established. From the system of generation it is easy to see that especial importance is laid on the fifteenth (God) figure, the first (querent) figure, and their resolution, or the attitude of the Gods to the fate of the individual, which is given in the sixteenth (Trano) figure.

Hence the first figure to be examined in any interpretation, is the fifteenth (Andriamanitra) figure which refers to God. In European geomancy the figure which falls into the First House is checked to see if it is the dreaded Dragon's Tail. If it is, the whole figure is immediately destroyed, and divination proceeds no further. The Malagasy equivalent is the finding of a Slave figure in the column of Andriamanitra, which likewise results in the instant destruction of the figure for fear that it may provoke an evil event. In fact, it is mathematically impossible to generate any of the following in the sixteenth column, a fact overlooked by earlier commentators who saw in this rule (which was actually designed to check errors in manipulation) just another superstition.

The slave figures are Alàhizàny, Votsíra (Vontsìra), Sàka, Alikísy, Kìzo, Adikasájy, Alaimòra and Adibijàdy. The remaining figures were 'noble' figures or 'Kings of *sikidy*' and were allowed to appear in the

Andriamanitra column.

Assuming that the figure is not destroyed owing to inaccurate manipulation, the interpretation proceeds by examining the four upper columns. From these one must be chosen to represent the nature of the question asked. To appreciate the significance of each column, it is necessary to investigate the structure of the divination grid more closely.

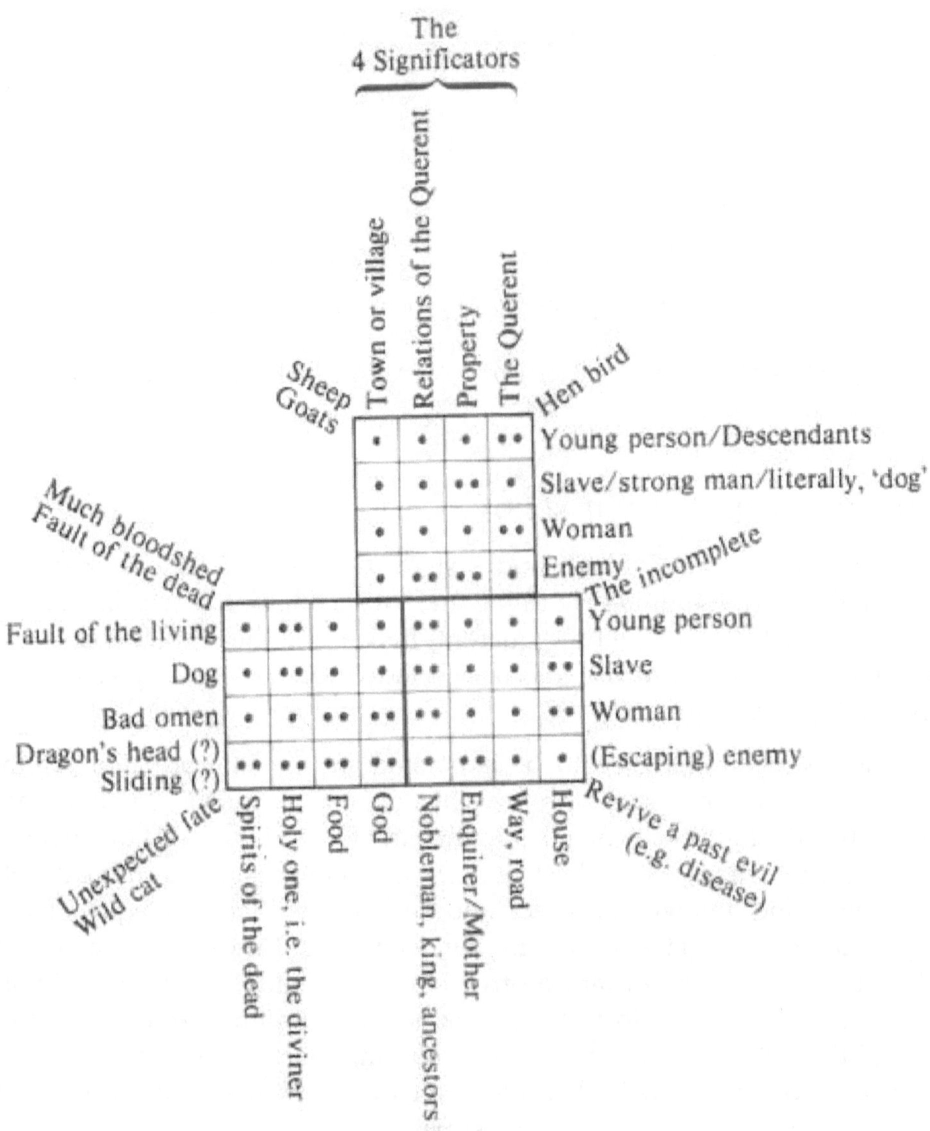

Figure 19: The interpretation of the toetry

The *toetry* has room for twelve vertical geomantic figures in all. These twelve positions correspond to the twelve Houses of astrology, inasmuch as they designate various categories of life into which a specific geomantic figure may fall. Each row has a specific Malagasy name thus associating each with a particular topic or everyday thing about which an answer may be sought (see Figure 19).

To complicate things a little, further figures can be discovered by reading sideways or even diagonally as well as vertically so that:

(a) The top 4 columns (Talè to Vòhitra) are read downwards. In this example they are (using the European names) respectively Acquisitio, Amissio, Cauda Draconis and Via.

(b) The bottom 8 columns (Trano to Fahasivy) are similarly read downwards.

(c) The right-hand 8 rows (Zatòvo to Firiariavana an-trano hafa) are read from right to left.

(d) The left-hand 4 rows (Kororozy to Tsinin'ny velona) are read from left to right.

(e) While all corner names are read according to the rules in Figure 20.

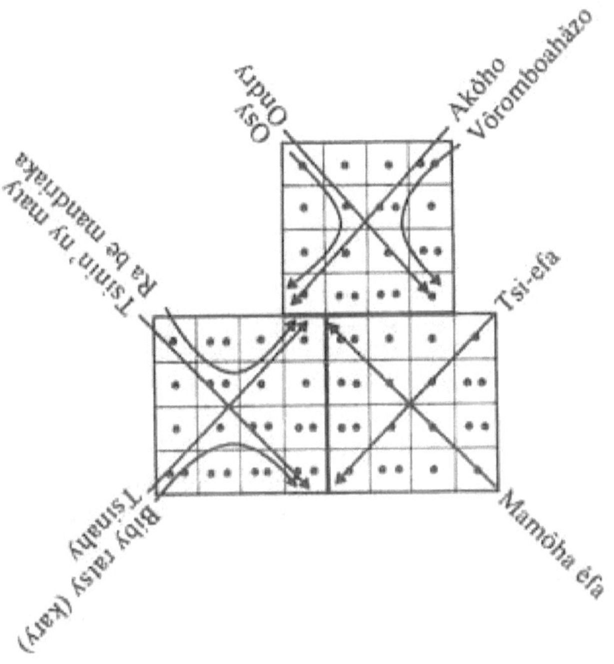

Figure 20: The structure of a toetry.

THE WORKING OF THE SIKIDY

To return to the actual divinatory operation, having selected one of the four Mother figures to represent the category of question asked, the geomantic figure in that column is examined. In our example, we have selected the Talè column as significator of the inquirer and we find the figure in it is Molahidy (i.e. Acquisitio).

o o

o

o o

o

Now as the Molahidy figure is in the column concerned with the question, the next job is to see if it also appears anywhere else in the figure (with the exception of the other three Mother figures). Looking through the grid in Figure 17, you will find that Molahidy is not lurking in any other position in the grid. Had it been, the subject associated with that column might have provided a clue to the nature of the problem to be resolved.

Lars Dahle explains this point more practically:[1]

> "If I expect a ship and am going to enquire about its coming by means of the *sikidy*, the rubric [i.e. column] *Harena* (property) is of course to represent it. If in this rubric [column] I find, for instance, the figure *Jamà* [Populus], and on further examination find the same figure in the rubric *Andro* [? = *Trano,* house] this gives me no answer, as there is no natural connection between the two conceptions. If, on the contrary, I find the same figure in the rubric [column] marked *Làlana* [way or road], then of course I know that the ship is at any rate already *on the way*. I have then got an answer to the chief question; but there may still be good reason for a sharp look-out, for there may be difficulties in its way. Suppose that I also find the same figure in the rubric [column] marked *Fahavalo* (enemy), my mind will immediately be filled with gloomy apprehensions of *pirates.* Not a bit more cheerful will be my prospects, if I find the same figure under *Ra be mandriaka* (much bloodshed). But what a consolation, on the other hand, if the same figure reappears under the rubric [column] *Nia* (food); for then I must certainly be a blockhead if I do not understand that, although the ship may have a long voyage, there is no fear of scarcity of food on board; and so on. It is easy enough to see that a man with much practice and a good deal of imagination could produce much 'information' in this manner; and I suppose that in a good many cases the *mpisikidy* were able to find an answer already in this first act of their proceedings, even if the means of finding it might seem scanty enough to ordinary mortals."

[1] Ibid., p. 231.

Dahle appears to have consulted the *sikidy* often enough for his own benefit, despite his rather patronizing attitude towards it when he says, 'I do not intend the reader to practise the *sikidy* (this secret I shall keep for my own use)': a rather incredible statement coming from a staid Christian missionary of the turn of the century!

It is an interesting point that the process of divination was a two-way operation, and not merely a passive questioning of an accepted 'kismet-type' fate. It was felt that not only the events and train of circumstances of the present shaped the outcome of the divination, but also that manipulation of the divination could alter the outcome of events.

The divination did not just stop at being simply a divination, but was used as a diagnostic tool, and finally became part of the prognosis. The *mpisikidy* actually uses it to manipulate, ease, or avert the evils which have been diagnosed or predicted by it. Hence *sikidy* becomes a doctor's aid, and a magical tool in its own right.

Following this identification of the key figure in its other possible locations on the *toetry* there comes a complex system of pairing and grouping, which although we will not detail here, because of the many variations in interpretation from *mpisikidy* to *mpisikidy,* leads none the less to a quite detailed analysis of the circumstances surrounding the main events, and the first hints of actions to circumvent some of them.

Having considered the various combinations of *sikidy* and the significance of those which fall in more than one position, it is now necessary to turn to the *sikidy tokana,* or the figures which stand alone. In our original example (Figure 17) the figure in the Talè or first column is such a *sikidy tokana* for it occurs nowhere else in the grid, it is unique. Special attention is again devoted to the Andriamanitra (fifteenth) column and the Talè (first) column.

Sikidy tokana in the first or Talè column as in our example, have a very direct effect on the querent. It will be seen that Mòlahidy (Acquisitio) is the *sikidy tokana* in the first column, and as this figure means gain in possessions, the outcome of the divination seems to imply a fairly speedy arrival of material possessions for the querent.

Similarly, a *sikidy tokana* in the fifteenth or Andriamanitra column has a very strong effect, and if this effect is malevolent, then the necessary *fadritras* will have to be paid the closest of attention, for here the querent is dealing with the god's attitude towards him and his question. Obviously none of the Slave figures can appear in the Andriamanitra column as that would have resulted in the instant destruction of the whole divination.

This limits the possibilities to eight figures. For example, if Asòravàvy (Fortuna Major) turned up, the execution of a *faditra,* in the form of a cooking pot of rice hurled by the querent, opens up the possibility of the acquisition of a lesser fortune in the immediate future.

Sometimes the four to eight beans actually making up the auspicious figure can constitute a talisman in their own right, for having fallen as a *sikidy tokana* into the incredibly powerful column of Andriamanitra they are charged with the necessary force. Thus the beans making up a *sikidy tokana* figure of Alokòla (Carcer) in the Andriamanitra column constitute a protection against gunshot if put into a bullock's horn and worn on the person. Similarly the beans of a *sikidy tokana* in the form of Mòlahidy (Acquisitio) if found in the Andriamanitra column and mixed with the herb *tambinoana* are supposed to be an excellent specific against illness if licked six times and then placed on the head! Likewise various parts of the divinatory layout are sometimes combined with other parts apparently at the whim of the diviner to derive or inspire further recipes for magical treatment or correction of the prevailing conditions. These ideas actually generated very elaborate rules specifically designed to 'rig' a particular divination in order to obtain the desired auspicious result and thereby claim the beans necessary for the charm!

The directions derived *from* the *sikidy* are of two kinds - the *sorora* which are intended to obtain favours and the *faditra* designed to avert predicted ills. The latter is analogous to the scapegoat ceremony of ancient Judaism and takes the form of ashes, cut money, a sheep, a pumpkin or almost anything else the *sikidy* might prescribe. If the *faditra* is ashes, then they are allowed to blow away, if a coin then it is thrown into the deepest water, if a pumpkin then it is dashed to the ground with mock fury, and if a sheep it is carried on the shoulders of a man as far as he can run: this then should discharge the evil.

The *sorora* on the other hand is either cooked and eaten or worn as a charm, the latter being a string of beads or pieces of silver, whilst the former can be a bullock, fowl, rice, milk, honey or any other foodstuff.

RAMIFICATIONS OF THE SIKIDY

From the table of meanings attributed to each section of the *toetry* we can see that the system is as complicated as the horary astrology of seventeenth century Europe. Like the *ifa* system of divination, which we have already considered, *sikidy* reaches much deeper into the lives of the people of Madagascar than would be expected. Not only will the divination prescribe remedies for the adverse fates, but a system of 'rigged divinations' can be used to provide favourable patterns of nuts or sand, which when collected form a charm in their own right. This is a facet of sympathetic magic superimposed on the classically elegant lines of the Arab *khatt al-raml,* so that the social impact of the *mpisikidy* is far more significant than merely that of a diviner. The Figures, especially fortunate ones like Fortuna Major can be used as a form of magic. For example, this figure is sometimes carved of roadside stones which guard the road near the entrance to a village. See Plate V.

Various other belief systems, including that of *vintana* have been associated with *sikidy,* but the former derives from the Malay origins of the Malagasy people, where possibly some elements of Chinese *feng-shui* had penetrated. In practice the only connection between *sikidy* and *vintana* is that *sikidy* is sometimes consulted to determine the best *vintana,* or location for house or burial plot, just as it might be used for any other purpose.

Malagasy geomancy occurs in an interesting connection in Richard Deacon's *The Book of Fate,* London, 1976. In chapter 8, he gives the history of a probably bogus early nineteenth-century character called 'Princess Caraboo' (1791-1864). *Alakaràbo* is the word for *puella,* or girl, in the Sakalava (or West Coast dialect) of Malagasy. It is conceivable that Caraboo derived her pseudonym from this Malagasy word for *puella.* Of course *al-* is the definite article in Arabic, leaving just *karabo.* She claimed to be from the island of Javasu in the Indian ocean. Even though it was later thought that she was actually an English servant girl called Mary Baker, it would be interesting if she was discovered to actually be of Malagasy origin, some of whose occupants descended from migrants from Java. Amongst her scribbling were some distinctly Arabic writing, and some patterns of vertical dots.

While some of the early missionaries in Madagascar, including a one-time Governor, wrote their reminiscences and descriptions of *sikidy* in European memoirs, to follow the development of geomancy in Europe we have to go back to the Middle Ages.

5. European Geomancy in the Middle Ages

Having traced the southward migration of geomancy through Africa, let us turn to the northward migration of geomancy from the world of Islam via the translators of part-Muslim Spain and the Byzantine Empire into Europe.

Isidore of Seville 560-636 CE lists geomancy along with other divinatory methods such as necromancy, hydromancy, aeromancy and pyromancy, without giving much detail about their *modus operandi.* It is tempting to deduce that the art had reached Spain by the seventh century, but it is certain that the geomancy mentioned by Isidore was the general type of 'divination by inspection of the element,' and not the elaborate type of divinatory art explored in this book. Isidore refers to divination by cracks in the earth, by observation of chance patterns, rather than the complete logical system of geomancy derived from *raml.* As we shall see later in this chapter, the word 'geomancy' did not take on its present meaning till the translation by Hugh of Santalla of an Arabic treatise on *raml.*[1]

The next major mention of geomancy in Europe occurs in the twelfth century when it is included in a breakdown and condemnation of the magical arts. Hugh of St. Victor (1096-1141 CE) divided magic rather pedantically into five main divisions, each then further sub-divided:

1. *Mantike*

    (a) necromancy

    (b) geomancy

    (c) hydromancy[2]

    (d) aerimancy [*sic*]

    (e) pyromancy

---

[1] See Plate XI.

[2] Not to be confused with 'hygromancy' which refers, in the opinion of the present author, to a form of spirit capture, to be found in the Greek grimoires, which were the predecessors of the *Key of Solomon.*

2. *Mathematica*

(a) *aruspicina horae* - which consists of the observation of hours

(b) *aruspicina hara* - which consists of the observation of entrails

(c) *augurato* - which consists of the observation of birds [as in Classical times]

(d) *horoscopia* - which consists of the observation of nativities [astrology]

3. *Sortilegia* or divination by lots [sometimes confused with geomancy]

4. *Maleficia* - defined by St Victor as "the performance of evil deeds by incantations to demons, or by ligatures [bindings] or any other accursed kind of remedies with the co-operation and instruction of demons."

5. *Praestigia* - in which "by phantastic illusions concerning the transformation of objects, the human senses are deceived by demoniacal art."

This early definition of the field of action of magic is very interesting for a number of reasons. First, *mantike* or divination grouped together the four elemental methods, of which geomancy came first, preceded only by necromancy which perhaps better belonged among the incantatory arts of *maleficia.*

Mathematica, far from being the abstract science of today, covered the practical interpretive arts which relied upon observation of natural phenomena, from birds and the intestines of sacrificed animals, to the movements of the stars *(horoscopia* or astrology) which partook of more actual calculation than the three other subdivisions of *Mathematica.* Here one can clearly see the gulf between formal geomancy and augury, which relies upon the chance movement of birds or animals across certain quarters of the sky or land.

The third main category, *sortilegia,* was also sometimes confused with geomancy, because occasionally a geomantic figure was generated to indicate the page or column of a book, which would just as easily be determined by lot or dice, hence artificially introducing geomancy into *sortilegia.* This has led to *libri delle sorti* or lot-books being dubbed 'geomancies,' a frequent source of academic confusion.[1]

[1] The study by Skeat, 'An Early Mediaeval *Book of Fate,*' in *Medieval and Renaissance Studies,* Vol. III, London, 1954, helps to iron out this confusion, whilst Richard Deacon's *Book of Fate,* 1976, only confuses the issue.

Maleficia and praestigia are those categories which have now come to be seen primarily as magic, the first operating through the actions of demons, the second being illusory and deceptive. *Maleficia* has always been 'black magic,' whilst *praestigia* has wavered between the contrived illusions of prestidigitators or legerdemain, and the more subtle magic of deceptions which may have been demoniacally inspired, or may have been natural. At various times sundry subjects, now become 'sciences,' have been the province of *praestigia. Maleficia* has always held its own, but has perhaps widened its field of action to dealing with elementals, genies, spirits, and more morally neutral inhabitants of the netherworld than mediaeval theology ever wished to concede it.

The arrival of the practice of *raml* in Europe had however to await the period of feverish translating activity which began in Spain. It was in the brilliant universities of Cordoba, Toledo and Seville that the scholars of the twelfth century translated the great Arabic works, such as the *Canon* of Avicenna and Ptolemy's *Almagest*, which introduced science and Muslim civilization to the Europe of the Middle Ages. Along with the natural sciences, many of the relics of Greek civilization, which had been translated into Arabic during the period of Haroun al-Raschid (763-809 CE), came the peculiarly Islamic contributions to astrology and the divinatory arts.

HUGH OF SANTALLA

The first geomancy translated into Latin from Arabic was Hugh of Santalla's *Ars Geomantiae* (see Plate XI). Hugh of Santalla (or Hugo Sanctelliensis) was an astrologer, alchemist and translator of the first half of the twelfth century born in Santalla in northwest Spain. He appears to have worked under the patronage of Michael the bishop of Tarazona, from 1119 to 1157. Although he to some extent translated the same works as his contemporaries, for instance the *Centiloquium* ascribed to Ptolemy (Latin versions of which have also been credited to Plato of Tivoli and John of Seville), he appears to have worked independently of the Toledo translators. Hugh's translations are undated but at least some of them, including his *Ars Geomantiae,* antedated the work of his more famous contemporaries. Hugh's seven known translations are concerned with works of astronomy, astrology and divination. Those on astrology include Albumasar's *Book of Rains,* Messahala on nativities, a book by pseudo-Aristotle, 'from 255 volumes of the Indians,' and *De spatula,* a treatise on divination from the shoulder-blades of animals.

Hugh of Santalla originally borrowed the term 'geomancy' to translate *'ilm al-raml.'* Prior to this 'geomancy' was used as one of the four *empty* categories of Elemental divination which mediaeval writers thought *ought* to exist: pyromancy, hydromancy, aeromancy and geomancy. These forms of divination were repeated in many lists but never expanded upon with actual techniques, at least not till New Age inventiveness dreamed them up.[1] In classical times there was not the slightest concrete information concerning the procedures constituting this [Elemental] geomancy. In fact Hugh's translation was an apt misnomer. In the preface to his geomancy he promises to write next on hydromancy but says that he has failed to find any books on aeromancy or pyromancy. This is understandable as it seems that the two last forms of divination were simply void categories carried over as labels from classical writers to satisfy the mediaeval craving for symmetry of classification. Finally, the *Emerald Tablet,* that archetypal alchemical text attributed to Hermes Trismegistus, was made available from the Arabic in the first Latin translation by Hugh.

There are *two* basic treatises on geomancy translated by Hugh of Santalla, the *Ars Geomantiae*[2] and the *Geomantia Nova:*[3] they are quite distinct texts.[4] In them Hugh mentions the art of spatulomancy which was taken by the Arabs from the Greeks, in contradistinction to geomancy, which was taken by the Greeks from the Arabs. Hugh mentions this derivation of spatulomancy, indicating how well informed he was on the origin of the various forms of divination. This considerably reduces any doubts as to the correctness of his ascription of geomancy to Arab sources. Further, his free use of the twenty-eight Mansions of the Moon in his geomantic work indicates an Arab source rather than Greek (to whom the twenty-eight Mansions were unknown).

From the incipit of the two works it seems likely that the *Ars Geomantiae* came before the *Geomantia Nova,* but further proof of its primacy is provided by later writers.

In the sixteenth century, Christopher Cattan, the Italian author on geomancy, only knew of the existence of the *Geomantia Nova* in an anonymous manuscript, which he held in great regard as a source work (together with the work of Bartholomew of Parma and a Hebrew work, *ha Veenestre).*

---

[1] In fact there is a hygromancy, but not in the sense intended by mediaeval writers.

[2] Bibliothèque Nationale, MS 7354. Copies also exist at Cambridge University, Magdalene MS 27 (late fourteenth century) and Vienna MS 5508 (fourteenth century).

[3] See Figure 22. Laurentian MS Plut. 30, codex 29. (Vienna MS 5327 contains a fragment of Hugh's geomancy in a fifteenth-century hand). See manuscript Bibliography for details of incipits.

[4] Both were edited and partly published by the French scholar and historian of mathematics, Paul Tannery, in his posthumous *Mémoires Scientifiques,* Vol. IV, Paris and Toulouse, 1920.

Map no	Location	Cent-ury	Contemporary mention[1]	20th century Academic study[2]
	Tours, France	12th	Bernard Silvestris (1085-1178)	
	Spain, Italy, France…	12th	Abraham ibn Ezra (1089-1164)	
	Santalla, Spain	12th	Hugh of Santalla (c.1100-1157)	
	Toledo, Spain	12th	Gerard of Cremona (1114-1187)	
	Ratisbon, Germany	13th	Albertus Magnus (1193-1280)	
	Greece	13th	William of Moerbeke (c.1215-1286)	
	Egypt, Mosul or Damascus	13th	Geomantic machine built 1241	Savage-Smith (1980)
	Paris & Padua	13th	Peter de Abano (1250-1317)	
	Morocco	13th	az-Zanātī	
	Constantinople	13th	Arsenius translates az-Zanātī to Greek (1266)	
	Palma, Spain & Bologna, Italy	13th	Bartholomew of Parma's *Summa* (1288)	
	Provence, France	14th	Provençal poem on geomancy (1332)	Tannery (1920)
	London	14th	King Richard II's geomancy (1391)[3]	
	Bohemia, Czech Rep.	14th	King Wenceslaus' geomancy (1392)	
	Byzantine Empire	15th	Georges Midiates 1462	Tannery (1920)
	Greece	16th	Pierre de Montdore 1552-67	Tannery (1920)
	Italy	16th	Christopher Cattan 1558	

Figure 21: Table showing the historical spread of geomancy across Europe from north Africa. This is just a selection to show the various countries penetrated by geomancy long before even the earliest Arab writers like Zanātī and Zunbul.

[1] Practitioner, author/translator, early explorer/colonial administrator.

[2] A selection of a few 20th century anthropologists and researchers.

[3] Royal acceptance of geomancy implies a fairly long period of prior usage. See Plate I.

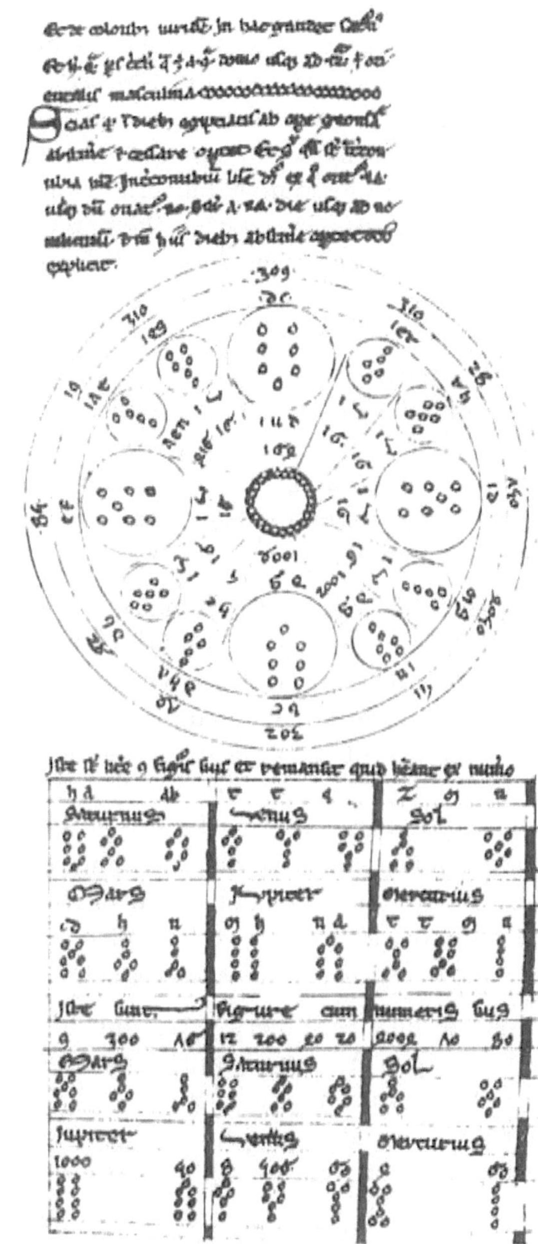

Figure 22: Mediaeval Latin geomantic MS of *Geomantia Nova* by Hugh of Santalla.[1]

[1] Florence, Laurentian MS Plut. 30.29 cod. F.25v.

On the other hand, two geomantic poems from Provence refer to a number of oriental authors, and amongst them only *one* Christian, Hugh of Santalla.[1] The reference however is in the form which indicates that the author of the Provençal poems has seen the *Geomantia Nova* rather than *Ars Geomantiae.* Although the name of Hugh of Santalla is quoted in the poems as the introducer of geomancy to the west, his own work is not quoted at length but rather subsequent and more modern treatises are subject to quotation. It seems certain that the *Ars Geomantiae* is the first work in Latin on geomancy with the *Geomantia Nova* being the second, but more popular, because in the latter Hugh's name is included in the titles, almost as if it were part of the *description* of the science of geomancy. It is possible, but unlikely, that the second treatise was not actually by Hugh, but his *name* was cited in the title to give it authority, and to indicate the nature of the science being written about. If this is so it further reinforces Hugh's primacy in the subject. Without doubt Hugh was the first translator to adapt the word 'geomancy' to its present use, being the author of the manuscript which has the oldest description of the geomantic technique derived from *raml.*

Basing his arguments on the *Ars Geomantiae,* Tannery makes two salient points.[2] The first is that the author of the prologue does not seem to know how to designate the art about which he wishes to speak, or at least he has at his disposal only vague circumlocutory expressions, until such time as he tries to use the term *'geomantiae inscriptionem aggredior,'* which he groups together with an enumeration as the other three types of divination which have already been given by Isidore of Seville. However, he qualifies this by saying that he has found nothing on pyromancy, aeromancy or hydromancy, which is quite understandable as the subject-matter of each of these forms of divination has either been well and truly lost, or was simply based on a type of intuitive inspection of the relevant element.

According to Tannery's epilogue, in which he sums up his conclusions, the scientific name 'geomantia' was *adopted* by Hugh of Santalla to render the initially untranslatable word *raml.* The better expression would have been *ars punctatoria* in Latin, a term which occasionally occurs in later works, and which very graphically means the art of divination by making points, either by stabbing or upon a writing tablet. In any case the term *ars punctatoria* soon dropped out of common use, but before it did so, it gave rise to the German term for geomancy which is *punktierkunst.*

---

[1] G. Contini, 'Un Poemetto provenzale di argomento geomantico' in *Collectanea Friburgensia,* 1940. See also T. Ebneter, *Poème sur les signes géomantiques en ançien provençale,* 1955.

[2] *Mémoires Scientifiques,* Vol. IV, 1920, pp. 324-6.

BERNARD SILVESTRIS

Very little is known about Bernard Silvestris (or Bernardus Sylvestris) (1085-1178), but his contribution to Mediaeval geomancy was significant. He is reputed to have written or translated three of the most widely distributed geomancies of the period. Bernard translated one text involving the twenty-eight Mansions of the Moon under the title *Experimentarius oder liber fortunae* and many manuscripts of this survive.[1] This however is a *libro delle sorti,* or book of 'lots', rather than a true geomancy. His other works are the *Desiderantibus* and possibly the *Estimaverunt Indi...*[2] Although these works were very influential, till very recently there has been no printed edition. Even now there is only one transcription of the Latin text,[3] and no translations. Charmasson is the first researcher to look at his work in detail.[4]

PLATO OF TIVOLI & ALFAKINI

Parallel with the intense translating activity in Toledo, which was preparing the ground for the breakthrough of scientific thought in Europe, translators also stirred in Barcelona. Plato of Tivoli was one such translator who sojourned in Barcelona from 1134 to 1145. Most of Plato's Arabic translations were astrological.[5] He was assisted by a Jew, Abraham bar Hiyya (or to use his Latin name, Savasorda). Included amongst his better known works is a divinatory geomancy entitled: *Alfakini arabici filii quaestiones geomantiae,* which was later published in the collection called *Fasciculus Geomanticus* along with Robert Fludd's work on geomancy. This collection later became the standard printed Latin source for the rules of geomantic practice, and Plato's contribution one of the earliest contained in it.

GERARD OF CREMONA

The only possible rival to Hugh's claim to primacy is the work translated by Gerard of Cremona (1114-1187). Gerard must however have been a much younger man than Hugh at the time, and it seems fairly certain that Hugh's translation preceded Gerard's.

Although Hugh was the father of geomantic texts in the Latin world, Gerard was far more important in terms of the range and volume of his

[1] There are nine MSS of this in the British library alone, with 7 in the Bodleian at Oxford, two more in Cambridge, and one in Paris.

[2] See the separate section on the *Estimaverunt indi,* below.

[3] Burnett (1996).

[4] Charmasson (1980), pp. 111-128.

[5] See Plate XVII.

translations. Gerard spent his early years in the great Moorish schools of Toledo, one of the main intellectual centres of Europe. Here, where magic and the divinatory arts were taught as a university subject to large groups of students, both Muslim and Christian, Gerard thrived and absorbed Latin and Arabic at a prodigious rate. Early in his career he determined to devote the rest of his life to translating Arabic scientific and magical treatises into Latin. Perhaps the most important translations were Ptolemy's *Almagest* and *Tetrabiblos,* which together formed the basis of the whole structure of astronomy and astrology in mediaeval Europe for centuries to come.

Gerard's contribution to the scientific and intellectual life of his century was enormous, for together with the school of translators which followed him, he was responsible for making available the bulk of the new scientific material in the twelfth and succeeding centuries. A biography appended by loyal pupils to his translation of Galen's *Tegni* contains a list of seventy-one works translated by him, some of them of immense size - for example the work of Ibn Sina's - and that list is far from being complete. Various other translations have been credited to him over the centuries, as was the fashion. Many of the Arabic recensions of the work of the great names of Greek science and philosophy, Aristotle, Euclid, Archimedes and Apollonius to mention just a few, found their way back into European thought via Gerard's translations.

Gerard himself, unassisted, could not possibly have made all the translations ascribed to him: he was tremendously active but we may assume that many other translations were made under his direction and that he was in fact the head of a school of translators. Later translations may have been ascribed to him because he was considered the translator par excellence of the period. However, some ascriptions to him are confusions with the work of the Italian astrologer Gerard of Sabbioneta who flourished in the second half of the thirteenth century.

GERARD OF SABBIONETA

Gerard of Sabbioneta composed or translated one treatise on geomancy, the *Geomantiae Astronomiae Libellus* (probably in 1294) and a summary of Ptolemaic astronomy as explained by al-Farghani and al-Battani, thus very closely paralleling the work of Gerard of Cremona, with whom he is sometimes confused.

The *Geomantiae Astronomiae Libellus* was first printed with the *Fourth*

Book of Occult Philosophy of Cornelius Agrippa,[1] and was the subject of a rather clumsy translation published first in Italian, then again in French in many editions (Paris 1615, 1664, 1687 to name a few) as *Géomancie Astronomique de Gérard de Cremone pour savoir les choses passées les présentes et les futures* by the Sieur de Salerne, an Italian refugee in Paris.

It can be immediately said that this book of astrological geomancy attributed to Gerard of Cremona and printed in *The Fourth Book of Occult Philosophy* is definitely by Gerard of Sabbioneta and not by Cremona, a fact firmly established by Prince Boncompagni. [2] Moreover the technique outlined by Gerard of Sabbioneta is a *special* practice which does not use the same technique as the geomancy of Gerard of Cremona.[3]

ESTIMAVERUNT INDI

An Arab work translated by Gerard of Cremona at Toledo, about 1160, which is to be found in a Latin Bodleian manuscript entitled *Liber geomantiae de artibus divinatoriis qui incipit Estimaverunt indi.*[4] This text, was first condemned by the Church in 1277. Some authorities attribute it to Hugh of Santalla others to Gerard of Cremona. The usual literal translation of this title is 'Book of geomancy and the art of divination which begins the Indians estimated...' Its incipit is therefore sometimes adduced as a proof that geomancy came from India. If this is truly the translation, one has to allow for the fact that India was one of this places that was assumed to be a source of things magical, but whose exact geographical location was not really known

However it is possible that this translation of the Latin is just too facile. Maybe the title should read *estimaverunt indi*[*cium*], meaning 'estimated indications or evidence,' i.e. divination. Alternatively, and more likely, *indi* could be the passive infinitive of *indo* 'to introduce.' In addition it is a mistake to translate *estimaverunt* simply as 'estimated', as if it was classical latin, because in the Middle Ages its meanings also included "very rare or of great value." Taking these together, the phrase would then mean something like "an esteemed or very valuable introduction," which sounds

---

[1] Reprinted by Askin Publishers, London, 1978, and again in an edition in modern English as *Agrippa his Fourth Book of Occult Philosophy,* edited by the present author, Berwick: Ibis, 2005.

[2] In *Atti dell' Accademia dei Nuovi Lincei IV,* 1851, p. 100 et seq.

[3] Details of which will be found in my *Oracle of Geomancy,* chapter 13.

[4] Bodleian Ashmole MS 4, ff. 49-70, not noted by Charmasson. There are three other copies in Florence, one in the British Library (Harley MS 4166), and one each in Aix, Erfurt and Munich.

a lot more likely than "the Indians estimated." The incipit may therefore has nothing to do with India, despite the apparent initial capital.

ROBERT OF CHESTER

In a British Library manuscript, one of Plato of Tivoli's translations is preceded by a translation of the *Judgements* of the astrologer Alkindi by one Robert of Chester.[1] Little is known of Robert except that he was an English mathematician, astronomer, alchemist and translator from Arabic into Latin. He lived in Spain about 1141-7 where he was archdeacon of Pamplona, before removing to London in 1150, so he could easily have come into contact with Plato of Tivoli.

Robert of Chester was also responsible in 1144 for translating perhaps the first work on alchemy into Latin. In *The Book of Morienus* Robert states that the Latin world does not yet know of the strange science of alchemy. However it took very little time for both these arts to 'catch on' in Europe.

MICHAEL SCOT

Geomancy, according to Lynn Thorndike "seems to have been nearly as popular in the mediaeval period as the ouija board is now," and so it is no surprise to find that Michael Scot (c.1175 - c.1235), a leading intellectual in Europe during the early thirteenth century also embraced the practice of geomancy. Scot has appeared as a shadowy and intriguing character to later generations, an alchemist, physician, astrologer and divine. His insistence on experience and experiment influenced the methods of such figures as Robert Grosseteste and Roger Bacon. On the other hand, Scot was also a man of his period and delighted "in the adulterine arts such as the interpretation of dreams, auguries and lots." He was born in Scotland and is thought to have studied at Oxford, and like Roger Bacon, taught and studied at the University of Paris. The earliest certain date in his cosmopolitan academic career is 1217 when he translated the work of al-Bitrugi, a twelfth century astronomer. He also introduced the works of Avicenna and Averroes to the Christian West. He was working in Toledo when he made his first translation, and later in Bologna, after which he probably served at the Court of Frederick II, at whose request many of his works were written.

Scot was often cited by many of the great scholars that followed him, including names which are also associated with the history of geomancy, such as Peter de Abano and Abraham ibn Ezra. His most popular works

[1] MS Cotton Appendix VI.

were *Liber Introductorius,* a general introduction to astrology, and *Liber Particularis,* a more popular version of the former, containing a series of questions and answers on astrology and allied natural sciences.

Although his main activities were as translator and experimental philosopher, Scot was especially famous in the following generations as an astrologer and magician. Many legends crystallized around his memory and he thus became in the popular mind one of the foremost magicians of the Middle Ages. Dante put him in Hell (Canto XX, 116), characterizing him as knowing magic rather than performing it:

> "Michele Scoto fù, che veramente
> Delle magiche frode seppe il giuoco."

Dante also speaks of geomancy in the first lines of Canto XIX of the *Purgatorio :*

> "In the hour when the day's heat overcome by the earth and sometimes by Saturn, can no longer temper the cold of the moon, when the geomancers see their *Fortuna Major* rise in the east before dawn by a path which does not long stay dark for it, there came to me in dream a woman, stammering, cross-eyed, and crooked on her feet, with maimed hands and of sallow hue."

The reference of course would be understood by Dante's contemporaries: the path or Via is of course attributed to the moon (night) while Fortuna Major is in the domain of the Sun (day).

But to return to Michael Scot, we find him defining magic as:

> "not found nor received in philosophy, because it is the mistress of all iniquity and evil, often deceiving and seducing the souls of its practitioners and injuring their bodies."

This identified the invocation of demons rather than the experimental natural magic which was the mediaeval parallel of today's science. On the other hand, it was the demons who form "various figures in the clouds, destroy bridges, uproot trees, and sometimes remove the roofs of houses."

Scot's attitude to magic parallels that of Hugh of St. Victor. Scot however extended the subdivisions of divination to a total of twenty-eight categories, of course including the four familiar elemental types of divination.

In his *Liber Introductorius* Scot neither condemned geomancy nor asserted its claim to an astrological basis, reminding his readers that geomancers were "apt to offend against the rule that once a question has been asked and answered, it should not be repeated." However, as Scot was not anti-geomancy, and interested in the art, he probably tried his hand at writing a geomancy. In fact, a manuscript which closely resembles his style of writing occurs in a (sixteenth century) collection of geomantic treatises at

Munich.[1] The text enumerates the sixteen geomantic figures, and Scot traditionally associated the sixteen geomantic figures with the twelve Signs of the Zodiac, giving two each to Taurus, Gemini, Virgo and Libra. Each geomantic Sign is also associated with one of the planets, a day, month, colour, odour, taste, stone, tree, metal and human type. Scot's geomancy goes into immense detail over the significance of each geomantic figure: in fact, more so than any other contemporary geomancy. Just to take one example,[2] Scot says of Acquisitio that it is:

> "of the planet Jupiter and the sign Aries. It is *optima,* fortunate, earthly [not in the elemental sense], fixed, masculine, oriental, airy, hot and wet like blood. Of colours it signifies white mixed with yellow declining to red; of tastes, sweet; of odours, fragrant; of stones, the hyacinth; of metals, gold and brass; of trees, fruit trees; of days, Thursday; of months, March; of time, years."

Scot continues with an extensive description of a typical Acquisitio man:

> "of mediocre stature, handsome, rather tall, with pleasing eyes, a thin nose, beautiful forehead, thin chin, long neck, hairy, and having two large upper teeth; extravagant, greedy of gain, desirous of some degree of honour and lordship, benign, faithful, and giving many goods to others for their service and friendship."

Acquisitio further:

> "signifies bodily health, pecuniary gain, male offspring, a hot illness and quick escape, reversion, the fugitive life of an absentee, a man of good condition who loves easily and faithfully..."

Although George Sarton[3] felt that the geomancy of Michael Scot was a doubtful ascription, the work itself is still a significant milestone in the history of geomancy, dealing as it does with such a wide spectrum of attributions for each of the geomantic figures.

ALBERTUS MAGNUS

From Scot we move on to a more illustrious contemporary, Albertus Magnus (1193-1280), Bishop of Ratisbon and intellectual luminary of the Church. Ironically Albertus Magnus took almost 700 years to live down his reputation as a magician and sorcerer, finally being canonized by the Church in 1935. Since then, what is reputed to be his bones have been moved to a crypt chapel in Cologne. Although his memory has been cleared

---

[1] CLM MS 489, f. 174-216v, *Incipit liber Geomantiae Michaelis Scoti, Geomantia dicitur ars judicandi per terram*, 'Geomancy said to be the art of judgement by earth.'

[2] Quoted by Lynn Thorndike, *Michael Scot,* London, 1965, p. 109.

[3] *Introduction to the History of Science,* 1927-47, Vol. II, p. 580.

of the charge of sorcery, a number of books on that subject still circulate under his name. However in his genuine works Albertus refers to magic and geomancy *(punctis terrae)* whilst defending the Magi against any suspicion of unwholesome magic. He shows an intimate grasp of the subject when he states:

> "in the science of geomancy the figures traced from the points are of no value unless they can be made to conform with astronomical images."[1]

Albertus appears to approve of the art of geomancy, the only qualification being that it was illicit and superstitious to utter prayers over the pen and ink employed in jotting down the lines of points, or to seek to divine only on a favourable day, or when the weather was settled (a frequent and favourite injunction of geomantic books). If these preliminaries were *not* observed then Albertus conceded that geomancy was no more superstitious than astrology, which on the whole he approved of in his writing.

THOMAS AQUINAS

His pupil, Thomas Aquinas (c.1226 - 74) was more careful and circumspect in his comments about the various magical arts. He admitted chiromancy to the category of 'natural,' and therefore acceptable, divination but he excluded geomancy, on the grounds that the original figures are based on either the outcome of chance or of voluntary human action. Geomancy is therefore regarded by him as a superstition, rather than as a divinatory art with a natural basis not influenced by the reason and will, like augury.

Aquinas cautions against casting of lots, a process which is similar in technique to geomancy, unless there is a "real necessity, or without due reverence and devotion" or for purely human and worldly purposes, excepting of course ecclesiastical elections. As Aquinas's censures are based on the theory that God is often supposed to influence the casting of lots, it follows that geomancy, which depends on voluntary human action, does not come under the heading of 'natural' divination.

WILLIAM OF MOERBEKE

One of St Thomas Aquinas's friends was William of Moerbeke (c.1215 - 1286), a Flemish Dominican translator from Greek into Latin. Many of his translations were made specifically at the request of Aquinas, and included the first translation of Aristotle's *Politics,* which had hitherto been unknown both to the Christian West and to the world of Islam. Some of the Greek

[1] *Treatise on Minerals,* Book II, iii, 3.

manuscripts of Aristotle disappeared after William translated them, leaving his version as the definitive text. His translations were very accurate as his style was to translate word for word, rather than summarise. Whilst Thomas Aquinas urged him to translate various books of a neo-Platonic persuasion, Moerbeke worked on a treatise on geomancy called *De Arte et Scientia* Geomantiae in 1276, making it quite likely that he and St Thomas both tried their hand at this divinatory art.

Not only were the clergy of this period obliged to fulminate against the divinatory arts, but they were also the most likely candidates to be practising them, especially given the limited literacy of the non-ecclesiastical population. It was not only Bishops (Albertus Magnus), Saints (Thomas Aquinas), or Dominican monks (William of Moerbeke), but also missionaries and martyrs such as Ramon Lull (1235 - 1315) who were involved in using and writing about the art of geomancy.

RAMON LULL

Ramon Lull was one of the most energetic and versatile characters of the thirteenth and early fourteenth centuries, as well as one of the most enigmatic. He was born in Palma on the island of Majorca, and remains the patron saint of that city till today. Having spent his youth as a libertine and pleasure-loving courtier, composing the long love poems in Catalan which make him a prominent figure in the history of Spanish literature, he like Saint Francis, underwent a conversion at about the age of thirty and thenceforth devoted himself to learning and religion.

The two driving forces in his life after this conversion were the method of his 'Art' *(ars nova)* and his urge to convert the Muslim world to Christianity and secure Jerusalem for Christendom. In pursuit of the latter objective he persuaded the King of Aragon to establish a school for the study of Arabic in Majorca, and the Pope himself to authorize chairs in Greek, Hebrew, Chaldean and Arabic at Rome, Paris, Oxford, Bologna and Salamanca Universities. This considerably accelerated the translation of valuable Greek and Arabic works into Latin. Further, in the pursuit of his aim to convert the whole Muslim world, he travelled extensively through Cyprus, Armenia and three times in north Africa. On his last trip to north Africa he achieved martyrdom by being stoned to death.

It was however for his 'Lullian Art' that the mediaeval world remembered him. This art is something which recurs again and again throughout the following centuries, as a theme or technique referred to by a number of different writers. Thorndike has explained it as:

"the invention of a logical machine which would constitute the same sort of labour-saving device in a scholastic disputation or mediaeval university as an adding machine in a modern bank or business office.'[1]

In fact it was an elaborate system of logic which could be applied mechanically by properly arranging concepts in categories, subjects and predicates in such a way that 'computer-like,' by the intermeshing of geared wheels upon which the categories were written, the answers to theological arguments could be derived. Lull even thought that such a machine might be able to convince a sceptical Muslim of the 'mechanical truth' of Christianity in a way that no missionary could. The Art was applied to every art and science Lull could lay his hands on, theology, medicine, logic, philosophy... even astrology and, of course, geomancy. The possibilities of combining Lullian wheels with geomancy might in fact prove a fruitful field for speculation, especially as twentieth-century French writers on geomancy have used such circles to explain the complementary and opposing relationships between the different geomantic figures.

Lull's treatment of astrology is typical of his desire to encompass all arts and sciences within his own scheme or *ars nova.* As Sarton says:

"It is clear that he had no real grasp of either mathematics or astronomy; he treated these subjects with the habitual conceit of a philosopher who believes he can dominate them without detailed and intimate knowledge.'[2]

Despite the fact that many of Ramon Lull's wheels and 'logic machines' look like geomantic wheels, often being divided into sixteen chambers, he talks slightingly of the art of geomancy and its practitioners. His wheels, however, are of interest to the geomancer. They are made of a number of card or wooden discs stuck with the same central pin, rotating independently but sometimes linked to other wheels by cogs. Each is marked with different categories or: [3]

"sixteen 'chambers' representing kindness, grandeur, eternity, power, wisdom, will, virtue, truth, glory, perfection, justice, beneficence, pity, humility, dominion and patience. One hundred and twenty more 'chambers' were formed by combining pairs of the foregoing. Another circle shows the rational soul in the centre represented by four squares and has its circumference divided into sixteen compartments representing appropriate qualities.[4] A third circle, devoted to principles and meanings, enclosed five triangles in a circumference of fifteen compartments; while a fourth circle divided fourteen compartments of its circumference between the seven

[1] Lynn Thorndike, *A History of Magic and Experimental Science*, Vol. II, p. 865.
[2] Sarton, *Introduction to the History of Science*, Vol. II, p. 909.
[3] Lynn Thorndike, *A History of Magic and Experimental Science*, Vol. I, p.865.
[4] Although not directly related to Lull, see Plate XV for such a circular arrangement.

> virtues and seven vices respectively rendered in blue and red. Other 'figures' dealt with predestination, fate, and free-will, truth and falsity. The following is a specific instance of the way in which these were combined. When the rational soul is troubled and uncertain in the circle of predestination, because the chambers of ignorance and merit, science and fault, mingle together, it forms a third figure representing doubt."

A similar arrangement can be used by a geomancer with the sixteen figures marked on four discs of different sizes. When any combination of four Mother figures come into line a Judge is revealed without the necessity of drawing up a full geomantic figure. Similarly, 'machines' for judging the figures generated in a horoscope have been used. The present writer has reconstructed several such 'Lullian geomantic machines.'

BARTHOLOMEW OF PARMA

Despite Ramon Lull's elaborate methodological treatises, probably the most elaborate treatise on geomancy written in the thirteenth century was the *Summa Breviloquium,* of Bartholomew of Parma. It was written at Bologna in 1288 at the express request of Theodosius de Flisco, bishop-elect of Reggio in northern Italy. Bartholomew also appears to have written summaries of this weighty work in 1294 and again in 1295 for other friends who wanted a slightly more concise text! Unfortunately Bartholomew's works were never printed, although a large number of the manuscripts are extant (see manuscript Bibliography). It is interesting that the bishop-elect of Reggio should have given his patronage and shown interest in the work, thereby indicating that such divinatory arts were at least not consistently condemned by the clergy of this period.

Bartholomew's work is quite detailed and begins by asserting quite emphatically that the art of geomancy originated from God and was taught to the sons of Noah by an angel who conveniently took on human form before the time of the flood. According to Bartholomew, the inventors of geomancy derived the sixteen figures "with great ingenuity and subtlety" from observation of the configuration of the constellations, an often repeated, but unlikely, claim designed to legitimize the connection between geomancy and astrology. As the figures are comparatively simple and do not appear to follow any obvious visual pattern in their astrological correspondences, this origin seems to be fallacious, but indicative of the connection between astrology and its terrestrial counterpart, which as we have seen dates back to Arab usage.

Bartholomew elaborates on the simple zodiacal and planetary correspondence to include with each figure's attributions, a day, month, colour, taste, stone, tree, metal and human type. Finally Bartholomew divides the figures into two basic groups:

Favourable	*Unfavourable*
Acquisitio	Amissio
Albus	Rubeus
Puella	Puer
Laetitia	Tristitia
Caput Draconis	Cauda Draconis
Populus	Via
Conjunctio	Carcer
Fortuna Major	Fortuna Minor

Such a table is of course an over-simplification of the elaborate rules and categorizations supplied by Bartholomew of Parma. Bartholomew's *Summa* has perhaps been copied more times than any other geomantic manuscript of this or any period, and was consequently responsible for spreading the practice of geomancy far and wide.

THE INQUISITION AND PETER DE ABANO

By the fourteenth century however the Inquisition had begun to busy itself with divination as well as magic and heresy. Nicholas Eymeric (1320-99), a Dominican professor of theology and inquisitor general of Aragon, seems to have been a stout opponent of any heresy, divination, magic or alchemy. Oddly, he describes 'geomancy'[1] as making use of a circle and a mirror; while the method of divining by chance markings of dots or scattering sand which is usually called geomancy, is strangely called by Eymeric 'geometrimancy.'

The Inquisition also affected Peter de Abano (1250 - 1317). He studied medicine in Paris before returning to Padua to practise as a physician. Towards the end of his life, he was actually accused of practising sorcery by

[1] Bibliothèque Nationale, MS 3171, fol. 90v-95r.

the Inquisition and was imprisoned. He was later acquitted but then re-arrested, and died in prison in 1317 whilst again awaiting trial.

A geomancy exists in several printed editions and manuscripts which is usually attributed to Peter de Abano. As Gabriel Naudé (1600-53), the French librarian, stated that Peter left treatises on "physiognomy, geomancy, and chiromancy," there seems to be no need to dispute the accuracy of this ascription. In his *Conciliator* (Diff. 156) Peter asserted that the future, and that which is absent, could be predicted by means of characters "as geomancy teaches." In his other great work, the *Lucidator,* he describes in some detail the method of geomancy, stating that its figures were produced under the influence of the constellations, and that not infrequently its judgments were verified. However, he regarded geomancy as a very difficult science, one requiring long experience and practice, although many of his contemporaries tried it simply because it looked so easy! As he had a well-paid practice as a physician, and a place in society to keep up, it is conceivable that the treatise remained in manuscript form till some time after his death, especially as he was in some trouble with the Inquisition.

Of the books of magic attributed to Peter de Abano, the *Heptameron* is the best known, but Naudé states that two other books of his were banned after his death, the *Elucidarium Necromanticum* and *Liber Experimentorum Mirabilium de Annulis Secundum* 28 *Mansiones Lunae,* or 'Book of marvellous experiments with rings according to the 28 Mansions of the Moon.' Amongst the less salubrious works from his pen was a work on poisons, commissioned by the then incumbent pope, possibly Honorius IV: ironical in view of Peter's treatment at the hands of the Pope's agents, the Inquisition.

Shortly after Peter's death, geomancy was immortalized in a Provençal didactic poem written in 1332 and running to 3,700 lines. This labour of love rather than art rhymes its way through all the possible combinations of the figures in the Houses of Heaven:[1] one wonders whether the poet sought immortality in art or in didactic verbosity. Nevertheless this exhaustive treatment escaped the flames to provide useful clues about the earlier writers on geomancy.

JOHN DE MORYS AND NICHOLAS ORESME

Jean de Murs (1290-1351/55) (often Latinized Iohannes de Muris or Anglicized as John de Morys) was a prominent Parisian astronomer and arithmetician of the first half of the fourteenth century. One of John's several claims to fame is the construction of a fifteen foot radius *Kardaja* for

[1] See Appendix VI for a listing of all the Figures in each of the 12 Houses.

astronomical observation. By way of comparison, Tycho Brahe employed one of only six foot and nine inch radius, although Dr John Dee (two centuries later) was reputed to have had a sextant of some forty feet radius.

John de Morys combined the study of astronomy with that of its terrestrial sibling, geomancy. Amongst manuscripts possibly attributable to John is one in which the sixteen geomantic figures are related in detail to the planets and signs.[1] John goes on to give the usual Christian mythical history of geomancy, stating that the art had its origins at the time of Noah. The relation of the geomantic figures to the twelve Houses of Heaven is considered, but much of the work is taken up with the interpretation of specific House/figure combinations, closely relating the concepts of astrology to geomancy. Amongst the traditionally geomantic material are other details on related astrological topics such as the 'Egyptian' or inauspicious days upon which it is not wise to cast geomantic figures, or in fact do much else!

Despite such works, the fourteenth century sported numerous sceptics such as Nicolas Oresme, philosopher and mathematician, who in his *Des Divinations* spoke disparagingly of geomancy as "nothing but the distinction between odd and even." He calls it "the game of philosophers" but concedes suggestively that certain problems in arithmetic can be worked out by using it. As he finds no reference to geomancy in classical writers, he rightly concludes that it is a mediaeval invention, although he doesn't spot its Arab origins. On the whole he spoke out against geomancy and similar divinatory practices.

LITERARY REFERENCES TO GEOMANCY

Such perception however went unheeded in popular circles. In *The Vision of Piers Ploughman* (c.1362), William Langland describes a series of moralistic visions in which geomancy is associated with guile and sorcery:

> "But astronomy is a hard thing and evil to know;
> Geometry and geomancy are guileful of speech;
> Who so works at these two must stay awake late,
> For sorcery is the sovereign book of that science.
> There are mechanical devices of many men's wits,[2]
> Experiments in alchemy of Albert's making,[3]
> Nigromancy and pyromancy which raise up ghosts.
> If you follow Dowel,[1] deal with these never.

---

[1] Venice, MS San Marco VIII, 44.
[2] Ramon Lull's logic machines.
[3] Albertus Magnus.

All these sciences I myself in sooth
Have found among the first to deceive folk."[2]

Other poets spoke of geomancy, and Chaucer[3] in 1386 in the *Parson's Tale* opined that:

"What say we of them that believe in divinations, as by flight or by noise of birds, or of beasts, or by sort [lot], by *geomancy*, by dreams, by chirking of doors, or cracking of houses, by gnawing of rats, and such manner of wretchedness? Certes, all this is defended [forbidden] by God and by all Holy Church."

ROYAL INTEREST IN GEOMANCY

Not only the popular tradition, but also royalty were interested in the intricacies of geomancy, for when Charles IV of Bohemia founded Prague University in 1348, geomancy featured amongst his scholarly interests. Charles died in 1378 leaving his son Wenceslaus IV to succeed him. Charles V of France also commissioned a geomancy.

Wenceslaus or Wenzel, the Holy Roman Emperor from 1378-1400, and king of Bohemia until 1419, was devoted to astrology and geomancy. This is amply testified by the existence in the National Library of Vienna of a superbly illuminated manuscript dated 1392/3 and marked with his initial. Illustrations include pictures of tubs and bathing girls which characterizes manuscripts associated with Wenceslaus, commemorating his imprisonment and supposed liberation by the bath-keeper Susanna. (There is an uncanny similarity to the infamous Voynich manuscript, whose provenance might well be traced back to the same source.) The manuscript is made up of a treatise upon constellations, the Alfonsine Tables (the standard Ephemeris of the period), and a beautifully illuminated geomancy, followed by a list of fixed stars and some details of aspects.

When Henry IV's daughter (Wenceslaus' sister), Anne of Bohemia, married Richard II of England in 1382 she found Richard more than sympathetic to geomancy. In fact an extremely elaborate astrological geomancy was compiled for Richard II in March 1391,[4] just one year before the execution of Wenceslaus's manuscript in 1392/3.

---

[1] The devil?

[2] *Piers Ploughman,* A. XI. 153.

[3] For further details see Mahmoud Manzalaoui, 'Chaucer and Science,' in *Geoffrey Chaucer,* ed. Derek Brewer, London, 1974.

[4] See Plate I. Richard II's geomancy is still preserved in the British Library as Royal MS 12. C. v.

ENGLISH GEOMANCERS

These two 'royal' geomantic manuscripts are amongst the most visually striking in existence. The interest of kings reflected an upsurge of interest by commoners, and under Richard's successor, Henry IV, a practitioner of medicine in Suffolk kept a notebook[1] record of details of methods for obtaining: "oracular answers prepared beforehand by this great Doctor for those of both Sexes who shall come to consult him," which included the "names of the 12 signs with such marks as shew that this John Crophill was a dabbler in Geomancy."

Crophill was not alone amongst a wide range of professional men and clerics who consulted geomancy. In a manuscript[2] of this period is a detailed description of the technique of 'astrological geomancy' broken down very conveniently into 125 chapters by [Walter] Cato who probably translated the work direct from Arabic, as it shows strong signs of Arabic influence, and is less likely to have been a recension of an earlier Latin work. The preceding treatise bound with it is also a manuscript on geomancy.

Other contemporaneous matter included references to the art in the *Apollogy for Lollard Doctrines (1400)* from which it appears that a number of Lollard sympathizers were also village 'cunning men' and practitioners of geomancy. In fact interest in England was so rife at this period that those who could afford it, such as the Dukes of Bedford and Gloucester, cultivated and employed such geomancers as they could find, sometimes even luring them away from overseas posts.

ROLAND SCRIPTORIS

Roland Scriptoris of Lisbon graduated in medicine from Paris University in 1424. After serving as a master and dean of the faculty for the next fifteen years, he became physician to John, Duke of Bedford.

---

[1] BL Harleian MS 1735, ff. 29-44v.

[2] All Souls College 96, ff. 16-41.

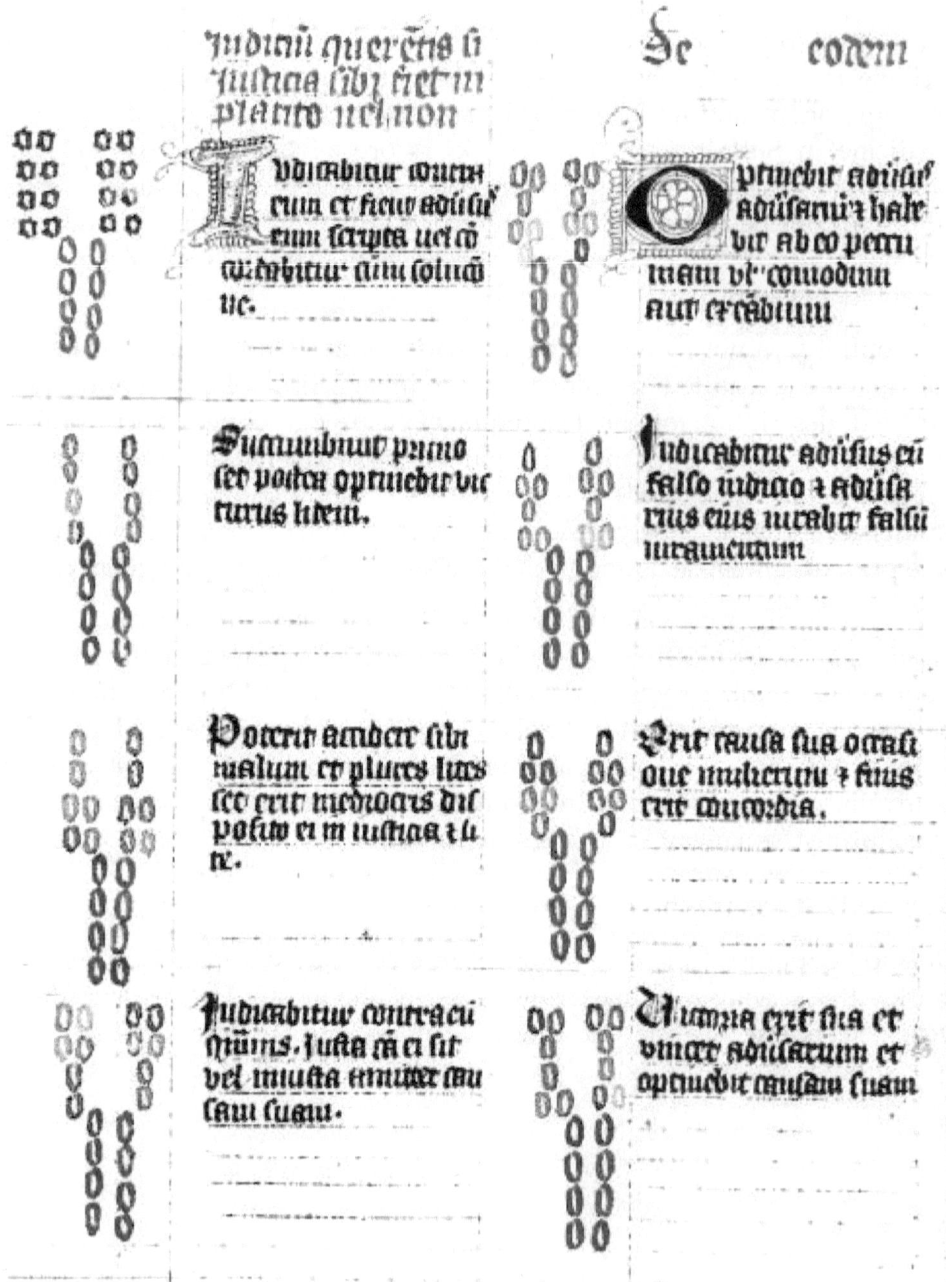

Figure 23: The geomancy of King Richard II commissioned by him in March 1391, showing the meaning of various Witness and Judge combinations.[1]

[1] British Library MS Royal 12. C.v., f. 26v. See also Plate I.

Whilst so employed he wrote one of the clearest early manuscript geomancies now in the British Library.[1] It is neatly written in a large hand with illuminated initials, and was probably executed some time in the 1430s. The treatise begins with details of the sixteen geomantic figures and their relationship with the seven planets and twelve Signs.

The rules for deriving the figures are then laid out before the tables of reference and sample answers, to various questions, categorized under the twelve Houses of Heaven, each House covering from six to forty different categories of question. Apparently Roland was attempting a fairly complete coverage of the divinatory arts, as he also wrote treatises on physiognomy, chiromancy and astrology for the Duke.

Not only Bedford, but also Humphrey Duke of Gloucester (1390-1447) had several geomancies drawn up for his use. One now resides in the British Library as part of one of the Arundel manuscripts,[2] and is entitled *Tabulae Humfridi Ducis Glowcestriae in judiciis artis geomansie* being bound with another geomancy, *Liber scientie arienalis* [?] *de judiciis geomansie ab Alpbarino filio Abrabe Judeo editus,* a translation from the Arabic of Alpharinus.[3]

Humphrey, who was very interested in the magic arts generally, bequeathed his library as the basis of what is now the Bodleian collection at Oxford, a notable repository of many magical and geomantic manuscripts. Less fortunately, in 1441 his wife Eleanor Cobham was accused, along with other members of the Duke's entourage, of attempting to kill Henry VI by sorcery and witchcraft. In the event, she was banished to perpetual imprisonment on the Isle of Man, while her husband survived the scandal to endow 'Duke Humphrey's library' in the Bodleian in Oxford with other examples of his early *geomantiae*.[3]

One of the earliest geomantic manuscripts was a Polish manuscript written in 1458-59 and bound together in 1460. Biblioteka Jagiellońska MS 793, kept in Kraków, contains four separate *Sortilegium geomanticum* (lot books which utilise the geomantic characters) and one *Geomantia*.[4]

---

[1] BL Sloane MS 3487.

[2] BL Arundel MS 66. See Figure 24.

[3] Critical notes on this manuscript may be found in Tanner *Bibl. Brit. Rib.* and the *Monthly Notes of the Royal Astronomical Society,* 80 (1920).

[3] Such as *Libellus Geomancie,* which also survives as Bodleian MS 581, ff. 9-89v.

[4] BJ 793, ff. 63v-67 and ff. 81-85v.

Figure 24: Humphrey Duke of Gloucester's geomantic table, the *Tabulae Humfridi Ducis Glowcestriae in Judiciis artis geomansie.* (fifteenth century).[1]

[1] British Library MS Arundel 66, f. 284.

However, sandwiched between these and other astrological selections is a beautifully drawn *Prognostica* by Socrates Basileus [1] which relates the geomantic figures to the Mansions of the Moon (see Plate XV) and zodiacal Signs (see Plate XVI). Fortune telling by 'lots', not geomancy.

COCLES

Meanwhile in Italy the art was alive and flourishing under the ministrations of a retired barber. Bartolommeo della Rocca, called Cocles, was born in 1467 near Bologna. Cocles made a speciality of forecasting doom. As the preface to his work on physiognomy and chiromancy puts it:[2]

> "Cocles left his country home (Tuguriolum) and came to Imola, to whose princes he predicted the loss of their dominion. He then went to Faenza, where Hieronymus de Manfredis was cousin of the prince, and foretold an ill fate for Astorgius of Faenza, who died soon after. As for Cocles, he proceeded to Cesena and Pesaro and visited Guido Ubaldi. To Julius Varanus of Camerino he forecast an evil fate for himself and his sons."

Needless to say, this kind of prediction acquired for Cocles a lot of enemies, so much so that his prediction of his own death came true when in 1504 he was murdered by order of the son of his patron, Giovanni Bentivoglio, to whom he had dedicated several of his works. According to one writer, Cocles even knew how he would be murdered, and foreseeing that he would be knocked over the head, he took to wearing a metal plate in his hat. Unfortunately for him, his assassin, disguised as a vendor of kindling wood, belaboured Cocles with the wood when he came to his front door, early one morning, unprotected by his hat. As for the rest of his predictions it was said that of a list of forty-five men who would die a violent death, all but two had reached their predicted sticky ends by the time that Jerome Cardan (1501-76) inspected the list, long after Cocles' own death.

Aside from his rather Saturnian predictions, Cocles made a practice of resurrecting antiquated methods of divination, which presumably he wielded with some dexterity. Of these, he is best known for his extensive and learned work on chiromancy and physiognomy, although according to

---

[1] See Additional 15236, ff. 95-108 and BJ 793, ff. 73v-81. See Thorndike 1923-1958, Vol. 2, pp. 116- 17; Bolte 1903, pp. 296-98.

[2] From a letter from Horatius Bichardus of Fano to Alessandro Bentivoglio, dated from Bologna on 15 December 1503, which is prefixed to Bartholomaeus Cocles, *Chryomantie ac physionomie Anastasis cum approbatione magistri Alexandri de Achillinis.* Bononiae, ex arte Ioannis Antonii de Benedictis, 1504.

writers such as Cardan, Cocles started life as a mendicant barber, "ignorant of letters."

For his work on geomancy he drew on Hali, Gerard of Cremona, Bartholomew of Parma, and the unidentifiable but ubiquitous 'Tundinus.' Apart from mentions of geomancy in his work on the arts of chiromancy and physiognomy, *Chryomantie ac Physionomie Anastasis*, Bologna 1504, there is a whole book on this subject, entitled *La Geomantia* (1550), which is ascribed to him. In the former book he lists exhaustively the different types of divination: [1]

> "several different modes of procedure...presented under pyromancy, hydromancy and necromancy. Long accounts are given of augury and interpretation of dreams. Spatulomancy is not defined as usual, as divination from the shoulder blades of sheep, but rather from the bone of a goat recently killed. Other less familiar varieties of divination are litteramancy and nomancy from letters and names respectively, solmancy from the rays of the sun, venamancy and umbilicomancy which are both connected with childbirth."

In the same work, Cocles defended Peter de Abano who also had a popularly attributed geomancy to his name. In fact Peter's geomancy was first published in 1542, after his death. Patricio Tricasso da Cerasari was later to re-publish both Cocles's work and Peter's geomancy. While Cocles defended geomancers and astrologers, he attacked other professions such as the clergy and lawyers whom he derisorily classified with 'rustics... mechanics, humanists, grammarians and women!' The clergy were of course prime targets because they opposed his art; and of them he said: [2]

> "we have at Bologna certain hypocrites in hoods who are supremely ignorant, whose names I pass over in silence, who under a certain appearance of sanctity are really fathers of deception. They daily deceive our citizens, especially idle women and most of all widows and insane old crones and some little men."

Cocles seems to have made a point of looking for trouble, and his death seems to have been more of a foregone conclusion than a fulfilled prophecy!

Jerome Cardan did not limit his study of geomancy to Cocles's prodigious predictions, but also examined other arguments for and against the subject in *De verum Varietate* where he conceded (XIV, 58, p. 270) that geomancy was a genuine form of divination, on the grounds that its figures stimulate the mind to "intent inquiry and truth telling," a faint echo of Ibn Khaldoun's limited praise of the art.

---

[1] Lynn Thorndike, *A History of Magic and Experimental Science*, Vol. V, p. 58.
[2] Ibid., p. 63.

Other contemporaries of Cardan such as Paracelsus (1493-1541) spoke favourably of the art. Gerhard Dorn, one of Paracelsus' disciples (who in fact edited in Latin translation his master's works) used geomancy to illustrate his points concerning the microcosm and anatomy of man in his *Clavis*. On the other hand, Erastus criticized Paracelsus' attitude to divination in general, seeing astrology as the foundation of all other magic arts, and geomancy as not much better.

Despite such clerical censure, the election of popes came within the province of geomancy, with not a few successes credited to its practitioners. The election of Giovanni de Medici (the son of Lorenzo the Magnificent) as pope was predicted by a geomancer of Bologna in 1513 to the sceptical philosopher Pietro Pomponazzi (1462-1525). The incident is reported in Pomponazzi's book *De Naturalium effectuum cousis sive de incantationibus,*[1] where he relates that on four successive days the geomantic figures gave the same answer, and in due course Giovanni was elected to the papacy as Leo X. A probably apocryphal story says that after his election, Leo offered the geomancer fifty gold pieces or a green hat of office to show his appreciation: the geomancer sensibly took the former.

[1] Basle, 1556, pp. 191-2.

6. The Renaissance: the Apogee of Geomancy

AGRIPPA

Henry Cornelius Agrippa (1468-1535), born just prior to the Renaissance, was in many ways an all round Renaissance man, being a writer, soldier and physician. However, his main influence on history, a claim to an important place in the development of the thought of the period is as a commentator on magic. As Agrippa himself says: [1]

> "some that are perverse... may take the name of Magic in the worse sense and, though scarce having seen the title, cry out that I teach forbidden Arts, sow the seed of heresies, offend the pious, and scandalize excellent wits; that I am a sorcerer, and superstitious and devilish, who indeed am a Magician: to whom I answer, that a Magician doth not, amongst learned men, signify a sorcerer or one that is superstitious or devilish; but a wise man, a priest, a prophet."

He was born in 1486 in Nettesheim, a small town south west of Cologne, of a family of scholars who ensured that he acquired the fundamentals of a good education, specifically Latin, together with the writings of the ascetics, scholastics and canonists. As printing was still a very new invention the dissemination of rarer texts depended very much on the scholar gaining access to patronage and private manuscript collections. Because Agrippa's accomplishments included foreign languages, he was taken from his studies in 1501 to serve the Holy Roman Emperor, Maximilian I of Germany, first as a secretary and then afterwards for seven years as a soldier. Towards the close of this period he travelled to Paris University, ostensibly as a scholar, but in fact as an observer of political developments there for Maximilian (a combination of activities which later occupied one of Agrippa's admirers, Dr John Dee, who undertook similar missions for Elizabeth I).

In 1509 Agrippa prepared a lecture on Reuchlin's *De Verbo Mirifico,* which he delivered at Dole. The University conferred a doctorate of divinity upon him, he was received by the archbishop of Besançon, and he attracted the attention and patronage of Margaret of Austria, the daughter of

[1] Cornelius Agrippa's address to the reader, in *Three Books of Occult Philosophy,* Vol. 1, Llewellyn, 1993, edited by Donald Tyson.

Maximilian I, to whom he had dedicated his lectures. He had chosen his theme well, for Reuchlin was not only a seminal influence, but was also well known in his own time, his book being eagerly devoured by Pope Leo X, Cardinal de Medici and other princes of the Church and State.

In pursuance of the patronage of Princess Margaret, Agrippa wrote his most frequently reproduced treatise on the *Nobility and Pre-excellence of the Female Sex,* a most ingeniously argued tract which was designed to ingratiate him with his patron. Having thus established himself, he married and settled down to work on his *De Occulta Philosophia,* which occupied him for the next two years (1509-10) but was not published until much later. Before the publication of this work Agrippa prospered, being elected regent by the University of Dole, held in high esteem by many learned men, and blessed with a clever and beautiful wife.

Fearing that *De Occulta Philosophia* might be misconstrued by the public he sent it to the Abbot John of Trittenheim, called Trithemius, with whom he had in the past conferred about "divers things concerning Chemistry, Magic, and the Cabala." Trithemius replied with enthusiasm: "your work, which learned men can sufficiently commend, I approve of," but he warned Agrippa that he should "communicate vulgar secrets to vulgar friends, but higher and secret to higher and secret friends only... lest you be trod under the oxen's feet," implying that persecution would follow the publication of this book, as indeed it did. For that volume contained a summary and popularisation of all the basic doctrines of magic, the qabalah, and divination known at that time. His book was practically the only starting point of qabalistic knowledge amongst Latin-reading scholars in Europe: it consequently enjoyed an immense repute, and for this reason was especially feared by the Church. Strangely, most of the information in the book came rather from the mythology and philosophy of Greece and Rome than the later Hebraic qabalah. In his third book, which he devoted to 'theology,' there is much about angels, demons and the souls of men, linked by an extremely competent system of correspondences, based wherever possible on the numbers one to twelve, and tied in extensively with classical mythology.

Agrippa divided his famous work on occult philosophy into three volumes, followed posthumously by a fourth volume, which contains his main treatise on geomancy with other works on magic and geomancy such as the *Magical Elements* of Peter de Abano. The first volume treats of Natural magic, the second of Celestial magic, and the third of Ceremonial magic, following the traditional division of philosophy into Natural (being concerned in large part with those subjects nowadays grouped under the physical sciences), Mathematical (including astrology, astronomy, geometry and akin subjects) and Theological or Metaphysical philosophy (concerned with speculations on Cosmology, Cosmogony and more religious issues). The fourth volume contains the practice, especially that of geomancy.

In his great rebuttal of all arts and sciences, *De Incentitudine,* Agrippa lists earlier geomancies by Hali, Gerard of Cremona, Bartholomew of Parma, and an unidentifiable Tundinus, and adds:[1]

> "I too have written a geomancy quite different from the rest but no less superstitious and fallacious or, if you wish, I will even say 'mendacious'."

This work is presumably the treatise published in Agrippa's *Fourth Book of Occult Philosophy.*[2] Despite numerous references to its 'spuriousness' it is genuinely a collection of six treatises by various authors; only two of which actually purport to be by Agrippa. Of these the *On Geomancy* at least is probably genuine. This treatise is possibly the one he sent to Metz for in 1526. At the same time he requested a copy of Trithemius' *Steganographia,* a work simultaneously devoted to cryptography and angel magic. Perhaps, to Agrippa, there was an obscure connection between this work by his old master and the art we are considering. In this treatise we have to thank Agrippa for one of the most concise definitions of geomancy ever penned:[3]

> "Geomancy is an Art of Divination, whereby the judgement may be rendered by lot or destiny, to every question of everything whatsoever, but the Art hereof consisteth especially in certain points whereof certain figures are deducted according to the reason or rule of equality or inequality, likeness or unlikeness; which Figures are also reduced to the Coelestiall Figures [astrological Signs and Houses], assuming their natures and properties, according to the course and forms of the Signs and Planets... the points of this Art to be made with signs in the Earth, wherefore this Art is appropriated to this Element of Earth... the hand of the Projector or Worker [the geomancer] to be most powerfully moved, and directed to the terrestrial spirits; and therefore they first used certain holy incantations and deprecations, with other rites and observations, provoking and alluring spirits of this nature..."

Agrippa's attitude to geomancy wavered between opposite extremes for, whilst doubting the complete efficacy of astrology and geomancy, he nevertheless both practised and wrote about them in some detail, and in his own practice he tended to rely upon the geomantic tables drawn up by Cornelius Schepper circa 1524.

---

[1] *De Incertitudine et vanitate scientiarum et artium*, Antwerp, 1531, chapter 13.

[2] Reprinted Askin Publishers, London, 1978.

[3] Agrippa, 'Of Geomancy' in *Fourth Book of Occult Philosophy,* London, 1655, reprinted Askin, London, 1978, pp. 1-2.

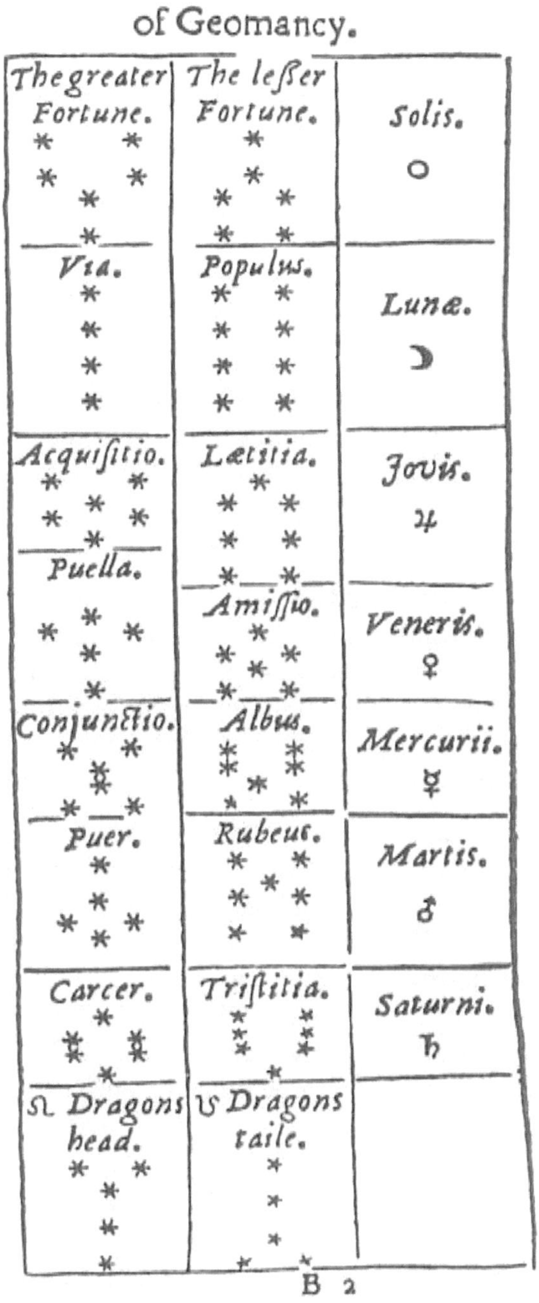

of Geomancy.

The greater Fortune. * * * * * *	The lesser Fortune. * * * * * *	Solis. ☉
Via. * * * *	Populus. * * * * * * * *	Lunæ. ☽
Acquisitio. * * * * * *	Lætitia. * * * * * * *	Jovis. ♃
Puella. * * * * *	Amissio. * * * * * *	Veneris. ♀
Conjunctio. * * * * * *	Albus. * * * * * * *	Mercurii. ☿
Puer. * * * * *	Rubeus. * * * * * * *	Martis. ♂
Carcer. * * * * * *	Tristitia. * * * * * * *	Saturni. ♄
☊ Dragons head. * * * * *	☋ Dragons taile. * * * * *	

B 2

Figure 25: The geomantic figures as portrayed in Henry Cornelius Agrippa's 'Of Geomancy' in the *Fourth Book of Occult Philosophy,* London 1655.

THE CHURCH AND OTHER PRACTITIONERS

Contemporary with Agrippa was the astrologer and master of geomancy, Luca Gaurico (c. 1531), who passed on his art to Gian Luigi de' Rossi. Another, but anonymous German practitioner of the art, published his magnum opus in Mayence in 1534, entitled *Künstlicher und rechtschaffner gebrauch der alten Kleynen Geomancey*. Such works however came under the condemnation of the Church.

The Catholic Indices of prohibited books did not begin to list works on occult subjects till the middle of the sixteenth century, till then contenting themselves with heresy and the works of religious reformers. The Indices of Venice and Milan of 1554 are amongst the first to condemn works of geomancy along with her sister arts of hydromancy, pyromancy, nigromancy, necromancy and the Notary art. Agrippa and Bartholomew Cocles were amongst the writers on geomancy so condemned.

In the Index of Paul IV issued at Rome in 1559, works of geomancy are again listed together with the above mentioned 'mancies' plus chiromancy, physiognomy, aeromancy, onomancy, sortilege, venefica, auguries, aruspicina, incantations and certain branches of judicial astrology. Interestingly enough alchemy is not mentioned in this Index. Of geomantic authors, Cocles and Agrippa are again singled out, together with Peter de Abano.

In 1580 the Congregation of Cardinals, perhaps fearing that divination was becoming too prominent an issue, wrote to the Inquisitor at Bologna, directing him not to interfere in cases of geomancy, but to leave them to the Ordinary. Additionally, if any person was charged both with using the divinatory arts and heresy, the latter charge was to be given precedence. Similar decrees highlight the fact that the Inquisition was primarily charged with the rooting out of heresy rather than magic, and prosecution for the latter was often based on the premise that those who professed magical beliefs were heretics.

Gaspar Peucer in his book *Les Devins* (Antwerp 1584), a commentary on the principal types of divination, fulminates against geomancy: "gens curiux [*sic*] et profanes, aux ridicules subtilitez." He gives several chapters to a refutation of its principles and attempts to demonstrate that the devil is its author!

The Indices were followed up in 1586 by the famous Bull of Sixtus V which was proclaimed generally against most forms of divination and magic. Ironically later ages were to accuse this Pope, who built the Vatican Library and published new editions of the *Septuagint* and *Vulgate* with being himself a magician!

Further internal decrees were issued, such as that of 1591 issued to the

Friars Minor of the Observance preventing them from having any writings or books on geomancy, chiromancy and similar subjects. Penalties ranged up to ten years in the galleys for those found flagrantly guilty. A year later all permits to read prohibited books which had been issued for bishops and local inquisitors were recalled, and even the official Jesuit censors themselves were instructed not to keep or use the books which they themselves had been responsible for expurgating or withdrawing from circulation. Hard times indeed for any scholar of the magic arts, be he lay or clerical!

Various defences of divination, particularly of astrology, were penned by such writers as Campanella who argued that astrology and hence its dependants, such as geomancy, are sciences, and that the suppression of astrology thereby brings all science and philosophy into disrepute. By an odd twist of fate Campanella met Urban VIII, the next pope to issue a comprehensive Bull against astrology and divination. Now, although Urban wished to suppress astrology, he was in fact a firm believer in it. He had horoscopes drawn up for all his cardinals resident in Rome and was in the habit of openly predicting the dates of their deaths from these horoscopes. By way of retaliation between 1626 and 1628 his own imminent death was astrologically predicted. This activity was probably the main cause behind his anti-astrology Bull of 1631, especially as the main target of the Bull was predictions of the deaths of princes (especially popes) and their families: the crime was however more one of *lèse-majesté* than either heresy or sorcery!

But to return to Campanella, whose interest in astrology more than matched that of the Pope. As 1628 drew to a close, Urban VIII became increasingly worried about the astrological and geomantic predictions of his death. He not only consulted Campanella a number of times, but actually engaged in ritual magic to circumvent the influences of the stars, taking measures against the "disease bearing eclipse and evil influences of Mars and Saturn." In his book *De Fato Siderali Vitando* (in *Astrologicorum Libri VI,* 1629) Campanella relates the events:[1]

> "First they sealed the room against the outside air, sprinkled it with rose-vinegar and other aromatic substances, and burnt laurel, myrtle, rosemary and cypress. They hung the room with white silken cloths and decorated it with branches. Then two candles and five torches were lit, representing the seven planets; since the heavens, owing to the eclipse, were [seen to be] defective... The other persons present had horoscopes immune to the evil eclipse. There was Jovial and Venereal music, which was to disperse the

[1] Quoted in Daniel P. Walker, *Spiritual and Demonic Magic from Ficino to Campanella*, London, 1958, p. 207.

> pernicious qualities of the eclipse-infected air and, by symbolising good planets, to expel the influences of bad ones. For the same purpose they used stones, plants, colours and odours, belonging to good planets (that is, Jupiter and Venus). They drank astrologically distilled liquors."

Obviously the magic was successful, as Campanella lived to be thrown into prison for publishing the details of the ritual (he was later pardoned), and the Pope lived to pass the Bull of 1631 against astrologers and other diviners. This however did little to check the spread of geomancy.

CHRISTOPHER CATTAN

In France from the end of the sixteenth to the end of the seventeenth century studies of geomancy multiplied, and many editions of the better known texts were published. The best known were those of the Italian Christopher Cattan (1558), the French translation of Cornelius Agrippa, and the indigenous works of De la Taille (1574) and De la Tayssonnière (1574).[1] Of these, only *The Geomancie of Maister Christopher Cattan* was translated out of French "into our English tongue" by Francis Sperry in 1591, immediately becoming a best-seller which necessitated its reprinting in 1608. Its popularity is also attested by the number of contemporary manuscript copies held in the British Library which owe their origins to this work.[2] The book is dedicated by Sparry to "Lord Nicat, Lord of Bosnay, and of Chesney, one of the Kinges Counsaile, and Maister of the Requests of the Housholde." Cattan himself was the soldier and servant of Lord Thais.

Cattan proposes in his preface to write in the future a Physiognomie and a Chiromancie, reinforcing the association between these three arts, which had grown since the time of Cocles: this he failed to do however. Following tradition, Cattan says "the Indians, Chaldeans, Hebrews, Arabians, Greekes, Egiptians and Latines" have written on geomancy.

---

[1] These were partly based on manuscripts of the sixteenth century (probably copies of earlier manuscripts) including *Introduction à la Géomancie* and *La Géomancie plaine et parfaicte*, translated by (Brother) Gilles de Morbeta, both now in the Bibliothèque Nationale. The Bibliothèque Mazarine also possesses amongst other texts on geomancy, a German manuscript of the sixteenth century, *Von der Geomancie*, together with a French work printed in Strasbourg in 1609: *Géomancie ou l'art de connaître les choses secrètes par points faits en terre.* The extraordinary *Manuscrit de Géomancie* of the Bibliothèque Arsenal dates from the early seventeenth century and has innumerable marginal signs, which give it the appearance of an antiphonal.

[2] Such as BL Sloane MS 2186.

THE

GEOMANCIE

of Maiſter Chriſtopher Cattan Gentleman.

A Booke, no leſſe pleaſant and recreatiue, then of a wittie inuention, to knowe all thinges, paſt, preſent, and to come.

Wherevnto is annexed the wheele of Pythagoras.

Tranſlated out of French into our Engliſh tongue.

LONDON

Printed by Iohn VVolfe, and are to be ſold at Edward VVhites ſhop, at the ſigne of the Gunne, at the little north doore of Paules.

1591.

Figure 26: Title page of Christopher Cattan' *Geomancy,* 1591. Pythagoras' wheel often accompanied manuscript geomancies.

He selected three of these works as the most important,

(a) the manuscript beginning '*Estimaverunt Indi*... written by the Indians;'

(b) the manuscript beginning '*Ha veenestre*... written by the Hebrewes;'

(c) the Latin work of Bartholomew de Pine [Parma].

An interesting choice of reference sources.

Cattan's work is divided into three books, being,

(i) A Treatise of the Art;

(ii) On the twelve Houses of Heaven; and

(iii) Judgment with examples.

The author is careful at the outset to explain that geomancy is not wrought

> "by diabolicke invocation, but [is] a part of Natural Magicke, and daughter of Astrology... and S[t]. Thomas of Aquine [Aquinas] himself, a Doctor of the Church of no small estimation, saith in his *Quodlibet,* that it [geomancy] may bee admitted, because it doth participate with Astrologie, and is called her daughter."

In his first chapter, Cattan defines geomancy:

> "Geomancie is a Science and art which consisteth of points, prickes, and lines, made in steade of the foure Elements, and of the starres and Planets of Heaven, called the Science of the Earth, because in times past it was made on it as we will hereafter declare. And thus everie pricke signifieth a Starre, and everie line an Element, and everie figure the faure quarters of the world, that is to say, the East, West, South, and North. Wherefore it is easie to know that Geomancie is none other thing but Astrologie, and a third meane, that is to say, participating of two, which is *Alquemy* [Alchemy].
>
> *Geomancy* is called *Gy* a Greek word, which signifieth earth: and *Mancie,* which is to say knowledge. Or defining it more properly, it is derived of *Gyos* and *Magos,* which signifieth knowledge of earthly things, by the power of ye superior bodies, of the foure Elements, the seaven planets, and of the twelve signes of heaven. And this Arte may be made upon the Earth, or in white Paper, or uppon any other thing, whereon it may commodiouslie bee done, so that the prickes and lines may be knowne."

In chapter 3, Cattan explains what equipment is needed and recommends pen, ink and paper, explaining that the use of 'beanes or other grains' to produce a geomantic figure is in "the manner of the curtizances [citizens] of *Bolognia.*" It is interesting that Cattan has come across a *modus operandi* similar to the palm nut and bean manipulation of African geomancy, perhaps found in the *Summa* of Bartholomew of Parma which was composed in Bologna.

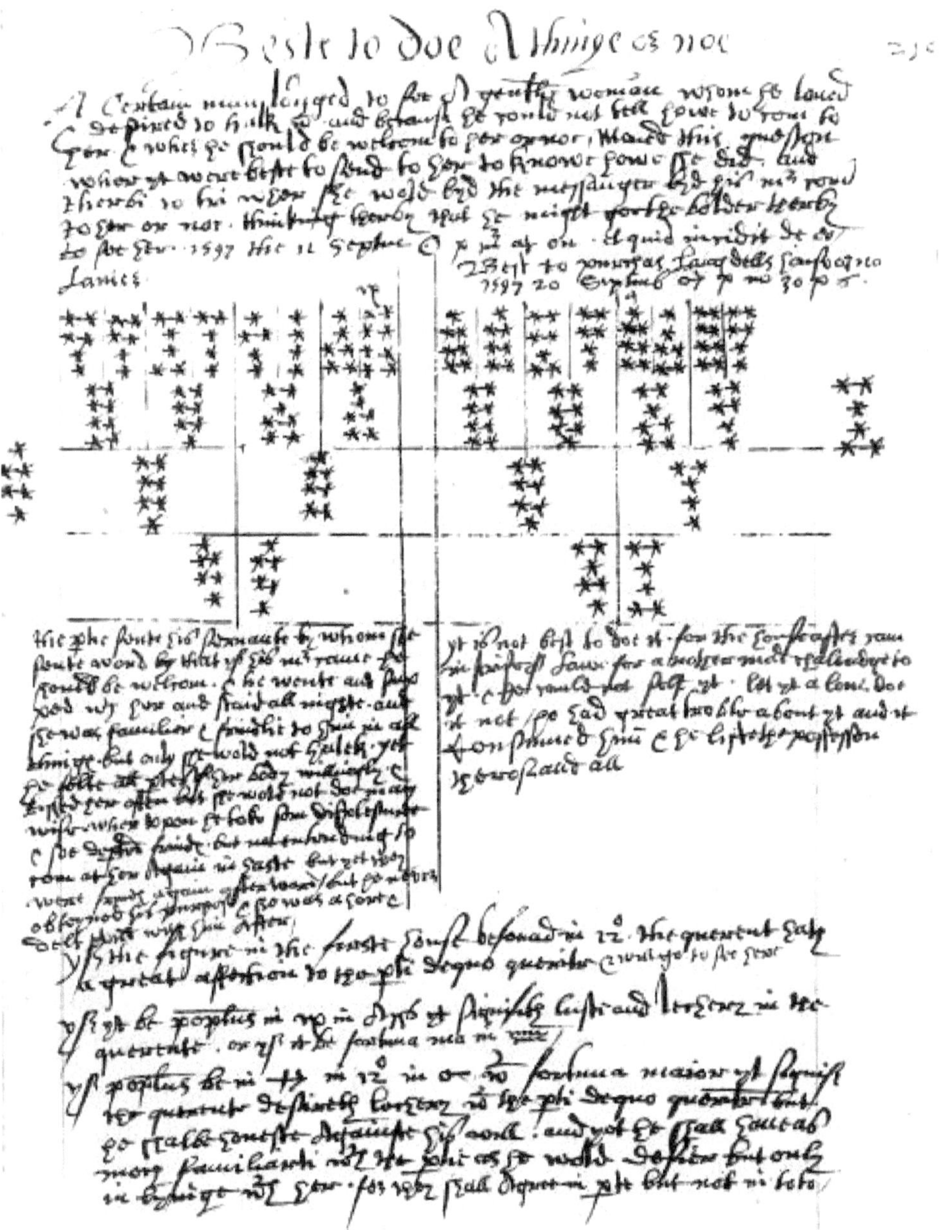

Figure 27: "Beste to doe a thing or noe," a geomantic consultation by Simon Forman dated 1597 relating to relationships.The left hand chart gives Carcer for both Witnesses and the Judge, a very bad configuration. The right hand chart yields Conjunctio as the Judge.[1]

[1] Bodleian Library Ashmole MS 354, f. 250r.

SIMON FORMAN AND THE NAPIERS

After a fairly traditional explanation of the generation of the figures, Cattan supplies extensive tables for use by the intending geomancer. Cattan's book being widely distributed would have been known to Simon Forman (1552-1611), the Elizabethan contemporary of John Dee who practised geomancy for clients, and as a diagnostic tool. Richard Napier, rector of Great Linford in Buckinghamshire, was Forman's pupil and colleague in these arts.

The line of transmission of geomancy in England at this time is clear. From library records and letters we know that Simon Forman, Richard Napier (who inherited Forman's books) and Robert Fludd, "formed a sort of succession especially in astrological and geomantic studies," as Craven (1902) points out in his study of Fludd. Not only did Napier inherit all of Simon Forman's papers, but Fludd (and Elias Ashmole) had access to them through Napier's son, and based their geomantic knowledge on them. Forman often used geomancy in his client consultations and medical practice,[1] and has left prolific records of these consultations (see Figure 27).

ROBERT FLUDD

Robert Fludd, physician and mystical philosopher, was born in Kent in 1574. He studied at St John's College, Oxford and then spent five years in Europe, taking his medical degree in 1605. He was a follower of Paracelsus whose advances in medicine were to revolutionize the whole mediaeval and classical attitude to medicine. Fludd was author of many obscure Latin works on theosophy, philosophy and mathematics. He approached these subjects however in a typical mediaeval manner, treating them as interrelated parts of one divine science, rather than separate fields of inquiry.

His father had been 'Treasurer of War' for Elizabeth I, and he was part of a reasonably important family, having therefore the money to travel widely and to study medicine in France, Spain, Italy and Germany. He poured out such an amazing stream of complex treatises that it was said that he employed an amanuensis regularly so that he could dictate his numerous works at odd moments throughout the day.

Apart from his interest in philosophy and medicine he became a supporter of the Rosicrucian cause and wrote several works supporting this almost mythical brotherhood of sages which had first come to the notice of the scholars in Europe in the early seventeenth century. As he was an

[1] Analysed in their historical context in A. L. Rowse, *Simon Forman*, London, 1974.

influential writer in his own time, much of what has later come to be considered as Rosicrucian was in fact based on Fludd's treatises.

He was also important in other fields of endeavour and became a close correspondent of the astronomer Kepler. Fludd's contribution to astronomy was more in the nature of cosmological speculations, but because of the logic of the time, Kepler felt that amongst Fludd's cosmological speculation were principles which he could possibly apply to deducing the physical nature of the universe. It was not unusual in the seventeenth century for thinkers to subscribe to the 'as above so below' theory, and use the conclusions of one science to answer questions in another.

Kepler was so fascinated with Fludd's theories explained in the *Utriusque Cosmi* that when he wrote his own treatise on the solar system he included an appendix specifically addressed to Fludd. However, where Fludd saw the universe animated by a living soul and ruled by spiritual essences, angelic powers and the whole machinery of planetary intelligences, Kepler took a more modern view and described the system in terms of mathematics. In some ways Fludd and Kepler represent the division between ancient and modern approaches to cosmology: on Fludd's side is the Platonic theory of the world soul integrated with the Christian ideas of his period, on the other side Kepler adheres rigorously to those things which he can prove with figures.

Fludd's speculation on Creation and natural history mixed theories of thunderbolts with addresses on anatomy, military manoeuvres, theological theories, religious rationalizations and qabalistic conjectures. For Fludd, there was no dividing line between science and religion.

As Fludd saw geometry and its attendant science, mathematics, at the root of the whole cosmos, it is not unusual that he felt that the binary mathematics of geomancy were a reliable means for probing the future.

Fludd describes one of his experiences with geomancy in the section on "the internal principle of terrestrial astrology or geomancy" in his *Historia Macrocosmi,* the translation of which is based on the work of C. H. Josten.[1]

> "In [1601-2]... I was compelled to spend the whole winter in the city of Avignon... With many other young men of good background, and of sound education (former pupils of the Jesuits) I received board and lodging at the house of a certain captain.

[1] *Journal of the Warburg and Courtauld Institutes*, Vol. XXVII, London, 1964, pp. 332-4.

TOMI SECVNDI

TRACTATUS PRIMI,

SECTIO SECUNDA,

De technica Microcoſmi hiſtoria,

in

Portiones VII. diviſa.

AUTHORE

ROBERTO FLUD aliàs de FLUCTIBUS

Armigero & in Medicina Doctore Oxonienſi.

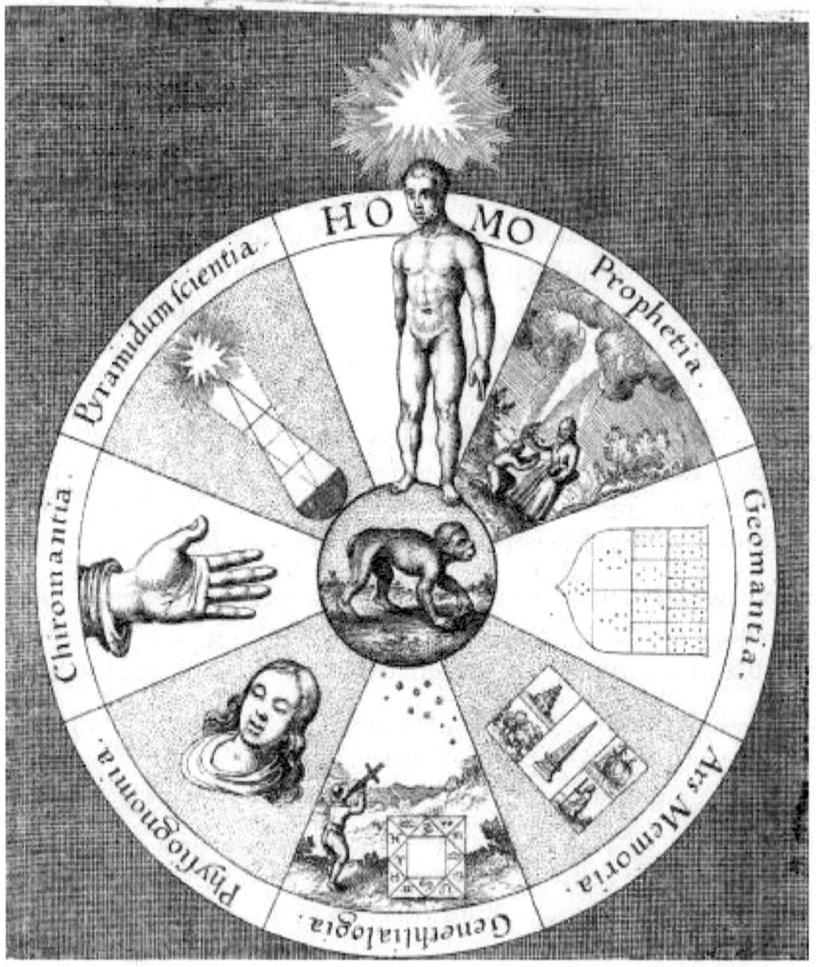

Figure 28: Robert Fludd's *Utriusque Cosmi,* 1618, showing geomancy as one of the seven predictive arts including prophecy, the art of memory (*Ars Memoria),* astrology (*Genethlialogia),* physiognonmy, chiromancy, and '*pyramidium scientia.*'

One evening, while we were drinking at table, I discussed philosophical subjects with the others and observed their various opinions on geomantic astrology. Some of them denied its usefulness altogether; others, with whom I sided, stoutly defended the truth of that art. I set out many arguments in which I proved myself fairly well versed in geomancy.

The meal being over. I had no sooner returned to my bedroom, when one of my companions followed me and asked me to try my skill [in geomancy] (which, he said, he had seen was considerable) in the resolution of a problem of some importance which greatly troubled him. Having made many excuses, I was at last prevailed upon by his entreaties. So, instantly I marked down geomantic dots for the question he had proposed. This question was: whether a girl with whom he had vehemently fallen in love returned his love with equal fervour with her entire mind and body, and whether she loved him more than anyone else.

Having drawn up the [geomantic] chart, I assured him that I could describe the nature and appearance of his beloved and, having duly described to him the stature and shape of the girl's body, I indicated also a particular and rather noticeable mark, a kind of wart on her left eye-lid, which he agreed was there. I said also that the girl loved vineyards, and this detail, too, was confirmed by him with pleasure. He said that her mother had for that very reason built her house among the vineyards. Finally I gave the following answer to the question: that his beloved was unfaithful and by no means steady in her love of him, and that she loved somebody else more than him. Whereupon he said that he had always very much suspected that this was the case and that he was [now] seeing it with open eyes.

He left my room in haste and then related to his companions with some admiration the truth and virtue of my art. Yet some of them, who knew the girl well, denied altogether that she had any such mark on her eye-lid as I had described, until they talked to her the following day and saw the correctness of that detail which I had foretold by the art of geomancy, and which even they had never previously noticed."

This interesting episode however could have led to serious trouble for Fludd as the papal town of Avignon contained a number of clergy who considered such practices unlawful and harmful, if not exactly demoniac. Fludd continues:

"Thus I became better known than I desired, so much so that rumours of this matter reached the ears of the Jesuits. Two of them went secretly to the Palace and, impelled by envy, reported to the Vice-Legate [Carlo Conti di Poli] that there was a certain foreigner, an Englishman, who had made predictions of future events by the science of geomancy, which science was not approved of by the Catholic Church. The following morning this was related to me by a captain of the Palace, named John."

John put Fludd's fears to rest for he had heard the Vice-Legate's reply:

> "Truly this is not so serious an offence as you are trying to make out. Is there indeed a single Cardinal in Italy who does not possess an interpretation of his nativity after the astrological or the geomantic method?"

A few days later di Poli invited Fludd to have a meal with him, and discuss geomancy. Just to be on the safe side, and to have a witness, in case his words should later be twisted in a court, Fludd took his old friend, Monsieur Malceau, the well-known papal apothecary. After the usual formalities the Vice-Legate broached the reason for his invitation and asked Fludd for his real opinion of geomancy. The Vice-Legate also wanted to know how a scientific method of divination could be based on an apparently random and accidental jotting. By this time Fludd saw that there was no trap concealed in the conversation, and that his questioner really wanted to know the inner mechanics and rationale of geomancy. Accordingly, Fludd replied:

> "the principle and origin of those dots made by the human hand was inward and very essential, since the movement [of the hand] emanated from the soul. I added that the errors of geomancy are not caused by the soul but by the unrefined nature of the body distorting the intention of the soul. For that reason it is a general rule in this art that the soul [of the geomancer] must be in a peaceful condition, and a condition in which the body is obedient to the soul; also that there must be no disturbance of body or soul, nor any bias concerning the question; that the [geomancer's] soul must be like a just and impartial judge... Likewise it is necessary for the practitioner to think intensely of the question that had been proposed so that he might not be seduced by any extraneous thoughts."

According to Fludd, geomancy was a "science of the intellectual soul in which intellectual rays emanated from the mind to mundane affairs and then returned to their centre with tidings of the future," a typically Fluddian rationalisation, attempting to make the occult sciences intellectually respectable. A state of almost prophetic rapture is, according to Fludd, needed as a pre-requisite of divining by geomancy. It is interesting to note that it is on record that despite Fludd's rationalisation of the reasons for geomancy's success, he preferred to use a wheel with sixteen projections which was spun, rather like a roulette wheel or a Lullian wheel to obtain the necessary geomantic figures. As with any art though, it is necessary to master completely all its details before any of its short-cuts can successfully be used.

Figure 29: Robert Fludd (1574-1637).

POPULARISERS AND THE DECLINE OF GEOMANCY

Richard Sanders (or Saunders), a fellow countryman of Fludd, was primarily a populariser in the field of physiognomy and chiromancy, but found time to insert casual references to geomancy in his *Physiognomie and Chiromancie* which was published in London in 1653. In it he included such odd pieces of information as "how to discover the physiognomy of anyone, or know the dreams of princes," both supposedly by geomancy![1]

Sanders dedicated his book to Elias Ashmole, the antiquarian and member of the Royal Society who combined these pursuits with a passionate love of magic and astrology. As mentioned earlier Ashmole was given Richard Napier's papers, along with Simon Forman's, and less directly John Dee's, most of which finished up in the Bodleian library in Oxford. It was in fact Ashmole was largely responsible for rescuing the magical diaries of Dr John Dee from oblivion.[2] Sanders referred to his dedicatee as "a real mercurial encyclopaedian".

Another populariser like Sanders was the self-avowed, and not a little pompous, John Heydon, who between 1662 and 1664 brought out three tomes entitled *Theomagia, or the Temple of Wisdom,* based primarily upon geomancy and the production of talismans or 'telesmes.' Not only is the book a hotch-potch of previous works, but it was only a small part of Heydon's voluminous output designed to promote alchemy, geomancy and a dubious brand of Rosicrucianism. Frances Yates, describes him as: [3]

> "that strange character, John Heydon, who abandoned all precedent by loudly claiming that he *was* a Rosicrucian, published a series of works in which the Rosicrucian tendency to fanciful utopianism reached unprecedented heights."

Heydon not only had an impact on his own time, but also (probably because of his reputed Rosicrucian connections) impressed S. L. MacGregor Mathers who used *Theomagia* as one of his prime sources when drawing up the papers on geomancy for the Hermetic Order of the Golden Dawn in the late nineteenth century. He also used Heydon's geomantic sigils (Figure 32).

---

[1] Similar instructions for determining someone's physiognomy or general complexion by geomancy can be found in Jean Belot's *Instruction familière et tres facile pour apprende les sciences de chiromance et phisiognomie*, Paris, 1819.

[2] The present author has just completed editing and correcting the diaries, to be published as *The Spiritual Diaries of Dr. John Dee (1583-1608),* Golden Hoard Press, Singapore, 2011, which is effectively a completely reset and corrected edition of Dr. Meric Casaubon's *A True and Faithful Relation of what passed between Dr. John Dee…and some Spirits,* 1659.

[3] Yates, *The Rosicrucian Enlightenment,* London, 1972, p. 189.

Figure 30: John Heydon (1629-1667).

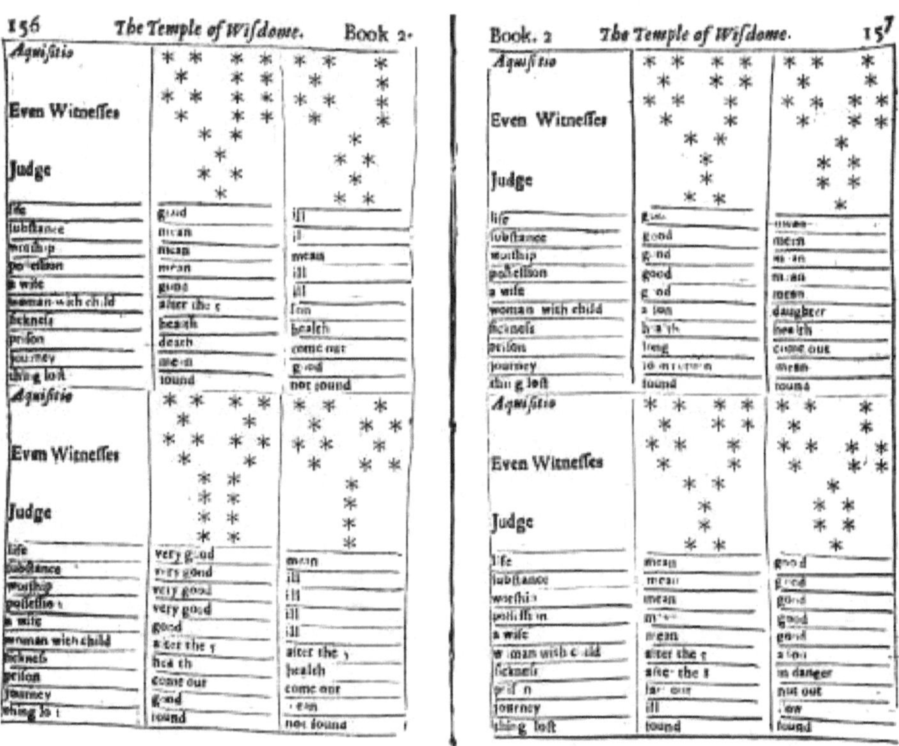

156 *The Temple of Wisdome.* Book 2.

Aquisitio / Even Witnesses / Judge		
life	good	ill
substance	mean	ill
worship	mean	mean
possession	mean	ill
a wife	good	ill
woman with child	after the [illegible]	son
sickness	health	health
prison	death	come out
journey	mean	good
thing lost	found	not found

Aquisitio / Even Witnesses / Judge		
life	very good	mean
substance	very good	ill
worship	very good	ill
possession	very good	ill
a wife	good	ill
woman with child	after the [illegible]	after the [illegible]
sickness	health	health
prison	come out	come out
journey	good	[illegible]
thing lost	found	not found

Book. 2 *The Temple of Wisdome.* 157

Aquisitio / Even Witnesses / Judge		
life	good	mean
substance	good	mean
worship	good	mean
possession	good	mean
a wife	good	mean
woman with child	a son	daughter
sickness	health	health
prison	long	come out
journey	[illegible]	mean
thing lost	found	found

Aquisitio / Even Witnesses / Judge		
life	mean	good
substance	mean	good
worship	mean	good
possession	mean	good
a wife	mean	good
woman with child	after the [illegible]	a son
sickness	after the [illegible]	in danger
prison	[illegible]	not out
journey	ill	slow
thing lost	found	found

Figure 31: Typical tabular layout, designed to interpret just the Witnesses and the Judge for a variety of fixed questions, from John Heydon's *Temple of Wisdom*, Book 2.

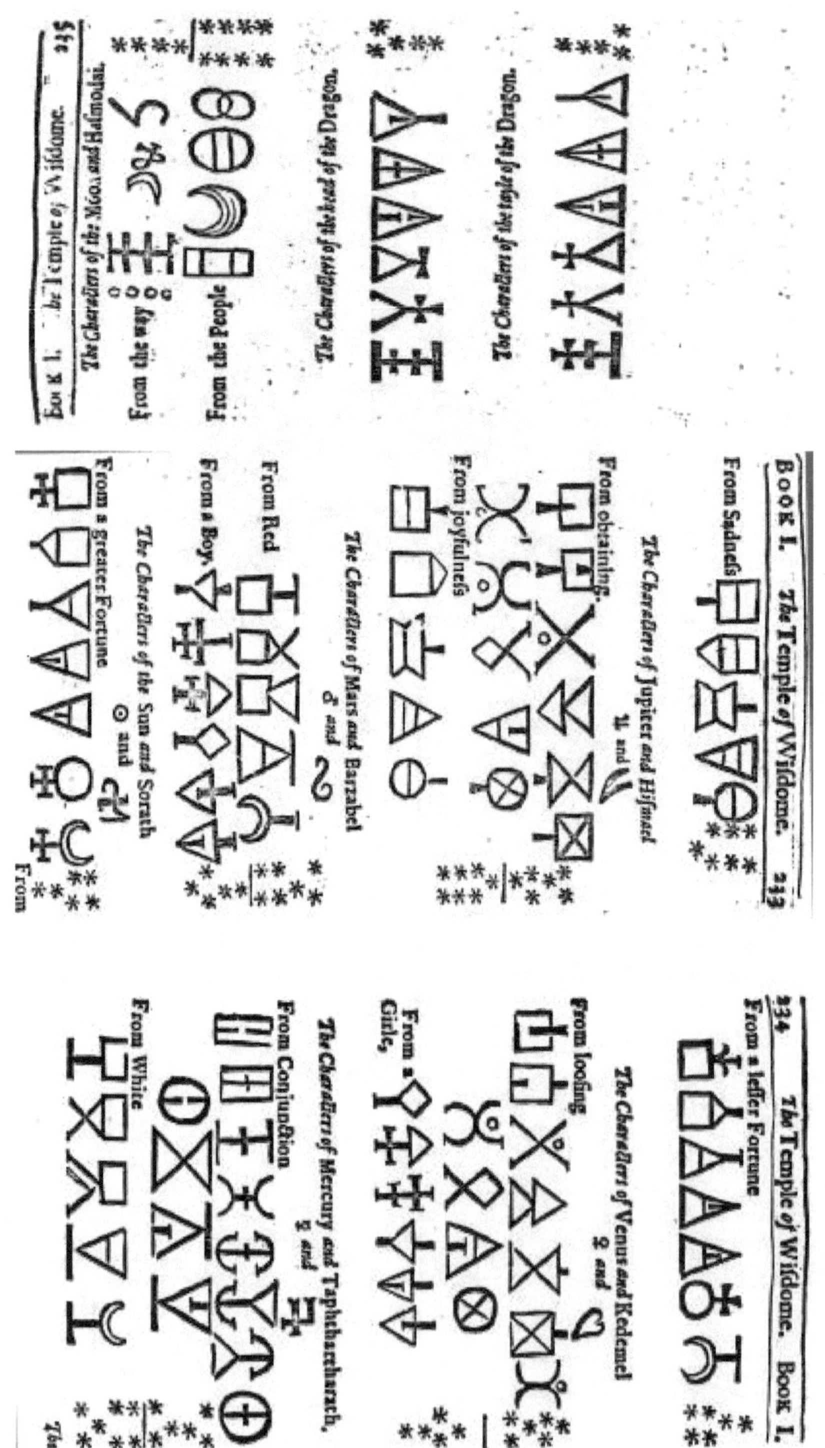

Figure 32: John Heydon's construction of geomantic sigils from the 16 Figures. These are intended for use in constructing talismans.

As a result the various spirits which Heydon spoke about, like Kedemel, Sorath and Bartzabel, were woven into those instructions on geomancy which later became the fountainhead of information for most of the magical groups of the twentieth century, despite the fact that these spirits have no part to play in traditional geomancy, and were borrowed by Heydon from other magical disciplines outlined in Agrippa.

The same popularisation occurred in continental Europe, where in 1657, and again in 1663, a work called *La chiromance, la physionomie et la géomance...* by de Peruchio, explained in some detail the art of astrological geomancy, together with 'astrological chiromancy' and physiognomy which had increasingly become its sister sciences since the days of Cocles. The mediaeval grouping of geomancy, pyromancy, hydromancy and aeromancy had given way to the above trilogy, mainly because of the dearth of information about these elusive and partly fanciful divination categories attributed to each of the four Elements. Peruchio supplements his geomancy with dice divination and the 'Wheel of Pythagoras,' a circular numerological arrangement falsely attributed to the Greek philosopher, but common in works of divination of the period.

Henry de Pisis, whose work on geomancy was first printed in 1638, appears reprinted in the *Fasciculus Geomanticus* (Verona, 1687) with the important treatise by Fludd already mentioned. De Pisis divides his geomancy into three books: theory, practice, and examples of questions taken from previous authors.

Instead of generating the geomantic figures by marking sixteen rows of dots at random, de Pisis uses a disc with the sixteen geomantic figures marked on it as a wheel to be spun four times to determine the four initial figures, reminiscent of Ramon Lull. This is a much faster way of generating the Mother figures, but far estranged from the sand-cutting of its forebear, *raml.* De Pisis relies heavily on authorities like the Arabic writers Geber and Aomar, mediaeval Latins like Gerard of Cremona and Peter de Abano, popularisers like Cocles, and recent contemporaries like Fludd.

Very late in 1704 the *Fasciculus Geomanticus,* followed by an additional *Tabulae Geomanticae,* was reprinted in Frankfurt: a handbook and compendium not since rivalled for clarity and completeness. Indeed the hour was very late for geomancy itself, since it was the eighteenth century with its growing rationalism which delivered the *coup de grace* to geomancy. It was just a short step from the Jesuit father Francois Ménétrier, who considered in his *Philosophie des images énigmatiques* in 1694 that all the operations of geomancy were diabolical, to the so-called Age of Reason when geomancies were relegated to the status of drawing-room diversions or bibliophile's curios. No original studies appeared in that century, and despite a flourishing trade in anonymous geomancies in German, they were, without exception, purely devised to delight, or while away the hours. These *'Punctierkunsts'* or *'Punctier-Buchs'*[1] were the first of a long line of thin anonymous or pseudonymous volumes often published with misleading imprints and unreliable dates. This tendency to popularise geomancy is part of the roots from which the English astrological revival of the early nineteenth century sprang.

[1] 'Punctier' literally means 'punctuation,' and refers to the rows of dots required to be done at the opening of any geomantic divination.

7. The Great Astrological Revival

Robert Cross Smith was born on 19 March 1795. The year was a vintage one for astrologers, as it also saw the birth of 'Dixon' and Richard James Morrison who later used the pseudonym 'Zadkiel' in his astrological books and pamphlets.

Very few new astrological books had been printed in the eighteenth century and the three men born in 1795 were to instigate a new flood of astrological writing and interest beginning in the 1820s. Smith is of greatest interest from our point of view as he also attempted to revive geomancy, another almost forgotten art, but now dressed up in a variety of new guises. Not content with geomancy by itself, Smith contrived to give the technique all sorts of fantastic pedigrees whilst omitting to mention that the subject of his text was in fact geomancy, which has as old a *genuine* pedigree as most forms of divination.

When Smith came to London circa 1820 he found employment as a clerk in Upper Thames Street. Before long he was being supported by G. W. Graham, the balloonist, who also encouraged him to take up astrology. In 1822 they collaborated in writing and publishing *The Philosophical Merlin* which was their first venture. The pamphlet outlined a method of geomantic fortune-telling with a simple *modus operandi.*

Ellic Howe says of Smith that he was

> "in the habit of 'discovering' pseudo-Napoleonic manuscripts, and was as assiduous in attributing occult interest to Napoleon as a later generation was in connection with Adolf Hitler.'[1]

The Philosophical Merlin...a Valuable Manuscript Formerly in the Possession of Napoleon Buonaparte...Fate: by the Rules of the Ancient Geomancy is a curious little tract first published in London in 1822 by Smith and Graham. It uses the sixteen geomantic figures to outline disposition, auspicious colours, favourable hours and days, and inherent qualities, much like astrological Sign descriptions. It was described as being 'the translation of a valuable manuscript, formerly in the possession of Napoleon Buonaparte' [sic], and

---

[1] In *Raphael, or the Royal Merlin,* London, 1964.

started a craze for such suppositious Napoleonic works. Graham and Smith certainly made up in publicity what they lacked in honesty concerning the origins of this work, and it became an instant success.

In the prologue 'to the ingenious reader' the authors built up their tale, making careful provision for future money-spinning publications should the demand warrant them:

> "At the decisive and to him [Napoleon], fatal, battle of Leipsic, nearly the whole of his curious, and valuable manuscripts fell into the hands of some Prussian officers; several of which have been already published; in different forms; [perhaps a reference to Kirchenhoffer's *Book of Fate* which will be examined later in this chapter] but none, so curious, or interesting as the present; which if patronized, by a discerning Public, will be only the prelude, to others, which when made known, cannot fail to excite the most intense interest, some of which are already nearly ready for the press, but awaiting the *fiat* of public opinion [before publishing further geomantic works by Smith with faked pedigrees]. The Editor does not pretend to establish the *fact* that Napoleon actually gained all his victorious laurels, by his knowledge of futurity; that point must be left to the candid attention of the impartial Reader. It is however a singular, but no less certain, fact, that after the above fatal battle, he never was victorious! So that the loss of his manuscripts, and [the loss of] victorious fame went hand in hand!"

The Philosophical Merlin was much less sophisticated in its divination techniques than those already outlined in this book. One arrives at the necessary divinatory figure by making only eight lines of random dots: the instructions suggest that each random line should have at least twelve dots in it. These lines of dots generated two figures in the usual manner (each odd line gave one dot, each even line, two dots). These two figures are joined together by adding each line (odd and even in the usual fashion) till you are left with your final figure. Then you look up the chapter relevant to the geomantic figure and see if the answer appears to coincide with your face and fortune. If it does, well and good - the rest of the text gives you all the details you need. If it doesn't, then the experiment should be repeated up to three times in all, with a delay of at least an hour between each try. The manuscript goes on to explain:

> "It is necessary for the Reader to observe that, if on trial, the answer does not correspond with the *known* part of his fate, (and particularly the disposition and bodily marks;) he may be sure that some mistake has been made by him in the process... This being the case, *(which sometimes will necessarily happen),* let him, if during the Summer Season, wait during the full *space of an hour and a half,* and if during the Winter Season, *one hour,* before he *again* makes his divining point. The Editor has also discovered from repeated trials, among his Friends, that it would be better for each person to make *three* trials, (after the proper time has intervened), and if *two,* out of the *three* trials, produce

> similar *figures*, let him choose *that particular* figure, which comes *twice* the same, for his Horoscope [in 1822 this word did not *only* mean an astrological chart]. But if all *three* are different, let him choose that which corresponds with his own ideas, and bodily marks or moles, as described in the Work.

The text occasionally refers to people "being born under one symbol" or another, thus betraying the fact that this material was obviously 'borrowed' from an earlier work of astrogeomancy rather than from Napoleon's bedside. Nevertheless the interpretations of each geomantic figure are quite unique, even if the *modus operandi* is somewhat over simplified.

When one particular geomantic figure is finally settled upon, the relevant chapter gives details of your most favourable astrological influences, qualities of mind and body, particular fads, fantasies or phobias, favourite colour, financial fortune, crucial ages, and fortunate times and hours. As an indication of the rather unique interpretation given to the figures by Smith, I quote here the text for Amissio:[1]

> "They who have this *figure* of Geomancy, arising, are under the spirits of the watery regions, and chiefly under the Moon and Venus. They will be of a studious, melancholic, patient, firm, and laborious disposition, rather inclined to obstinacy, and very amorous, votaries of Venus. - Part of their life, will be much fatigued, with getting riches; which they shall obtain; but often lose again, and that suddenly, without great caution is used. - However, as they sink into the vale of years, fortune shall again smile on them; and they shall again re-gain, even more than they lost; seeing their most bitter enemies utterly subjected, and cast down, while they shall descend to the silent tomb, surrounded by happiness.
>
> They shall have moles on the neck, throat, arms, and breast; are subject to scorbutic and hereditary diseases, heartburn, liver complaints, and hypochondria; but generally enjoying good health.
>
> In the south angle of their horoscope, they will have the sorrowful figure Tristita, of the airy Triplictie, chiefly governed by the cold and rigid Saturn; which will make them remarkable for having dreams of dead things, sepulchres, church-yards, ghosts, and terrific, yet unnatural appearances: and of lofty places, troubled and muddy waters, and destruction. Their dreams shall indeed, for the most part, be ominous, and troublesome. Let them beware of disappointments, when they dream of money - and of deceit, after having dreamed of flattering notice.
>
> They, shall be fortunate in finding hidden, and lost things, and shall at some period of their life, discover a treasure. In their gait, they shall generally appear stooping, and looking, as if towards the earth. They shall arrive to great honor, and dignity, and experience great favor, and friendship,

---

[1] The full text for each geomantic figure is reprinted in the appendices of my *Oracle of Geomancy*, Warner Destiny, New York, 1977.

from rich and noble persons, bearing rule in public affairs or offices, and fortunate in the science of hydraulics, and in liquids and fluids in general. - They will be successful in houses, lands, gardens, and earthly things, and should reside in low, crowded and dark places, where they are much frequented.

They will be in danger from an ox, and from other beasts, chiefly those who ruminate, to violent blows and falls, they will be much subject, especially at the ages of *five* and *eight* years. They must be careful of water, at the ages of *nine* and *thirty-six.*

In the west angle, will be found the deceitful and violent figure *Rubeus,* which will cause them at times to be very enviously accused, in some measure through their own seeking, as they shall at times, court hostility, but though not very courageous shall overcome their adversaries. This figure also gives many false friends, with danger of law suits, or public contentions, and will cause them during some period of their life to appear before a Court of Justice, either on the offensive or defensive.

At *ten, fifteen, twenty-one, thirty,* and *forty-six* years of age, they will meet with changes and good fortune, removals, or journeys. At *two, four, five, seven, eleven, sixteen, twenty-eight, thirty-five,* and *forty-two* years of age, they will meet with sickness and trouble; at *eighteen* or *twenty-eight* [they will] take a long voyage, or go to reside near the water. They shall marry well, but to persons of hasty temper, occasionally devoted to Bacchus, but rigidly careful. At *nineteen,* if a woman, she shall be in love, and marry previous to *twenty-four* years of age. They shall have more than one marriage, and bury their first child.

In the north angle they will have *Fortuna Major,* belonging to the region of the fire, foreshowing a legacy, or some considerable property - trifling gain by the lottery, or games of chance, - they shall be fortunate in *white, purple, red,* and *citron* colours, - and in bay horses.

They shall have much trouble through their relations, and survive the greatest part of their kindred, - they will be liable to stings from insects, and especially bees or wasps, - they will generally however, die an easy death.

If they travel, let it be by land, and not on horseback, but in some conveyance, let them also beware of fair women, on their travels.

Friday, is their fortunate day, and chiefly about sun-setting, they will prevail. Let them also chose the Moon in *Taurus,* if they would overcome any obstacle, and going to the *full.*

If born in the night time, they will be more fortunate, and successful, than those who are born between sun-rising and sun-setting.

The name of this Angel, or Tutelary Spirit is *Anael.*"

Because of the uniqueness of this text, the attributions of all of the figures have been given in tabular form in Figure 33.

It is interesting to note from this table, in the full text for Conjunctio, (not reproduced here) that if one is born at midnight, with a new Moon in conjunction with the Sun, Conjunctio for Ascendant and Albus for mid-heaven, "the dead in their graves shall scarcely rest for them, such will be their desire for mysterious intercourse, magic and necromancy." The text then asserts that 'the manuscript [*sic*] here relates that Edward Kelly, Chiancungi, and Agrippa, were born under this horoscope, with similar configurations, one of which, the second, was crushed to atoms by infernal spirits.' An odd reference, but interesting inasmuch as the mention of Agrippa points to a possible source of the geomantic borrowings. Where Kelly fits in is not so obvious, except for his well-known interest in necromancy (which incidentally was not embraced by his mentor Dr. John Dee). It is probably not coincidence that the infamous engraving depicting Kelly and Paul Waring raising spirits in a churchyard, which is often erroneously captioned as "John Dee and Edward Kelly raising spirits" first appeared in an astrological magazine edited by Smith.

The Emperor Napoleon himself is reputed by the text to have been born with Puella in his ascendant with Puer in the Seventh House, but in a later chapter is said to have had Cancer in Ascendant, demonstrating a rather careless insertion of the Emperor's name into an already existent text, for the purposes of confirming the book's false pedigree.

Finally the last four figures, Via, Fortuna Minor, Cauda and Caput Draconis are considerably abridged, having no attributions for their South, West or North points, almost as if upon running short of space towards the end, or getting tired of inventing material, the chapters on these four figures were confined to a page apiece. Altogether a rather singular, albeit bogus, variation on the theme of geomancy.

Geomantic figure of the Ascendant	*Elemental region*	*Planets ruling*	*Figure of the South Angle or Mid-heaven*	*Figure of the West Angle or Seventh House*
Amissio	water	Moon Venus	Tristitia	Rubeus
Puer	fire	Mars	Carcer	Puella
		Sun		
Populus	water	Moon Jupiter (or Moon only if born during the day)	Puer	Carcer
Albus	air	Saturn Mercury	Letitia [sic]	Acquisitio
Fortuna Major	fire	Sun Jupiter (or Sun only if born during the day)	Amissio	Tristitia
Conjunctio	earth	Mercury Venus (or Moon and Mercury if born at night)	Albus	Letitia [sic]
Puella	air	Venus	Via & Populus	Puer
Acquisitio	fire	Jupiter (in Sagittarius)	Conjunctio	Albus
Rubeus	water	Mars	Fortuna Minor	Amissio
Tristitia	air	Saturn	Rubeus	Fortuna Major
		Mercury		
Carcer	earth	Mars	Puella	Via
		Saturn		
Letitia [sic]	water	Jupiter & Venus (if born at night)	Acquisitio	Conjunctio
Via	water	Moon	[not listed]	
Fortuna Minor	?	Sun (at night)	[not listed]	
Cauda Draconis	fire	South Node of Moon	[not listed]	
Caput Draconis	earth	Jupiter	[not listed]	
		Venus		

Figure of the North Angle or Fourth House	*Fortunate day*	*Favourable lunar configuration*	*Angel or tutelary spirit*
Fortuna Major	Friday	Moon in Taurus	Anael
Populus	Tuesday	Moon in Capricorn and in her first quarter	Samael
Amissio	Monday & Thursday night	Moon waxing in Cancer or Pisces in good aspect to Jupiter	Gabriel
Conjunctio	Wednesday & Saturday	Moon in Scorpio or Aquarius	Raphael
Rubeus	Sunday	Moon in Aries or Sagittarius and in her first Sextile	Michael
Acquisitio	Wednesday & Saturday night	Moon waxing in Cancer by day, and Virgo by night & in Trine to the Sun	Raphael
Carcer	Friday & Monday night	Moon in Cancer or Capricorn at night) approaching conjunction with Venus and Trine with the Sun	Anael
Letitia [sic]	Thursday	Moon in Pisces in Trine to Jupiter or the Sun, but not the new Moon	Zadkiel
Tristitia	Tuesday & Friday night	Moon in Cancer approaching full Moon	Samael
Amissio	Saturday	Moon in Capricorn and sextile to the Sun	Cassiel
Puer	Saturday & Wednesday night	Moon in Aries, and Trine to Jupiter. Avoid Moon in Cauda Draconis	Samael
Albus	Thursday & Sunday	Moon in Libra, and Sextile to the Sun, also Trine Saturn	Zadkiel & Anael
	Monday night	Moon in Capricorn or Virgo. Avoid the new Moon	Gabriel
	Saturday night & noon Thursday	Moon waxing in Leo or Pisces	Michael
	Tuesday	New Moon, or Eclipse only	Barzabel
		Moon waxing in Gemini	Raphael & Uriel

Figure 33: Table of the attributions of the geomantic figures from *The Philosophical Merlin.*

NAPOLEON'S OTHER BOOK OF FATE

In the same year as *The Philosophical Merlin* came out, another book appeared, edited by Herman Kirchenhoffer, also purporting to have belonged to Napoleon: it was called *Napoleon's Book of Fate.* Both books make use of geomantic figures, but both are quite different in structure and style.

The Book of Fate by Kirchenhoffer claims an Egyptian origin and was allegedly discovered by Napoleon in a royal tomb near Thebes during his Egyptian campaign in 1798. It was then supposed to have been translated out of the hieroglyphics into French by a Copt (about a thousand years after the knowledge of the meaning of the hieroglyphs had died out amongst the indigenous Coptic population, and almost a quarter of a century before Champollion *re*discovered their meaning). The manuscript was then translated into German (for safety!) and in this form found its way into Kirchenhoffer's hands. Unfortunately the book is simply an extension of geomancy, with a simplified system for generating one Mother figure, and is almost certainly a translation from one of the many earlier German books on geomancy. It consists of a series of questions to which a long list of possible answers are appended, appropriately glamorized by the addition of Napoleon and Egyptology, both of which were very fashionable at the time. As Richard Deacon says of it: [1]

> "The Book of Fate became a talking point at fashionable London dinner parties, for the moment that Napoleon died a fickle British public turned him from an ogre through which they threatened recalcitrant children into a romantic legend of chivalry and genius. They became eager to learn every possible scrap of gossip about the man who so very nearly became Master of the World. The book itself was sometimes used, as *The Fashion Gazette* had suggested, for party games and refined but shy young ladies surreptitiously consulted it in the privacy of their bedrooms to find out what kind of husbands they could expect. There were plenty who scoffed, of course, but they were outnumbered by those who actually consulted the book."

Both *The Book of Fate* and *The Philosophical Merlin* claim that the manuscript belonged to the French Emperor and was lost by him at the battle of Leipzig, after which (of course) he was never again completely victorious. It is however rather difficult to see how he won battles using the technique described in either book, for *The Book of Fate* specializes in questions like:[2]

> "Inform me of any or all particulars relating to the woman I shall marry.

[1] In *The Book of Fate: its Origins and Uses,* London, 1976, p. 19.
[2] 'Ibid., pp. 115-16.

Shall I live to an old age?
Shall I have to travel far by sea or land, or reside in foreign territories?
Shall I make or lose my fortune by gambling?
Will the patient recover from illness?
Does the person whom I love, love and esteem me?
Have I any, or many enemies?
Will my name be immortalised and will posterity applaud it?
Will my beloved prove true in my absence?
Shall I ever recover from my present misfortunes?"

Although *The Philosophical Merlin* is not constructed in the same manner, consisting as we have seen of an interpretation of the sixteen traditional geomantic figures, it seems however equally useless for determining military strategy!

Such were some of the manifestations of geomancy in the nineteenth century: masquerading as Napoleon's bedside book, or as the secrets of an ancient Egyptian papyrus. As we have already seen, Europe knew the secrets of geomancy long before either Robert Cross Smith, or Napoleon.

A similar system appeared as recently as 1962 disguised as *The Ladies Oracle* erroneously ascribed to "Cornelius Agrippa, being an infallible prophet of the male sex"; enough to make the original Agrippa turn in his grave! While Kirchenhoffer's volume remained a 'one off' effort, Smith and Graham contrived to work at popularising astrology and geomancy.

Graham combined ballooning with astrology (no doubt consulting his chart before going aloft) and a touch of alchemy, all of which he found quite practical arts. Smith, under the pseudonym of Raphael, meanwhile became the editor of a periodical, the *Straggling Astrologer of the Nineteenth Century*. Immediately Smith's genius for 'invoking' the names of the famous came to the fore and he apparently enlisted as contributors Her Royal Highness the Princess of Cumberland, the celebrated clairvoyant Mademoiselle Lenormand, not to mention the "Members of the Mercurii... and other celebrated astrologers." Her Royal Highness was none other than Mrs Olivia Serres, an eccentric lady who claimed to be the daughter of the Duke of Cumberland; Mademoiselle Lenormand was probably not even aware of the magazine; and the 'Members of the Mercurii' were Smith's friends who formed a little astrological society, of which Lieutenant R.J. Morrison, R. N. ('Zadkiel') was a member, and Smith probably the founder. Nevertheless circulation was greatly boosted!

An interesting example of the application of geomancy to political prognostication is to be found in *The Straggling Astrologer*, in an article entitled a 'Singular Fulfilment of Predictions respecting the Spitalfields Silk-weavers.' The geomantic figure was cast on the earth in Kensington Gardens on 20 March 1824, to ascertain the result of the Bill pending in Parliament that year concerned with the regulation of the Spitalfields silk-weavers.[1]

Another of Smith's ideas was a column, the 'Weekly Astrological Calendar: founded on Celestial influence' carried by the *Straggling Astrologer* which became the forerunner of the modern daily newspaper astrology column. After the decease of the *Straggling Astrologer,* Smith wrote for yet another magazine produced by the same publisher in 1824-5, and called *Urania;* or, *The Astrologer's Chronicle and Mystical Magazine,* edited by 'Merlinus Anglicus, Junior,' yet another of Smith's pseudonyms.

By 1827, Smith was short of funds and so agreed to write an annual publication called the *Prophetic Messenger,* which found numerous purchasers when it finally made its appearance. The instant success of this meant that a number of publishers now rushed to commission new books from him, a number of which are listed in the Bibliography. Amongst them was *Raphael's Witch, or the Oracle of the Future,* 1831, which provided a geomantic form of oracle and was delightfully advertised by its publisher as the archetypal coffee-table book of the 1820s:

> "adapted to lay about in *drawing rooms* - to be read in *gardens* and *groves* - to ornament the *boudoir* - to be consulted *in* every mood of mind and temper...it removes *ennui* and low spirits, by cheering the heart - brightening the ideas, and alluring to virtue, happiness and bliss."

The original formulators of geomancy could never have foreseen this application! Many of Smith's friends however were averse to his interest in geomancy, for shortly after his death in 1832 Dixon wrote,

> "In professing the science of *geomancy* and *magic* Raphael made many enemies among his astrological friends."

Despite this, the *Prophetic Messenger* became so well known that when Smith died there was great competition to succeed him as its editor. Indeed so well known was his pseudonym that not only are a number of astrological and geomantic publications still in print today under that name, but also no less than five other writers adopted it as their own. They included John Palmer (1807-37), Medhurst who took over the editorship of the *Prophetic Messenger* from 1838-1847, Edwin Wakeley who called himself 'Edwin Raphael,' Sparkes (1820-75) and Robert T. Cross (1850-1923) who

---

[1] Full details of the interpretation and conclusion of the matter may be found in my *Oracle of Geomancy,* pp. 301-305.

wrote a number of books on astrology and issued a cyclostyled manuscript on *The Art of Talismanic Magic* which extracted much material from earlier writers, and has been reprinted a number of times since. He also acquired the copyrights of the well-known *Raphael's Ephemeris* which persists to this day and is published every year in September.

A post-script to the story of Robert Cross Smith is provided by an item in the 1899 *Notes and Queries*[1] which relates the existence of a geomantic manuscript which was transcribed from an original by 'R. C. S.,' quite possibly our Raphael, and which belonged at one time to the painter and astrologer John Varley, the original having been sold with the library of the second Earl of Essex. It would be interesting if this turned out to be the original inspiration for Napoleon's bedside prognosticator.

Mlle Lenormand again features in the history of geomancy, albeit without her knowledge, for B.P. Grimaud issued a pack of cards rejoicing in the name *The Secret and Astro-Mythological Practices* by Mademoiselle Lenormand, dated (incorrectly) 1845. Each card bears either the picture of a figure or a compartmentalized design which includes a mythological or historical scene, flowers, an ordinary playing card design, two lesser scenes, a star constellation, and a letter, occasionally accompanied by a geomantic figure (see Figure 34). The latter are not explained in the accompanying rather frivolous explanation booklet.

BULWER LYTTON

While geomancy was being thus popularised, its more serious students were carefully studying earlier works on the subject in an attempt to build geomancy into an overall philosophical and magical system. One such student was the novelist Bulwer Lytton (1803-73). He was best known as the author of a number of historical romances and occult novels, a successful playwright and a politician who rose to be Secretary for the Colonies. During his life, his novels dealing with the supernatural were dismissed as aberrations that would soon be forgotten. Today his occult works such as *Zanoni, A Strange Story* and *Zicci* are as well known, if not better known than all his other works.

---

[1] *Notes and Queries,* Ninth Series, Vol. IV, pp. 328-9.

Figure 34: Two cards from the Astro-Mythological Game by Mademoiselle Lenormand showing geomantic squeezer marks.

Lytton first became interested in mesmerism at Cambridge where he met the mesmerist Chauncey Hare Townshend. His marriage in 1827 against his mother's wishes resulted in the withdrawal of his allowance and the subsequent need to write to support himself and his wife. In 1838, two years after separation from his wife, he was created a baronet. Greater financial freedom gave him time to study the mediaeval and Renaissance writers on divination and magic. His novels increasingly reflected his interest in these subjects.

His favourite method of divination was geomancy, combining this method with astrology. He wrote a long prediction of the career of Disraeli which proved to be amazingly accurate, and drew up horoscopes for various personal friends.

Amongst the books of his library was a well-thumbed copy of *The Geomancie of Master Christopher Cattan* published by John Wolfe in 1591, together with John Heydon's *Theomagia* which also contains much geomancy. From a letter he sent to Hargrave Jennings, author of a now almost forgotten two-volume work on the Rosicrucians, it appears that Lytton belonged to at least one Rosicrucian organization. He is also reputed to have organized a club for the practice and investigation of ceremonial magic, to which he recruited the occultist Eliphas Levi among others.

Members are said to have attempted to evoke elemental spirits on the roof of a building in Oxford Street in London, in 1853.

His reputation for being interested in magic grew and he was invited to take part in the Society for Psychical Research's investigation of the amazing medium D. D. Home.

However, when the Societas Rosicruciana in Anglia appointed him as their Honorary Patron he refused the honour, which is not surprisingly considering that the Society decided on the appointment without consulting him, only actually notifying him of the appointment, on a letterhead on which his patronage was already printed! However the Society, or some of its members, helped in the founding of one of the best known magical fraternities, the Hermetic Order of the Golden Dawn.

8. Geomancy in the Twentieth & Twenty-first Century

The Golden Dawn was the brainchild of S. L. MacGregor Mathers and two of his Masonically inclined associates, Dr Wynn Westcott and Dr Woodman. The history of the formation of this Order, based on alleged German Rosicrucian manuscripts, is too well known to bear repeating here: suffice it to say that Mathers was the synthesizing genius who amassed an encyclopaedic knowledge of magic, from the manuscripts and printed books of the British Library (or the British Museum as it was then). He combined this avid scholarship with a Celtic turn of mind, an ascetic life-style, and an enthusiasm for all matters military. Not only was Mathers' breadth and depth of knowledge about magic and other mediaeval arts of divination, invocation and evocation, essential to the founding of the Golden Dawn, but also his ability to synthesize previously disparate views and apparently unconnected ideas, into a monolithic schema, would have done credit to the most intricate of the Renaissance memory systems.

Mathers resorted to the rather quaint distortions of Arab magic that had filtered through to Europe via Spain in the eleventh and twelfth centuries, the fragments of classic tradition which had become part of magic, the Jewish Qabalah (for which he had a very special passion), the intricate symbolism of alchemists, and the fantasies of the Rosicrucians, and welded them together into a coherent and living whole which used as its framework the Tree of Life, or *Otz Chiim (Etz 'Hayyim),* and the complex pantheon of Egyptian gods.

For Mathers, the magical dictum 'as above so below' was as strong an article of faith as his belief in the reality of the earth beneath his feet. As a result of this view of the world, Mathers was able to draw the most complicated parallels between previously diverse systems, using the numerical classification of the thirty-two Paths and Spheres of the Tree of Life which brought together systems based on the Triad, the Heptad, the Dodecad, the twenty-two Tarot Trumps, or letters of the Hebrew alphabet, the sixteen figures of geomancy, twenty-five elements and sub-elements, pantheons both European and Oriental, and the bewildering maze of spirits,

Dukes, Earls and other Lords of Hell in the Grimoires.

From John Heydon's *Theomagia,* Christopher Cattan's *Geomancy,* and various manuscript geomancies in the British Library, Bibliothèque d'Arsenal and Bibliothèque Nationale in Paris, he drew together a concise document on geomancy. This has had a number of recensions with Israel Regardie's and Aleister Crowley's printed works relying on it for geomantic source material, but it was basically in the form of a 'knowledge lecture' circulated amongst the members of the Hermetic Order of the Golden Dawn that Mathers's work served its primary purpose.

One of the early associates of the Golden Dawn was Franz Hartmann whose *Principles of Astrological Geomancy* (1913) includes a rather Theosophically flavoured astrological introduction, with material from Agrippa, and a large appendix "containing two thousand and forty-eight answers to questions translated from the German of the sixteenth century," in reality just a Judge/Witness table providing answers to sixteen basic questions.

In 1909 Crowley began publishing his series of bi-yearly magazines called the *Equinox,* which resembled in their bulk a book rather than a magazine. In the second number, published in that year there was a short sketch called *A Handbook of Geomancy* which relied for most of its information on the Golden Dawn 'knowledge lecture' given to Crowley after his initiation. In the course of transcribing this material Crowley abridged most of the instructions, and according to his own admission, omitted a number of pertinent points. To quote his introduction to the Handbook:

> "This MS. is now first printed from the private copies of certain adepts, after careful examination and collation. It is printed for the information of scholars and the instruction of seekers. By the order of the A∴A∴ [Crowley's magical Order] certain formulae have been introduced into it, and omissions made, to baffle anyone who may seek to prostitute it to idle curiosity or to fraud. Its practical use and the method of avoiding these pitfalls will be shown to approved students by special authority from V.V.V.V.V. [Crowley] or his delegates."

It is strange that Crowley chose this particular 'instruction' to obfuscate, as he published much of the Golden Dawn material of a much more recondite nature elsewhere in the *Equinox.* Obviously his note was also designed to attract students who wished to know more, to his Order.

The work was also prefaced by completely unrelated items such as a quote from the *Oracles of Zoroaster,* a square from the *Sacred Magic of Abra Melin the Mage,* and a sketch by Austin Osman Spare; none of these having much, if anything, to do with geomancy. The quote from Zoroaster is actually a diatribe *against* divination and augury, for it says:

> "Direct not thy mind to the vast surfaces of the earth; for the Plant of Truth grows not upon the ground. Nor measure the motions of the Sun, collecting rules, for he is carried by the Eternal Will of the Father, and not for your sake alone. Dismiss from your mind the impetuous course of the Moon, for she moveth always by the power of Necessity. The progression of the Stars was not generated for your sake. The wide aerial flight of birds gives no true knowledge, nor the dissection of the entrails of victims; they are all mere toys, the basis of mercenary fraud..."

Presumably, had Zoroaster been familiar with geomancy, he would have also decried its use as a technique of divination.

The use of an Abra-Melin square is even more odd, for this particular square is drawn from the tenth chapter of the third book of Abra-Melin, and is a square designed 'to hinder Sorcerers from operating,' presumably a safeguard against the mis-use of geomancy! The sketch by Spare is the so called 'Death Posture' from Spare's work *The Book of Pleasure (Self-love); The Psychology of Ecstasy* which was published in 1913 *after* the *Equinox* article. At the time of the *Equinox* article Spare was one of Crowley's A∴A∴ pupils, a fact confirmed by Crowley's manuscript comments on the copy of this work held by the Mitchell Library in Sydney.

The main text of Crowley's *Equinox* commences with a table of zodiacal Sign, and Element, with the corresponding geomantic figure, its sex, name and meaning, presiding Genius, ruler and planet; quite conventional in itself. The second chapter rapidly outlines the method of generating the geomantic figures from the four Mothers to the Judge, with the exception that Crowley introduces the Golden Dawn prescription to:

> "place an appropriate Pentagram (either with or without a circumscribed circle) invoking. If a circle, draw this first. Sigil of ruler to which nature of question most refers should be placed in the Pentagram."

This stipulation has been repeated by other writers of the Golden Dawn tradition, including Israel Regardie, but there appears to be no precedent for this particular operation before the synthesizing genius of S. L. MacGregor Mathers put together the Golden Dawn, except for Heydon whose work he mined for most of his geomantic information.

Crowley then quickly summarizes the determination of the Part of Fortune and the Reconciler before moving onto his third chapter, where he attributes the first twelve geomantic figures to the twelve Houses of heaven. His method of attribution is the traditional Golden Dawn attribution and summarized in Appendix III.

Then comes the part of the handbook which Crowley might well have "designed to baffle anyone who may seek to prostitute it," for it consists of sets of interpretative tables whose main claim to fame is that they are an incomplete summary of an earlier text. The tables of Witnesses and Judge are set out in such a way that you can derive answers to ten different categories of questions which are, 'Life, Money, Rank, Property, Wife, Sex of Child, Sickness, Prison, Journey, Thing Lost.' These ten categories of question, rather oddly assorted in themselves, are actually a bastardized version of the twelve categories of the astrological Houses into which any particular geomantic figure could fall.

Additionally one would have hoped that anyone slightly versed in geomancy should have been able to combine the basic meanings of two Witness and one Judge figure and use their own intuition to derive a much more specific answer than the extremely bare 'mod,' 'good,' 'bad,' 'evil,' etc. Even this scheme breaks down and occasionally a number appears in the column indicating that the judgment should be determined, 'by the figure in that House of Heaven.' As the text was in its original form designed to be a table of Houses, this is a fair indication of the degree of debasement which has occurred to the text. Regardie in *The Golden Dawn* says of these tables: 'I have found them most untrustworthy, giving answers in utter contradiction to the proper divination worked out by the readings.' Not surprising.

In Chapter V Crowley gives tables of the meanings of the sixteen figures when they fall in each of the twelve Houses. These are basically accurate but extremely abridged.[1]

The last five pages of Crowley's *Handbook of Geomancy* cover extremely rapidly the astrological interpretation of the figures, aspects, essential dignities, friendship and enmity of the planets and figures, and other matters: an extremely sketchy treatment culminating in yet another sketch by A.O. Spare. Nevertheless this text on geomancy was one of the few available in the 20th century, and was therefore quite influential, appearing again by itself at a later date in a card-covered edition.

Crowley's interest in geomancy was also reflected in his work of Qabalistic correspondences *Liber 777*,[2] and in *Magick in Theory and Practice,* where he praises geomancy as being 'rigorously mathematical.'

He goes on to explain:

---

[1] The full version occurs in Agrippa's *Fourth Book of Occult Philosophy* and is reproduced in my *Oracle of Geomancy,* pp. 272-93.

[2] The tables in Crowley's *777* have been superseded by the much more detailed *Complete Magician's Tables,* Golden Hoard, 2006, by the present author.

"The objection to its use lies in the limited number of the symbols. To represent the Universe by no more than 16 combinations throws too much work upon them. There is also a great restriction arising from the fact that although 15 symbols appear in the final figure, there are, in reality, but 4, the remaining 11 being drawn by an ineluctable process from the 'Mothers'... Some Adepts, however, appear to find this system admirable, and obtain great satisfaction from its use. Once more, the personal equation must be allowed full weight."[1]

Crowley claims to have used geomancy extensively, but never felt wholly at ease with it, finding interpretation very difficult, which is not to be wondered at if he used his own tables! He conceded that the tables given in his *Handbook* are "exceedingly vague on the one hand, and insufficiently comprehensive on the other," but justified his inability to get on with geomancy in terms of the low order of the geomantic intelligences involved, who were far from sympathetic to his work.

If Crowley lacked success in his practice of geomancy, then one of his pupils, Thomas Windram (or Frater Semper Paratus), did not. To quote from Crowley's *Confessions:*[2]

"this brother possessed the most remarkable magical faculties, within a certain limited scope. It was natural for him to bring into action those forces which impinge directly upon the material world. For instance, his ability to perform divination by means of geomancy (which presumes the action of intelligences of a gross type) has no parallel in my experience..."

By profession Frater Semper Paratus was a chartered accountant. He would be called in to audit the finances of some firm. He would find himself confronted by an overwhelming mass of documents. "It means three weeks' work," he would say to himself, "to discover the location of the error..." Instead of exploring the mass of material at random, he would set up a series of geomantic figures and, after less than an hour's work, would take up the volume geomantically indicated and put his finger at once upon the origin of the confusion.

Formerly one might not have associated the 'geomantic intelligences' with accountancy, their nature being more associated with the earth, consequently it comes as no surprise that:

"On another occasion, he bethought himself that, living as he did in Johannesburg, surrounded by gold and diamonds, he might as well use geomancy to discover a deposit for his own benefit. Indifferent as to whether he found gold or diamonds, he thought to include both by framing his

---

[1] *Magick in Theory and Practice,* Lecram, Paris, 1929, pp. 158-9.
[2] Routledge & Kegan Paul, London, 1979, p. 693.

> question to cover 'mineral wealth.' He was directed [by the geomantic intelligences] to ride out from the city by a given compass bearing. He did so. He found no indication of what he sought. He had given up hope and determined to return when he saw a range of low hills before him. He decided to push on and see if anything was visible from their summit. No, the plain stretched away without promise, a marshy flat with pools of stagnant water dotted about it. At this moment of complete disappointment, he noticed that his pony was thirsty. He therefore rode down to the nearest pool to let him drink. The animal refused the water, so he dismounted to find out the reason. The taste told him at once that he had discovered an immensely rich deposit of alkali. His geomancy had not misled him; he had found mineral wealth. He proceeded to exploit his discovery."

However, as is often the case with such magically acquired information, his practical exploitation of this find was, according to Crowley, baulked by Brunner, Mond and Company, who presumably were also interested in these deposits. A similar experiment undertaken by the present author with the intention of locating gold, using a combination of geomantic intelligence and pendulum, coupled with a map, resulted ironically enough in a perfect fix being obtained on a point on the map, which subsequently turned out to be the vaults of a rather large bank!

Israel Regardie, a member of the Stella Matutina, a later offshoot of the Golden Dawn, later published a version of its geomancy 'knowledge lecture' in the fourth volume of his *The Golden Dawn*. This was a useful source of information on geomancy succinctly packed into twenty-four pages, which Regardie subsequently reworked into a short booklet.

The first edition of the present book, published in 1985, was however the first attempt in English to present a detailed history of geomancy. Many of the books written on geomancy in the last two decades have utilised material from it, often unacknowledged, but few have progressed the subject further.

While English adepts applied geomancy to magical ends, their French counterparts were reaping the harvest of their anthropologists' labours in Madagascar, in what was then French West Africa, and Northern Africa. Because of this, the French literature on geomancy has long been aware of the history of the subject, stretching as it does from the Arab culture of North Africa, south to sub-Saharan regions and Madagascar. It is interesting that ex-colonial settlement patterns still have an influence on cultural orientation, although studies of *ifa* and *fa* in English do not seem to have ever been correlated with European geomancy except as a footnote or passing remark by writers such as Burton, who was not blinkered by a particular 'discipline.'

Some two years after Caslant produced his study of geomancy,[1] drawn from the work of Christopher Cattan, we find a hefty two-volume tome published by Dom Néroman, an 'ingénieur civil des mines' called *Grande Encyclopédie Illustrée Des Sciences Occultes.* Oddly enough this volume is one of the few 'occult' books which were actually shelved in the British Library's open reference section, and although it is very much a reflection of its period, and of French occultism generally, the Library has seen fit to have this as almost sole reference work over and above many similar English compilations. Nevertheless the work contains a large chapter on geomancy whose main claim to an original contribution is a systematization of the generation of the figures of geomancy which was later taken up and carried to its logical conclusion by Robert Jaulin in his work *La Géomancie: Analyse-Formelle* in 1966, the best work so far on the logical relationships between the figures. Apart from this, Néroman contributes some interesting circular drawings of the sixteen geomantic figures opposing each other in various relationships such as might have been part of a Lullian disc. He includes a large table which links up the geomantic figures with more than the usual planets and elements, by including metals, colours, months of the year, days, lengths of time and typical occupations associated with each figure.

[1] Eugène Caslant, *Traité élémentaire de géomancie,* Paris, 1935.

PART TWO

Practice

9. Method and Manipulation

CONDITIONS FOR PRACTICE

Before divining you should make sure that external circumstances are favourable. Agrippa suggests that you should not divine on:

> " a cloudy or rainy day, or when the weather is stormy, nor while the mind is disturbed by anger or oppressed with cares."

Gerard of Cremona likewise explains:

> "you must alwayes take heed, that you do not make a question in a rainy, cloudy, or a very windy season, or when thou art angry, or the minde busied with many affairs; nor for tempters or deriders, neither that you may renew and reiterate the same Question again under the same figure or forme; for that is error."[1]

More specifically, a fourteenth-century work on geomancy by Nicholas Oresme suggests that if a man who is about to put a question to the oracle walks about in the quiet of the night and thinks the matter over thoroughly with all the reasons pro and con, and then suddenly casts his points without noting their number, the 'motion of the sky' will lead him to the right number and hence the right answer.

It is easy to see why the diviner should be in a calm state of mind, for obviously the intuition is going to function better if the person is not depressed, thinking of other things, or acting in an offhand manner. For the same reasons, geomancy or any form of divination should not be attempted light-heartedly at a party, for gratifying idle curiosity or mere amusement. All of these circumstances will tend to destroy any feeling or faculty you have for divination. Similarly, do not keep asking the same question, hoping that a 'better answer' will be produced. If the first answer is not easy to understand, then the second will not be any easier; besides repeated asking of the oracle is as impolite as continually demanding the same thing from a person, who may be answering you, but whom you cannot understand. If an answer is genuinely perplexing, try asking a different

---

[1] Gerard of Cremona (i.e. Sabbioneta) 'Astronomical Geomancy' in Agrippa's *Fourth Book of Occult Philosophy,* London, 1655, reprinted Askin, London, 1978, p. 157.

corroborative question rather than using the same form.

The first half of Agrippa's stipulations are however harder to understand: not only is the diviner to be in a peaceful mood, but also the weather! This specification is the same as that made for evocation in many of the grimoires, so it seems that disturbed weather makes it difficult to attract and get answers from the earth elementals necessary for the divination. Aleister Crowley suggests that the diviner:

> "must banish all thoughts which concern himself, those of apprehension no less than those of ardour... So long as his mind is stirred, however slightly, by one single aspect of the subject, he is not fit to begin to form the figure... he must await the impulse to trace the marks on the sand; and, as soon as it comes let it race to the finish. Here arises another technical difficulty. One has to make 16 rows of dots; and, especially for the beginner, the mind has to grapple with the apprehension lest the hand fail to execute the required number. It is also troubled by fearing to exceed; but excess does not matter. Extra lines are simply null and void, so that the best plan is to banish that thought and make sure only of not stopping too soon!"[1]

THE EQUIPMENT

Having established the right conditions for practice, it is necessary to consider the equipment of divination. In its original form, geomancy used the earth itself, or a sand tray in which to make the initial marks.

A. If you want to be this authentic you should obtain a shallow square box, several inches deep and up to a couple of feet square, filled with dry sand obtained from an inland site.

B. Traditional sub-Saharan *raml* equipment is a chalk and slate (both products of the earth) which are even easier to use for marking rows of dots.

C. The *ifa* board covered with flour or termite dust is another possible instrument, to be used in conjunction with palm nuts.

D. For European practice one can do no better than quote Christopher Cattan's *Geomancie:*

> "The instrument of this Arte is a Penne, Incke, and Paper, or a board wel shaven, and a little bodkin or punchin, or else upon the ground in dust, or sand well purged and made cleane, with a little sticke, which is the verie manner which was used in the olde time... But now the best way for to practice the same is, with Penne, Incke, and Paper..."

> "Beanes or other grains is the manner of the curtizances [citizens] of

[1] *Magick in Theory and Practice,* Lecram, Paris, 1929, pp. 165-6.

> Bolognia, when they would know newes of their friends absent, and as yet it is used throughout all Italie."

The latter is a practice strangely reminiscent of the techniques used for consulting *ifa!*

E. Two other methods for producing the initial geomantic figures have been suggested by Israel Regardie. The first consists of using a bowl full of large pebbles. From it are drawn a handful of pebbles one at a time for each line. If the number of pebbles drawn is uneven, then one dot is written down, if even then two dots. Sixteen draws are needed to complete the initial geomantic figures as will be explained later in this chapter.

F. His second suggestion was simply to use two dice to produce odd or even number combinations, with the same result in terms of dots.

Both E and F are considerably simpler than the traditional methods, but the pebbles have more of the quality of earth about them than the dice.

G. Throughout the rest of this book, however, the more simple equipment of pencil and paper will be used to make the initial sixteen lines of points.

Whichever method you have selected from those given above, according to which appeals most to your temperament, stick to it and don't flit from one method to another.

Having assembled your equipment, you may now like to consecrate it to the service of the Earth elementals, thereby establishing a point of contact between them and the equipment. A simplified form of consecration could consist of anointing them with olive oil or sprinkling salt over them whilst reading an Invocation to the Gnomes of your own devising.[1] When your equipment is 'charged,' it should be kept wrapped or covered and out of sight, unless in use.

Before going any further you should acquire a book in which to keep your geomantic exercises, in which the questions, charts and interpretations should be fully and truthfully recorded. There is no good in deceiving yourself about your correct predictions, if you forget your less accurate answers. Keep a fair score as to the correctness or otherwise of each of your divinations. This will give you a clear indication if you need to refine your technique, or conversely will demonstrate beyond doubt the emergence of your intuitive faculty. As you improve this ability your score should rise to at least 80 per cent accuracy, or even better.

---

[1] Tolkien's *Lord of the Rings* or Eliphas Levi's *Doctrine and Ritual of Transcendental Magic*, part II, chapter 4 offer inspiration along these lines.

THE QUESTION

Among the questions which geomancy undertakes to answer are:

> "how long will one live, whether one will better one's present position, whether one should enter the clergy or remain a layman, whether a journey will be dangerous, whether a rumour is true or false, whether you buy or not, whether the year will be a fertile one, and concerning gain and loss, hidden treasure, the condition of a city or castle, and which side is stronger in a war. Whether a child will be born or not, of what sex it will be, and whether it is legitimate or a bastard. Which of two magistrates is superior in wisdom, whether a scholar can by study become an honour to the convent or not, whether the soul of some dead person is in paradise or before the doors of paradise or in purgatory or in hell."[1]

Of course these questions rather quaintly reflect the hopes, fears and desires of several centuries ago and the oracle could equally well be asked for news of possible promotion, success of a business venture, trustworthiness of a partner, employees or a spouse, the development of a love affair, marriage, the whereabouts of a thief or of stolen goods and so on: the range of possible questions is limitless.

Let us assume that you are provided with the necessary equipment, be it pencil and paper, sand-tray, chalk and slate, pebbles, or dice. Now you must formulate your question. It is no good just trying out geomancy for fun. If you want a reliable device to give you serious answers to your serious questions and serve you well, then you must treat it as such. Imagine that your tools of divination are in fact a person whose advice you respect. Immediately it is obvious that you should not ask it fatuous questions or invent questions whose answers you already know, just to try it out. If you have no faith in its abilities to reveal the unknown to you, it will treat your flippant questions to a dose of nonsense or flippant answers.

So, when selecting your question, think seriously, write down the question in your book of geomantic exercises so that there is no possible ambiguity in it or room for evasive answers, then check to see which of the following categories it falls into:

Questions of Mars

Concerned with war, struggle, fighting, victory, weapons, dissension, energy, haste, anger, destruction, danger, accidents, surgery and vitality.

---

[1] Lynn Thorndike, *History of Magic and Experimental Science*, Vol. II, p. 838.

Questions of Jupiter

Concerned with good fortune, general happiness, church matters, or holding office in an organization concerned with spiritual matters, abundance, plenty, growth, expansion, generosity and some forms of spirituality.

Questions of Saturn

Concerned with gardening, farming, crops, sorrow, bereavement, death, legacies, long-standing problems, older people and old plans; debts and their repayment, real estate, wills, stability, inertia, time and patience.

Questions of Mercury

Concerned with science, learning, trickery, theft, knowledge, gambling, business matters, writing, contracts, judgment, short travels, buying, selling, bargaining, neighbours, giving and obtaining information, literary capabilities and intellectual friends, libraries, books, papers, communications, publications.

Questions of Venus

Concerned with love, music, pleasure or luxury, social affairs, affections and emotions, women, younger people, the arts, music, beauty, extravagance and self-indulgence.

Questions of the Moon

Concerned with travelling, fishing, childbirth, reproduction or tidal change, the general public, women, short journeys and removals, changes, fluctuations, the personality, visions and dreams.

Questions of the Sun

Concerned with music, feasting, success, power and rulership, employers, executives, power and success, life, money, growth of all kinds, illumination, imagination, mental power, creativity and health.

If you wish to take great pains with your divination, then you might choose to perform it at certain times, which are more propitious for some types of question than others. The time is dependent on the planetary category into which the question falls. Why the time should make a difference is hard to say, but magicians and diviners have been using certain days or hours for certain types of question or operation for many centuries now. Perhaps the constant usage has 'worn into' the time, the associated qualities. Details of such times may be found in Appendix IV for those who care to use them.

THE ACTION

The physical process of geomantic divination is similar to the trial-run simple divination outlined in the Introduction, except that instead of drawing only four lines to generate one figure, we use sixteen lines to generate four figures. Greater complexity generates greater accuracy.

Having decided on the planet relevant to your question, take a clean piece of paper and write out your question as specifically as possible.[1] Then make a row of random dots or points, at the same time thinking clearly of the question. In all a total of sixteen rows of dots should be made. The pen is to be held firmly in the hand, which should not rest on the paper, while making the dots quickly and mechanically, from right to left, without counting.

The right-left direction is obviously a carry-over from geomancy's Arabic origins. It is best to avoid the temptation of anticipating or counting them, which can result in unconscious manipulation of the divination. If you are working with the sand tray you may have to note the number of digs (points made in the sand) every four lines or so, and after transferring the numbers to your paper, rub them out and proceed to the next four lines.

However, if you are working solely with a pencil and paper you can go ahead until you have done at least sixteen lines of dots. A few more won't matter as you just discount any lines after the sixteenth. It is however, advisable to have at least something in the vicinity of a dozen dots per line. Next cancel the points in each line, a pair at a time, until only one or two points are left. (Alternatively you can count the total number of points in the line. If the total is odd, mark one point as the remainder; if even, mark two points as the remainder.) Observing the operation from right to left we get:

[1] Golden Dawn sources suggest that a planetary sigil with invoking encircled pentagram be inscribed at this point, but this is not a traditional essential of the process, being derived from John Heydon's *Theomagia*, 1662-4.

		Figures generated	*Points*	*Row*
Fire (South)	Fire	o	o oo oo oo oo	1
	Air	o	o oo oo oo oo oo	2
	Water	o o	oo oo oo oo oo oo oo	3
	Earth	o o	oo oo oo oo oo oo	4
Air (East)	Fire	o o	oo oo oo oo oo oo	5
	Air	o o	oo oo oo oo oo	6
	Water	o	o oo oo oo oo	7
	Earth	o o	oo oo oo oo oo	8
Water (North)	Fire	o	o oo oo oo oo	9
	Air	o	o oo oo oo oo oo	10
	Water	o	o oo oo oo oo oo	11
	Earth	o o	oo oo oo oo oo oo	12
Earth (West)	Fire	o o	oo oo oo oo oo oo	13
	Air	o o	oo oo oo oo	14
	Water	o	o oo oo oo oo oo	15
	Earth	o	o oo oo oo oo oo oo	16

Here ends the physical work of the divination. From here on, the figures formed from the above dots are manipulated to give an answer to the question, so you can lay aside your sand tray, slate, pebbles or dice and work solely on paper.

In order to understand the details on the left-hand side of the page it is useful to quote Christopher Cattan: "everie pricke [point] signifieth a Starre, and everie line an Element, and everie figure the foure quarters of the world," so that a system of symbolism may be imposed upon the lines of points. Thus, the first line is attributed to Fire, the second to Air, the third to Water, and the fourth to Earth. The same sequence repeats for the fifth to eighth line, the ninth to twelfth line, and also the last four lines.

Similarly, each group of four lines which is to become a geomantic figure in its own right is attributed to an element: the first figure of four lines to Fire, the second to Air, and so on. A further level of meaning can be added to the figures by giving cardinal directions to the lines and figures, south to Fire lines and figure, east to Air, north to Water and west to Earth.

10. Generation of the Judge

MOTHERS[1]

The four geomantic figures so formed are called the four Mothers and are the basis for the whole geomantic chart. From here on the geomantic figures and calculations are generated solely out of these four figures. Put them *side by side* from right to left and examine them carefully:

	Earth	Water	Air	Fire
	IV	III	II	I
Head	o o	o	o o	o
Neck	o o	o	o o	o
Body	o	o	o	o o
Feet	o	o o	o o	o o
	West	North	East	South

Look at each Mother: you will see that each line containing either one or two dots is labelled according to the parts of the body. From these four figures the rest of the chart is formed, and although the operations which follow look complex, in fact they only take about three minutes once you have got the hang of them. Read the instructions through first, then come back to this point and using a pencil and paper, construct each of the figures given in this example as outlined in the instructions.

DAUGHTERS[2]

The Mothers 'give birth' to the first Daughter, which is generated by taking all the heads from Mothers I to IV and placing them one on top of the other.

First Daughter – figure V

o	from the head of I
o o	from the head of II
o	from the head of III
o o	from the head of IV

[1] In Latin *Matre,* in Arabic *ummahāt.*

[2] In Latin *Filiae,* in Arabic *banāt.*

Then take all the necks from Mothers I to IV and place them on top of each other to produce the second Daughter.

Second Daughter – figure VI

o	from the neck of I
o o	from the neck of II
o	from the neck of III
o o	from the neck of IV

Similarly use the bodies for the *Third Daughter* – figure VII

o o	from the body of I
o	from the body of II
o	from the body of III
o	from the body of IV

And use the feet for the *Fourth Daughter* – figure VIII

o o	from the feet of I
o o	from the feet of II
o o	from the feet of III
o	from the feet of IV

The Daughters assume the same element and directional qualities as the Mothers:

Daughters				*Mothers*			
VIII	VII	VI	V	IV	III	II	I
o o	o o	o	o	o o	o	o o	o
o o	o	o o	o o	o o	o	o o	o
o o	o	o	o	o	o	o	o o
o	o	o o	o o	o	o o	o o	o o
Earth	Water	Air	Fire	Earth	Water	Air	Fire
West	North	East	South	West	North	East	South

NEPHEWS[1]

Next comes the generation of the Nephews, which are produced in a different manner. Look at the eight figures laid out above, take them two at a time and 'add' them together thus:

[1] Latin is *Nepotes.* In Arabic they are called Neices.

Mother I	plus		*Mother II*		*Nephew IX*
head	o	+	o o	= odd	=	o
neck	o	+	o o	= odd	=	o
body	o o	+	o	= odd	=	o
feet	o o	+	o o	= odd	=	o o

In this example, the heads together make up three dots *(odd)*, so mark down one dot. Taking the necks of these Mothers, we again have an *odd* number, so again mark down one dot. Likewise the bodies make one dot *(odd)*. But the feet together make up four dots *(even)* so mark down two dots. The figure of the first Nephew appears above.

For the next Nephew repeat the same process, but with Mothers III and IV.

Mother III	plus	*Mother IV*			*Nephew X*
o	+	o o	= odd	=	o
o	+	o o	= odd	=	o
o	+	o	= odd	=	o o
o o	+	o	= odd	=	o

For the next two Nephews, repeat the same process, but with the Daughters.

DaughterV	plus	*Daughter VI*			*Nephew XI*
o	+	o	= odd	=	o o
o o	+	o o	= odd	=	o o
o	+	o	= odd	=	o o
o o	+	o o	= odd	=	o o

And:

Daughter VII	plus	*Daughter VIII*			*Nephew XII*
o o	+	o o	= odd	=	o o
o	+	o o	= odd	=	o
o	+	o o	= odd	=	o
o	+	o	= odd	=	o o

So far we have got:

Daughters				*Mothers*			
VIII	VII	VI	V	IV	III	II	I
o o	o o	o	o	o o	o	o o	o
o o	o	o o	o o	o o	o	o o	o
o o	o	o	o	o	o	o	o o
o	o	o o	o o	o	o o	o o	o o

Adding these together in pairs we get the 4 Nephews, as follows:

VIII + VII	VI + V	IV + III	II + I

This gives 4 Nephews:

XII	XI	X	IX
o o	o o	o	o
o	o o	o	o
o	o o	o o	o
o o	o o	o	o o
Earth & Water	Fire & Air	Earth & Water	Fire & Air

WITNESSES[1]

From the four Nephews are constructed the two Witnesses in the same manner, that is the first Witness from IX and X, and the second from XI and XII.

Nephew IX	plus	*Nephew X*		*Witness XIII*
o	+	o	= even =	o o
o	+	o	= even =	o o
o	+	o o	= even =	o
o o	+	o	= even =	o

and then

Nephew XI	plus	*Nephew XII*		*Witness XIV*
o o	+	o o	= even =	o o
o o	+	o	= even =	o
o o	+	o	= even =	o
o o	+	o o	= even =	o o

The two Witnesses look like this, and are attributed to all four Elements which make up their nature:

Witness XIV	*Witness XIII*
o o	o o
o	o o
o	o
o o	o

JUDGE[2]

Finally, from the Witnesses is formed the Judge, again by addition.

---

1 Latin *Testes* or *Coadjutrices*.

2 Latin *Judex*.

Witness XIV	plus	*Witness XIII*		*Judge XV*
o o	+	o o	= even =	o o
o	+	o o	= even =	o
o	+	o	= even =	o o
o o	+	o	= even =	o

Thus are formed the figures required for judging the outcome of the geomantic divination, the Four Mothers, Four Daughters, Four Nephews, the Right Witness, Left Witness and the Judge.

The Judge gives a general answer to the question as to whether the matter will come to a good or bad end. If the Judge's figure is compatible with the first Mother, and the other figures generally on the right hand side of the chart, then one can expect a good outcome with benefit to the querent. If however the Judge agrees in nature with the Daughters and those figures to be found generally on the left-hand side of the geomantic chart then matters are likely to go against the querent and in favour of his enemies as signified by the left Witness. In short:

1. A good Judge made of two good Witnesses is good.
2. A bad Judge made of two bad Witnesses is bad.
3. A good Judge made of one good Witness and one bad Witness means success, but delay and vexation.
4. If the two Witnesses are good and the Judge bad, the result will be obtained; but it will turn out unfortunately in the end.
5. If the first Witness is good and the second bad, the success will be very doubtful.
6. If the first Witness is bad and the second one good, the unfortunate beginning will take a good turn.

Sometimes if the divination still provides conflicting answers, it is possible to construct a Reconciler (or Supreme Judge) which is constructed by adding together the first Mother (I) and the Judge (XV). Only consult the Reconciler if there is no clear answer. Never consult it just because you do not like the answer you have.

Judge XV	plus	*Mother I*			*Reconciler XVI*
o o	+	o	= odd	=	o
o	+	o	= odd	=	o o
o o	+	o o	= odd	=	o o
o	+	o o	= odd	=	o

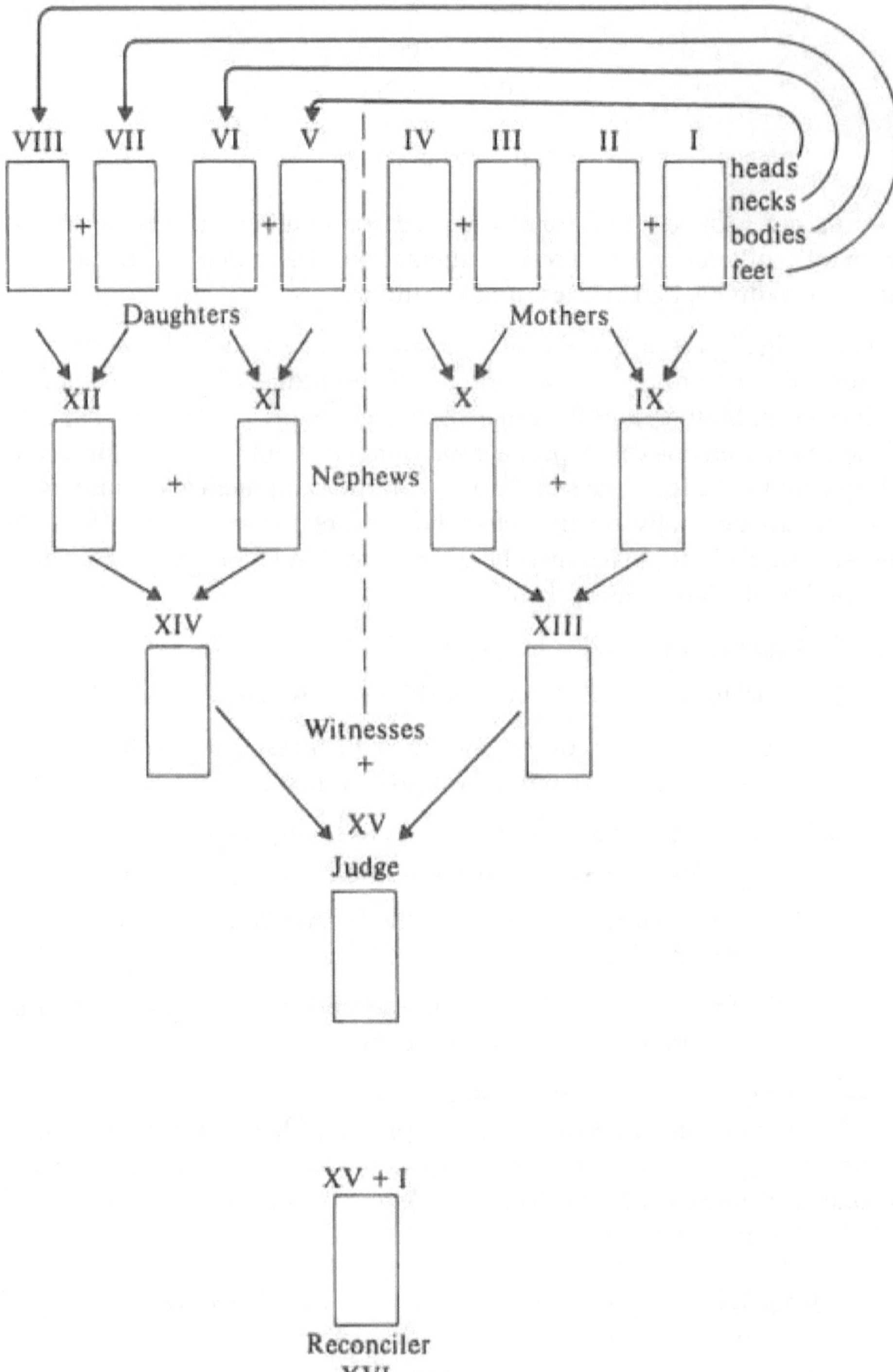

Figure 35: The format for the generation of the geomantic figures.

All this sounds complex but it isn't; it just takes a long time to explain. If we set out the evolution of the figures in a graphic form, the simplicity of the whole operation becomes apparent (see Figure 35).

Because of the manner in which the Judge is formed, being composed of various parts of all the other figures, it can only come out as one of eight possible figures: Acquisitio, Amissio, Fortuna Major, Fortuna Minor, Populus, Via, Conjunctio or Carcer - in fact only those whose *total* number of dots add to either 4, 6 or 8. This provides a rough but handy check, because if a Judge with an odd number of points turns up, you should check your calculations. Because of the binary mathematics involved it is certain that a mistake has been made if any other figure is generated as a Judge.

It is worth noting that the figures generated by geomancy have some interesting mathematical properties:[1]

a) There are $16^4 = 65{,}536$ possible combinations.
b) The Judge must be made of an even number of points, so Tristitia for example, will never appear as a Judge.
c) No geomantic spread can ever contain every one of the 16 Figures.
d) There will always be at least one Figure that appears twice in every spread.

The Path from the Judge

In Arabic *raml* texts there are a number of more sophisticated techniques for deriving more details from the geomantic spread, and only a few of these found their way into European geomancy practice. One such method was to look for the 'path' from the 'head' of the Judge back to either the Mothers or Daughter.

Let us look at the example shown in Figure 23. The Judge is Fortuna Minor. The head is a single point.[2] Now look at the line above (Witnesses) and find the character whose head is a single point: its Witness XIII, Puer. Then move up another line, and see which of the Figures it was generated from has a single point for its head: Figure Nephew IX, Via. Lastly move up to the next line of Mothers/Daughters. Here you will see that Figure I, Fortuna Minor has a single point for its head.

The next procedure is to find the astrological House of that Mother or Daughter. In this case its House 1, the House of the querent. How to evaluate the Figures in the Houses will be outlined in the next Chapter and

[1] For proof see Jaulin (1961), pp. 22-23, 27.

[2] If the head of the Judge was a double point, then the path is traced by the double point heads instead.

in Appendix VI. Suffice it to say that in this particular case, the fact that the Judge and the Figure traced by the 'path' were both Fortuna Major, confirms this Figure as the definite answer. If the path led back to the House of marriage, for example, this would add a new dimension to the answer.

Geomantic Figures in the Mansions of the Moon

Although the 16 geomantic Figures have been attributed to the 28 Lunar Mansions in Arabic texts and by Hugh of Santalla, the fit is not comfortable. Only three attributions agree between Hugh and those of the *raml* machine (shown in Plates VIII-X). The *raml* machine shows the following attributions (reading clockwise):

Direction	Figure	Mansion	Figure	Direction
E1	Laetitia	4	Tristitia	W1
E2	Caput Draconis	16, 17	Cauda Draconis	W2
E3	Acquisitio	6	Amissio	W3
E4	Conjunctio	7, 8, 9	Carcer	W4
S1	Fortuna Minor	3	Fortuna Major	N1
S2	Populus	<20 13>	Via	N2
S3	Rubeus	5	Albus	N3
S4	Puella	21	Puer	N4

Each pair of Figures share one or more Mansions, with Via and Populus (the most important Figures in *raml*) having one Mansion each. Obviously Caput and Cauda Draconis also get a double allocation.

Geomantic Figures and Directions

There are a clear correspondences between the seasons and the directions in Arabic manuscripts,[1] and these are also documented on the *raml* machine. See Figure 5 for the folio that shows the original Arabic directional correlations:

[1] The Arabic manuscript which most closely relates to the *raml* machine in these correspondences is the *Kitāb darb al-raml* ('Book of *Raml*') by Tumtum al-Hindī.

11. The Sixteen Figures in Detail

The most basic attribution is that of the four Elements to the sixteen figures of geomancy, not the circumstantial attribution which we examined in the previous chapter (which changes from divination to divination) but the permanent attribution of Element to figure according to the significance and nature of that figure. (Variant arrangements may be found in Appendix II.) The following are the four figures of:

Fire in the South

Fortuna Minor
Amissio
Rubeus
Cauda Draconis

Air in the East

Conjunctio
Puer
Laetitia
Acquisitio

Water in the North

Puella
Populus
Via
Albus

Earth in the West

Caput Draconis
Fortuna Major
Carcer
Tristitia

So far we have the techniques for creating the four Mothers using sand tray, slate, paper, pebbles or dice. Then we have the analysis and manipulation which forms the four Daughters, four Nephews, two Witnesses, Judge, and possibly the Reconciler.

We must now be able to read the hieroglyphs so created. If you look back to the Introduction, you can recognize the rough meanings of each of the sixteen possible figures which may turn up in any geomantic divination. To these basic meanings can be added a host of traditional attributions, which help to explain the meaning of specific figures found in the various parts of the geomantic chart drawn up for a particular question.

Each of the seven classical planets has two of the geomantic figures allocated to it:

The Greater and Lesser Fortunes are ascribed to the Sun; Fortuna Major when the Sun is above the horizon and astrologically dignified, Fortuna Minor during the night when the sun is below the horizon or placed in lesser dignities.

The Moon rules Via (street or way) and Populus (people or crowds) during her waxing and her waning respectively.

The Jupiterian figures of Acquisitio (gain and profit) and Laetitia (joy) are both bountiful figures respectively of material success and happiness; the former when the planet has direct motion, the latter when moving retrograde.

Puella (girl) and Amissio (loss) are respectively the fortunate and retrograde (or less fortunate) aspects of Venus.

Similarly, Conjunctio (union) and Albus (white) are the two sides of Mercury, both good figures, but the first more propitious than the second.

The good and evil aspects of Mars are represented by the Puer (boy) and Rubeus (red) figures respectively.

Saturn's two figures are by the very nature of the planet, both evil. They are Carcer (prison) and Tristitia (sorrow); the first being the more evil of the two.

The remaining figures, Caput Draconis and Cauda Draconis are represented in the heavens by the nodes of the Moon, the point where the Moon crosses the Ecliptic. These last two are strange concepts inasmuch as they are not heavenly bodies but mathematical points in the sky. They are not used much in modern astrology but their old meanings are still very necessary parts of a divination.

The reason for the introduction of astrological terms at this point is twofold. First, they will be of great help later when applying the geomantic figures to the Houses of Heaven. Second, and most importantly, they help to bring alive the rather stilted geometric shapes of the geomantic figures.

Now look at Figure 36 and notice the pairs of figures which are brought together by their association with a particular planet. Take the geomantic figures one at a time, and add in their divinatory meaning and further attributes. In the case of zodiacal ascriptions, the various authorities do not agree. Consequently the ascriptions of the Hermetic Order of the Golden Dawn have been used here, and a table of alternate ascriptions has been provided in Appendix I, for those who want to pursue them further.

The traditional ascriptions are based on the rulership of the zodiacal Sign by the planet ascribed to that geomantic figure. Thus, in each case, the planet, Sign and Element should be in perfect agreement.

As the zodiacal Signs have traditional dominion over the parts of the body, trees, plants, geographical regions and similar categories, the answer to a question obtained in the form of a geomantic figure can in turn refer to any of these other categories of things, thereby extending the possibilities for a precise answer from a geomantic divination. It is for this reason that the following information about each figure is tabulated.

Direct or dignified	Planet	Retrograde or adverse
Fortuna Major	Sun ☉	Fortuna Minor
Via	Moon ☾	Populus
Acquisitio	Jupiter ♃	Laetitia
Puella	Venus ♀	Amissio
Conjunctio	Mercury ☿	Albus
Puer	Mars ♂	Rubeus
Carcer	Saturn ♄	Tristitia
Caput Draconis	Dragon's Head and Tail ☊ ☋	Cauda Draconis

Figure 36: Planetary groupings of the sixteen geomantic figures.

In each case, the geomantic figure is given first with its Latin name, planet, Element and astrological Sign. Following these are the various divinatory meanings which will 'decode' the answer given each time. The simplest form of decoding is simply to locate the Judge amongst these sixteen possible forms and read off the meaning of the figure, ignoring for the moment the associated astrological material. If more information is required, read off the meaning of each of the Witnesses which contributed to the judgment of the Judge.

One can either use geomancy to form a snap judgment from the Judge and two Witnesses, or at greater length to encourage your intuitive abilities by combining the more detailed meanings of these three figures from the following explanations of each figure, for a richer and more detailed answer.

I

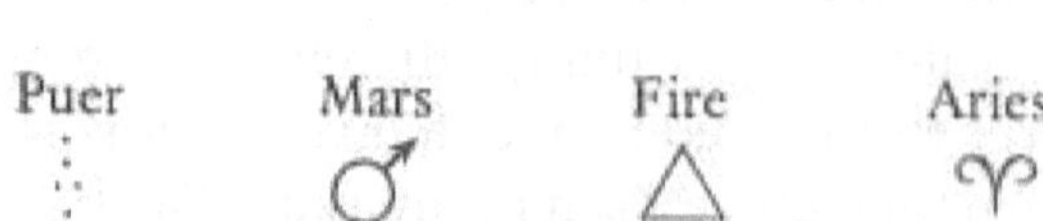

Puer means 'boy' in Latin. The figure also means yellow, beardless, rash and inconsiderate. The nature of the figure depends upon its position in the geomantic spread. The figure is basically neutral, but is rather bad than good. The traditional description of Puer is "evil in most demands, excepting those relating to war or love." Puer is the malevolent and destructive side of Mars. Associated ideas include son, servant, slave, page and bachelor. More detailed meanings for this and the following figures, as found in various cultures, may be consulted in Appendix V.

II

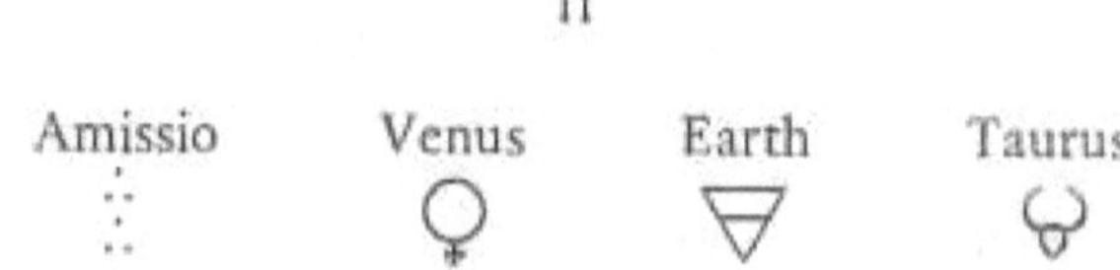

Amissio means 'lost,' comprehended without, and that which is taken away: it is a bad figure. Although Venus is astrologically a benefic, the geomantic figure Amissio means quite the opposite. Traditionally it is "good for loss of substance and sometimes for love, but very bad for gain." Regardie gives a telling example of the action of Amissio: "if a woman were seeking counsel as to whether she should divorce her husband, Amissio in the appropriate house would indicate a positive answer. On the other hand, so far as the possibility of alimony is concerned the figure would be negative." This is also a warning to the inquirer to phrase his questions carefully. Amissio is the less fortunate side of Venus, or as it used to be put, it is 'retrograde or combust.' Associated ideas include that of loss through death.

III

Albus ∴ Mercury ☿ Air 🜁 Gemini ♊

The Latin literally means 'white, dead white.' Its divinatory meanings include 'white head,' fair, wisdom, sagacity, clear thought, all Mercurial concepts. As the traditional explanation has it, "good for profit and for entering into a place or undertaking." Associated ideas include pale, bright (as in Lucifer's brightness), white paint, and egg whites.

IV

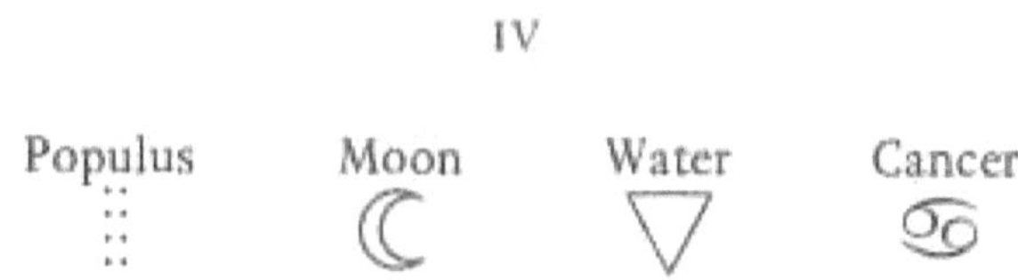

The Latin means 'the people,' forming a community or state, a congregation or crowd. It is essentially a neutral figure and reflects its surroundings (or the adjoining geomantic figures), as does a crowd or gathering. The element water and the Moon which are attributed to this figure demonstrate its reflective properties. Populus is "sometimes good and sometimes bad; good with good, and evil with evil." It rules the waning part of the Moon's cycle, and is therefore less auspicious than Via who rules the Moon with it. Associated meanings include: a host, a multitude, a free state, the people as opposed to their rulers.

V

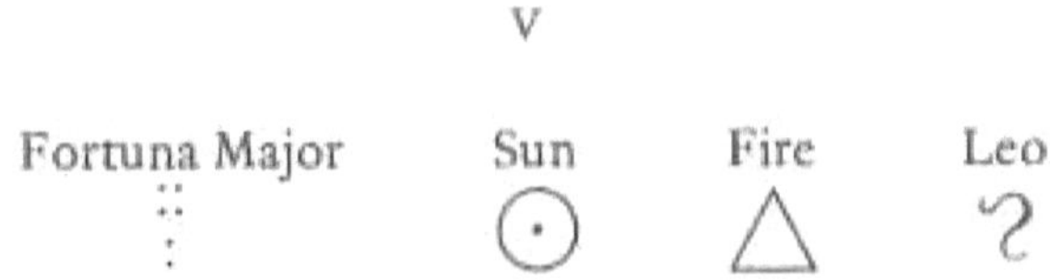

Fortuna means "chance, luck, lot, fate, or fortune." Fortuna Major means the greater fortune: it is attributed to the Sun which is the source of light and life, and is a very good figure. Fortuna Major also means safeguard, entering, success, and interior aid and protection. This figure is ascribed to the Sun during its daylight hours when it is "posited in his dignities." Associated ideas include: property, possessions and a good position in life.

VI

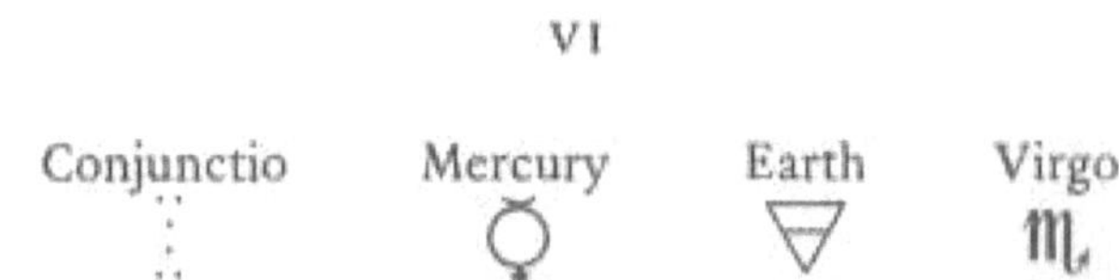

Conjunctio means assembling, 'uniting or joining together.' It is rather good than bad, and its old definition was "good with good or evil with evil, recovery of things lost." Conjunctio is more fortunate than Albus which is the second geomantic figure of Mercury. Ideas associated with Conjunctio include marriage, allies and relationships.

VII

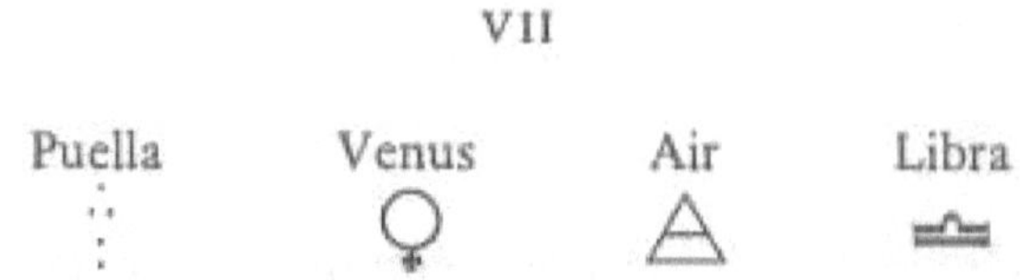

Puella means 'a girl or a maiden.' Its divinatory meanings include a pretty face, pleasant, a daughter, or a young wife. It is not very fortunate, and the mere possession of beauty does not promise underlying beneficence. Puella is the better side of Venus and used to be considered "good in all demands, especially in those relating to women."

VIII

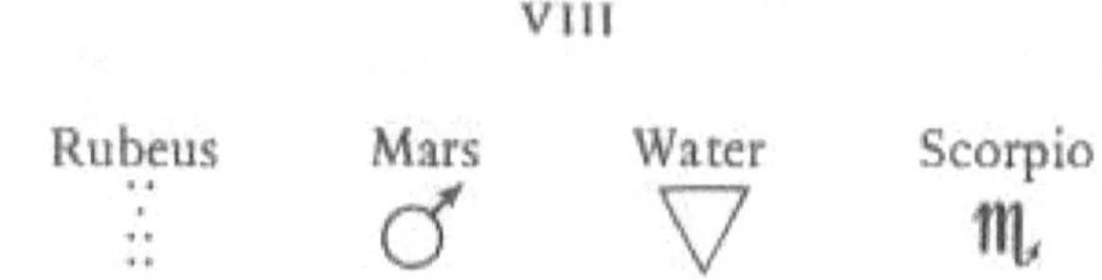

Rubeus means red or reddish and has the divinatory meaning of redhead, passion, vice and fiery temper: it is a bad figure, and covers the traditionally evil associations of Scorpio. The violently sexual aspects of Scorpio are also implied.

IX

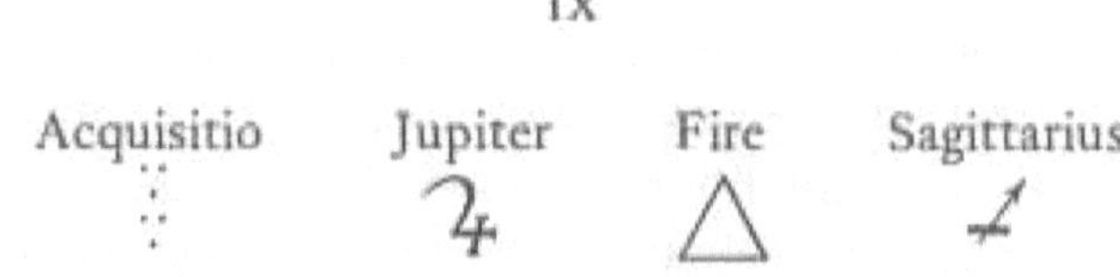

Acquisitio means "acquisitions or additions to existing possessions, or money." Its divinatory meanings include success, comprehending within, obtaining, absorbing, receiving, gain and good fortune, all attributes of Jupiter: it is a very good figure. The old meaning was "generally good for profit and gain." If it appears as the significator in a geomantic figure, or as the Judge then great success is indicated. Acquisitio is the better half of the two figures which are ruled by Jupiter. In a sense the gain or acquisition occurs as a direct result of inquiry or supplication.

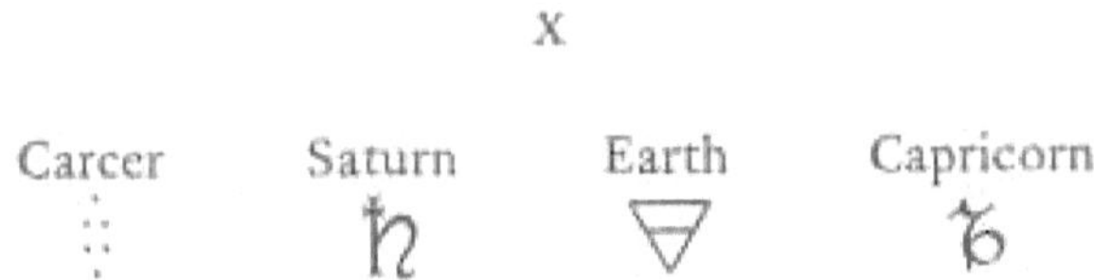

Carcer means 'a prison, jailor cell.' Its divinatory meanings include: being bound or confined, and it is good or bad according to the nature of the question. Traditionally, if Carcer occurs in the first House of the geomantic map then the divination is to be immediately discontinued and the details destroyed. No further attempt to ask the question should be made for some hours. The old meaning was "generally evil, delay, binding, bars, and restriction." Carcer has the distinction of being the more malevolent of the two Saturnian figures.

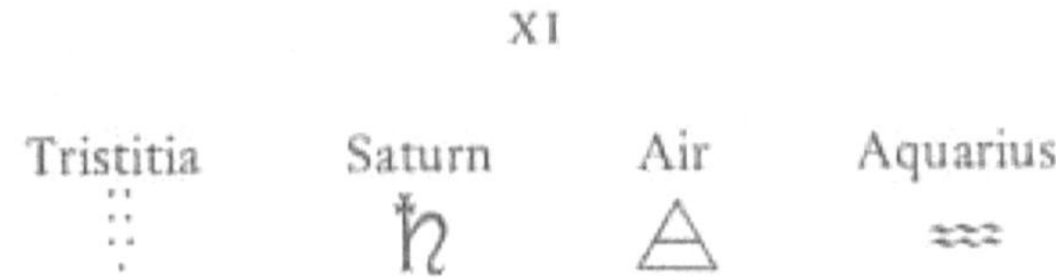

Tristitia means in Latin sadness, sorrow and melancholy. Its divinatory meanings also include: damned, cross, perversion and condemnation, with the old meaning 'evil in all things' except usefully Saturnian qualities like fortification, earthworks, retrenchment, or strangely enough, debauchery. Additionally it can apply to moroseness, ill-humour, severity and sternness.

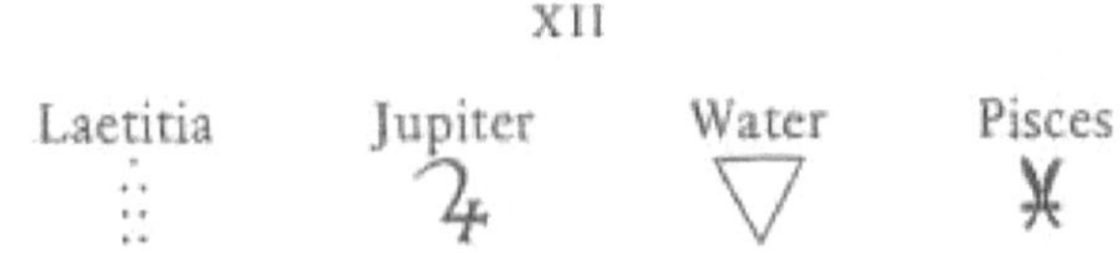

Laetitia literally means joy, expressed and unrestrained gladness or delight. It implies health and laughter, bearded, and is a very fortunate figure, "good for joy, present, or to come." Additional meanings include: a pleasing appearance, beauty and grace.

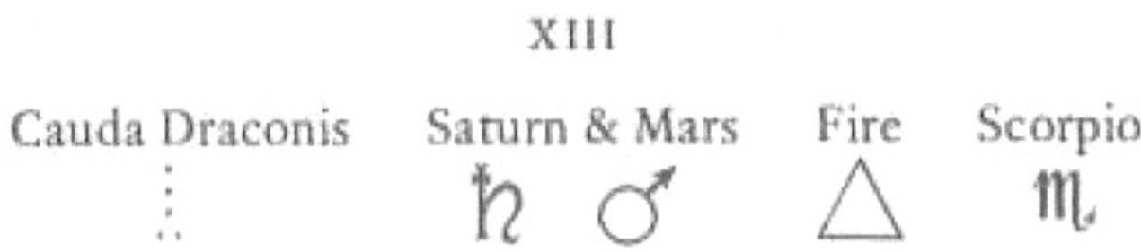

Cauda Draconis, the Dragon's Tail, has as its divinatory meanings the exit, lower kingdom or outer or lower threshold. It is "good for evil, and for terminating affairs of any kind." It represents the harbinger of disaster and is thoroughly evil. If this symbol occurs in the first House, the divination should be abandoned and the forms destroyed. Again, the planetary ascription is convenient, the two so-called 'malefics' being the strongest kind of planetary attribution applicable, but nowhere near as strong as the meaning of the Dragon's Tail.

XIV

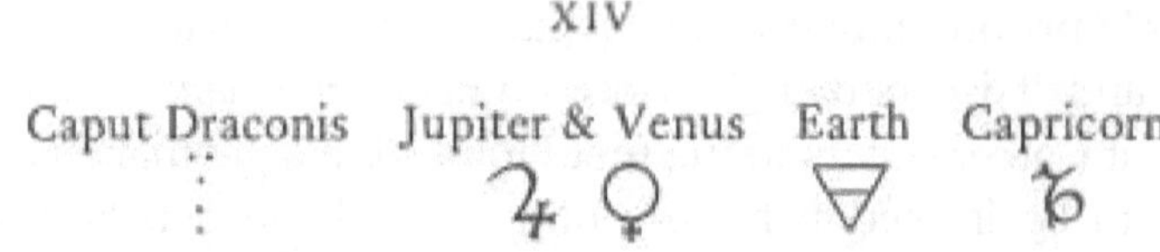

Caput Draconis is the Dragon's Head, and is named after the constellation Draco. It refers to the Moon's northern node, which is the point at which the Moon's orbit intersects the plane of the ecliptic. Its divinatory meanings include: the entrance, upper threshold or upper kingdom. The planetary ascription is tentative and mainly for the sake of tidiness: in effect the Head and Tail of the Dragon are points in the sky in their own right.

XV

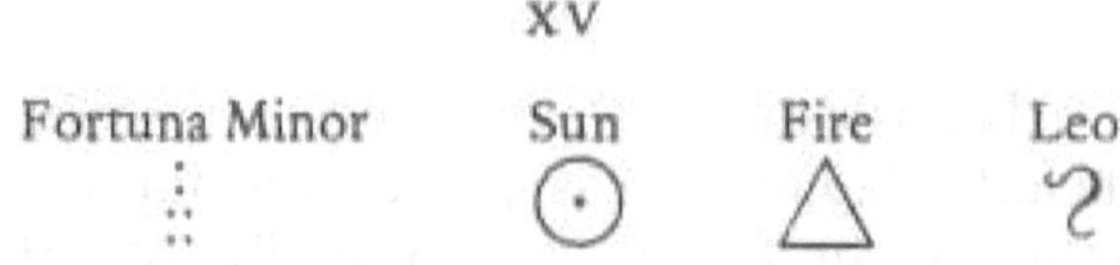

Fortuna Minor means the lesser fortune, safeguard going out, external aid and protection, and is not nearly as good a figure as Fortuna Major. Like the latter, it is also attributed to the Sun, but the Sun at night, "or placed in lesse dignities." Sometimes Fortuna Minor has Air attributed to it, which balances the attribution of geomantic figures to elements better by providing four figures per element, rather than a surplus of figures for Fire.

XVI

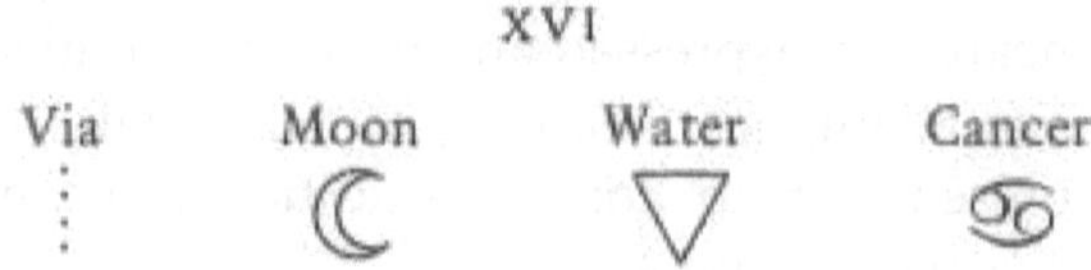

The Latin means 'street or way,' literally the way along which one goes, and hence its divinatory meaning also includes journey. Again it is essentially neutral, being reflective like the Moon. Via is "injurious to the goodness of other figures generally, but good for journeys and voyages." Via governs the waxing half of the Moon's cycle. Associated meanings include: a highway, a way through, a wind-pipe, a march and a method.

For easy reference these details and meanings have been tabulated together with the name of the ruler of each figure; in accordance with Golden Dawn attributions as listed in Appendices I and II.

The logical grouping of some of the figures in pairs is obvious from the figures themselves, but is made more evident if the original Arabic names for the figures (see Appendix V) are considered in detail. Here it becomes immediately apparent that three figures (Caput Draconis, Acquisitio and Fortuna Major) all have the word *dakil* in their title which carries the meaning of interior, whilst the figures formed by inverting these figures (Cauda Draconis, Amissio and Fortuna Minor) all contain the word *kharga* with the meaning of exterior. The Latin names for these figures do not so obviously display this polarity. Other pairs, however, are obvious such as Populus and Via, being the figures with the most and least points respectively; Albus and Puella, being the two 'colour' figures; the boy and girl combination of Puer and Puella; leaving the last two pairs of Tristitia and Laetitia (obvious in the Latin but not in the Arabic), Carcer and Conjunctio. It is interesting to compare the interaction of meaning between such pairs.

An idea of the way individual Figures will behave in a divination, or in response to particular questions, can be had by reading through Appendix VII.

Geomantic figure	*Name*	*Meaning*
· · · · ·	Puer	Boy, yellow, beardless, rash and inconsiderate, is rather good than bad
· · · · · ·	Amissio	Loss, comprehended without, that which is taken away, a bad figure
· · · · · · ·	Albus	White, fair, wisdom, sagacity, clear thought, is a good figure
· · · · · · · ·	Populus	People, congregation, an indifferent figure
· · · · · ·	Fortuna Major	Greater fortune, greater aid, safeguard entering, success, interior aid and protection, a very good sign
· · · · · ·	Conjunctio	Conjunction, assembling, union or coming together, rather good than bad
· · · · ·	Puella	A girl, beautiful, pretty face, pleasant, but not very fortunate
· · · · · · ·	Rubeus	Red, reddish, redhead, passion, vice, fiery temper, a bad figure
· · · · · ·	Acquisitio	Obtaining, comprehending within, success, acquisition, absorbing, receiving, a good figure
· · · · · ·	Carcer	A prison, bound, is good or bad according to the nature of the question
· · · · · · ·	Tristitia	Sadness, damned, cross, sorrow, grief, perversion, condemnation, is a bad figure
· · · · · · ·	Laetitia	Joy, laughing, healthy, bearded, is a good figure
· · · · ·	Cauda Draconis	The threshold lower, or going out, dragon's tail, exit, lower kingdom, is a bad figure
· · · · ·	Caput Draconis	The head, the threshold entering, the upper threshold, dragon's head, entrance, upper kingdom, is a good figure
· · · · · ·	Fortuna Minor	Lesser fortune, lesser aid, safeguard going out, external aid and protection, is not a very good figure
· · · ·	Via	Way, street, journey, neither good nor bad

Figure 37: Table of geomantic figures and attributions.

Sign	*Element*	*Ruler*	*Planet*
♈	🜂	Bartzabel	♂
♉	🜃	Kedemel	♀
♊	🜁	Taphthartharath	☿
♋	🜄	Chashmodai	☽
♌	🜂	Sorath	☉
♍	🜃	Taphthartharath	☿
♎	🜁	Kedemel	♀
♏	🜄	Bartzabel	♂
♐	🜂	Hismael	♃
♑	🜃	Zazel	♄
♒	🜁	Zazel	♄
♓	🜄	Hismael	♃
☋	🜂	Zazel & Bartzabel	♄ ♂
☊	🜃	Hismael & Kedemel	♃ ♀
♌	🜂	Sorath	☉
♋	🜄	Chashmodai	☽

Figure 38: Table of Sign, Element, Spirit and Planet of each Geomantic Figure.

12. Practical Divination

To make the operation of the oracle clearer, and to explain its interpretation in detail, let us take a sample divination: in this case, to determine if the querent should marry a specific person. Suppose that the lines of dots were traced and the figures generated, as in the first seven steps of the divining process (see Chapter 14 for a summary). This gives us the four Mothers which must be written from right to left. We can commence our example at *Step 8:*

Mothers

IV	III	II	I
o o	o o	o	o o
o	o o	o	o o
o	o	o	o
o o	o	o o	o

STEP 9

Now you will remember that the Daughters are formed from the Mothers by taking:

all the heads of the Mothers for the first Daughter
all the necks of the Mothers for the second Daughter
all the bodies of the Mothers for the third Daughter
all the feet of the Mothers for the fourth Daughter

Daughters

VIII	VII	VI	V
o	o	o o	o o
o o	o	o	o
o	o	o o	o o
o o	o	o	o o

STEP 10

Now for the Nephews, which are formed using the 'addition formula':

Mother I + Mother II = Nephew IX
Mother III + Mother IV = Nephew X
Daughter V + Daughter VI = Nephew XI
Daughter VII + Daughter VIII = Nephew XII

These are also written right to left:

Nephews

STEP 11

Likewise Witnesses are formed by addition:

Nephew IX + Nephew X = Witness XIII
Nephew XI + Nephew XII = Witness XIV

Witnesses

XIV	XIII
o o	o
o	o o
o o	o o
o o	o o

STEP 12

These two are then added to form the Judge.

Witness XIII + Witness XIV = Judge *XV*

Judge

XV
o
o
o o
o o

Layout the full fifteen figures as shown in Figure 39.

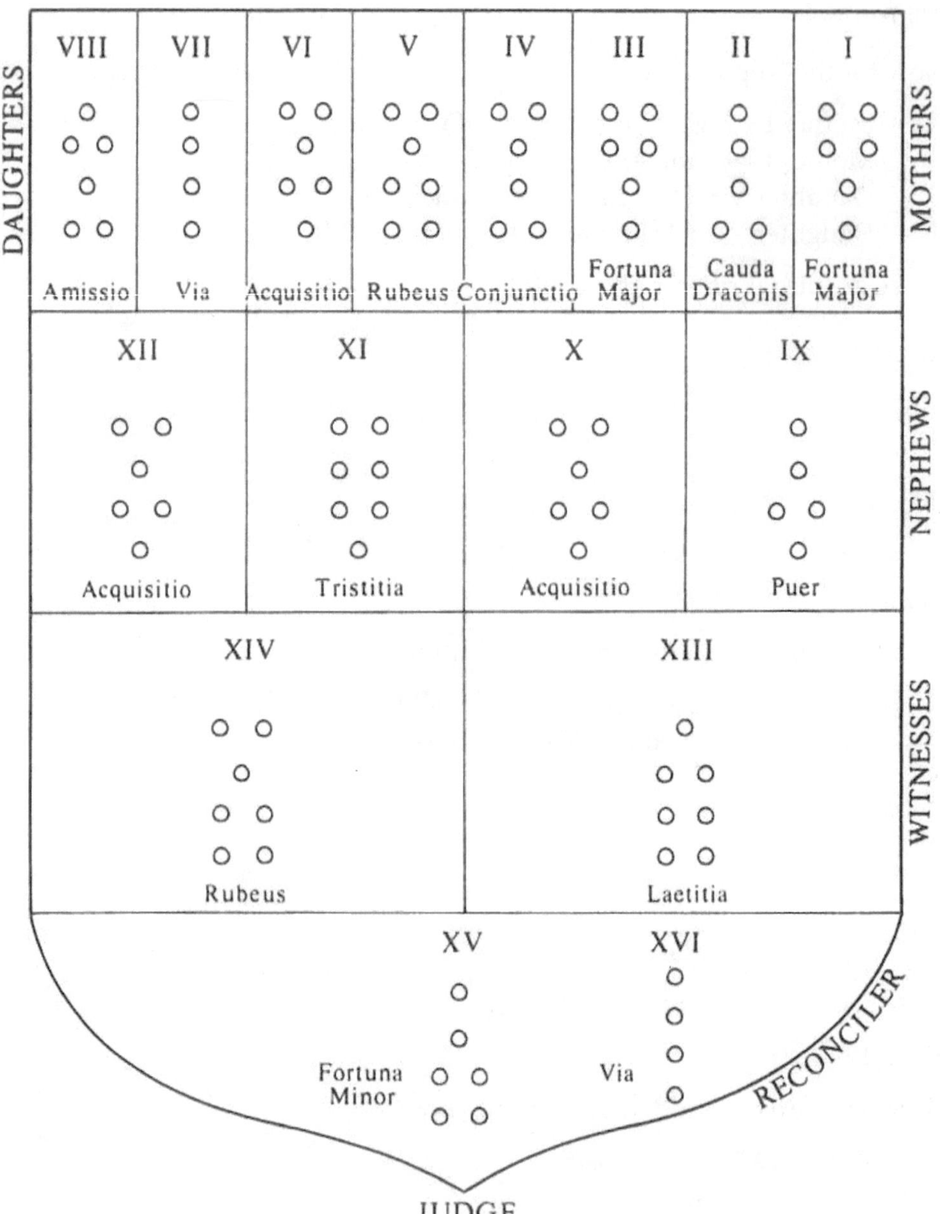

Figure 39: Plan of a sample 'shield' shaped geomantic divination.

Interpretation

Having gone through the mechanical generation of the fifteen figures of the geomantic spread, now comes the work of interpretation. Before we can determine the meaning of the chart we have to identify the name of each of the fifteen figures. On the chart each figure has been given its name. Observe particularly the figures that are in the Witnesses and Judge.

The Judge is Fortuna Minor which is grouped amongst the unfavourable figures by Bartholomew of Parma (chapter 5) as a general indication of its nature. In detail it means "the lesser fortune, safeguard going out, external aid and protection," and is attributed to the Sun at night, that is the cold, hidden or vanquished Sun. This does not sound very promising for a marriage, so let us examine the Witnesses which contributed to the production of this Judge.

Left Witness: This is Rubeus, which means "red, reddish, redhead, passion, vice and fiery temper; it is a bad figure, and covers the traditionally evil associations of Scorpio. The violently sexual aspects of Scorpio are also implied." Here we have considerable light thrown on the question. The nature of attraction is strong sexual desire of a violent kind rather than love.

Right Witness: This is Laetitia which literally means "joy, expressed and unrestrained," and its additional meanings include "a pleasing appearance, beauty and grace." Although it is a good figure it confirms beautifully what we now know, that it is basically sexual attraction at the root of the proposed marriage with no depth of feeling or long-lasting good fortune implied. This also explains how Fortuna Minor can be listed as a partly favourable figure, for here the sexual attraction and pleasure is pleasant, but does not bode well for the success of the marriage, which after all is what the question is about.

STEP 13

Who could ask for greater clarity? If the answer were ambiguous, don't forget that you could always resort to that back-stop, the Reconciler (figure XVI), which is formed by 'adding' together figures I and XV, that is, the first Mother and the Judge. However don't form a Reconciler if you have already got a satisfactory answer, as this is rude persistence in the face of a perfectly adequate reply by the oracle!

If more detail is required, refer back to the first Mother (figure I) for the beginning of the matter. This figure is Fortuna Major, indicating that the relationship commenced with a good figure which means 'the greater fortune' and is attributed also to Leo and the Sun, but the Sun during the day. Thus both this figure and the Judge are attributed to the Sun and Leo, but the relationship moves from the Sun during the day to the Sun at night, in short the relationship cools off and dies. Fortuna Major also includes among its divinatory meanings "safeguard, entering success, and interior aid and protection," indicating the beginning of the relationship, which perhaps commenced with some elements of a desire on the part of one partner to protect or look after the other.

The termination or end of the relationship is indicated by figure IV which is Conjunctio or 'uniting or joining together,' more good than bad, but "good with good or evil with evil," Associated ideas include marriage.

This is interesting because it indicates clearly that although the Judge warns against the marriage as being the lesser fortune, the likely upshot of the matter is that the marriage will take place nevertheless. As Conjunctio is "good with good or evil with evil," the mixture of Rubeus and Laetitia (violent sexual attraction and good looks) will draw the two into a marriage which will nevertheless wane in quality as the Sun at day (figure I, Fortuna Major) reverts to the Sun at night (figure XV, Fortuna Minor).

Crowley neatly sums up the operation of judgment, emphasizing the need of a meditative frame of mind untouched by bias in assessing the correct interpretation of the information supplied by the geomantic chart:

> "In the judgment, the diviner stands once more in need of his inmost and utmost attainments. He should exhaust the intellectual sources of information at his disposal, and form from them his judgment. But having done this, he should detach his mind from what it has just formulated, and proceed to concentrate it on the figure as a whole, almost as if it were the object of his meditation. One need hardly repeat that in both these operations, detachment from one's personal partialities is as necessary as it was in the first part of the work."[1]

[1] Crowley, *Magick in Theory and Practice,* Lecram, Paris, 1929, p. 166.

13. Astrogeomancy

When skill has been achieved in the manipulation of ordinary geomantic divination, it will become increasingly obvious that the Judge and Witness figures are really not much more than artificially derived summaries of the primary figures, the Mothers, and consequently a shade mechanical.

It is traditional to flesh out the interpretation of a geomantic spread by referring it to the Houses of judicial astrology. Robert Fludd actually called geomancy, 'terrestrial astrology,' and therefore a knowledge of astrology outside of that contained in this chapter is helpful, and some background reading would be useful. There is however no need for complex calculations, for that part of astrology is not utilized in geomantic interpretation. As far as geomancy is concerned, astrology is an interpretive tool and it is therefore not necessary to go into it in depth.

If we ignore the relative positions of the solar system in which the planets revolve around the Sun, and think instead of the universe from the point of view of a man standing on the earth and gazing up at the dome of the sky we will get a clearer picture of astrology. It does not matter what the complex orbital systems are which result in planets and stars being in certain parts of the sky at certain times; what does matter is the angles they make with each other and their relationship with the spot on the Earth where we are standing.

If we had to devise a system of astrology for people born on the surface of the Sun, then the present scientific model of the (heliocentric) solar system would be a perfect start. However, we are dealing with the relationship of the planets and stars *with the Earth,* so it is irrelevant to talk about their orbital relationship with the Sun.

Having disposed of this unnecessary complication, let us imagine that we are standing at night with feet firmly planted on the earth, some time before Copernicus, looking up into the blue-black dome of the night. The stars gradually move across the sky, each star keeping the same position relative to the other stars. Those who watched this phenomenon did not think in terms of the rotation of the earth but, taking the earth as their reference point, chose to examine particular groups of stars fixed, as they thought, into the crystal sphere of the stars which ceaselessly turned around the earth. These groups of stars they called constellations.

SIGNS OF THE ZODIAC

Obviously as the dome of the sky moved it was necessary to find a fixed point of reference for measuring the movement of the Sun, Moon and planets. Twelve particularly outstanding constellations in a rough band about 16° wide round the earth were chosen as 'markers' in the sky by which to plot the movement of the planets, Sun and Moon. These twelve constellations are the twelve signs of the Zodiac.

HOUSES OF HEAVEN

Astronomers also needed another system of measurement, for although we have the Signs of the Zodiac, they are moving as part of the sphere of stars and are therefore not a fixed system of measurement. For this purpose astrologers have devised the 'House' system. These Houses form an imaginary but fixed grid centred on the earth and orientated according to the spot of ground on which you are standing. The twelve fixed House divisions are projected out into the sky forming the ribs of the system:

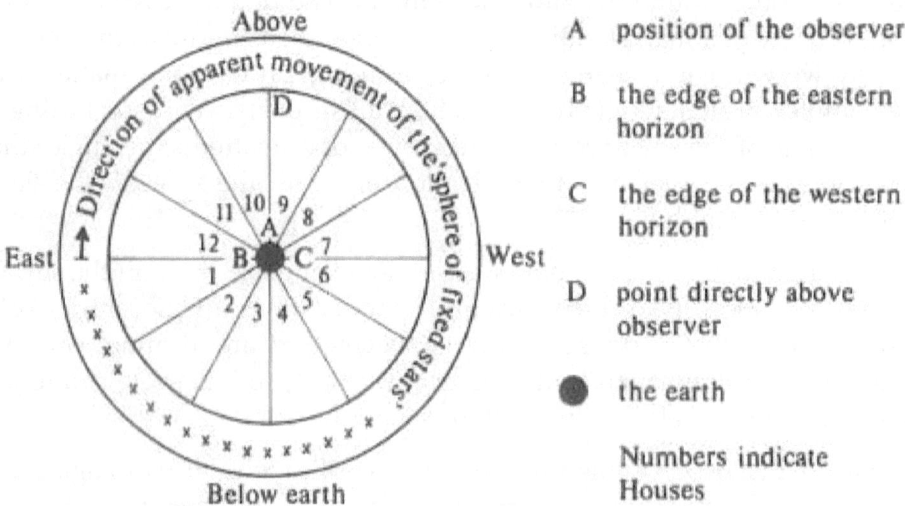

Figure 40: The numbering of the twelve Houses of Heaven.

The First House is always located just under the eastern horizon (left-hand side of chart) with the rest numbered in order around the earth till House 12 is just *above* the eastern horizon. This is fixed, for the Houses are a manmade fixed grid, whilst the Zodiac is based on the natural phenomena of the moving zodiacal Signs. These then provide two systems of reference for plotting the position of the planets; as a planet's position in the sky may be indicated by both its House and its Zodiacal Sign location.

Each of the Houses is given a meaning, so that each sector of the sky both above the earth and under the earth is associated with a particular type of question or function, as follows:

First House The person himself, his life, health, behaviour, habits, disposition, personal characteristics and apparent personality.

Second House Money, property, personal wealth, financial profit and loss, income and expenditure, and associated ideas of theft, loss or negligence.

Third House Brothers, sisters, blood relatives, news, letters, communication, short journeys, languages, writing, publicity, agencies, and similar mercurial pursuits.

Fourth House Home environment, fathers and grandfathers, inheritances, possessions, especially buildings, land and hidden treasure. It also gives details about thefts and thieves. Retirement, the grave. The *conclusion* of any matter is also included in the significations of this house.

Fifth House Women, luxury, eating, drinking. Creation, recreation, procreation; love affairs, courtship; pregnancy and childbirth; children and the young in general, creative artistic work; amusements and pleasures, sexual compatibility, gambling or speculation.

Sixth House Servants and employees; sickness and recovery; which parts of the body are most likely to suffer in illness or injury, aunts and uncles, and domestic animals.

Seventh House Wedlock, whoredom and fornication, love, marriage, partnerships and associations. Public enemies, law suits, company business, war, conflict, opponents and controversies. Thieves, robbers, dishonour.

Eighth House Deaths and financial matters connected with death, such as wills, legacies, the estate of the deceased, or business connected with death such as undertakers, executors or spirit mediums. Poverty.

Ninth House Long journeys, voyages, relations with foreigners. Science, philosophy, the Church, religion, art, visions, dreams and divinations.

Tenth House Fame or notoriety, reputation, rank, honour, trade or profession, authority, employment, and worldly position generally. Also signifies the querent's mother.

Eleventh House Friends, acquaintances and social contacts, hopes and wishes. Also patronage by the rich or well placed. Philanthropic or altruistic organizations.

Twelfth House Sorrows, fears, punishments, imprisonment, intrigue, enemies in secret, servants, prostitutes, institutions, asylums, orphanages, hospitals, prisons, secret societies, unseen dangers, restrictions, and misfortune generally (for details refer to the Sixth and Eighth Houses).

It is also necessary to understand the terms Angular, Succedent and Cadent. They refer to the three types of Houses. Those on the Angles, that is the horizon in the east and west and the Houses at the midheaven and directly below the earth, are the strongest Angular Houses and are the First, Fourth, Seventh and Tenth. Those Houses following or succeeding the Angular Houses are called Succedent Houses and are the Second, Fifth, Eighth and Eleventh Houses. Finally those furthest away from the first mentioned Angular Houses are called Cadent, and are the Third, Sixth, Ninth and Twelfth Houses (see Figure 41).

When interpreting the meaning of the geomantic figures in the twelve Houses it is useful to remember that if the figure falls in an Angular House, then its action will be strong and "profitable for the question propounded," in the Succedent House it is less effective, and if the figure falls into a Cadent House its action is positively retarded.

Having considered the framework of astrology, the time has come to apply the figures derived in ordinary geomantic divination to this framework to derive a more detailed interpretation.

In almost every case a greater clarification is necessary than can be obtained merely by reading off the meaning of the Judge and Witnesses. One such method of clarification is to allocate the first twelve geomantic figures to the twelve Houses of Heaven on an astrological chart.

As already explained, the only fixed framework which marks out the sky in astrology is the House system, through which revolves the Zodiac, and against which the planets move with complex motions. The Houses traditionally represent the departments of everyday life, and it is the Houses which contain the answers to the mundane questions with which geomancy deals; questions such as the number and sex of children, the outcome of a business deal, the success of a journey, and so on.

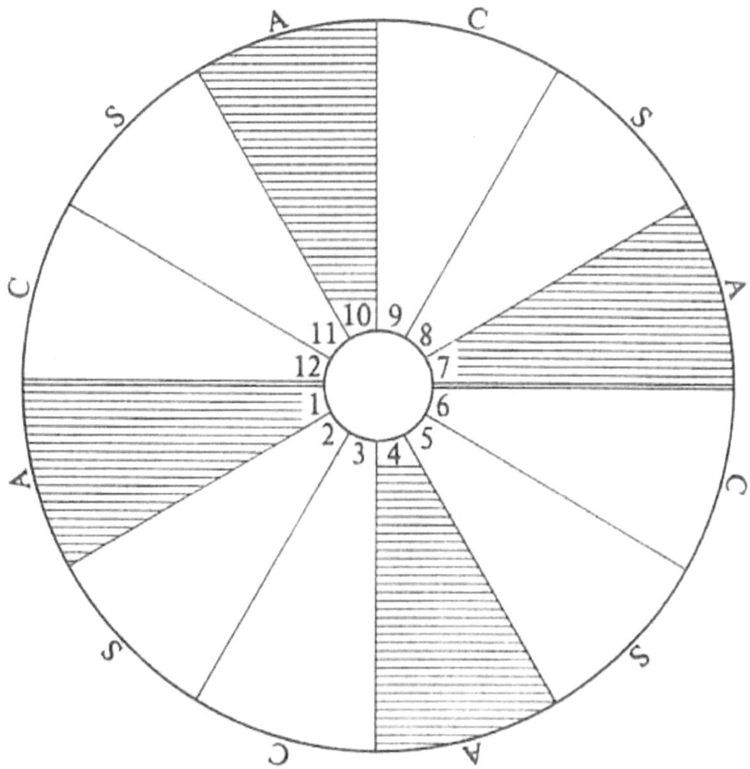

Figure 41: Angular, Succedent and Cadent Houses.

Therefore, the geomantic figures which have been derived by divination are to be put into this House grid system, and the figure which is allocated to the House most relevant to the question asked, becomes the major significator. With the addition of the seven planets and twelve Signs of the Zodiac to the House system, more information can be derived concerning the question.

The seven planets are the *forces* that act on human beings, the twelve Signs show *how* they act, whilst the Houses show *where* they act, and in what department of life their action will be felt. In this manner the static answer of the plain geomantic divination is fleshed out with background information and associated causes and conditions.

Now, there are several systems for allocating the geomantic figures derived in an ordinary divination to the twelve Houses of astrology. It has often been said that the correct method of allocation is the real secret of geomancy which has never been published. Even Aleister Crowley, who was in the habit of "telling everything like it is," admitted that a major key had been left out of his explanation of the technical side of astro-geomancy. That key was the House allocation system. Amongst the systems outlined in this book is the major key which was omitted. For the present we will simply use the House allocation system prescribed by the Golden Dawn. In Appendix III you will find the alternative systems. You may find, with practice, that one of those systems gives you more consistently accurate results. It is up to you to choose one system and stick with it.

Using the Golden Dawn system (Appendix III) and the example used in chapter 12, place the first Mother, Fortuna Major, into the Tenth House. Then mark in the second Mother, Cauda Draconis, in the First House. Follow through anti-clockwise with the two other Mothers in the Angular Houses. Then draw in the Daughters (in the Succedent Houses) and Nephews (in the Cadent Houses).

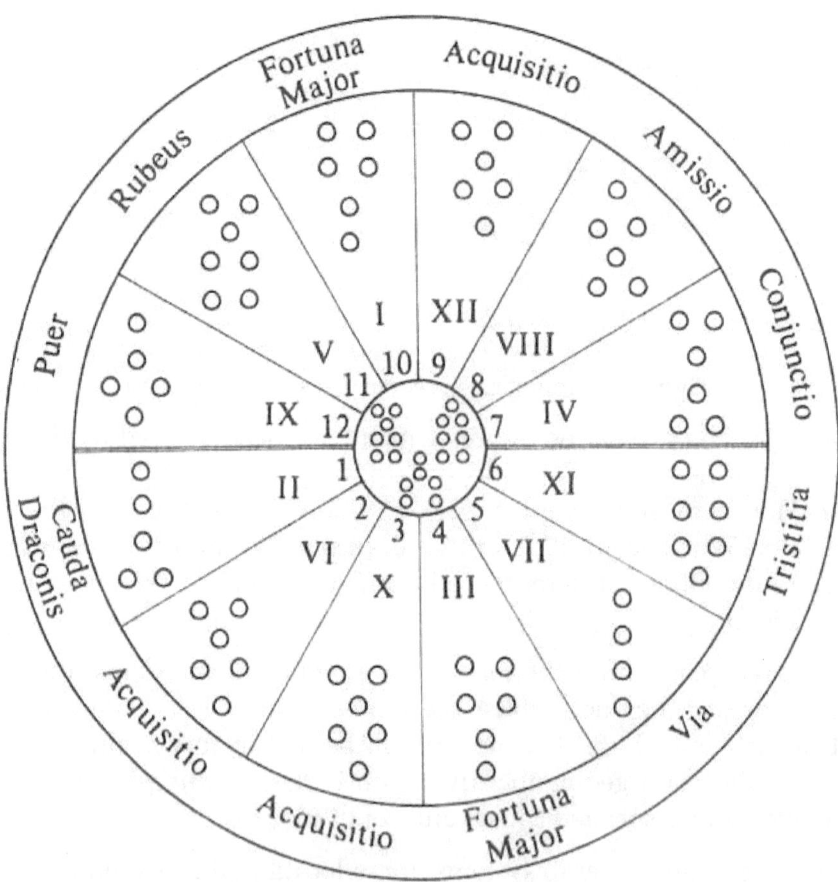

Figure 42: The geomantic figures distributed amongst the Twelve Houses of Heaven. The House numbers are in Arabic numerals, and the geomantic figures are designated by Roman numerals.

One word of warning here, whichever House system you decide to use, remember always that if Rubeus or Cauda Draconis fall in the first House or Ascendant, the chart is *not fit for judgment* and it should be destroyed without any further calculation or consideration. You should not attempt divination again concerning this question for at least a couple of hours and preferably not for a day or so. Presumably the question is important for such a result to have happened, and therefore you should think about it very seriously before re-attempting the divination.

Why such an extreme reaction? Well, Cauda Draconis in the First House means a short life and bad fortune, in fact impending death for the person asking the question. Rubeus in the First House means the same, and it became the practice to destroy these two answers which occasionally crop up, on the principle that with these two particularly nasty outcomes, it is as well not to tempt fate by examining them in detail.

You will notice that only the first twelve figures are used in astrological geomancy, that is the Mothers, Daughters and Nephews. You may if you like, place the two Witnesses and the Judge in the central circular space to remind you of the general interpretation of the geomantic layout.

Having inserted the geomantic figures into the House framework it is now necessary to translate them into astrological terms of reference.

ZODIACAL SIGNS

To add in the astrological data, first find which geomantic figure has been allocated to House I (the Ascendant). Look in the Table of Zodiacal Correspondences in Appendix I and (using the column you have already elected to use as your own standard attribution) find the Zodiacal Sign attributed to this figure. Write this Sign in the First House. Then following the Houses round in order of number (i.e. anti-clockwise) write in the Zodiacal Signs in order. For example, if the Sign attributed to the First House was Pisces, then the Second House would receive Aries, the Third Taurus, the Fourth Gemini and so on round the Zodiac.

Returning to our example, look in the First House and you will see that it contains Cauda Draconis. Now although a chart with Cauda Draconis in the First House should not be used, let us continue for the moment with this just to illustrate the method. Look up Cauda Draconis in Appendix I (col. 2) and we find that Cauda Draconis = Scorpio. Therefore place Scorpio in the First House. Now take the Signs in order, placing Sagittarius in the Second House, Capricorn in the Third House, and so on till we have filled in the whole chart.

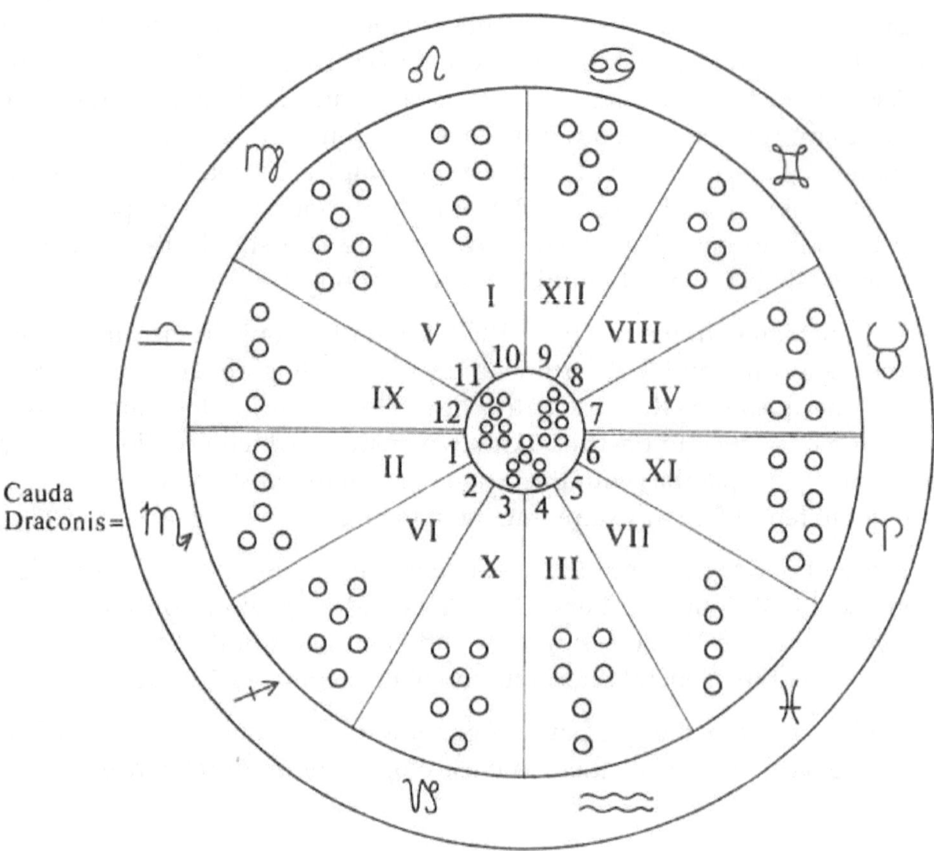

Figure 43: Zodiacal attributions of the 16 geomantic figures, from Appendix I.

PLANETS

The translation of the geomantic figures into their planetary equivalents is quite straightforward. Merely refer back to chapter 11, or Appendix I, and write down the planet corresponding to the geomantic figure. In our example, it is resolved as shown in Figure 44.

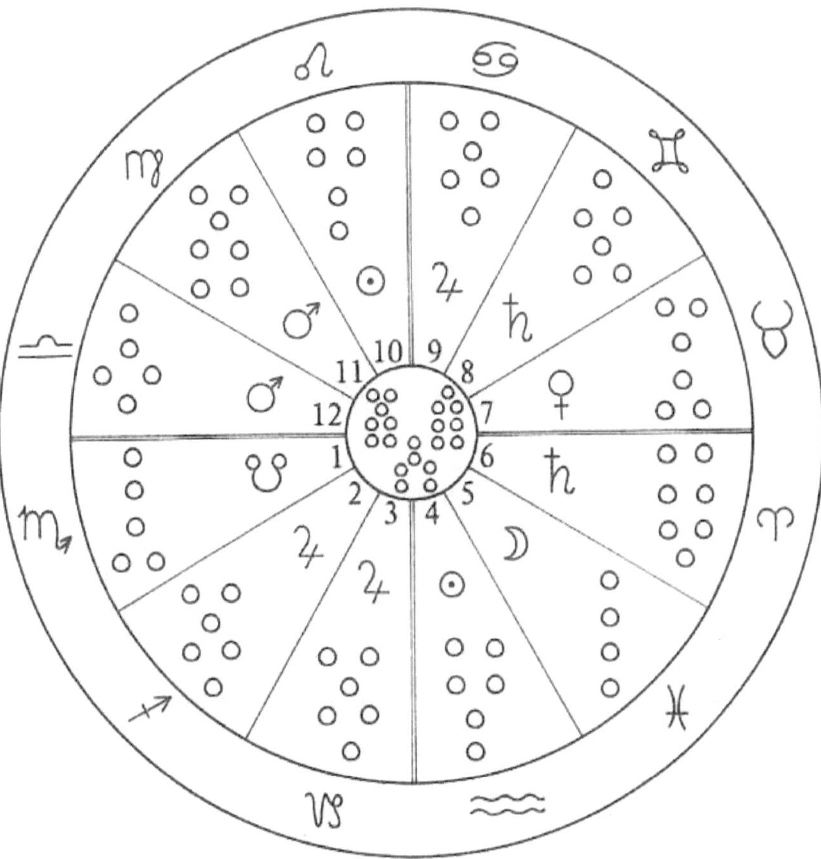

Figure 44: The complete astrogeomantic figure including planetary equivalents.

14. Summary of Technique and Interpretation

First, to recap on the technique:

1. Choose the time, hour and day in which to carry out the divination (see Appendix IV).

2. If it is decided to go ahead immediately, layout your equipment, paper and pencil.

3. Formulate the question precisely and write it down at the top of the page. Decide which House and planet the question belongs to: write this down also.

4. Inscribe pentagram and appropriate sigil, if so desired.

5. Make 16 rows of random dots with eyes half closed and mind concentrating on the question, right to left.

6. Divide the 16 rows into 4 groups of 4 lines.

7. Count each line and mark down two points for an even number and one point for an odd number.

8. Write the 4 figures so formed on the paper from right to left, side by side. These are the 4 Mothers. It is useful to make some copies of the blank chart in Figure 45, and fill in the figures in the appropriate boxes, as they are worked out.

9. Form the Daughters. The first Daughter is formed from the heads of each Mother written down one above another, the second Daughter from the necks of the Mothers, the third Daughter from their bodies, and the last Daughter from their feet.

10. Form the Nephews. The first Nephew is created by 'adding together' Mothers I and II, the second from adding together Mothers III and IV. The third Nephew is formed from adding together the first and second Daughters (figures V and VI). The fourth Nephew is formed from adding together the third and fourth Daughter (figures VII and VIII).

11. Form the two Witnesses. The Right Witness is formed by adding

together the first and the second Nephews (figures IX and X). The Left Witness is formed by adding together the third and the fourth Nephew (figures XI and XII).

12. Form the Judge by adding together the two Witnesses.

13. If the answer is not clear at this point, form a Reconciler by adding together the first Mother (figure I) and the Judge (figure XV).

14. Using the chosen House system (see Appendix III) place the geomantic figures in the Houses, check to see if Rubeus or Cauda Draconis are in the First House (in which case the figure should be destroyed).

15. Determine the corresponding Zodiacal Sign of the geomantic figure in the First House (using Appendix I), and write in the rest of the Zodiac Signs sequentially in an anti-clockwise direction.

16. Translate each geomantic figure into its planetary equivalent (Appendix I).

Although the above method looks fairly complex at first glance, you will find as soon as you have done two or three divinations that the manipulation becomes almost automatic. It is simply a matter of getting the sequence right.

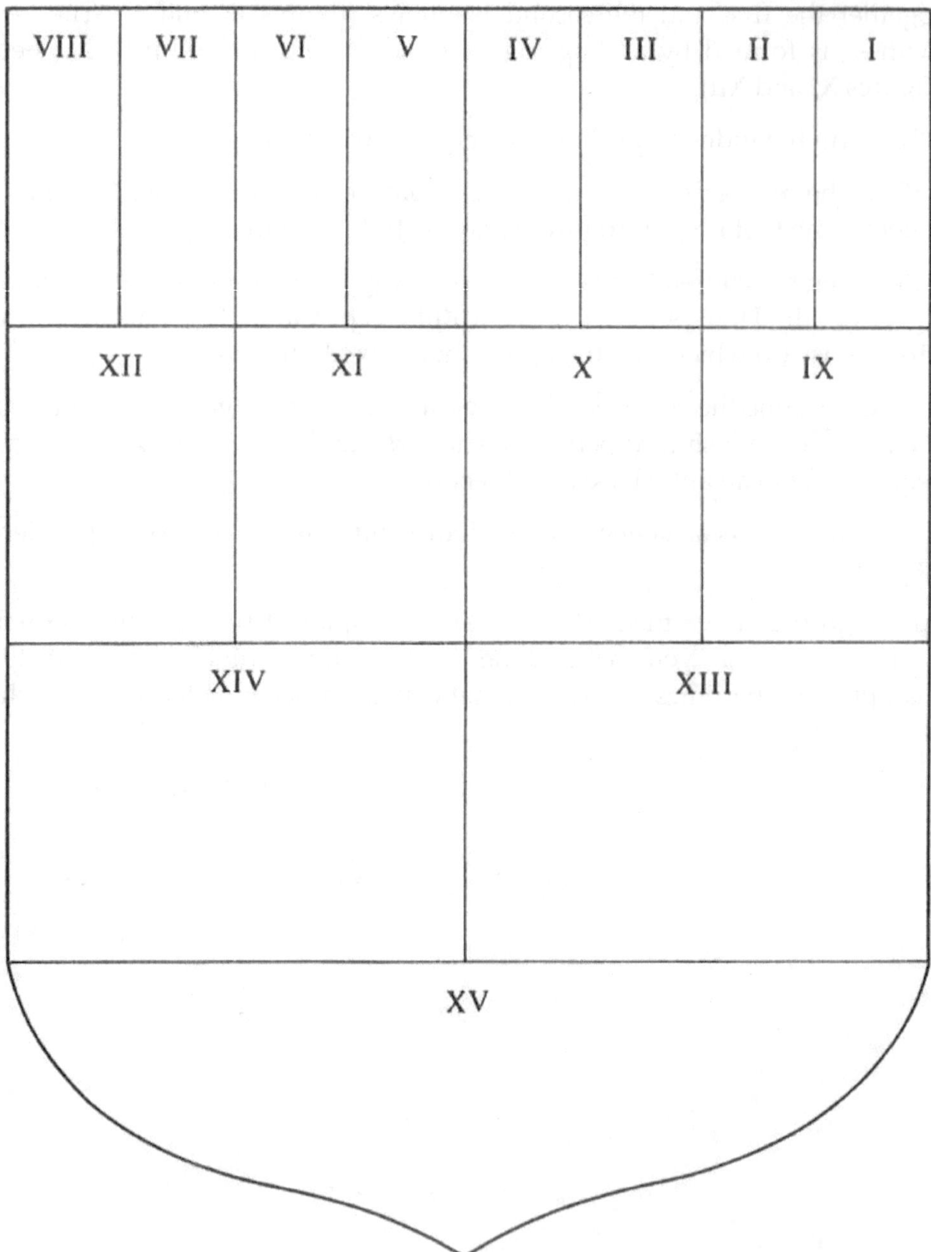

Figure 45: A blank traditional shield shaped geomantic chart.

INTERPRETATION

Having completely drawn up the astrogeomantic chart, and entered the geomantic figures, Zodiacal Signs and Planets in the correct Houses, then:

1. Check the Witnesses and Judge to see if the latter is favourable or otherwise.[1] Note that the Right Witness signifies the querent whilst the Left Witness symbolizes the thing asked about. It is said by some writers that if Populus appears as a Judge then the figure should be judged solely on its interaction with the Houses, and the significance of Populus as a Judge *per se* should be ignored, but this is not a universally accepted rule.

2. If more detail is required, refer back to the Mothers (figures I-IV) for details of the commencement (figure I) and termination of the matter (figure IV).

3. Note which geomantic figure falls in the House relating to the question (the Significator) and write it down along with its accompanying Sign and Planet.

4. If it is a question of money the Part of Fortune should be consulted. This is done by calculating the total number of points in the twelve geomantic figures in the Houses, and then dividing this total by twelve. The number remaining after this division indicates the House in which the Part of Fortune will be found: the geomantic figure in this House is the Index for questions of money.

5. If the Index figure appears elsewhere on the chart, that is 'passes' or 'springs' into another House, then the significance of that House is to be taken into account when interpreting the figure. Cattan and several other writers give elaborate tables for the passing of each and every figure from one House to the next, but careful consideration of the meaning of the figure in relation to the meaning of the relevant House should suffice for an accurate interpretation. For example, in a question concerning stolen money, if the figure in the Second House (money and movable possessions) is also found in the Sixth House (servants and employees) it might indicate that the thief was a servant or employee.

6. Check the figure falling in the Ascendant or First House for information about the querent.

7. Look in a Table of Geomantic figures in the Houses[2] to see the

---

[1] Or refer to Judge/Witness tables such as those printed in my *Oracle of Geomancy,* chapter 8, or Franz Hartmann's *Geomancy,* appendix.

[2] See Appendix VI, or such tables as appear in Agrippa's *Fourth Book of Occult Philosophy* (1655, reprinted 1978), pp. 157-75 or my *Oracle of Geomancy,* pp. 272-93.

significance of the geomantic figure which falls into the House of the question under consideration. Write this down in full.

8. Check the Table of Essential Dignities (Figure 46) to determine the strength of the figure in that House. This will tell you how much weight to give any factor in the final analysis.

9. Check to see if the same geomantic figure as figure XV, the Judge (which has not been placed in a House but in the centre of the chart) actually turns up anywhere else. If it does, then the meaning of the House it appears in is highly significant.

10. The planets interact with the Houses so that if a figure of Mercury falls in the First House, it is a particularly good omen. Likewise if the Moon falls in the Third; Venus in the Fifth; Mars in the Sixth; the Sun in the Ninth; Jupiter in the Eleventh; or Saturn in the Twelfth.

11. Determine the aspects made between figures and note the Houses in which they fall.

12. It is possible, if the divination is still not clear at this point, to form a new Reconciler figure by adding together the points of the Judge and the Significator figure in the House of the question.

RELATIVE STRENGTH OF FIGURES IN HOUSES

Sometimes the interpretation of the meaning of an answer given by an astrogeomantic chart is difficult because a number of competing pieces of information can be extracted, but it is difficult to see the overall picture because of apparently conflicting items in the chart.

To give a simple example, you may find Acquisitio in the Second House, boding very well for gain of money or property. However, the same figure, Acquisitio, may also turn up in another House, for example House 6, illness and employees. In principle you know that Acquisitio is "acquisition as a result of your own effort" and that employees are unlikely to be part of the work indicated, while illness could even be a strong factor preventing you exercising this effort. However, this still leaves you with an uncertainty as to whether that effort is going to be strongly baulked by the effects of House 6 or only mildly retarded. To assess this, provided there is not a clear indication elsewhere in the chart, it is necessary to have some measure of the relative strength of one influence versus another. This measure of strength is given in the Table in Figure 46 which relies on the 'essential dignity' of the planets and their associated geomantic figures. From the table, Acquisitio is *strong* in the Second House but at its *weakest* in the Sixth, therefore fortunately the influence of the Second House will prevail.

The essential dignity of a figure in a particular House is a measure of its strength, the degree to which it will influence the judgment. It could in fact be invoked as a 'tie-breaker'

Essential dignity means the strength of a figure when found in a particular House. A figure is therefore strongest when in its own House; very strong when in its Exaltation; strong in its Triplicity; very weak in its Fall; weakest of all in its Detriment. A figure is in its Fall when in a House opposite to that of its Exaltation, and in its Detriment when opposite to its own House. These terms are only given by way of explanation to those who like to know the underlying astrological reasons. It is sufficient for the moment merely to use the table to determine which of two apparently conflicting situations shown in a chart is the stronger and therefore the more likely to overcome the other. The numbers refer to the House in which the geomantic figure is strong or weak.

Table of essential dignities*

Geomantic figure	*For reference: corresponding planet*	Strongest: ruler of own House	Very strong: exaltation	Strong: triplicity	Very weak: fall	Weakest: detriment
Puer	Mars	1, 8	10	5	4	2, 7
Amissio	Venus	2, 7	12	9, 11	6	1, 8
Albus	Mercury	3, 6	6	4, 10	12	9, 12
Populus	Moon	4	2	12	8	10
Fortuna Major	Sun	5	1	8	7	11
Conjunctio	Mercury	3, 6	6	4, 10	12	9, 12
Puella	Venus	2, 7	12	9, 11	6	1, 8
Rubeus	Mars	1, 8	10	5	4	2, 7
Acquisitio	Jupiter	9, 12	4	1, 2, 7	10	3, 6
Carcer	Saturn	10, 11	7	3, 6	1	4, 5
Tristitia	Saturn	10, 11	7	3, 6	1	4, 5
Laetitia	Jupiter	9, 12	4	1, 2, 7	10	3, 6
Cauda Draconis	–	–	9	–	3	–
Caput Draconis	–	–	3	–	9	–
Fortuna Minor	Sun	5	1	8	7	11
Via	Moon	4	2	12	8	10

*To arrive at this table, the twelve Houses are considered as answering to the twelve Signs of the Zodiac, the First House to Aries, Second to Taurus and so on.

Figure 46: Table of Essential Dignities.

The table thus has five categories of essential dignity, ranging from the strongest to the weakest. The planets appear only as a guide, and the main use of the table is to settle judgments made complicated by several factors. Thus if Puer was in the First House and the Fourth House, from the first line of the above table, it is obvious that Puer has a much stronger significance in the First House (in connection with the nature and characteristics of the person himself) than in the Fourth House (where it shows the outcome of the matter or the nature of the home environment or property owned by the querent).

Compatibilities

Further aid to interpretation can be derived from the relationships between the planets.

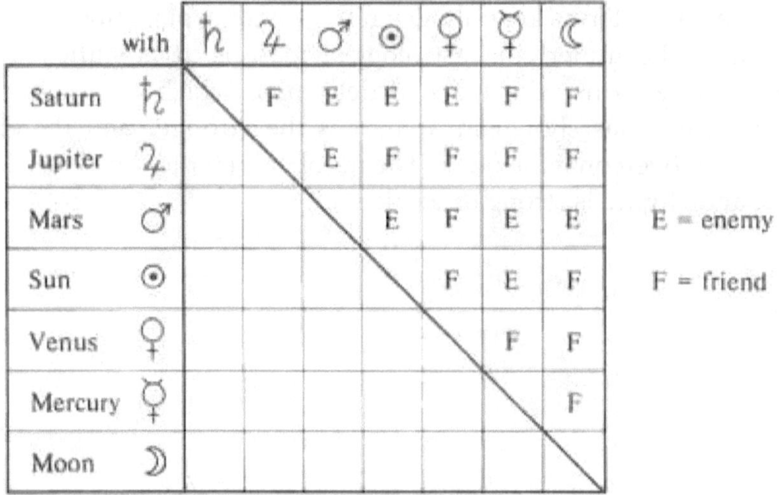

with	♄	♃	♂	☉	♀	☿	☾
Saturn ♄		F	E	E	E	F	F
Jupiter ♃			E	F	F	F	F
Mars ♂				E	F	E	E
Sun ☉					F	E	F
Venus ♀						F	F
Mercury ☿							F
Moon ☽							

E = enemy

F = friend

Figure 47: Planetary compatibility according to Francis Sperry, 1608.

QUESTIONS OF MONEY

As money is such an important factor in life and perhaps the most subject to vicissitudes, astrologers have in the past devised a special calculation and symbol for ready money, or easily available cash belonging to the person asking the question. This is called the Part of Fortune and symbolized by a circle with a cross dividing it into quarters.

For geomantic purposes, it is not necessary to perform the astrological calculations to find the Part of Fortune. It is just necessary to add together all the points of the first twelve geomantic figures, that is the total number of points of the four Mothers, four Daughters and four Nephews.

Divide your total by twelve and note down the remainder. The number of the remainder will give you the number of the House in which the Part of Fortune is to be found. If there is no remainder, it goes in the Twelfth House. The nature of the House it falls in tells you the direction from which ready cash might come, or be obtained. The geomantic figure, the sign and the planet in the House, give you details of the likelihood of the ready cash turning up (geomantic figure) and the sequence of events involved in its appearance (the planet).

THE ASPECTS OF THE HOUSES

It is traditional, but not very productive, to examine the aspects formed between the Ascendant and the other Houses, and sometimes also those formed in relation to the Significator found in the House of the question. Obviously the aspects are not the exact ones of conventional astrology, but whole Houses are considered in their aspect to each other. This means that if you consider the First House, it will be aspected by the Eleventh (as sextile), Tenth (as square) and Ninth (as trine) in a *dexter* (i.e. clockwise) direction. It is also similarly aspected to the Third (sextile), Fourth (square) and Fifth (trine) in a *sinister* (or anti-clockwise) direction.[1] Additionally it is aspected by the Seventh House in opposition and the Second House in a sort of 'conjunction' which in geomancy is always considered in an anti-clockwise direction in House pairs (First and Second, Third and Fourth, and so on).

This leaves exactly *three* Houses unaspected by the First House. It is for this reason that judging aspects geomantically is not exactly rewarding, but the details are given below nevertheless:

1. The *Trine* (△) aspect is formed by the fifth House from and including the Significator in both directions (clockwise and anti-clockwise), thereby forming two trines. The *dexter* trine is stronger in effect than the *sinister* trine. The trine is a favourable aspect.

2. The *Square* (□) aspect is formed by the fourth House from and including the Significator in both directions. Usually it is a bad aspect, representing a challenge of some sort, an obstacle that may or may not be overcome successfully, depending on the geomantic figures found in those Houses.

3. The *Sextile* (⚹) aspect is to be found three Houses from and including the Significator in both directions. The sextile is a mildly beneficent aspect.

4. *Opposition* (☍) is of course directly opposite to the Significator, 180° away, and indicates the nature of the chief difficulties to be expected by the querent.

[1] *Sinister* here just means left, rather than the current English meaning of the word.

5. *Conjunction* (☌) is a mutually supportive arrangement, only taking place between the pairs of Houses already specified, and not for example, the Second and Third, or Fourth and Fifth Houses.

Each aspect can be counted in a clockwise direction (Dexter aspects) or a counter-clockwise direction (Sinister[1] aspects).

Home House[2]	**Sextile 60^0**	**Square 90^0**	**Trine 30^0**	**Opposition 180^0**	**Sextile 60^0**	**Square 90^0**	**Trine 30^0**
	Dexter Aspects				**Sinister Aspects**		
1	11	10	9	7	3	4	5
2	12	11	10	8	4	5	6
3	1	12	11	9	5	6	7
4	2	1	12	10	6	7	8
5	3	2	1	11	7	8	9
6	4	3	2	12	8	9	10
7	5	4	3	1	9	10	11
8	6	5	4	2	10	11	12
9	7	6	5	3	11	12	1
10	8	7	6	4	12	1	2
11	9	8	7	5	1	2	3
12	10	9	8	6	2	3	4

Figure 48: The Geomantic House aspects. The numbers are the House numbers. Interpretation of specific figures in particular House will be found in Appendix VI.

[1] Meaning left-handed rather than evil.

[2] The House from which the Aspects are being counted.

15. Astrogeomantic Examples

Let us take an example and try to judge it thoroughly by using the steps outlined in the last chapter. Suppose we were to ask: "Will the proposed business partnership be a success for me?" As before, we generate the four basic Mother figures from the sixteen lines of dots, going on to generate the Daughters, Nephews, Witnesses and Judge (see Figure 49).

These in turn can be translated to the astrological chart form placing the figures I-XII in the twelve Houses, with the Witnesses and Judge in the centre. Using the Golden Dawn system of Figure to House allocation (Appendix III), the Figure in the First House is Fortuna Major, which is Leo. Therefore the zodiacal signs may be inserted from the First House as Leo, in their proper order, through the Second House as Virgo, Third House as Libra and so on to the Twelfth House as Cancer. The planets, of course, are simply the translation of each figure into its appropriate planet (Appendix I). The resulting astrogeomantic chart can be seen in Figure 50.

Now we can begin the judgment, taking our interpretation step by step.

1. First, neither Rubeus nor Cauda Draconis are in the First House, so the figure is safe to proceed with.

2. Noting planets in Signs we have:

Sun in Leo, Capricorn and Taurus

Venus in Virgo

Mercury in Libra and Aries

Jupiter in Scorpio, Sagittarius and Gemini

Moon in Cancer, and

Caput Draconis in Aquarius and Pisces.

VIII	VII	VI	V	IV	III	II	I
o o o o o	o o o o o o	o o o o o	o o o o o o o	o o o o o	o o o o o o	o o o o o o	o o o o o o

XII	XI	X	IX
o o o o o o o	o o o o o o	o o o o o o o	o o o o

XIV	XIII
o o o o o o o	o o o o o

XV
o o o o o o

Figure 49: Geomantic chart: Will the proposed business partnership be a success for me?

So far so good, as all these are neutral or beneficent with the notable exception of Venus in Virgo and Jupiter in Gemini. In both these cases the planet is located either in the Sign of its fall or detriment, that is, the effect of the planet is considerably weakened or opposed. Note especially that these two weaknesses occur in the Second and Eleventh House, that is, the Houses of money, property and financial profit and loss (Second House) and friends, acquaintances, social contacts, hopes and patronage (Eleventh House). Already the clouds have gathered, just on this first inspection.

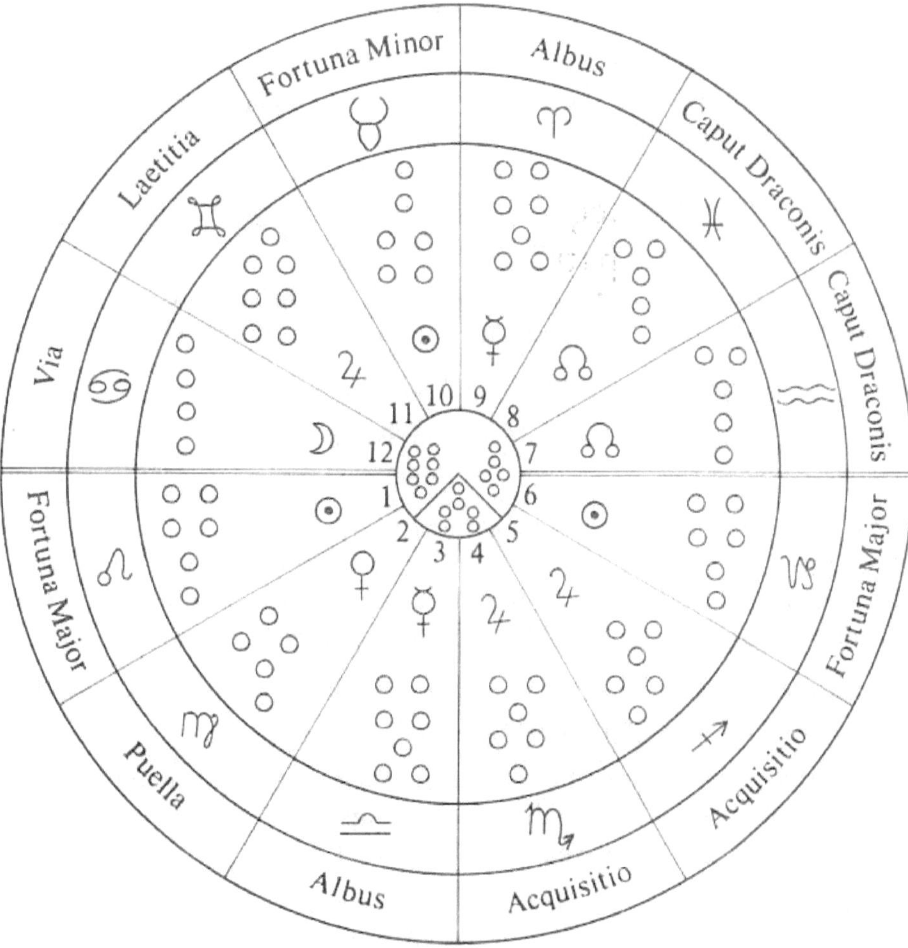

Figure 50: Astrogeomantic chart: Will the proposed business partnership be a success for me?

3. The Judge (in the centre) is Fortuna Minor, which means the lesser fortune, lesser (or not very successful) aid... not a very good figure.

4. Now let us look in the Houses relevant to the question. These are:

House 2: money, property, personal wealth, financial profit and loss, income and expenditure.

House 7: partnerships, amongst other things.

House 11: friends, acquaintances and social contacts, hopes and wishes, and patronage.

Interestingly we find the same two Houses that sprang to our attention when we examined the planet and Sign combination (point 2). This is a typical example of the way in which a successful geomantic divination begins unmistakably to 'fall into place.' Again and again the same elements come to our attention confirming and strengthening our verdict.

But to continue, as we have identified the three relevant Houses, to interpret the meaning of the geomantic figures found in these three Houses.

Puella in House 2: (Venus in Virgo) No increase of riches nor greater poverty.

Caput Draconis in House 7: (in Aquarius) There are many adversaries and lawsuits.

Laetitia in House 11: (Jupiter in Gemini) Many friends among the highly placed, protection. This might be interpreted that either your partnership is with someone well placed or that you may escape the worst results of such a partnership by appealing to friends in high places.

Again the picture is one of warning against the partnership: it will not be profitable and may involve you in costly lawsuits.

5. Of the three geomantic figures in the three relevant Houses, only Caput Draconis appears elsewhere or 'springs into' another House. Puella and Laetitia only occur once each in the whole figure.

Caput Draconis 'springs into' House 8 where its meaning is: "death is certain; legacies and inheritances; prospects of a wealthy wife." Those parts relevant to financial matters indicate that legacies (inheritance due to someone's death) or a financially advantageous marriage are more likely to be of profit than the proposed business partnership. This may indicate that the venture is better financed from family money rather than that of the partner, although this possibility would involve a second complete reading in itself.

6. To determine the Index (or as it is a money question, the Part of

Fortune), add up the total number of dots used in forming the first twelve figures. In this example, the total comes to 151 dots. Dividing by 12 gives an answer of 12 with a remainder of 7. The remainder is significant because it places the Part of Fortune in the Seventh House. Again we have the Seventh House (of the twelve possible Houses) cropping up to reinforce the reading of Caput Draconis in the Seventh House, which was, "There are many adversaries and lawsuits." Again our answer is confirmed: don't enter the partnership.

7. As the interpretation so far has been in complete accord with itself there is no need to use the 'tie-breaker' table of Essential Dignities, but just for practice look up:

Puella in the Second House
Caput Draconis in the Seventh House
Laetitia in the Eleventh House.

The first two are listed as the strongest possible combinations, whilst Laetitia in the Eleventh House is neither strong nor weak. This confirms the inadvisability of the partnership without offering much hope of it being salvaged by high-placed friends. Here it is useful to have an assessment of the weight to place on each piece of the interpretation, and the message of Puella and Caput Draconis is unequivocal.

8. The outcome, which is the Fourth House, shows Acquisitio. In the tables it reads "a large inheritance... a hidden treasure shall be found, a rich, but covetous father." This harks back to the earlier remarks that in this case inheritance is a more likely source of wealth than the business partnership, and in fact confirms that this will be the eventual outcome.

9. Although the occurrence of the Judge (Figure XV) elsewhere in the figure is a very minor indication, here we will follow it up, just to be complete. Figure XV, Fortuna Minor, does in fact appear in House 10. This suggests the death of the parents (the idea of inheritance again) and lawsuits and contentions (outcome of the partnership if undertaken).

10. A Reconciler is not necessary as we already have a wealth of confirmation.

11. The answer is clear: such a partnership would result in no profit, but lawsuits and contention. It is better not to enter into it and money will come from an inheritance instead.

PART THREE
Appendices

Appendix I - Zodiacal Attributions of the Geomantic Figures

Geomantic figure	*Planet*	*1 Golden Dawn*	*2 Agrippa by Ruler*	*3 Agrippa Esoteric*	*4 Agrippa Book II*	*5 Gerard of Cremona*	*6 Christopher Cattan*
Populus	☽	♋	♋	♒	♑	♑	♉
Via	☽	♋	♋	♍	♌	♌	♋
Conjunctio	☿	♍	♍	♎	♍	♍	♍
Carcer	♄	♑	♑	♓	♓	♓	♒
Fortuna Major	☉	♌	♌	♉	♒	♒	♌
Fortuna Minor	☉	♌	♌	♉	♉	♉	♈
Acquisitio	♃	♐	♓	♈	♈	♈	♓
Amissio	♀	♉	♎	♐	♎	♏	♍
Tristitia	♄	♒	♒	♐	♏	♏	♑
Lactitia	♃	♓	♐	♊	♉	♉	♐
Rubeus	♂	♏	♏	♋	♊	♊	♏
Albus	☿	♊	♊	♌	♋	♋	♓
Puella	♀	♎	♉	♋	♎	♎	♎
Puer	♂	♈	♈	♏	♈	♊	♈
Caput Draconis	☊	☊	♑	♎	♍	♍	♊
Cauda Draconis	☋	☋	♏	♑	♐	♐	♒

Figure 51: Golden Dawn ascriptions derived from the rulership of the planets

The sources of the columns in Figure 51 are:

1. The Golden Dawn ascriptions logically derived from the rulership of the planets as follows:

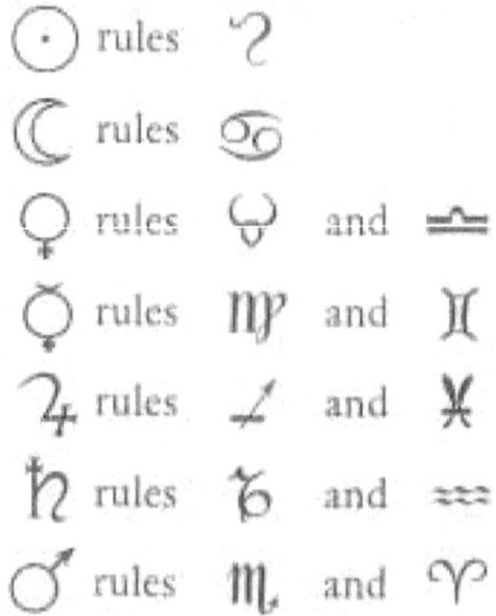

2. Agrippa's attribution from his 'Geomancy' in the *Fourth Book of Occult Philosophy* is also drawn from the above rulership of the planets, but with some differences in the case of joint rulership. There is a misprint in the English edition of Agrippa, as Puer is omitted from the series so the only remaining sign, Aries has been inserted there.

3. A second attribution of Agrippa's given as traditional but 'vulgarly used,' in other words, these attributions though common in books on geomancy, are not the 'initiated' version.

4. This system is derived from Agrippa Book II, and was used by Franz Hartmann (with Aquarius mistakenly attributed to Tristitia). It is also the system of attribution proposed by Christopher Cattan (with the reversal of Fortuna Minor and Major) and subsequently utilized by Eugene Caslant.

5. Was used by Gerard of Cremona (i.e. Sabbioneta) in his system of astrological geomancy, by Peter de Abano (with Puer and Puella interchanged), and by Robert Fludd in his *Tractatus de Geomantia.*

6. Christopher Cattan's (1608) version of the rules of 'Gerard of Cremona.'

7. The table in Socrates Basileus' *Prognostica*[1] shows the same attributions as Gerard of Cremona, except that Socrates puts Puella = Gemini and Puer = Libra.

[1] BJ 793, f. 71v. See Plate XVI.

Appendix II – Element Attributions of the Geomantic Figures

Element	*Arrangement* 1 Golden Dawn (according to Sign) derived from John Heydon		2 Agrippa (according to Sign)		3 Agrippa (according to Planet and Figure)		4 Agrippa 'Esoteric Arrangement'
Fire 🜂	Puer	♈	Puer	♈	Puer	♂	Fortuna Minor
	Fortuna Major	♌	Fortuna Major	♌	Fortuna Major	☉	Amissio
	Acquisitio	♐	Laetitia	♐	Amissio		Rubeus
	Cauda Draconis	☋	Fortuna Minor	♌	Rubeus	♂	Cauda Draconis
Air 🜁	Albus	♊	Albus	♊	Conjunctio	☿	Conjunctio
	Puella	♎	Amissio	♎	Puella		Acquisitio
	Tristitia	♒	Tristitia	♒	Laetitia	♃	Laetitia
	Fortuna Minor	♌			Fortuna Minor	☉	Puer
Water 🜄	Populus	♋	Populus	♋	Populus	☽	Populus
	Rubeus	♏	Rubeus	♏	Acquisitio		Albus
	Laetitia	♓	Acquisitio	♓	Via	☽	Puella
	Via	♋	Via	♋	Cauda Draconis	☋	Via
			Cauda Draconis	♏			
Earth 🜃	Amissio	♉	Puella	♉	Albus		Fortuna Major
	Conjunctio	♍	Conjunctio	♍	Tristitia	♄	Tristitia
	Carcer	♑	Carcer	♑	Carcer	♄	Carcer
	Caput Draconis	☊	Caput Draconis	♑	Caput Draconis	☊	Caput Draconis

Figure 52: Various ascriptions of the Elements to the Geomantic Figures.

The sources of the columns in Figure 52 are:

1. Attributions according to John Heydon's *Theomagia* (1664), later adopted by the Hermetic Order of the Golden Dawn. This arrangement depends for its rationale on zodiacal attributions. Fortuna Minor is an exception: as it is attributed to Leo which belongs with Fire, but is classed with Air for the sake of an even division.

2. Agrippa's elemental attributions, but based on Agrippa's zodiacal arrangement.

3. This arrangement brings into consideration the shape of the figures (e.g. the two upward-pointing triangles of Amissio suggesting Fire) or of the divinatory meaning (e.g. Rubeus belonging in fire because of the red colour). Interesting, for it is not as mechanical as the other systems.

4. Agrippa says of this arrangement that "this order is also far more true and rational than that which vulgarly is used." It is also the attribution favoured by Christopher Cattan. With the exception of Puer (which is placed in Fire), this is the arrangement used by Franz Hartmann. It is likewise used by Robert Fludd, with Puer and Puella interchanged.

Appendix III - Allocation of the Geomantic Figures to the 12 Houses

ORDINARY HOUSE ALLOCATION

The simplest method of allocating the geomantic figures to the twelve Houses is simply to take the Mothers, Daughters and Nephews and allocate them in order.

Mothers:	I	House 1
	II	House 2
	III	House 3
	IV	House 4
Daughters:	V	House 5
	VI	House 6
	VII	House 7
	VIII	House 8
Nephews:	IX	House 9
	X	House 10
	XI	House 11
	XII	House 12

The Witness and Judge (figures XIII-XV) are placed in the centre of the chart, not in any specific House.

ESOTERIC METHOD OF HOUSE ALLOCATION

This system of House allocation relies on the division of the Houses into Angular, Succedent and Cadent as explained in Chapter 15.

To allocate the geomantic figures to the Houses by this method it is merely necessary to place them in turn thus:

4 Mothers in the 4 Angular Houses
4 Daughters in the 4 Succedent Houses
4 Nephews in the 4 Cadent Houses

Laid out in full the twelve Houses contain these figures:

Angularity	*Figure*	*Relationship*	*House*
Angular	I	Mother	1
Succedent	V	Daughter	2
Cadent	IX	Nephew	3
Angular	II	Mother	4
Succedent	VIII	Daughter	5
Cadent	XII	Nephew	6
Angular	III	Mother	7
Succedent	VII	Daughter	8
Cadent	XI	Nephew	9
Angular	IV	Mother	10
Succedent	VI	Daughter	11
Cadent	X	Nephew	12

THE GOLDEN DAWN SYSTEM OF HOUSE ALLOCATION

Relationship	*Figure*	*House*	*Angularity*
Mothers:	I	House 10	Angular
	II	House 1	Angular
	III	House 4	Angular
	IV	House 7	Angular
Daughters:	V	House 11	Succedent
	VI	House 2	Succedent
	VII	House 5	Succedent
	VIII	House 8	Succedent
Nephews:	IX	House 12	Cadent
	X	House 3	Cadent
	XI	House 6	Cadent
	XII	House 9	Cadent

This system relies on the Mothers, the primary geomantic figures, being placed at the most powerful points on the chart, the four so-called Angular Houses (the Houses at the East and Mid-heaven and their opposite points, i.e. Houses 10, 1, 4 and 7). The secondary figures, the Daughters, are given to the Succedent Houses, that is the next House round in an anti-clockwise direction from each of the Angular Houses (Houses 11, 2, 5 and 8). Finally the four remaining or Cadent Houses are allocated to the four Nephews (Houses 12, 3, 6 and 9).

Appendix IV - Times of Planetary Days and Hours

An important consideration for geomancers, which would have been obvious in the Middle Ages, is underlined by Peruchio when he explains that geomancers, like magicians, must reckon the hours of the day from dawn to dawn rather than midnight to midnight. Thus the first hour of the day is under the planetary influence of that day, with each successive hour changing its allegiance to the planets in the usual order of Saturn, Jupiter, Mars, Sol, Venus, Mercury, Luna. The questions of geomancy should if possible be put in the planetary hour most appropriate to the question, for example, literary questions in the hour of Mercury, those of agriculture in the hour of Saturn and so on.

The planetary days are as follows: Monday - questions of the Moon; Tuesday - Mars; Wednesday - Mercury; Thursday - Jupiter; Friday - Venus; Saturday - Saturn; Sunday - the Sun.

To determine planetary hours find out the time of sunrise and sunset from an ephemeris or the daily newspaper and calculate the number of minutes in the day between those two times. Divide the number of minutes by 24 to give you the exact length of a planetary 'hour,' which will be less than sixty minutes in winter but more than sixty minutes during the summer. On two days of the year (the Equinox), the length of a planetary daylight 'hour' will be exactly sixty minutes.

Counting off each planetary 'hour' (calculating according to the number of minutes in the planetary hour), you find that the first and the eighth 'hour' of each day is dedicated to the planetary ruler of that day. For example, the first and eighth hour of Monday is sacred to the Moon, whilst the first and eighth hour of Friday is dedicated to Venus.

If you wish to choose an appropriate night hour, again count the number of minutes of darkness from sunset to sunrise. Divide this by twelve to get the length of a planetary night 'hour.' Then counting off these 'hours,' take the third and the tenth 'hours' of the night. Thus the third and tenth 'hours' of Monday night are dedicated to the Moon, whilst the third and tenth night hours of Friday are dedicated to Venus, and so on.

Appendix V - Full Tables of the Sixteen Geomantic Figures[1]

Geomancy Order.		G1. Geomantic Binary Figures.		G2. Traditional Meaning.	G3. Geomantic Elements.	G4. Geomantic Attributions to the Zodiac.			
						Golden Dawn	**Agrippa Esoteric**	**Gerard of Cremona**	**Christopher Cattan**
♋	18	Populus		Crowd	Water	Cancer	Aquarius	Capricorn	Taurus
♋	18	Via		Road	Water	Cancer	Virgo	Leo	Cancer
♍	20	Conjunctio		Conjunction	Earth	Virgo	Libra	Virgo	Virgo
♑	26	Carcer		Prison	Earth	Capricorn	Pisces	Pisces	Aquarius
♌	19	Fortuna Major		Great Fortune	Fire	Leo	Taurus	Aquarius	Leo
♌	19	Fortuna Minor		Lesser Fortune	Air	Leo	Taurus	Taurus	Aries
♐	25	Acquisitio		Acquisition	Fire	Sagittarius	Aries	Aries	Pisces
♉	16	Amissio		Loss	Earth	Taurus	Sagittarius	Scorpio	Virgo
♒	28	Tristitia		Sorrow	Air	Aquarius	Sagittarius	Scorpio	Capricorn
♓	29	Laetitia		Joy	Water	Pisces	Gemini	Taurus	Sagittarius
♏	24	Rubeus		Red	Water	Scorpio	Cancer	Gemini	Scorpio
♊	17	Albus		White	Air	Gemini	Leo	Cancer	Pisces
♎	22	Puella		Girl	Air	Libra	Cancer	Libra	Libra
♈	15	Puer		Boy	Fire	Aries	Scorpio	Gemini	Aries
☾	13	Caput Draconis		Head of the Dragon	Earth	Caput Draconis	Libra	Virgo	Gemini
☾	13	Cauda Draconis		Tail of the Dragon	Fire	Cauda Draconis	Capricorn	Sagittarius	Aquarius

[1] Taken from Stephen Skinner, *Complete Magician's Tables*, Golden Hoard, 2006, pp. 94-104. The original column numbers have been retained for ease of cross-reference.

Geomancy Order.		Geomantic Figures.	G5. Latin Names from Hugh of Santalla (fl. 1119-1157).	G6. Latin from *Geomantiae Nova* and *Estimaverunt Indi* (12th century).	G31. Latin from Gerard of Cremona (1114-1187)
♋	18	Populus	Congregatio	Aggregatio	Populus, Aggregatio, Congregatio
♋	18	Via	Via	Via (Iter)	Via
♍	20	Conjunctio	Conjunctio	Coadunatio, Conjunctio	Conjunctio, Coadunatio, Associatio
♑	26	Carcer	Constrictus	Carcer	Carcer, Constrictus
♌	19	Fortuna Major	Auxilium intus	Tutela intrans	Fortuna Major, Auxilium Intus, Tutela Intrans, Omen Majus
♌	19	Fortuna Minor	Auxilium foris	Tutela exiens, Tutela Foris	Fortuna Minor, Auxilium Foris, Tutela Exiens, Omen Minus
♐	25	Acquisitio	Comprehensum intus	Comprehensum intus	Acquisitio, Comprehensum intus
♉	16	Amissio	Comprehensum foris	Comprehensum foris	Amissio, Comprehensum foris
♒	28	Tristitia	Transverses, Diminutus	Diminutus	Tristitia, Transversus, Caput Imum
♓	29	Laetitia	Barbatus	Barbatus, Ridens Canus	Leticia, Barbatus, Caput Altum
♏	24	Rubeus	Rubeus	Rubeus	Rubeus, Ruffus
♊	17	Albus	Candidus	Candidus, Albus	Albus, Candidus
♎	22	Puella	Mundus facie	Mundus facie, Puella	Mundus facie, Puella
♈	15	Puer	Imberbis	Imberbis, Gladius erigendus, Flavus	Imberbis, Puer Flavus, Puella, Belliger
☾	13	Caput Draconis	Limen interius	Limen intrans, Intus	Caput Draconis, Limen intrans, Limen superius
☾	13	Cauda Draconis	Limen exterius	Limen exiens	Cauda Draconis, Limen inferius

Geomancy Order.		Geomantic Figures.	G32. Latin Names from William of Moerbeke (1276)	G33. Latin Names from John de Morys (1290-1351/55).	G34. Latin Names from Roland Scriptoris (fl. 1424).
♋	18	Populus	Populus, Congregatio	Populus	Populus, Congregatio, Duplex Via
♋	18	Via	Via	Via	Via
♍	20	Conjunctio	Conjunctio, Feretrum, Coadunatio	Conjunctio	Conjunctio, Feretrum, Coadunatio
♑	26	Carcer	Carcer, Constrictus	Carcer	Carcer, Constrictus
♌	19	Fortuna Major	Fortuna Major, Auxilium Intus, Tutela Intrans, Omen Intrans, Honor Intus	Major Fortuna	Fortuna Major, Auxilium Intus, Tutela Intrans, Omen Majus, Honor Intus
♌	19	Fortuna Minor	Fortuna Minor, Tutela Exiens, Omen Minus, Honor Extra/Apparens	Minor Fortuna	Fortuna Minor, Omen Minus, Honor Extra/Apparens
♐	25	Acquisitio	Acquisitio, Comprehensum Intus	Acquisitio	Acquisitio, Comprehensum Intus
♉	16	Amissio	Amissio, Comprehensum Extra	Amissio	Amissio, Comprehensum Extra
♒	28	Tristitia	Tristitia, Tristis, Diminutus, Transversus	Tristitia	Tristitia, Tristis, Caput Imum Diminutus, Transversus
♓	29	Laetitia	Leticia, Ridens, Canus Barbatus, Senex, Caput Altum	Leticia	Leticia, Ridens, Barbatus, Senex, Caput Altum
♏	24	Rubeus	Rubeus, Ruffus	Rubeus	Rubeus, Ruffus
♊	17	Albus	Albus, Candidus	Albus	Albus, Candidus
♎	22	Puella	Puella, Mundus Facie, Maxilla Munda	Puella	Puella, Mundus Facie, Maxilla Munda
♈	15	Puer	Puer, Flavus	Puer	Puer, Imberbis, Belliger
☾	13	Caput Draconis	Caput, Limen Superius	Caput	Caput, Limen Superius
☾	13	Cauda Draconis	Cauda, Limen Inferius	Cauda	Cauda, Limen Inferius

Geomancy Order.		Geomantic Figures.	G7. Traditional Arabic Names.	G8. Traditional Arabic Meanings.
♋	18	Populus	Jama'a	group of people, band, party, gang
♋	18	Via	Tariq	way, road, highway, trail
♍	20	Conjunctio	Ijtima	meeting, get together, gathering, social life, conjunction
♑	26	Carcer	'uqla	prison, arrest, bond, tie
♌	19	Fortuna Major	El nusra el-dakila	interior, inside, inmost, hidden help or assistance (interior personal victory)
♌	19	Fortuna Minor	El nusra el-kharga	external, outer, outside, foreign, exterior, help, aid or assistance (exterior victory)
♐	25	Acquisitio	Qabd el-dakil	interior, grasping, taking possession, receiving, receipt (taken forcibly)
♉	16	Amissio	Qabd el-kharge	'giving outside,' to take outside, or give away
♒	28	Tristitia	Mankus el-kharga, ankis, rakiza kharga	change, turn, upside-down, to fall, inverted, reversed, relapsing or suffering a relapse
♓	29	Laetitia	El-dakila, janubi fariha	joy, southern happiness (happiness in the south?) rejoicing, gladness/bearded
♏	24	Rubeus	Humra	redness, red implying a bad omen, danger
♊	17	Albus	El-bayad	whiteness, or writing paper, or blank space in a manuscript, barren, desolate, wasteland
♎	22	Puella	Naqiy el-kadd	clear cheek (complexion), pure, clean, immaculate, unstained, free of dirt or impurity (young girl)
♈	15	Puer	Jud lahu, kausaj	literally 'generosity is for him,' open-handedness, *liberality/kausaj* is a swordfish/ beardless
☾	13	Caput Draconis	El 'ataba el-dakila	the interior threshold (the step to go inside)
☾	13	Cauda Draconis	El 'ataba el-kharga	the exterior threshold (the step to go out)

Geomancy Order.		Geomantic Figures.	G9. Arabic Names in Kordofan (Sudan).	G10. Divinatory Meaning in Kordofan (Sudan).
♋	18	Populus	Tiql	an ape, a man of empty talk
♋	18	Via	Tariq	a road, indicating a journey
♍	20	Conjunctio	Damir	a hungry man on a journey
♑	26	Carcer	Surra	a woman of good omen
♌	19	Fortuna Major	Rasn	a head-rope, indicating a journey
♌	19	Fortuna Minor	Jebbar	a powerful sheikh or notable
♐	25	Acquisitio	Qabid	indicating a successful seizure of an animal, etc.
♉	16	Amissio	Kharij	an indication of a journey, or selling, or loss of a stolen animal
♒	28	Tristitia	Jihin or abu heila	a fikih, red in colour *abu heila*
♓	29	Laetitia	Hurr	a tall yellow man with a fire-mark or pock-mark in mid forehead
♏	24	Rubeus	Humra'	a red woman, with red face markings, an indication of blood, a successful hunt
♊	17	Albus	Beyyad	a poor unimportant man
♎	22	Puella	Mahzum	a stout-hearted man, the thief (if found in the enemy's houses), but weaker than jebbir
♈	15	Puer	Jodala	a woman of no importance
☾	13	Caput Draconis	Raiya	A tall woman, like a flag, full of words
☾	13	Cauda Draconis	Rakiza	a woman who brings news

Geomancy Order.		Geomantic Figures.	G11. Greek Geomantic Names - Pierre de Montdore, 1552-67.	G12. Greek Geomantic Names - Georges Midiates, 1462.	G13. French Provençal Names (1332).
♋	18	Populus	(ν)τζαμαάτ τζμαάτης		Poble
♋	18	Via	ταριχ		Via
♍	20	Conjunctio	ἰστιμᾶ(ς) (η)		Conjunction
♑	26	Carcer	οὐχλᾶς ῾ιουχλᾶ	φυλαχή fulachē	Carcer
♌	19	Fortuna Major	(ταρχάνα) νουσρατουλταχήλ	ἔξοδος τῆς δόξης exodos tēs doxēs	Aventura major
♌	19	Fortuna Minor	(σάμψαν) νουσρατουλχάριτς	εἴσοδος τῆς δόξης eisodos tēs doxēs	Aventura minor
♐	25	Acquisitio	β χαπδουλταχήλ	εἴσοδος τῶν χρημάτων eisodos tōn chrēmatōn	Aquisicio
♉	16	Amissio	β χαπδουλχάριτζ	εξοδος τῶν χρημάτων exodos tōn chrēmatōn	Perda
♒	28	Tristitia	ἀγγῆς (ἀγχίς) (ἀγχῆς)	χατωφερές chatōferes	Tristetia
♓	29	Laetitia	λαχιάμ λαχιάν	ἀνωφερές anōferes	Alegria
♏	24	Rubeus	χουμπρᾶ(ς)	ἐρυθροτής ἤγουν ὁ πόλεμος eruthrotēs ēgoun ho polemos	Ros
♊	17	Albus	παγιάδ (θ)	λευχότης leuchotēs	Blancor
♎	22	Puella	ναχιουλχάτ	ἄνηδος ἤγουν ὁ ἀρσενιχός anēdos ēgoun ho arsenichos	Donzel
♈	15	Puer	φαρά(ρ)χ(ης) φαράχη φαράχ	σπανάς, ἤγουν ὁ θηλυχός spanas, ēgoun ho thēluchos	Donzela
☾	13	Caput Draconis	χαιτ(σ)μᾶς	εἰσερχόμενον ἀνώφλιον eiserchomenon anōflion	Portal alzat
☾	13	Cauda Draconis	(δαμσάπητα) θεπιτά(ς)	εξερχόμενον ἀνώφλιον exerchomenon anōflion	Portal reversat

Geomancy Order.		Geomantic Figures.	G14. Hebrew Names.	G15. Hebrew Names – Meaning.	G16. Hebrew Names – in Hebrew Characters.
♋	18	Populus	Kehila	Congregation	קהלה
♋	18	Via	Derech	Way	דרך
♍	20	Conjunctio	Chibur [Kibbutz]	Collective	[קבוץ] חבור
♑	26	Carcer	Beit ha-sohar	Prison	בית הסהר
♌	19	Fortuna Major	Kabod nichnas	Honour or fortune enters (incoming)	כבוד נכנס
♌	19	Fortuna Minor	Kabod yotze	Honour or fortune exits (goes out)	כבוד יוצא
♐	25	Acquisitio	Mamun nichnas	Incoming monetary fortune	ממון נכנס
♉	16	Amissio	Mamun yotze	Exiting monetary fortune	ממון יוצא
♒	28	Tristitia	Shefel rosh	Main humiliation	שפל ראש
♓	29	Laetitia	Nisho rosh	Main joy (wife)	נשוא ראש
♏	24	Rubeus	Ha-adom	Red one	ה אדום
♊	17	Albus	Ha-laban	White one	ה לבן
♎	22	Puella	Bar ha-lechi	Beautiful one	בר הלחי
♈	15	Puer	Nilcham	Fighter	נלחם
☾	13	Caput Draconis	Sof nichnas	Enters the threshold	סף נכנס
☾	13	Cauda Draconis	Sof yotze	Exits the threshold	סף יוצא

Geomancy Order.		Geomantic Figures.	G17. Malagasy: Hova Interior Dialect Names.	G18. Malagasy: Antanosy & Sakalava West Coast Names.	G19. Malagasy: Fort Dauphin Region.
♋	18	Populus	Jamà (or zomà)	Asombòla	Assomboulo
♋	18	Via	Taraiky	Taraiky	Tareche
♍	20	Conjunctio	Aditsimà (aditsimay)	Alatsimay	Alissima
♑	26	Carcer	Alokòla	Alikòla	Alocola
♌	19	Fortuna Major	Asòravàvy	Adabàra	Adabara
♌	19	Fortuna Minor	Asóralàhy	Asóralahy	Alaazadi
♐	25	Acquisitio	Vandal miòndrika (= Mòlahidy)	Alahòtsy	Alohotsi
♉	16	Amissio	Vandal mitsàngana (= Mikarija)	Adálo	Adalou
♒	28	Tristitia	Alikisy	Alikisy	Alinchissa
♓	29	Laetitia	Alàhizàny	Alizàha	Alihiza
♏	24	Rubeus	Alaimòra	Alihimòra	Alohomore
♊	17	Albus	Adibijàdy	Alabiàvo	Alibiauou
♎	22	Puella	Kizo	Alakaràbo	Al acarabo
♈	15	Puer	Adikasájy	Bètsivóngo	Alicozaza (Alimiza)
☾	13	Caput Draconis	Sàka	Alakaosy	Alacossi
☾	13	Cauda Draconis	Votsira (= Vontsira)	Karija	Cariza

Geomancy Order.		Geomantic Figures.	G20. Central African Tribal Names: from Sara Madjingaye (South Chad).	G21. Central African Tribal Names: from Sara Deme (South Chad).	G22. Central African Names: from Dakhel (North East Chad).
♋	18	Populus	jama'a - dead ancestors	tigil - [under] the shadow of a village tree	tigil - the crowd
♋	18	Via	tarik - little children	terek - all the men of the village	terik - exit, door, path, passage
♍	20	Conjunctio	danhur - meat	danhur - drink of bilibili (food)	dam'r - famine, lean person, empty stomach
♑	26	Carcer	sura - chiefs	sura - plenty of food	sura - small pregnant woman
♌	19	Fortuna Major	arshan - highways	rashan - all the young men of the village	rashan - wealth, assets, cattle
♌	19	Fortuna Minor	djobar - byways	djobar - weapons of the village	djabur - light colour and short hair (=enemy/infidel)
♐	25	Acquisitio	gab - objects of iron	gabat = qabdah - highway	gabat - strong and intelligent man, conqueror
♉	16	Amissio	harija - men of other villages	harija - war	harija - chiefs, men with authority and prestige
♒	28	Tristitia	djahiliti - death, foreign	djuhiliti - village hut	djuhiliti - a sign of bad omen, misfortune, lack of courage
♓	29	Laetitia	lahica - interior of huts, joys and possessions	pure - recovery from sickness	hurr - health
♏	24	Rubeus	homra - red	homra - people sleeping in huts	homra - red, blood, injury blood
♊	17	Albus	bahiti - world in the village, whiteness, death	bayada - injury	bayada - white, chance, joy, happiness
♎	22	Puella	metason - high place on the earth	madjum - anger of the village men, but not about hunger	mazum - ill men and women, suffering
♈	15	Puer	kosaje - shadow of a village tree	djoalla - thinking of something	djoalla - welcome during travel
☾	13	Caput Draconis	raya - men in the village	Raya - the bush or scrub outside the village	raya - beautiful man or woman
☾	13	Cauda Draconis	arkis - women of the tribe	rakis = kharija - men (servants?) of the village	rakis - woman with large buttocks, delay, expectation, deception

Geomancy Order.		Geomantic Figures.	G23. West African Tribal Names from Dahomey.	G.24. Islamic Patriarchs - Bambara (Mali).
♋	18	Populus	yeku - west, night.	Moussa - Moses
♋	18	Via	gbe - life, east, day	Abachim
♍	20	Conjunctio	woli - ferocious animals, south	Ali
♑	26	Carcer	di - woman, copulation, north	Sulaymann - Solomon
♌	19	Fortuna Major	wele - illnesses	Nouhoun - Noah
♌	19	Fortuna Minor	loso - a hole, accident, misfortune	Kalantala - Muhammad
♐	25	Acquisitio	fu - white, maternal principle	Ousmane
♉	16	Amissio	ce - breakable, bad smell	Issa - Jesus
♒	28	Tristitia	akla - twins	Yacouba - Jacob
♓	29	Laetitia	abla - rope, duration, possessions	Adana - Adam
♏	24	Rubeus	ka - snake, filial piety, filial love	Amara - Amar
♊	17	Albus	turukpe - pregnancy, anything protruding	ldrissa - Idris
♎	22	Puella	tula - speech, mouths	Ladari (?)
♈	15	Puer	lete - earth, death	Jonas
☾	13	Caput Draconis	sa - black magic (ill-omen), feminine fire	Madi - the messenger
☾	13	Cauda Draconis	guda - sword, testicle, erection	Lassima al Houssein

Geomancy Order.		Geomantic Figures.	G25. Dr. Rudd's Geomantic Intelligence - Hebrew.	G26. Dr. Rudd's Geomantic Intelligence - Transliteration.	G27. Dr. Rudd's Geomantic Intelligence - Translation.
♋	18	Populus	מוריאל	MVRIAL	Muriel
♋	18	Via	מוריאל	MVRIAL	Muriel
♍	20	Conjunctio	חמליאל	HMLIAL	Hamaliel
♑	26	Carcer	חנאל	HNAL	Haniel
♌	19	Fortuna Major	ורכיאל	VRKIAL	Verachiel/Verakiel
♌	19	Fortuna Minor	אדוכיאל	ADVKIAL	Advachiel
♐	25	Acquisitio	אדוכיאל	ADVKIAL	Advachiel
♉	16	Amissio	אסמודאל	ASMVDAL	Asmodiel
♒	28	Tristitia	כאמבריאל	KAMBRIAL	Cambriel
♓	29	Laetitia	אמניציאל	AMNITzIAL	Amnitziel[1]
♏	24	Rubeus	ברכיאל	BRKIAL	Barachiel/Barakiel
♊	17	Albus	אמבריאל	AMBRIAL	Ambriel
♎	22	Puella	זוריאל	ZVRIAL	Zuriel
♈	15	Puer	מלכידאל	MLKIDAL	Malchidiel
☾	13	Caput Draconis	גבריאל	GBRIAL	Gabriel
☾	13	Cauda Draconis	גבריאל	GBRIAL	Gabriel

[1] Or Vakabiel וכביאל.

Geomancy Order.		Geomantic Figures.	G28. Dr. Rudd's Enochian Letter Correspondence.	G29. Planetary Spirit.	G30. Astrological Correspondence.
♋	18	Populus	[illegible]	Chasmodai	Moon in Cancer (waxing)
♋	18	Via	[illegible]	Chasmodai	Moon in Cancer (waning)
♍	20	Conjunctio	[illegible]	Taphthartharath	Mercury in Virgo
♑	26	Carcer	[illegible]	Zazel	Saturn in Capricorn
♌	19	Fortuna Major	[illegible]	Sorath	Sun in Leo (in Northern Declination)
♌	19	Fortuna Minor	[illegible]	Sorath	Sun in Leo (in Southern Declination)
♐	25	Acquisitio	[illegible]	Hismael	Jupiter in Sagittarius
♉	16	Amissio	[illegible]	Qedemel/Kedemel	Venus in Taurus
♒	28	Tristitia	[illegible]	Hismael	Saturn in Aquarius
♓	29	Laetitia	[illegible]	Hismael	Jupiter in Pisces
♏	24	Rubeus	[illegible]	Bartzabel	Mars in Scorpio [Pisces]
♊	17	Albus	[illegible]	Taphthartharath	Mercury in Gemini
♎	22	Puella	[illegible]	Qedemel/Kedemel	Venus in Libra
♈	15	Puer	[illegible]	Bartzabel	Mars in Aries
☾	13	Caput Draconis	[illegible]	Hismael and Qedemel/Kedemel	Caput Draconis
☾	13	Cauda Draconis	[illegible]	Zazel and Bartzabel	Cauda Draconis

Appendix VI - Agrippa's Interpretation of the Significance of the 16 Geomantic Figures in the 12 Houses[1]

The first House shows the person of the Querent[2], as often as a question shall be proposed concerning himself of his own matters, or any thing appertaining to him. And this House declares the Judgement of the life, form, state, condition, habit, disposition, form and figure, and of the colour of men[3].

The second House contains the Judgement of substance, riches, poverty, gain and loss, good fortune and evil fortune: and of accidents in substance,[4] as theft, loss or negligence.

The third House signifies brethren, sisters, and Collaterals in blood:[5] It judges of small journeys, and [the] fidelities of men.

The fourth House signifies fathers and grandfathers, patrimony and inheritance, possessions, buildings, fields, treasure, and things hidden: It gives also the description of those who want[6] any thing by theft, losing, or negligence.

The fifth House gives judgement of Legats[7], Messengers, Rumours, News; of Honour, and of accidents after death: and of Questions that may be propounded concerning women with child, or creatures pregnant.

The sixth House gives Judgement of infirmities, and medicines; of familiars and servants; of cattle and domestic animals.

The seventh House signifies wedlock, whoredom, and fornication; [it] renders Judgement of friends, strife, and controversies; and of matters acted before Judges.

The eighth [House] hath signification of death, and of those things which come by death of Legats, and hereditaments; of the dowry or portion of a wife.

The ninth House shows journeys, faith, and constancies; dreams, divine Sciences, and Religion.

---

[1] From Agrippa, 'Geomancy' in *The Fourth Book of Occult Philosophy*. The English spelling has been modernised.

[2] The person asking the question.

[3] This House was also thought to be able to describe the physical features of the Querent.

[4] Property.

[5] Relatives.

[6] Loose.

[7] This relates to legacies or inheritance.

The tenth House hath signification of Honours, and of Magisterial Offices.

The eleventh House signifies friends, and the substance of Princes.

The twelfth House signifies enemies, servants, imprisonment, and misfortune, and whatsoever evil can happen besides death and sickness, the Judgements whereof are [also] to be required in the sixth House, and in the eighth [House].

It rests now, that we show you what every figure before spoken of signifies in these [House] places; which we shall now unfold.

Fortuna Major: the Greater Fortune[1]

Fortuna major being found in the first House, gives long life, and frees from the molestation of Diseases: it demonstrates a man to be noble, magnanimous, of good manners, mean of stature, complexion ruddy, hair curling, and his superior members greater then his inferior. In the second House, he[2] signifies manifest riches and manifest gain, good fortune, and the gaining of any thing lost or mislaid; the taking of a thief, and recovery of things stolen. In the third House, he signifies brethren and kinsmen, Nobles, and persons of good conversation; journeys to be prosperous and gainful with honour: it demonstrates men to be faithful, and their friendship to be unfeigned. In the fourth House, he represents a father to be noble, and of good reputation, and known to many people: He enlarges possessions in Cities, increases Patrimonies, and discovers hidden treasures. In this place he likewise signifies theft, and recovers everything lost. In the fifth House, he gives joy by children, and causes them to attain to great Honours: Embassies he renders prosperous; but they are purchased with pains, and prayers: He notes rumours to be true: he bestows public Honours, and causes a man to be very famous after death: foreshows[3] a woman with child to bring forth a man-child. In the sixth House, he frees from diseases; shows those that have infirmities shall in a short time recover; signifies a Physician to be faithful and honest to administer good Physick,[4] of which there ought to be had no suspicion; household-servants and ministers to be faithful: and of animals, he chiefly signifies Horses. In the seventh House, he gives a wife rich, honest, and of good manners; loving and pleasant: he overcomes strife and contentions. But if the

[1] Agrippa now examines the meaning of each Figure in each of the 12 Houses. The name of the 16 Figures are found as a margin note in the original text, but have here been converted to a sub-heading for ease of reading.
[2] Fortuna Major.
[3] The Figure shows.
[4] Medicine.

Question be concerning them, he signifies the adversaries to be very potent, and great favourites. In the eighth House, if a Question be proposed of the death of any one, it signifies he shall live: the kind of death he shows to be good and natural; an honest burial, and honourable Funerals: He foreshows a wife to have a rich dowry, legacies and inheritance. In the ninth House, he signifies journeys to be prosperous; and by land on horseback, rather than on foot, to be long, and not soon accomplished: He shows the return of those that are absent; signified men to be of good faith, and constant in their intentions; and religious; and that never change or alter their faith; Dreams he presages[1] to be true; signifies true and perfect Sciences. In the tenth House, he foreshows great Honours, bestows public Offices, Magistracies, and Judgements; and honours in the Courts of Princes: signifies Judges to be just, and not corrupted with gifts: brings a Cause to be easily and soon expedited: shows Victory to be certain: signifies a mother to be noble, and of long life. In the eleventh house, he signifies true friends, and profitable; a Prince rich and liberal; makes a man fortunate, and beloved of his Prince. In the twelfth House, if a Question be proposed of the quality of enemies, it demonstrates them to be potent and noble, and hardly to be resisted: But if a Question shall be concerning any other condition or respect to the enemies, he will deliver from their treacheries. It signifies faithful servants; reduces fugitives; hath signification of animals, as horses, lions, and bulls; frees from imprisonments; and eminent dangers he either mitigates or takes away.

The Lesser Fortune

Fortuna minor in the first house, gives long life, but encumbered with divers molestations and sicknesses: it signifies a person of short stature, a lean body, having a mold or mark in his forehead or right eye. In the second House, he signifies substance, and that to be consumed with too much prodigality: hides a thief; and a thing stolen is scarcely to be recovered, but with great labour. In the third House, he causes discord amongst brethren and kinfolks; threatens danger to be in a journey, but escapes it: renders men to be of good faith, but of close and hidden minds. In the fourth House, he prejudices Patrimonies and Inheritances; conceals treasures; and things lost cannot be regained, but with great difficulty: He signifies a father to be honest, but a spender of his estate through prodigality, leaving small portions to his children. *Fortuna minor* in the fifth House gives few children; a woman with child he signifies shall have a woman-child; signifies Embassies to be honourable, but little profitable; raises to mean[2] honours; gives a good fame after death, but not much divulged; nor of lasting memory.

---

[1] Predicts.

[2] Middling honours.

In the sixth House, he signifies diseases, both Sanguine and Choleric[1]; shows the sick person to be in great danger, but shall recover: signifies faithful servants, but slothful and unprofitable: And the same of other animals. In the seventh House, he gives a wife of a good progenies descended[2]; but you shall be encumbered with many troubles with her: causes love to be anxious & inconstant: prolongs contentions, and makes ones adversary to circumvent him with many cavillations[3]; but in process of time he gives victory. In the eighth House, he shows the kind of death to be good and honest; but obscure, or in a strange place, or [whilst on a] pilgrimage: discovers Legacies and Possessions; but to be obtained with [legal] suit and difficulty: denotes Funerals and Buryings to be obscure; the [dowry] portion of a wife to be hardly gotten, but easily spent. In the ninth House, he makes journeys to be dangerous; and a party absent slowly to return: causes men to be occupied in offices of Religion: shows Sciences to be unaccomplished; but keeps constancy in faith and Religion. In the tenth House, he signifies Kings and Princes to be potent; but to gain their power with war and violence: banished men he shows shall soon return: it likewise discovers Honours, great Offices and benefits; but for which you shall continually labour and strive, and wherein you shall have no stable continuance: A Judge shall not favour you: [legal] Suits and contentions he prolongs: A father and mother he shows shall soon die, and always to be affected with many diseases. In the eleventh House, he makes many friends; but such as are poor and unprofitable, and not able to relieve thy necessities: it ingratiates you with Princes, and gives great hopes, but small gains; neither long to continue in any benefice or offices bestowed by a Prince. In the twelfth House, he shows enemies to be crafty, subtle, and fraudulent, and studying to circumvent you with many secret factions: signifies one in prison to be long detained, but at length to be delivered: Animals he shows to be unfruitful, and servants unprofitable; and the changes of fortune to be frequent, from good to evil, and from bad to good.

Way

Via in the first House, bestows a long and prosperous life; gives signification of a stranger; lean of body, and tall of stature; fair of complexion, having a small beard: a person liberal and pleasant; but slow, and little addicted to labour. In the second, he increases substance and riches; recovers any thing that is stolen or lost; but signifies the thief to be

---

[1] Two of the four medical 'humours,' respectively bloody and heated.

[2] A wife from a good family.

[3] Frivolous objections.

departed without the City[1]. In the third, he multiplies brethren and kinfolks; signifies continual journeys, and prosperous; men that are publically known, honest, and of good conversation.

Via in the fourth House, signifies the father to be honest; increases the Patrimony and Inheritance; produces wealthy fields; shows treasure to be in the place enquired after; recovers any thing lost. In the fifth, he increases the company of male-children; shows a woman with child to bring forth a male-child; sends Embassies to strange and remote parts; increases public honours; signifies an honest kind of death, and to be known thorow[2] many Provinces.

In the sixth House, *Via* preserves from sickness; signifies the diseased speedily to recover; gives profitable servants, and animals fruitful and profitable. In the seventh House, he bestows a wife fair and pleasant, with whom you shall enjoy perpetual felicity: causes strife and controversies most speedily to be determined; adversaries to be easily overcome, and that shall willingly submit their controversies to the Arbitration of good men. In the eighth House, he shows the kind of death to proceed from Phlegmatic diseases; to be honest, and of good report; discovers great Legacies, and rich Inheritances to be obtained by the dead: And if any one hath been reported to be dead, it shows him to be alive.

In the ninth House, *Via* causes long journeys by water, especially by Sea, and portends very great gains to be acquired thereby: he denotes Priesthoods, and profits from Ecclesiastical employments; makes men of good Religion, upright, and constant of faith: shows dreams to be true, whose signification shall suddenly appear: increases Philosophical and Grammatical Sciences, and those things which appertain to the instruction and bringing up of children. In the tenth House if *Via* be found, he makes Kings and Princes happy and fortunate, and such as shall maintain continual peace with their Allies; and that they shall require amity and friendship amongst many Princes by their several Embassies: promotes public Honours, Offices, and Magistracies amongst the vulgar and common people; or about things pertaining to the water, journeys, or about gathering Taxes and Assessments: shows Judges to be just and merciful, and that shall quickly dispatch Causes[3] depending before them: and denotes a mother to be of good repute, health, and of long life. In the eleventh House, he raises many wealthy friends, and acquires faithful friends in foreign Provinces and Countries, and that shall willingly relieve

---

[1] Departed beyond the city.

[2] Through.

[3] Legal cases.

him that requires them, with all help and diligence.[1] It ingratiates persons with profit and trust amongst Princes, employing him in such Offices, as he shall be encumbered with continual travels. *Via* in the twelfth House, causes many enemies, but such as of whom little hurt or danger is to be feared: signifies servants and animals to be profitable: whosoever is in prison, to be escaped, or speedily to be delivered from thence: and preserves a man from the evil accidents of Fortune.

Populus - People

Populus being found in the first House, if a Question be propounded concerning that House, shows a mean[2] life, of a middle age, but inconstant, with divers sicknesses, and various successes of Fortune: signifies a man of middle stature, a gross body, well set in his members; perhaps some mold or mark about his left eye. But if a Question shall be propounded concerning the figure of a man, and to this figure if there be joined any of the figures of *Saturn* or *Rubeus*, it shows the man to be monstrously deformed; and that deformity he signifies to proceed from his birth: but if in the fifth House, if he be encompassed with malevolent Aspects, then that monstrousness is to come. In the second House, *Populus* shows a mean substance[3], and that to be gotten with great difficulty: makes a man also always sensible of laborious toil: things stolen are never regained: what is lost shall never be wholly recovered: that which is hidden shall not be found.

But if the Question be of a thief, it declares him not yet to be fled away, but to lie lurking within the City. In the third House, *Populus* raises few friends, either of brethren or kindred: foreshows journeys, but with labour and trouble; notwithstanding some profit may accrue by them: denotes a man unstable in his faith, and causes a man often to be deceived by his companions. In the fourth House, it signifies a father to be sickly, and of a laborious life, and his earthly possessions and inheritances to be taken away: shows profit to be gained by water: shows treasure not to be hid; or if these be any hidden, that it shall not be found: A patrimony[4] to be preserved with great labour. In the fifth House, he shows no honest Messages, but either makes the messengers to be Porters, or public Carriers: he divulges false rumours, which notwithstanding have the likeness of some truth, and seem to have their original from truth, which is not reported as it is done: It signifies a woman to be barren, and causes such as are great with child to

---

[1] SB.
[2] An average life.
[3] Average income.
[4] Inheritance.

be abortive: appoints an inglorious Funeral, and ill report after death.

In the sixth House, *Populus* shows cold sicknesses; and chiefly affects the lower parts of the body: A Physician is declared to be careless and negligent in administering Physick to the sick, and signifies those that are affected with sickness to be in danger of death, and scarcely recover at all: it notes the deceitfulness of servants, and detriment of cattle. In the seventh House, it shows a wife to be fair and pleasant, but one that shall be solicited with the love of many wooers: signifies her loves to be feigned and dissembling: makes weak and impotent adversaries soon to desert prosecuting. In the eighth House, it denotes sudden death without any long sickness or anguish, and oftentimes shows death by the water; gives no inheritance, possession or legacy from the dead; and if any be, they shall be lost by some intervening contention, or other discord: he signifies the dowry of a wife to be little or none.

Populus in the ninth House, shows false dreams, personates[1] a man of rude wit, without any learning or science; In religion he signifies inferior Offices, such as serve either to cleanse the Church, or ring the bells; and he signifies a man little curious or studious in religion, neither one that is troubled with much conscience. In the tenth House he signifies such Kings and Princes, as for the most part are expulsed out of their Rule and Dominions, or either suffer continual trouble and detriment about them: he signifies Offices and Magistracy, which appertain to matters concerning the waters, as about the Navy, bridges, fishings, shores, meadows, & things of the like sort; makes Judges to be variable and slow in expediting of Causes before them; declares a Mother to be sickly, and of a short life. In the eleventh House he gives few friends, and many flatterers; and with Princes gives neither favour nor fortune. In the twelfth House he shows weak and ignoble enemies; declares one in prison not to be delivered, discovers dangers in waters, and watery places.

---

[1] Indicates.

Aquisitio - Gain

Aquisitio found in the first House, gives a long life and prosperous old age; signifies a man of middle stature, and a great head, a countenance very well to be distinguished or known, a long nose, much beard, hair curling, and fair eyes, free of his meat and drink, but in all things else sparing and not liberal. In the second House, he signifies very great riches, apprehends all thieves, and causes whatsoever is lost to be recovered. In the third House, many brethren, and they to be wealthy; many gainful journeys; signifies a man of good faith. In the fourth is signified a Patrimony of much riches, many possessions of copious fruits; he signifies that treasure hid in any place shall be found; and shows a Father to be rich, but covetous. In the fifth House, *Aquisitio* signifies many children of both Sexes, but more Males then Females; shows a woman to be with child, and that she shall be delivered without danger: and if a question be propounded concerning any Sex, he signifies it to be Masculine; increases gainful profitable Embassies and Messages, but extends same not far after death, yet causes a man to be inherited of his own, and signifies rumours to be true.

In the sixth House he signifies many and grievous sicknesses, and long to continue, makes the sick to be in danger of death, and often to die: yet he declares a Physician to be learned and honest; gives many servants and chattel[1], and gains to be acquired from them. In the seventh House he signifies a wife to be rich, but either a widow, or a woman of a well-grown age; signifies [legal] suits and contentions to be great and durable, and that love and wedlock shall be effected by lot. In the eighth House, if a man be enquired after, it shows him to be dead, signifies the kind of death to be short, and sickness to last but a few days; discovers very profitable legacies and inheritances, and signifies a wife to have a rich dowry. In the ninth House he signifies long and profitable journeys; shows if any one be absent he shall soon return; causes gain to be obtained from Religious and Ecclesiastical Persons or Scholars, and signifies a man of a true and perfect Science. In the tenth House, he makes Princes to enlarge their Dominions; a Judge favourable, but one that must be continually presented with gifts; causes Offices and Magistracy to be very gainful; signifies a Mother rich and happy. In the eleventh House, *Aquisitio* multiplies friends, and brings profit from them, and increases favour with Princes. In the twelfth House he signifies a man shall have many powerful or potent enemies; reduces and brings home servants fled away, and cattle strayed; and signifies he that is in prison shall not be delivered.

[1] Possessions.

Laetitia - Joy

Laetitia in the first House signifies long life with prosperity, and much joy and gladness, and causes a man to out-live and be more victorious than all his brethren; signifies a man of a tall stature, fair members, a broad forehead, having great and broad teeth; and that hath a face comely and well coloured. In the second House it signifies riches and many gains, but great expenses and various mutations of one state and condition; theft and any thing lost is recovered and returned: but if the Question be of a thief, it declares him to be fled away. In the third House *Laetitia* shows brethren to be of a good conversation, but of short life; journeys pleasant and comfortable; men of good credit and faith. In the fourth he signifies happy Patrimonies and possessions, a Father to be noble, and honoured with the dignity of some princely office; shows treasure to be in the place enquired after, but of less worth and value then is supposed, and causes it to be found. In the fifth House he gives obedient children, endued with good manners, and in whom shall be had the greatest joy and comfort of old age; signifies a woman with child to bring forth a daughter; shows honourable Embassies, and declares rumours and news to be altogether true, and leaves a good and ample fame after death.

In the sixth House it shows the sick shall recover, denotes good servants, good and profitable cattle and animals. In the seventh House *Laetitia* gives a wife fair, beautiful and young; overcomes strife and contentions, and renders the success thereof to be love. *Laetitia* in the eighth House gives Legacies and possessions, and a commendable portion with a wife: if a Question be proposed concerning the condition of any man, it signifies him to be alive, and declares an honest, quiet, and meek kind of death. In the ninth House *Laetitia* signifies very few journeys, and those that do apply themselves to travail[1], their journeys either are about the Messages and Embassies of Princes, or Pilgrimages to fulfil holy vows; shows a man to be of a good religion, of indifferent knowledge, and who easily apprehends all things with natural ingenuity. In the tenth House, it raises Kings and Princes to honour and great renown; makes them famous by maintaining peace during their times; signifies Judges to be cruel & severe; honest Offices and Magistracy; signifies those things which are exercised either about Ecclesiastical affairs, schools, or the administration of justices; shows a mother if she be a widow, that she shall be married again. In the eleventh House *Laetitia* increases favour with Princes, and multiplies friends. And in the twelfth House *Laetitia* gives the victory over enemies; causes good servants and families, delivers from imprisonment, and preserves from future evils.

---

[1] Travel, not work.

Puella – the Maid

Puella in the first House signifies a person of a short life, weak constitution of body, middle stature, little fat, but fair, effeminate and luxurious, and one who will incur many troubles and dangers in his life-time for the love of women. In the second House, it neither increases riches, nor diminishes poverty; signifies a thief not to be departed from the City, and a thing stolen to be alienated and made away: if a Question be of treasure in a place, it is resolved there is none. In the third House *Puella* signifies more sisters then brethren, and increases and continues good friendship and amity amongst them; denotes journeys to be pleasant and joyous, and men of good conversations. In the fourth House *Puella* signifies a very small patrimony, and a Father not to live long, but makes the fields fertile with good fruits. In the fifth House a woman with child is signified to bring forth a woman-child; denotes no Embassage, causes much commerce with women, and some office to be obtained from them.

Puella in the sixth House signifies much weakness of the sick, but causes the sick shortly to recover; and shows a Physician to be both unlearned and unskilful, but one who is much esteemed of in the opinion of the vulgar people; gives good servants, handmaids, cattle and animals. In the seventh House *Puella* gives a wife fair, beautiful and pleasant, leading a peaceable and quiet conversation with her husband, notwithstanding one that shall burn much with lust, and be coveted and lusted after of many men; denotes no suits or controversies, which shall depend before a Judge, but some jars [arguments] and wrangling with the common people one amongst another, which shall be easily dissolved and ended. In the eighth House, if a Question be of one reputed to be dead, *Puella* declares him to be alive: gives a small portion with a wife, but that which contents her husband.

In the ninth House *Puella* signifies very few journeys, shows a man of good religion, indifferent skill or knowledge in sciences, unless happily Music, as well vocal as instrumental. In the tenth House *Puella* signifies Princes not to be very potent, but notwithstanding they shall govern peaceably within their Dominions, and shall be beloved of their Neighbours and Subjects; it causes them to be affable, mild and courteous, and that they shall always exercise themselves with continual mirth, plays, and hunting; makes Judges to be good, godly and merciful; gives Offices about women, or especially from noble women. In the eleventh House *Puella* gives many friends, and increases favour with women. In the twelfth House *Puella* signifies few enemies, but contention with women; and delivers Prisoners out of prison through the intercession of friends.

Amissio - Loss

Amissio in the first House signifies the sick not to live long, and shows a short life; signifies a man of disproportioned members of his body, and one of a wicked life and conversation, and who is marked with some notorious and remarkable defect in some part of his body, as either lame, or maimed, or the like.

Amissio in the second House consumes all substance, and makes one to suffer and undergo the burden of miserable poverty, neither thief, nor the thing stolen shall be found; signifies treasure not to be in the place sought after, and to be sought with loss and damage.

In the third House *Amissio* signifies death of brethren, or the want of them, and of kindred and friends; signifies no journeys, and causes one to be deceived of many. In the fourth House *Amissio* signifies the utter destruction of ones Patrimony, shows the Father to be poor, and Son to die.

Amissio in the fifth House shows death of children, and afflicts a man with divers sorrows; signifies a woman not to be with child, or else to have miscarried; raises no fame or honours, and disperses false rumours.

In the sixth House *Amissio* signifies the sick to be recovered, or that he shall soon recover; but causes loss and damage by servants and cattle. In the seventh House *Amissio* gives an adulterous wife, and contrarying her husband with continual contention; nevertheless she shall not live long; and it causes contentions to be ended.

In the eighth House *Amissio* signifies a man to be dead, consumes the dowry of a wife; bestows or sends no inheritances or legacies. In the ninth House *Amissio* causes no journeys, but such as shall be compassed with very great loss; signifies men to be inconstant in Religion, and often changing their opinion from one sect to another, and altogether ignorant of learning.

In the tenth House *Amissio* renders Princes to be most unfortunate, and shows that they shall be compelled to end their lives in exile and banishment; Judges to be wicked; and signifies Offices and Magistracy to be damageable, and shows the death of a Mother.

In the eleventh House *Amissio* signifies few friends, and causes them to be easily lost, and turned to become enemies; and causes a man to have no favour with his Prince, unless it be hurtful to him. In the twelfth House *Amissio* destroys all enemies, detains long in prison, but preserves from dangers.

Conjunctio - Conjunction

Conjunctio in the first House makes a prosperous life, and signifies a man of a middle stature, not lean nor fat, long face, plain hair, a little beard, long fingers and thighs, liberal, amiable, and a friend to many people. In the second House *Conjunctio* doth not signify any riches to be gotten, but preserves a man secure and free from the calamities of poverty; detects both the thief and the thing stolen, and acquires hidden treasure. In the third House he gives various journeys with various success, and signifies good faith and constancy. In the fourth House *Conjunctio* shows a mean Patrimony; causes a Father to be honest, of good report, and of good understanding. In the fifth House he gives Children of subtle ingenuity and wit, shows a woman pregnant to have a male-child, and raises men to honours by their own mere proper wit and ingenuity, and disperses their fame and credit far abroad; and also signifies news and rumours to be true.

In the sixth House *Conjunctio* signifies sicknesses to be tedious and of long continuance; but foreshows the Physician to be learned and well experienced; and shows servants to be faithful and blameless, and animals profitable. In the seventh House he gives a wife very obedient, conformable, and dutiful to her husband, and one of a good wit and ingenuity; [it] causes difficult suits and controversies, and crafty, subtle and malicious adversaries. In the eighth House, him of whom a Question is propounded, *Conjunctio* signifies him to be dead, & pretends some gain to be acquired by his death; shows a wife shall not be very rich. In the ninth House he gives a few journeys, but long and tedious, and shows one that is absent shall after a long season return. *Conjunctio* in this House increases divers Arts, Sciences, and Mysteries of Religion; and gives a quick, perspicuous, and efficacious wit.

In the tenth House *Conjunctio* makes Princes liberal, affable and benevolent, and who are much delighted and affected with divers Sciences, and secret Arts, and with men learned therein; causes Judges to be just, and such who with a piercing and subtle speculation, do easily discern causes in controversy before them; enlarges Offices which are concerned about Letters, Learning, sound Doctrines and Sciences; and signifies a Mother to be honest, of good ingenuity and wit, and also one of a prosperous life. In the eleventh House *Conjunctio* signifies great increase of friends; and very much procures the grace and favour of Princes, powerful and noble Men. In the twelfth House *Conjunctio* signifies wary and quick-witted enemies; causes such as are in prison to remain and continue so very long, and causes a man to eschew very many dangers in his life.

Albus - White

Albus in the first House signifies a life vexed with continual sickness and grievous diseases; signifies a man of a short stature, broad breast, and gross arms, having curled or crisped hair, one of a broad full mouth, a great talker and babler, given much to use vain and unprofitable discourse, but one that is merry, joyous and jocund, and much pleasing to men. In the second House *Albus* enlarges and augments [increases] substance gained by sports, plays, vile and base arts and exercises, but such as are pleasing and delightful; as by plays, pastimes, dancing and laughter: he discovers both the thief, and the theft or thing stolen, and hides and conceals treasure.

In the third House *Albus* signifies very few brethren; gives not many, but tedious and wearisome journeys, and signifies all deceivers. In the fourth House he shows very small or no Patrimony, and the Father to be a man much known; but declares him to be a man of some base and inferior Office and Employment. In the fifth House *Albus* gives no children, or if any, that they shall soon die; declares a woman to be servile, and causes such as are with young to miscarry, or else to bring forth Monsters; denotes all rumours to be false, and raises to no honour.

In the sixth House *Albus* causes very tedious sicknesses and diseases; discovers the fraud, deceit and wickedness of servants, and signifies diseases and infirmities of cattle to be mortal, and makes the Physician to be suspected of the sick Patient. *Albus* in the seventh House gives a barren wife, but one that is fair and beautiful; few suits or controversies, but such as shall be of very long continuance. In the eighth House if a question be propounded of any one, *Albus* shows the party to be dead; gives little portion or dowry with a wife, and causes that to be much strived and contended for.

In the ninth House *Albus* denotes some journeys to be accomplished, but with mean profit; hinders him that is absent, and signifies he shall not return; and declares a man to be superstitious in Religion, and given to false and deceitful Sciences. In the tenth *Albus* causes Princes and Judges to be malevolent; shows vile and base Offices and Magistracies; signifies a Mother to be a whore, or one much suspected for adultery. In the eleventh House *Albus* makes dissembling and false friends; causes love and favour to be inconstant. *Albus* in the twelfth House denotes vile, impotent and rustic enemies; shows such as are in prison shall not escape, and signifies a great many and various troubles and discommodities of ones life.

Puer - Child[1]

Puer in the first House gives an indifferent long life, but laborious; raises men to great fame through military dignity; signifies a person of a strong body, ruddy complexion, a fair countenance, and black hair. In the second House *Puer* increases substance, obtained by other men's goods, by plundering, rapines, confiscations, military Laws, and such like; he conceals both the thief and the thing stolen, but discovers no treasure. In the third House *Puer* raises a man to honour above his brethren, and to be feared of them; signifies journeys to be dangerous, and denotes persons of good credit. In the fourth House *Puer* signifies dubious inheritances and possessions, and signifies a Father to attain to his substance and estate through violence. In the fifth House *Puer* shows good children, and such as shall attain to honours and dignities; he signifies a woman to have a male-child, and shows honours to be acquired by military discipline, and great and full fame. In the sixth House *Puer* causes violent diseases and infirmities, as wounds, falls, contusions, bruises, but easily delivers the sick, and shows the Physician and Surgeon to be good; denotes servants and animals to be good, strong and profitable. In the seventh House *Puer* causes a wife to be a virago, of a stout Spirit, of good fidelity, and one that loves to bear the Rule and Government of a house; makes cruel strife and contentions, and such adversaries, as shall scarcely be restrained by Justice. *Puer* in the eighth House shows him that is supposed to be dead to live, signifies the kind of death not to be painful, or laborious, but to proceed from some hot humour, or by iron, or the sword, or from some other cause of the like kind; shows a man to have no legacies or other inheritance. In the ninth House *Puer* shows journeys not to be undergone without peril and danger of life, yet nevertheless declares them to be accomplished prosperously and safely; shows persons of little Religion, and using little conscience, notwithstanding gives the knowledge of natural philosophy and physick, and many other liberal and excellent Arts. *Puer* in the tenth House signifies Princes to be powerful, glorious, and famous in warlike achievements, but they shall be inconstant and unchangeable, by reason of the mutable and various success of victory. *Puer* in this House causes Judges to [be] cruel and unmerciful; increases offices in warlike affairs; signifies Magistracy to be exercised by fire and sword; hurts a Mother, and endangers her life. In the eleventh House *Puer* shows Noble friends, and Noble men, and such as shall much frequent the Courts of Princes, and follow after warfare; and causes many to adhere to cruel men: nevertheless he causes much esteem with Princes; but their favour is to be suspected. *Puer* in the twelfth House causes Enemies to be cruel and pernicious; those that are in Prison shall escape, and makes them to eschew many dangers.

[1] Usually translated as 'boy' rather than child.

Rubeus - Red

Rubeus in the first House, signifies a short life, and an evil end; signifies a man to be filthy, unprofitable, and of an evil, cruel and malicious countenance, having some remarkable and notable sign or scar in some part of his body. In the second House *Rubeus* signifies poverty, and makes thieves and robbers, and such persons as shall acquire and seek after their maintenance and livelihoods by using false, wicked, and evil, and unlawful Arts; preserves thieves, and conceals theft; and signifies no treasure to be hid nor found. In the third House *Rubeus* renders brethren and kinsmen to be full of hatred, and odious one to another, and shows them to be of evil manners, & ill disposition; causes journeys to be very dangerous, and foreshows false faith and treachery. In the fourth House he destroys and consumes Patrimonies, and disperses and wastes inheritances, causes them to come to nothing; destroys the fruits of the field by tempestuous seasons, and malignancy of the earth; and brings the Father to a quick and sudden death. *Rubeus* in the fifth House gives many children, but either they shall be wicked and disobedient, or else shall afflict their Parents with grief, disgrace and infamy.

In the sixth House *Rubeus* causes mortal wounds, sicknesses and diseases; him that is sick shall die; the Physician shall err, servants prove false and treacherous, cattle and beasts shall produce hurt and danger. In the seventh House *Rubeus* signifies a wife to be infamous, publicly adulterate, and contentious; deceitful and treacherous adversaries, who shall endeavour to overcome you, by crafty and subtle wiles and circumventions of the Law. In the eighth House *Rubeus* signifies a violent death to be inflicted, by the execution of public Justice; and signifies, if any one be enquired after, that he is certainly dead; and wife to have no portion or dowry. *Rubeus* in the ninth House shows journeys to be evil and dangerous, and that a man shall be in danger either to spoiled by thieves and robbers, or to be taken by plunderers and robbers; declares men to be of most wicked opinions in Religion, and of evil faith, and such as will often easily be induced to deny and go from their faith for every small occasion; denotes Sciences to be false and deceitful, and the professors thereof to be ignorant. In the tenth House *Rubeus* signifies Princes to be cruel and tyrannical, and that their power shall come to an evil end, as that either they shall be cruelly murdered and destroyed by their own Subjects, or that they shall be taken captive by their conquerors, and put to an ignominious and cruel death, or shall miserably end their lives in hard imprisonment; signifies Judges and Officers to be false, thievish, and such as shall be addicted to usury; shows that a mother shall soon die, and denotes her to be blemished with an evil fame and report. In the eleventh House *Rubeus* gives no true, nor any faithful friends;

shows men to be of wicked lives and conversations, and causes a man to be rejected and cast out from all society and conversation with good and noble persons. *Rubeus* in the twelfth House makes enemies to be cruel and traitorous, of whom we ought circumspectly to beware; signifies such as are in prison shall come to an evil end; and shows a great many inconveniences and mischief to happen in a mans life.

Carcer - Prison

Carcer in the first House being posited, gives a short life; signifies men to be most wicked, of a filthy and cruel unclean figure and shape, and such as are hated and despised of all men. *Carcer* in the second House causes most cruel and miserable poverty; signifies both the thief and thing stolen to be taken and regained; and shows no treasure to be hid. In the third House *Carcer* signifies hatred and dissention amongst brethren; evil journeys, most wicked faith and conversation. *Carcer* in the fourth House signifies a man to have no possessions or inheritances, a Father to be most wicked, and to die a sudden and evil death. In the fifth House *Carcer* gives many children; shows a woman not to be with child, and provokes those that are with child to miscarry of their own consent, or slays the child; signifies no honours, and disperses most false rumours.

In the sixth House *Carcer* causes the diseased to undergo long sickness; signifies servants to be wicked, rather unprofitable; Physicians ignorant. In the seventh House *Carcer* shows the wife shall be hated of her husband, and signifies suits and contentions to be ill ended and determined. In the eighth House *Carcer* declares the kind of death to be by some fall, mischance, or false accusation, or that men shall be condemned in prison, or in public judgement, and shows them to be put to death, or that they shall often lay violent and deadly hands upon themselves; denies a wife to have any portion and legacies. *Carcer* in the ninth House, shows he that is absent shall not return, and signifies some evil shall happen to him in his journey; it denotes persons of no Religion, a wicked conscience, and ignorant of learning. In the tenth House *Carcer* causes Princes to be very wicked, and wretchedly to perish, because when they are established in their power, they will wholly addict themselves to every voluptuous lust, pleasure, and tyranny; causes Judges to be unjust and false; declares the Mother to be cruel, and infamous, and noted with the badge of adultery; gives no Offices nor Magistracies, but such as are gotten and obtained either by lying, or through theft, and base and cruel robbery. In the eleventh House *Carcer* causes no friends, nor love, nor favour amongst men. In the twelfth House it raises enemies, detains in prison, and inflicts many evils.

Tristitia - Sorrow

Tristitia in the first House doth not abbreviate life, but afflicts it with many molestations; signifies a person of good manners and carriage, but one that is solitary, and slow in all his business and occasions; one that is solitary, melancholy, seldom laughing, but most covetous after all things. In the second House it gives much substance and riches, but they that have them, shall not enjoy them, but shall rather hide them, and shall scarce afford to themselves food or sustenance therefore; treasure shall not be found, neither shall the thief nor the theft. *Tristitia* in the third House signifies a man to have few brethren, but shows that he shall outlive them all; causes unhappy journeys, but gives good faith. In the fourth House *Tristitia* consumes and destroys fields, possessions and inheritances; causes a Father to be old and of long life, and a very covetous hoarder up of money. In the fifth House it signifies no children, or that they shall soon die; shows a woman with child to bring forth a woman-child, gives no fame nor honours.

In the sixth House *Tristitia* shows that the sick shall die; servants shall be good, but slothful; and signifies cattle shall be of a small price or value. In the seventh House *Tristitia* shows that the wife shall soon die; and declares suits and contentions to be very hurtful, and determining against you. In the eighth House it signifies the kind of death to be with long and grievous sickness, and much dolour and pain; gives legacies and an inheritance, and endows a wife with a portion.[1] Tristitia in the ninth House, shows that he that is absent shall perish in his journey; or signifies that some evil mischance shall happen unto him; causes journeys to be very unfortunate, but declares men to be of good Religion, devout, and profound Scholars. In the tenth House *Tristitia* signifies Princes to be severe, but very good lovers of justice; it causes just Judges, but such as are tedious and slow in determining of causes; brings a Mother to a good old age, with integrity and honesty of life, but mixed with divers discommodities and mis-fortunes; it raises to great Offices, but they shall not be long enjoyed nor persevered in; it signifies such Offices as do appertain to the water, or tillage, and manuring of the Earth, or such as are to be employed about matters of Religion and wisdom. In the eleventh House *Tristitia* signifies scarcity of friends, and the death of friends; and also signifies little love or favour. In the twelfth House it shows no enemies; wretchedly condemns the imprisoned; and causes many dies-commodities and dies-profits to happen in ones life.

---

[1] Dowry.

Caput Draconis - Dragon's Head

Caput Draconis in the first House augments [increases] life and fortune. In the second House he increases riches and substance; saves and conceals a thief; and signifies treasure to be hid. In the third House *Caput Draconis* gives many brethren; causes journeys, kinsmen, and good faith and credit. In the fourth House he gives wealthy inheritances; causes the Father to attain to old age. In the fifth House *Caput Draconis* gives many children; signifies women with child to bring forth women-children; and oftentimes to have twins; it shows great honours and fame; and signifies news and rumours to be true.

Caput Draconis is the sixth House increases sicknesses and diseases; signifies the Physician to be learned; and gives very many servants and chattel. In the seventh House he signifies a man shall have many wives; multiplies and stirs up many adversaries and suits. In the eight House he shows the death to be certain, increases Legacies and inheritances, and gives a good portion with a wife.

In the ninth House *Caput Draconis* signifies many journeys, many Sciences, and good Religion; and shows that those that are absent shall soon return. In the tenth House he signifies glorious Princes, great and magnificent Judges, great Offices, and gainful Magistracy. In the eleventh House he causes many friends, and to be beloved of all men. In the twelfth House *Caput Draconis* signifies men to have many enemies, and many women; detains the imprisoned, and evilly punishes them.

Cauda Draconis - Dragons Tail

Cauda Draconis, in all and singular the respective Houses aforesaid, gives the contrary judgement to Caput. And these are the natures of the figures of Geomancy, and their judgements, in all and singular their Houses, upon all manner of Questions to be propounded, of or concerning any matter or thing whatsoever.

Appendix VII - General Indications of the Figures[1]

Indication	Figures
Good and quick for a voyage	Acquisitio, Caput Draconis, Fortuna Major, Laetitia
Good for Land Journey	Populus, Laetitia, Albus, Conjunctio, Via
Good for Water Journey	Populus, Puella, Albus, Acquisitio, Laetitia
Slow for a Voyage, but profitable	Puella
Ill for the Way	Albus, Conjunctio, Populus, Tristitia
Robbing on the Way	Cauda Draconis, Rubeus
Ill for Fear	Conjunctio, Acquisitio, Rubeus, Caput Draconis, Fortunsa Major, Albus
Good for Honour and Dignity (Promotion)	Acquisitio, Fortuna Major, Fortuna Minor, Laetitia, Albus, Caput Draconis, Conjunctio
Ill for Honour	Amissio, Via, Rubeus, Puer, Tristitia
Good to be set free, or come out of Prison	Fortuna Minor, Via, Cauda Draconis, Puer, Amissio, Laetitia
Ill to come out of Prison	Acquisitio, Fortuna Major, Tristitia, Carcer
Mean (average) to come out of Prison	Rubeus, Puella, Albus
Good for the Body	Populus, Conjunctio, Fortuna Minor
Better than before (for the Body)	Via, Cauda draconis, Laetitia, Tristitia
Evil for the Body	Carcer, Rubeus, Amissio
Mean (average) for the Body	Fortuna Major, Albus, Puella, Puer
Good for a Woman with Child	Amissio, Fortuna Minor, Via, Laetitia
The Child (of the pregnancy) will die	Tristitia
Mean (average) for the Child	Amissio, Fortuna Major, Cauda

[1] From John Heydon, *Theomagia,* Vol. III, pp. 84-96.

Indication	Figures
	Draconis, Populus
Good for Marriage	Fortuna Major, Laetitia, Caput Draconis
Best for Marriage	Tristitia,[1] Conjunctio
Mean (average) for Marriage	Caput Draconis, Carcer
Ill for Marriage	Fortuna Major,[1] Amissio, Via, Fortuna Minor, Rubeus
Good for Love of Women	Laetitia, Tristitia, Caput Draconis, Puer, Fortuna Major
Ill for Love of Women	Amissio, Via, Rubeus, Caput Draconis
Good for dread and fear	Amissio, Via, Cauda Draconis, Puer, Fortuna Minor
Good to Recover a thing Stolen	Acquisitio, Caput Draconis, Conjunctio, Carcer, Puer, Fortuna Minor
Mean (average) to Recover a thing Stolen	Puella
Ill to Recover a thing Stolen	Fortuna Minor, Laetitia, Caput Draconis, Populus, Via
Good to take shipping	Acquisitio, Laetitia, Fortuna Major, Fortuna Minor, Via
Mean (average) to take shipping	Cauda Draconis
Ill to take to ship, for they shall be drowned	Conjunctio, Populus, Amissio, Tristitia
Good to remove (move house)	Fortuna Major, Cauda Draconis, Laetitia, Caput Draconis, Acquisitio
Mean (average) to remove (move house)	Albus, Conjunctio, Puer, Amissio
Ill Figure to remove (move house)	Fortuna Minor, Tristitia, Rubeus, Carcer, Populus, Via, Puella
Good in suspicion of war	Carcer, Rubeus, Conjunctio, Acquisitio
Evil in suspicion of war	Fortuna Minor, Populus
Good for Victory	Fortuna Major, Rubeus, Caput Draconis

[1] Maybe a printer's mistake.

Indication	Figures
Evil for Victory	Tristitia, Carcer
Mean (average) for Victory	Conjunctio
Signifying Showers	Fortuna Major, Tristitia, Cauda Draconis, Puella, Conjunctio, Acquisitio
A good end by an ill beginning	Caput Draconis, Cauda Draconis, Tristitia, Carcer
Amendment of Sickness	Via, Cauda Draconis, Amissio, Fortuna Major, Carcer, Conjunctio
Ill for sickness, and good for bloody flux[1]	Populus, Rubeus, Caput Draconis, Tristitia
Death (in the Eighth House)	Acquisitio
Good for (signifying) the Year	Fortuna Major, Acquisitio, Laetitia, Tristitia, Caput Draconis, Albus, Carcer
Signifying Months	Puella, Puer, Fortuna Minor, Rubeus, Populus, Via
Signifying Weeks	Cauda Draconis
Signifying Days	Conjunctio
Signifying Hours	Amissio
Good for signifying Loyalty	Acquisitio, Albus, Laetitia, Puella, Populus, Caput Draconis, Fortuna Major, Fortuna Minor
Evil Figures signifying Evil	Via, Carcer, Puer, Tristitia, Cauda Draconis, Rubeus, Amissio
Mean Figures	Conjunctio
Figures of Chastity and Virginity	Albus, Fortuna Major, Laetitia, Carcer, Caput Draconis, Tristitia, Puella
Figures of Incontinence and Lechery	Puer, Cauda Draconis, Amissio, Rubeus, Populus, Conjunctio, Via, Acquisitio, Fortuna Minor
Figures of True Love	Acquisitio, Conjunctio, Puella, Laetitia
Figures signifying False Love	Amissio, Puer, Cauda Draconis, Rubeus, Fortuna Minor

[1] Dysentery.

Indication	Figures
Figures signifying there is no Thief	Acquisitio, Fortuna Major, Albus, Caput Draconis, Laetitia
Figures signifying War	Tristitia, Rubeus, Puer, Cauda Draconis, Fortuna Minor, Amissio
Figures of Peace	Fortuna Major, Acquisitio, Caput Draconis, Laetitia, Albus, Puella
Figures of Gain	Acquisitio, Fortuna Major, Tristitia, Puella, Caput Draconis
Figures of Loss[1]	Carcer, Conjunctio, Albus, Laetitia, Populus, Via, Amissio, Puer, Cauda Draconis, Rubeus, Fortuna Minor
Figures of Nobility	Acquisitio, Laetitia, Puella, Fortuna Major, Fortuna Minor, Caput Draconis
Figures of Ignobility	Tristitia, Carcer, Via, Cauda Draconis, Conjunctio
Figures of Life	Albus, Fortuna Major, Laetitia, Puella, Acquisitio, Populus, Caput Draconis, Via
Figures of Death (only if the Eighth House agrees)	Tristitia, Cauda Draconis, Carcer, Rubeus, Puer, Conjunctio, Amissio, Fortuna Minor, Acquisitio
Figures of Liberality (extravagance)	Amissio, Cauda Draconis, Fortuna Minor, Via
Figures of Covetousness and Avarice	Tristitia, Carcer, Conjunctio, Fortuna Major
Figures of Justice	Puer
Of Prudence	Acquisitio
Of Force	Laetitia
Of Temperance	Conjunctio
Good to buy Cattle	Puella, Populus, Caput Draconis
Loss to buy Cattle	Tristitia, Carcer

[1] Some of these do not make sense.

Bibliography

It is very difficult to draw up a complete bibliography of works on geomancy, as it would include magical, historical, anthropological and sociological works in a number of different languages covering Africa, the Middle East and Europe. Likewise it is undesirable simply to list such works alphabetically. They are here divided into the basic cultural areas, in much the same way that chapters 1-5 are broken down according to cultural region. In each case the most relevant and fruitful texts are marked with an asterisk, and where any of these have extensive bibliographies this is also noted, so that the student of geomancy can pursue his researches in greater detail.

For a general historical background to divination the reader should consult Bouché-Leclercq, *Histoire de la divination dans l'antiquité* (4 volumes) Paris, 1880-2.

For Hebraic sources the reader should consult the bibliographic references in the geomancy article in the *Encyclopaedia Judaica.* Likewise for extensive bibliographic references to Arabic manuscripts, the reader should consult the *Encyclopaedia of Islam* (new edition: the article on Khatt by Toufic Fahd) and specially Savage-Smith (1980), pp. 1-5, 87-88.

Paul Tannery's *Mémoires Scientifiques* is one of the best introductions to the early history of geomancy in Europe and the connection between Arab sources and their Greek and Latin derivatives.

For extrapolations, worked examples and tables connected with practical European geomancy see my own *Oracle of Geomancy,* Warner/Destiny, New York, 1977. See my *Guide to the Feng Shui Compass,* Golden Hoard, Singapore, 2008 for history of the completely unrelated system of Chinese feng shui, sometimes called 'geomancy.'

Thérèse Charmasson has produced a very worthwhile study of the early development of geomancy in Europe in *Recherches sur une technique divinatoire: la géomancie dans l'Occident medieval,* which includes a list of manuscripts arranged by both author or incipit, and location, which supplements the manuscript bibliography of the present volume.

The works of George Sarton and Lynn Thorndike are of course invaluable historical frames of reference.

Raml and Islamic origins (chapter 2)

The most important source works are in Arabic, being those of az-Zanātī and Ahmad ben 'Alī Zunbul, with the works of Tannery, Toufic Fahd and Carra de Vaux being the most useful of the French critical works on *raml*. Unfortunately there is little material in English on *raml*, and the few magazine articles that have appeared range from sketchy to downright misleading. Not all Arabic texts have full bibliographic details.

Al-Adhami. *Mizan al-adl fi masqasis ahkam al-raml* (1322 A.H.)

Al-Afandi, Ahmad (fl. 1290 A.H.). *Ilm al-raml.*

Al-Buni, Ahmad ibn `Ali. *Kitāb shams al-ma`ārif al-kubra* ('The Great Book of the Sun of Gnosis'). Manshurat Mu'assat al-Nur li'l-Matbu`at al-Thaqafiyya, Beirut, 2000. 616 pp.

Al-Buni, Ahmad ibn `Ali. *[Kitab] Shams al-ma`ārif al-kubrá wa-lata'if al-`awarif* `Abd al-Qadir al-Husayni al-Adhami. 4 vols. in one. Mustafá al-Bābī al-Halabi, Cairo, 1945. 576+16 pp.

Al Sudi, Muhammad. *A treatise on astrology and divination.*

Al Tounsi, Muhammad ibn Omar. *See* Perron.

Barakat, Robert A. *Tawula: A Study in Arabic Folklore,* (F.F. Communications, No. 214) Tiedeakatemia, Helsinki, 1974.

Ben Choaib, Abou Bakr. 'La bonne aventure chez les musulmans' in *R.A.*, 1906, pp. 62-70.

Brenner, Louis. 'Muslim Divination and the Religion of Sub-Saharan Africa' in *Insight and Artistry in African Divination.* ed. John Pemberton III. Smithsonian Institution Press, 2000. pp. 50-1.

Brockelmann, C. *Geschichte der arabischen Litteratur,* Vol. II, Leiden, 1949, pp. 298, 326 ff.

Carmody, F. J. *Arabic Astronomical and Astrological Sciences in Latin Translation: a critical bibliography,* Cambridge, 1906. [Useful bibliography]

Carra De Vaux, Bernard. 'La Géomancie chez les Arabes,' *see* P. Tannery, *Mémoires Scientifiques.* *

Cruzet, V. 'Du *khet-er-raml* ou art de lire l'avenir sur le sable' in *R. T.*, 1920, pp. 267-76.

Davies, R. 'A System of Sand Divination,' in *Sudan Notes and Records,* Vol. III, 1920, pp. 157-62 and in *Moslem World,* Vol. XVII, Missionary

Review Publishing, New York, 1927, pp. 123-9.

Decourdemanche, J. A. 'Sur quelques pratiques de divination chez les Arabes,' in *Revue des traditions populaires,* 1906, Vol. 21, pp. 66-73.

Doutté, Edmond. *Magie et religion dans l'Afrique du Nord.* Algiers, 1909, pp. 377 ff.

Elisseéff, N. *Thèmes et motifs des Mille et Une Nuits. Essai de classification.* Beirut, 1959, pp. 127-8.

Fahd, Toufic. 'Khatt' in *Encyclopedia of Islam* (new edition), pp. 1128-30. *

Fahd, Toufic. 'La Divination Arabe' in *Études religieuses, sociologiques et folkloriques sur le milieu natif de l'Islam*, Sindbad, Paris, 1987.

Fahd, Toufic. 'La Magie Comme "Source" de la Sagesse d'Apres l'Oeuvre d'al-Būnī' in *Charms et Sortileges Magie et Magiciens,* (Res Orientales XIV), Bures-sur-Yvette, 2002, pp. 61-108.

Fahd, Toufic. *La Divination Arabe,* Brill, Leiden, 1966, pp. 195-204. **

Hadjdji, Khalifa. *Encyclopedia of Islam* (new edition) Vol. III, pp. 478 ff.

Ibn Khaldun, Abd Al-Rahman Ibn Muhammad. *The Muqaddimah,* ed. Franz Rosenthal, 3 Vols, Routledge & Kegan Paul, London, 1958, Vol. 1, pp. 226 ff, Vol. 2, p. 201.

Idriss, Prophet. *Geomancy: Elm Al-raml*, FAR Publishing, London, 2006.

Khamballah, Hadji. *La Géomancie traditionelle...Traite pratique d'enseignement et dictionnaire d'interpretation géomantique,* Editions Véga, Paris, 1947.*

Klein-Franke, Felix. 'The Geomancy of Ahmad ben 'Alī Zunbul. A Study of the Arabic Corpus Hermeticum,' in *Ambix,* London, Vol. 20, 1973. *

LeLubre, M. 'La Géomancie chez les Touareg' in *Bulletin de Liaison Saharienne, Paris,* No. 10, 1952.

Lemay, Richard. 'Books of Magic in translation from the Arabic, and the birth of a theology of the Sacraments of the Church in the twelfth century' in *Charms et Sortileges Magie et Magiciens* (Res Orientales XIV), Bures-sur-Yvette, 2002, pp. 165-192.

Leroux, H. 'Animisme et Islam dans la subdivision de Maradi (Niger),' in *Bulletin de l'Institut Français d 'Afrique Noire,* Vol. X, Paris, 1948, pp. 652-6.

Lewicki, T. 'Prophètes, divins et magiciens chez les Berbères médiévaux,' in *Folia orientalia,* 1966, Vol. 8, pp. 3-27.

Maddison, Francis, Emilie Savage-Smith, Ralph Pinder-Wilson, & Tim Stanley. *Science, Tools And Magic: Part One: Body and Spirit, Mapping the Universe.*

Part Two: Mundane Worlds. Khalili Collection of Islamic Art, Vol XII, Oxford University Press & Azimuth, London, 1997. pp. 106-7.

Madrus, Jean-Charles. *Sucre d'Amour,* 1926.

Mahfūf, 'Abdallah ibn. *Muthallathat Ibn Mahfuf fi'-l-raml*[1] aka *Risalat raml.*[2]

Margoliouth, D. S. 'Divination (Muslim)' in *Encyclopaedia of Religion and Ethics,* ed. J. Hastings *et al.,* 1908, Vol. 4. pp. 816-18.

Maupoil, Bernard. 'Contribution à l'étude de l'origine musulmane de la géomancie dans le Bas-Dahomey,' in *Journal de la Société des Africainistes,* Vol. XIII, Paris, 1943, pp. 1-94. *

Maxwell, J. *La Divination,* Paris, 1927, pp. 135-7.

Mercadier, Captain. 'Un Procédé de divination par le sable, en usage chez les peuplades sahariennes,' in *Bulletin de liaison saharienne,* no. 10, Paris, 1952.

Mouls, Jean-Pierre. 'Nouvelles orientations pour une typologie formelle des séquences fixes de figures des premiers traités de géomancie arabe' Nov-Dec, 2004.

Nasr, Seyyed Hossein & Chittick, William. *An Annotated Bibliography of Islamic Science* (Section XF & XG The Occult Sciences), Imperial Iranian Academy of Philosophy, Kazin, New York, 1985.

Osman, Ben Ali (pseud.). *Grosses Punktir-Buch des weisen Arabers Osman Ben Ali oder Blicke in die Zukunft,* Landsberg, n.d.

Perron, Dr. *Voyage au Darfour,* Paris, 1845.

Porter, Venetia. `Islamic Seals: Magical or Practical' in Alan Jones (ed.) *University Lectures in Islamic Studies,* Vol. 2, Alatair World of Islamic Trust, London, 1988. pp. 135-149.

Rescher, O. *Der Islam,* Vol. IX, 1919, p. 37.

Ruska, J. *Arabische Alchemisten,* Vol. II, Heidelberg, 1924.

Sarton, George. *Introduction To The History of Science,* vols. 1-3, (Carnegie Institute Pub. No. 376) Williams & Wilkins, Baltimore, 1927-47. [A standard reference work.]

Savage-Smith, Emile. (ed.) 'Magic and Divination in Early Islam' in *Journal of Islamic Studies,* 17, 2006, No. 3, Aldershot. pp. 366-368.

---

[1] Rağip Paşa MS 964, copy made by Ahmad 'Isā.
[2] Esat Ef. MS 1988, copy made by Ahmad 'Iyād at the al-madrasa al-Zāhiriyya.

Savage-Smith, Emilie and Marion B. Smith. *Islamic geomancy and a thirteenth-century divinatory device.* Studies in Near Eastern Culture and Society, 2, Undena, Malibu, 1980.

Savage-Smith, Emilie. *Magic and divination in early Islam,* Ashgate, Burlington, 2003. [An useful collection of essays]

Sayyid `Abd al-Qadir al-Husayni al-Adhami, 'Risālah Mīzān al-`adl fī maqāsid askām al-raml' in *Majmū`a Arba` Rasā'il* ('Compendium of Four Treatises'). pp. 537-552.

Smith, Marion B. 'The Nature of Islamic Geomancy with a Critique of a Structuralist's Approach' in *Studia Islamica,* No. 49, 1979, pp. 5-38. [She clearly distinguishes geomancy from feng shui.]

Steinschneider, Moritz. 'Die S[i]kidy oder Geomantischen Figuren,' in *Zeitschrift der Deutschen Morgenländischen Gesellschaft,* Vol. 31, Leipzig, 1877, pp. 762-5. *

Steinschneider, Moritz. *Europäiscbe Übersetzungen,* 35-37, 1904. *

Tannery, Paul. *Mémoires Scientifiques,* Vol. IV, Sciences Exactes chez Les Byzantins. Mémoire No. 14 - 'Le Rabolion (Traités de Géomancie arabes, grecs, et latins),' pp. 295-411 (includes 'La géomancie chez les arabes' by Baron Carra de Vaux, p. 299) Heiberg & Zeuthen, Toulouse and Paris, 1920. *

Trancart, Andre. 'Sur un procédé de divination de l'Adrar Mauritanien, le gzân,' in *Bulletin du Comité d'études historiques et scientifiques de l'Afrique occidental française,* Vol. XXI, no. 104, Paris, Oct-Dec 1938, pp. 489-98.

Zanātī, Abu 'Abdallāh Muhammad (ben 'Uthman?). *al-Aqwāl al-mardīyah fī al-ahkām ar-ramlīyah,* Cairo, 1908-9. *

Zanātī, Abu 'Abdallāh Muhammad (ben 'Uthman?). *Kitāb al-Fasl fī usūl 'ilm ar-raml,* Cairo, 1863-4 & 1927. *

Zunbul, Ahmad Ben 'Alī. *Kitāb lamm aš-šaml fī 'ilm al-raml.*

Zunbul, Ahmad Ben 'Alī. *Kitāb al-māqālat fī hall al-muškilāt* ('Treatise on the Solution of Problems').

Zunbul, Ahmad Ben 'Alī. *Kitāb ad-dahab al-ibrīz al-muharrar.*

Zunbul, Ahmad Ben 'Alī. *Kitāb 'aga'ib al-mahluqāt.*

Africa: *Fa, ifa* and voodoo (chapter 3)

The outstanding work in this section is that by Bernard Maupoil, followed by the comparative work of J. C. Hébert, Ardant du Picq and René Trautmann. In English the most comprehensive text on *ifa* divination is that by William Bascom (1969), who is also the most extensive periodical writer on the subject. Extensive bibliographies will be found in all the above texts. Herskovits (1938) is of course the classic writer on Dahomey, and Dennett (1910) and Spieth are also well worth consulting. Finally there are several texts listed which are written by Yoruba writers, of which the two most notable are those of Bishop Johnson (1899) and Abayomi Cole (1898). The Yoruba sources missing bibliographic details are ones I have not been able to consult.

Adedoja Aluko, Chief. *The Sixteen (16) Major Odu Ifa from Ile-Ife.*

Alapini, Julien. *Les Noix Sacrées. Etude complète de Fa-Ahidégoun. Génie de la Sagesse et la Divination au Dahomey,* Regain, Monte-Carlo, 1950, p. 126.

Ambimbola, 'Wande. *IFA: an exposition of the Ifa Literary Corpus.* OUP, Ibadan, 1976.

Awo Fa'Lokun Fatunmbi. *Awo: Ifa & the Theology of Orisha Divination.*

Awo Fasina Falade. *Ifa: The Key to Its Understanding.*

Bascom, William. *Ifa Divination: Communication between Gods and Men in West Africa,* Indiana University Press, Bloomington and London, 1969. [Extensive bibliography.] *

Bascom, William. 'Ifa Divination: Comments on the Paper by J. D. Clarke,' *Man,* Vol. XLII (21), 1942, pp. 41-3.

Bascom, William. 'Odu Ifa: The Names of the Signs,' in *Africa,* London, Vol. XXXVI, 1966, pp. 408-21.

Bascom, William. 'Odu Ifa: The Order of the Figures of Ifa,' in *Bulletin de l'Institut Français d'Afrique Noire,* Paris, Vol. XXIII, 1961, pp. 676-82.

Bascom, William. 'The Relationship of Yoruba Folklore to Divining,' in *Journal of American Folklore,* Vol. LVI, 1943, pp. 127-31.

Bascom, William. 'The Sanctions of Ifa Divination,' in *Journal of the Royal Anthropological Institute,* London, Vol. LXXI, 1941, pp. 43-54.

Bascom, William. 'Two Forms of Afro-Cuban Divination,' in *Acculturation in the Americas,* in Sol Tax (ed). *Proceedings and Selected Papers of the XXIXth International Congress of Americanists,* Vol. 1, 63-9, University of Chicago Press, Chicago, 1952.

Bascom, William. *Sixteen Cowries,* Indiana University Press, Bloomington, 1993.

Beaujard, Philippe. 'Les manuscrits arabico-malagaches (*sorabe*) du pays antemoro' in *Omaly sy Anio (Hier et Aujourd'hui),* No. 28, 1988, pp. 123-49.

Beier, Ulli. *Yoruba Myths.* CUP, Cambridge, 1980.

Bertho, Jacques. 'La Science du Destin au Dahomey,' *Africa,* London, Vol. IX, no. 3, July 1936, pp. 359-78.

Bertho, Jacques. 'La Science du Destin chez les Noirs du Dahomey,' in *Écho des Miss. Afric. de Lyon,* Lyon, no. 10, Dec. 1936, pp. 162-4; & No. 1, Jan. 1937, pp.9-10.

Beyioku, Fagbenro. *Ifa.* Hope Rising Press, Lagos, 1940.

Binger, Louis Gustav. *Du Niger au Golfe de Guinée par le pays de Kong et le Mossi.* Hachette, Paris, 1892.

Binsbergen, Wim van. *The Astrological origin of Islamic Geomancy.* Binghamton University, 1996.

Boehmer, J. *Religions - Urkunden Der Völker,* Section 4, Book 2, 1909*; see also* Spieth, J.

Brenner, Louis. 'The Esoteric Sciences in West African Islam' in B. M. Du Toit & I Abdalla (eds.) *African Healing Strategies.* Trado-Medic, Buffalo, 1985.

Brenner, Louis. 'Histories of Religion in Africa' in *Journal of Religion in Africa,* XXX, 2. Brill, Leiden, 2000.

Brenner, Louis. 'Muslim Divination and the Religion of Sub-Saharan Africa' in *Insight and Artistry...of Divination in Central and West Africa.* ed. John Pemberton. Smithsonian, New York, 2000. pp. 50-1. *

Burton, Richard Francis. *A Mission to Gelele, King of Dahome. With notices of the so called 'Amazons,' the Grand Customs, the Yearly Customs, the Human Sacrifices, the Present State of the Slave Trade, and the Negro's place in Nature,* Tinsley, London, 1864; Routledge & Kegan Paul, London, 1966 (2 vols); Vol. I, pp. 161, 330-7.

Chief Solagbade Popoola Foundation, *Ifa Dida,* Volume One of seventeen, Asefin Media, 2008.

Clark, J. D. 'Ifa Divination' in *Journal of the Royal Anthropological Institute,* London, Vol. LXIX, part 2, plate XIII, 1939, pp. 235-56.

Cole, J. Abayomi. *Astronomical Geomancy in Africa,* 1898, rpt. Edited Kali Sichen-Andoh, Northscale, San Francisco, 1990.

Crosley, Dr. Reginald O. *The Voudou Quantum Leap,* 2000.

Dennett, R. E. *At the Back of the Black Man's Mind, or Notes on the Kingly Office in West Africa,* Macmillan, London, 1906. [Appendix].

Dennett, R. E. *Nigerian Studies, or the Religious and Political System of the Yoruba,* Macmillan, London, 1910. *

Dieterlen, Germaine. *Textes Sacres d 'Afrique Noire,* Gallimard, Paris, 1965.

Dupire, Marguerite. 'Divination et pouvoir local: variations sénégalaises, le *siltigi* peul' in *Islam et Sociétés au Sud du Sahara,* No. 12, pp. 109-128.

El-Zein, A. H. M. *the Sacred Meadows: a Structural Analysis of Religious Symbolism in an East African Town.* Northwestern, Evanstown, 1974.

Eglash, Ron. 'Bamana Sand Divination: Recursion in Ethnomathematics' in *American Anthropologist,* New Series, Vol. 99, No. 1, March 1997, pp. 112-122.

Ellis, Alfred Burton. 'How the Yoruba Count and the Universal Order in Creation' in *Journal of the African Society,* London, Vol. XVII, 1917-18.

Ellis, Alfred Burton. *The Ewe-speaking Peoples of the Slave Coast of West Africa, their Religion, Manners, Customs, Laws, Languages.* Chapman & Hall, London, 1890.

Ellis, Alfred Burton. *The Yoruba-speaking Peoples of the Slave Coast of West Africa, their Religion, Manners, Customs, Laws, Languages, etc..... with an Appendix containing a comparison of the Tshi, Ge, Ewe and Yoruba Languages.* Chapman & Hall, London, 1894, rpt Charleston: BiblioBazaar, 2007. *

Epega, Afolabi A. *Ifa: the Ancient Wisdom.* Omole Oluwa, New York, 1987.

Epega, D. Olarimwa. *The Basis of Yoruba Religion.* Ijamido, Lagos, n.d.

Epega, D. Onadele. *Ifa-amọna 'awọn Baba wa.* Imọlẹ Oluwa Institute, Ode Rẹmọ, Hope Rising Press, Lagos, Nigeria, 1931.

Epega, D. Onadele. *The Mystery of Yoruba Gods,* Hope Rising Press, Lagos, 1931.

Epega, M. Lajuwon. 'Ifa - The light of my Fathers,' in *The Nigerian Teacher,* Vol. I, no. 5, 1935, pp. 11-14.

F. S. 'Ifa,' in *Nigerian Chronicle,* Lagos, Mar 1909.

Fagg, William & Willett, Frank. 'Ancient Ife. An Ethnographical Summary,' in *Odu,* No. 8, 1960, pp. 21-35.

Fama, Chief. *Fundamentals of the Yoruba Religion (Orisa Worship)*

Fama, Chief. *Fundamentos de la Religion Yoruba (Adorando Orisa).*

Fama, Chief. *Practitioners' Handbook for the Ifa Professional.*

Fama, Chief. *Sixteen Mythological Stories of Ifa (Itan Ifa Merindinlogun).*

Farrow, Stephen Septimus. *Faith, Fancies and Fetish or Yoruba Paganism,* Macmillan, London, 1926.

Frobenius, Leo. *Auf den Trümmern des klassichen Atlantis,* Berlin, 1912, pp. 254-91.

Frobenius, Leo. *Das Unbekannte Afrika. Aufhellung der Schicksale eines Erdteils,* Oskar Beack, Munich, 1923, table, 185-92.

Frobenius, Leo. *Histoire de la Civilisation Africaine* (trans. H. Back and D. Ermont), Gallimard, Paris, 1936.

Frobenius, Leo. *Kulturgeschichte Africas,* Phaidon-Verlag, Zurich, 1933, pp. 169-73. Plate 88, 113, 123, 128.

Gaillard, Dr. 'Étude sur les Lacustres du Bas-Dahomey,' in *L'Anthropologie,* Paris, Vol. XVIII, 1907, pp. 99-125.

Gorer, Geoffrey Edgar. *Africa Dances,* Faber & Faber, London, 1935.

Gleason, Judith. *A Recitation of Ifa Oracle of the Yoruba.* Grossman, New York, 1973.

Hazoumé, Paul. 'Annales Dahoméennes. La conquête du royaume houéda par les Dahoméens au XVIIe siècle,' in *Bulletin de l'enseignement de l'Afrique Occidental Française,* Gorée, No. 45, Jan 1921, p. 43.

Hazoumé, Paul. 'La Mentalité du Dahoméen, Bokano, le Prêtre du Fa (Divinité des Oracles),' in *Conférence,* Cotonou, Dec 1941.

Hazoumé, Paul. 'La Mentalité du Dahoméen. La Consultation du Fa,' in *Conférence,* Cotonou, Dec 1941 & Jan 1942.

Hazoumé, Paul. 'Le Calendrier Dahoméen,' in *La Reconnaissance Africaine,* Cotonou, No. 43, Oct 1927, pp. 2-3, No. 44; Nov 1927, pp. 3-5.

Hazoumé, Paul. *Le Pacte de Sang au Dahomey,* Institut d'Ethnologie, Paris, 1937.

Hébert, J.C. 'Analyse structurale des géomancies comoriennes, malgaches, et africaines,' in *Journal de la Société des Africainistes,* Vol. XXXI, fasc. II, 1961, pp. 115-208. [Extensive bibliography.] *

Herskovits, Melville J. & Herskovits, Frances. 'An Outline of Dahomean Religious Belief,' in *Memoirs of the American AnthropologicaL Association,*

Menasha, Vol. III, no. 41, 1933.

Herskovits, Melville J. & Herskovits, Frances. 'The Art of Dahomey I,' in *American Magazine of Arts,* Washington, Vol. XXVII, No. 2, Feb 1934, pp. 67-76.

Herskovits, Melville J. 'The Art of Dahomey II,' in *American Magazine of Arts,* Washington, Vol. XXVII, No. 3, Mar 1934, pp. 124-31.

Herskovits, Melville J. 'African Gods and Catholic Saints in New World Negro Belief' in *American Anthropologist,* Menasha, new series, Vol. XXXIX, No. 4, Oct-Dec 1937, pp. 635-43.

Herskovits, Melville J. *Dahomey: An ancient West African Kingdom,* Augustin, New York, 1938, 2 vols; Vol. II, chapters XXX & XXXI, & passim. *

Herskovits, Melville J. *Life in a Haitian Valley,* Knopf, New York and London, 1937, p. 30.

Hounon-Amengansie, Chief & Mama Zogbé. *Mami Wata: Africa's Ancient Goddess Unveiled,* Vol. I. (*see* Vivian Hunter-Hindrew).

Hunter-Hindrew, Vivian (Mama Zogbé/Mama Issii). *Mami Wata: Africa's Ancient Goddess Unveiled.* 2nd Edition, MWHS, New York, 2005.

Iyalaja Ileana Alcamo, *The Source Iya Nla Primordial Yoruba Mother*, Athelia Henrietta Press, 2007.

Johnson, James. *Yoruba Heathenism,* Townsend, London, 1899.

Kassíbo, Bréhima. 'La géomancie ouest-africaine. Formes endogènes et emprunts extérieurs (West African Geomancy: Endogenous and Borrowed Forms)' in *Cahiers d'Etudes Africaines,* Vol. 32 (4), Cahier 128, 1992. pp. 541-596.

Labouret, Henri & Travélé, Moussa. 'Quelques aspects de la magie Africaine: Amulettes et Talismans au Soudan Français,' *Bulletin du Comité d'études historiques et scientifiques de l'Afrique Occidental Française,* Paris, Vol. X, Nos. 3-4, Jul-Dec 1927, pp. 480-545. *

Le Hérissé, A. *L'Ancien Royaume du Dahomey. Moeurs, Religion, Histoire.* Larose, Paris, 1911. *

Marcelin, Emile. 'Les Grands dieux du vodou haitien,' *Journal de la Société des Africainistes,* Paris, 1947 (?), pp. 51-135.

Maupoil, Bernard. *La Géomancie à l'ancienne Côte des Esclaves,* Institut d'Ethnologie, Paris, 1943, Travaux et Mémoires de l'Institut d'Éthnologie, Vol. 42. Extensive bibliography.*

Maupoil, Bernard. 'Contribution à l'étude de l'origine musulmane de la géomancie dans le Bas-Dahomey,' in *Journal de la Société des Africainistes,* Vol. XIII, Paris, 1943-6, pp. 1-94. *

Maupoil, Bernard. 'L'Ethnographie Dahoméenne et la probité scientifique,' in *L'Afrique Française,* Paris, No. 7, Jul 1937, pp. 358-60.

Maupoil, Bernard. 'Le Culte du vaudou,' in *M. J. Herskovits et l'Ethnographie Afro-américaine,* Outre-Mer, Paris, 3rd quarter, 1937, p. 2.

McClelland, E. M. 'The cult of Ifa among the Yoruba,' *Ethnographica,* Vol. I, London, 1982.

McClelland, E. M. 'The Significance of Number in the Odu of Ifa,' in *Africa,* Vol. XXXVI, No. 4, 1966, pp. 421-30.

Meek, C. K. *A Sudanese Kingdom. An Ethnographical Study of the Jukun-speaking Peoples of Nigeria,* Kegan Paul, London, 1931.

Mercier, Paul. 'Procédé de divination observé à Boutilimit-Mauritanie,' in *Notes Africaines,* Paris, 1947, No. 33, pp. 12-13.

Metraux, Alfred. *Voodoo in Haiti,* Deutsch, London, 1959, p. 29.

Monteil, Charles. 'La Divination chez les Noirs de l'Afrique occidentale française' in *Bulletin du Comité d'éudes historiques et scientifiques de l'Afrique occidentale française,* Paris, Vol. XIV, Nos. 1-2, Jan-Jun 1931. pp. 72 *et seq*., especially pp. 82-95, 108.

Monteil, Charles. *La Divination chez les Noirs de l'Afrique occidentale française,* Larose, Paris, 1932.

Osamaro, Ibie. *Ifism the Complete Works of Orunmila.*

Peek, Phillip M, 'African Divination Systems' in *African Divination Systems,* Indiana University Press, Bloomington, 1991.

Pemberton, John. *Insight and Artistry in African Divination.* Smithsonian, New York, 2000.

Prévaudeau, Marie-Madeleine. *Abomey La Mystique. Préf. de Pierre Mille,* Albert, Paris, 1936.

Prince, Raymond. *Ifa. Yoruba Divination and Sacrifice,* Ibadan University Press, Ibadan, 1963, p. 18.

Quénum, Maximilien Possy-Berry. 'Au pays des Fons,' *Bulletin du Comite d'Études historiques et scientifiques de l'Afrique Occidentale Française,* Paris, Vol. XVIII, Nos. 2-3, Apr-Sep 1935, reprinted Larose, Paris, 1938.

Regourd, Anne. 'La géomancie comme voie d'accès à un savoir ésotérique: un cas isolé au nord du Yémen?' in *Quaderni di Studi Arabi. Studi e Testi,* 3,

Venice, pp. 5-16.

Ribeiro, René. 'Projective Mechanisms and the Structuralization of Perception in Afro-brazilian Divination,' in *Revue Internationale d'Ethnopsychologie Normale et Pathologique,* Vol. I, (2), 1956, pp. 3-23.

Rosenthal, J. *Possession Ecstasy & Law in Ewe Voodoo.* University of Virginia, Charlottesville, 1998.

Sissoko, Filly Dabo. 'La Géomancie,' in *Bulletin de recherches soudanaises,* Paris, nos. 5-6, 1936, pp. 248-68.

Skertchly, J. A. *Dahomey as it is...,* Chapman & Hall, London, 1875, pp. 474-7, *et seq.*

Solichon. 'Croyances et superstitions dans le Bas-Dahomey,' in *Bulletin du Comite d'Études historiques et scientifiques de l'Afrique Occidentale Française,* Paris, Vol. IV, No. 4 , Oct-Dec 1921, pp. 667-71, 674.

Şowande, Fẹla. *Ifa,* Forward Press, Yaba, c.1964, p. 74.

Şowande, Fẹla. *Ifa. Odu Mimọ,* Ancient Religious Societies of African Descendants Association, Lagos, 1965, pp. viii, 70.

Spieth, Jakob. *Die Religion der Eweer in Süd-Togo,* Vandenhoek & Ruprecht, Gottingen, 1911. *See also* Boehmer, J.

Talbot, Percy Amaury. *The Peoples of Southern Nigeria,* Oxford University Press, London, 1926, 3 vols, Vol. II, p. 33-4, 185-8, 357 and *passim;* Vol. III, pp. 431-3.

Tegnoeus, Harry. 'Le Héros civilisateur.' *Contribution à l'étude ethnologique de la religion et de la sociologie africaine,* Stockholm, 1950, pp. 65-81.

Thompson, Frederick William. *West African Secret Societies. Their organisation, officials and teaching,* Witherby, London, 1929.

Tounsi, *see* Perron.

Trancart, André. 'Sur un procédé de divination de l'Adrar Mauritanien, le gzân,' in *Bulletin du Comité d'études historiques et scientifiques de l'Afrique Occidentale Française,* Paris, Vol. XXI, No. 104, Oct-Dec 1938, pp. 489-98.

Travélé, Moussa. *See* Labouret.

Verger, Pierre. 'Notes sur le culte des orisa et vodun à Bahia, la baie de tous les saints, au Brésil, et à l'ancienne Côte des Esclaves en Afrique,' in *Mémoires de l'Institut Français d'Afrique Noire,* No. 51, Dakar, 1957, rpt. Ifan, Dakar, 1957.

Verger, Pierre. *Dieux d'Afrique Culte des orishas et vodouns à l'ancienne Côte des Esclaves en Afrique et à Bahia, la baie de Tous les Saints au Bresil,* Paris, 1954.

Vigné d'Octon, Paul. *Terre de Mort (Soudan et Dahomey),* Lemerre, Paris, 1892.

Vincent, Jeanne Françoise. 'Divination et possession chez les Mofu, montagnards du Nord-Cameroun,' in *Journal de la Société des Africainistes,* Vol. LVI, Paris, 1971, pp. 71-132.

Wyndham, John. 'The Divination of Ifa (A Fragment),' in *Man,* Vol. XIX (80), 1919, pp. 151-3.

Madagascar: *Sikidy* (chapter 4)

With the exception of the work of a few writers like Lars Dahle, William Ellis and James Sibree, the most relevant works on *sikidy* are all in French, due no doubt to the colonial history of the island. Of these, Caquot has some of the few extant photographs of diviners practising *sikidy,* and Ferrand and Hébert are the most comprehensive. Flacourt is interesting particularly because his position as Governor of Madagascar gave him access to more information, and the fact that writing in the mid seventeenth century he was able to recognize the presence of a similar divinatory mode (geomancy) in Europe.

Ardant Du Picq, J. J. J. 'Etude comparative sur la divination en Afrique et à Madagascar,' *Bulletin du Comité d'études historiques et scientifiques de I 'Afrique Occidentale Française,* Paris, Vol. XIII, No. 1, Jan-Mar 1930, pp. 9-25. *

Ardant Du Picq, J. J. J. *L'influence islamique sur une population malayapoly-nésienne de Madagascar,* Charles-Lavauzelle, Paris, 1933.

Ascher, Marcia. *Malagasy Sikidy: A Case in Ethnomathematics,* in *Historia Mathematica,* 24, 1997, pp. 376-395. rpt. Academic Press, New York, 1997.

Berthier, Hughes. 'Notes sur les destins des quatre éléments, in *Bulletin de l'Académie malgache,* Vol. X, Paris, 1913, pp. 185-6.

Berthier, Hughes. *Notes et impressions sur les moeurs et coutumes du peuple malgache,* Tananarive, 1933. *

Bloch, Maurice, 'Astrology and Writing in Madagascar' in *Literacy in Traditional Societies,* ed. Jack Goody, CUP, Cambridge, 1968, pp. 278-297.

Caquot, André & Leibovici, Marcel. *La Divination,* Presses Universitaires de France, Paris, 1968, pp. 331-427, 473-551. *

Chemillier Marc, 'Divination et rationalité à Madagascar' in K. Chemla (éd.), *Actes du colloque de synthèse Histoire des savoirs,* Dec 2007, p. 241-258.

Chemillier Marc, 'Mathématiques de tradition orale' in *Mathématiques et sciences humaines,* 178, 2007 (2), p. 11-40.

Chemillier Marc, Jacquet D., Randrianary V., Zabalia M., 'Aspects mathématiques et cognitifs de la divination sikidy à Madagascar,' in *L'Homme,* 182, 2007, p. 7-40.

Chemillier Marc, Jacquet D., Randrianary V., Zabalia M., 'L'art des devins à

Madagascar, in *Pour la science,* dossier n° 47 'Mathématiques exotiques,' 2005, p. 90-95.

Chemillier Marc, *Les Mathématiques naturelles,* Paris, Odile Jacob, 2007.

Dahle, Lars. 'Sikidy and Vintana: Half-Hours with Malagasy Diviners,' in *The Antananarivo Annual* (ed. Rev. J. Sibree and Rev. R. Baron), Nos. X-XII, LMS Press, Antananarivo, pp. 219-34 (1886), 315-24 (1887) and 457-67 (1888). *

Dandouau, André. 'Le Sikidy sakalava,' in *Anthropos,* Vol. IX, nos. 3 & 6, Paris, 1914, pp. 546-63 & 833-72.

Dandouau, André. 'My famboazan'ny Sikidy (région d'Analava),' in *Bulletin de l'Académie malgache,* Vol. V, Paris, 1908, pp. 61-72.

Decary, Raymond. *La Divination malgache par le sikidy,* Geuthner, Paris, 1970. (Series 6. Vol. 9, Pub. du Centre Universitaire des langues orientales vivantes).

Decary, Raymond. *Moeurs et coutumes des Malgaches,* Payot, Paris, 1951.

Devèze, P. LA. 'Scènes de divination à Madagascar - Les Mpisikidy,' in *Le mois littéraire,* Paris, Mar 1913, pp. 244-50.

Douliot, H. *Journal du voyage fait sur la côte ouest de Madagascar,* 1891-1892, Paris, 1895.

Ellis, William. *History of Madagascar,* 2 vols, Fisher, London, 1838. *

Faublée, Jacques. 'Techniques divinatoires et magiques chez les Bara de Madagascar,' in *Journal de la Société des Africainistes,* Paris, 1952, Vol. XXI, pp. 127-38.

Ferrand, Gabriel. 'Les Destins des quatre éléments dans la magie malgache,' in *Revue des études ethnographiques et sociologiques,* Paris, 1908, pp. 277-8.

Ferrand, Gabriel. *Les Musulmans à Madagascar et aux iles Comores,* Algiers, 1891, pp. 73-100. Paris, 1902, Appendix, pp. 141-50. *

Ferrand, Gabriel. 'Madagascar,' in *Encyclopedia of Islam* (old edition), Vol. 3, pp. 70-4.

Ferrand, Gabriel. 'Un chapitre d'astrologie arabico-malgache,' in *Journal asiatique,* Paris, Sep-Oct 1905, pp. 193-273. *

Flacourt, Étienne de. *Histoire de la grande isle Madagascar...,* Paris, 1661, pp. 171-8. *

Gardenier, William J, 'Divination and Kinship among the Sakalava of West

Madagascar' in *Madagascar: Society and History,* edited Kottack, Rakotoarisoa, Southall, Vérin, Carolina Press, Durham, 1986, pp. 337-351.

Grandidier, Alfred & Guillaume. 'Ethnographie de Madagascar,' in *l'Histoire physique, nationale et politique de Madagascar,* vols. III, IV, Paris, 1917, pp. 458-507. *

Hébert, J. C. 'Analyse structurale des géomancies comoriennes, malgaches, et africaines,' in *Journal de la Société des Africainistes,* Vol. XXXI, (II), 1961, pp. 115-208. [Extensive bibliography.] *

Leibovici, Marcel. *See* Caquot, A.

Pennick, Nigel. *Madagascar Divination,* Fenris-Wolf, Cambridge, 1976 (?).

Pennick, Nigel. *The Oracle of Geomancy: The Divinatory Arts of Raml, Geomantia, Sikidy , and I Ching.* Capall Bann, 1995.

Rabedimy, J. F., *Pratiques de divination a Madagascar: Technique du Sikidy en pays Sakalava-Menabe,* ORSTO, Paris, No 51, 1976.

Russillon, Henri. 'Le Sikidy malgache,' in *Bulletin de l'Académie malgache,* Vol. VI, Paris, 1909, pp. 115-62.

Sibree, James. *Madagascar before the Conquest,* Fisher Unwin, London, 1896. [copied almost verbatim from Lars Dahle].

Southall, Adrian, 'Common Themes in Malagasy Culture' in *Madagascar: Society and History,* edited Kottack, Rakotoarisoa, Southall, Vérin, Carolina, Durham, 1986, pp. 411-426.

Steinschneider, Moritz. 'Die S[i]kidy oder geomantischen Figuren,' in *Zeitschrift der Deutschen Morgenländischen Gesellschaft* 31, Leipzig, 1877, pp. 762-5. **

Sussman, Robert. 'Divination among the Sakalava of Madagascar' in *Extrasensory Ecology,* ed. J. K. Long, Scarecrow, New Jersey, 1977, pp. 271-291.

Trautmann, René. 'La Divination à la Côte des Esclaves et à Madagascar. La Vôdou - le Fa - le Sikidy,' in *Mémoires de l'Institut Français d'Afrique Noire,* No. 1, Larose, Paris, 1939. *

Vérin, P & N. Rajaonarimanana. 'Divination in Madagascar: the Antemoro Case and the Diffusion of Divination' in P. M. Peek, *African Divination Systems.* Indiana University, Bloomington, 1991.

European Geomancy (chapters 5-8)

Texts here are too numerous to mention, but the seminal ones are those of Henry Cornelius Agrippa, Christopher Cattan, Bartholomew of Parma, Cocles, Robert Fludd, Gerard of Cremona (or Sabbioneta) and Peter de Abano.

In French the work of Tannery, Caslant (taken from Cattan), Delatte and Charmasson are important for the historical details and bibliographies. The work of John Heydon is mainly derivative, as are most twentieth-century works in English, with writers like Deacon contributing towards the general confusion between geomantic books and *libri delle sorti*, rather than clarifying the issue.

Lynn Thorndike's monumental work remains the most reliable background work on the history of European geomancy.

Abano, Pietro. *'Modo Judicandi Questiones Secundum Petrum de Abano Patavinum'* in Charmasson, *Recherches sur une Technique Divinatoire: La Geomancie dans l'Occident Mediaeval,* Droz, Geneva, 1980.

Agrippa, Henry Cornelius. 'On Geomancy,' in *Fourth Book of Occult Philosophy,* London, 1655; reprinted Askin Publishers, London, 1978. Edited by Stephen Skinner, Ibis Press, Berwick, 2005. *

Agrippa, Henry Cornelius. *Of The Vanitie and Uncertaintie of Artes and Sciences,* California State University, Berkeley, 1974, pp.60, 109, 408.

Agrippa, Henry Cornelius. *Opera* (Latin ed. Richard H. Popkin), Hildesheim, 1970, Vol. I, pp. 500-26. *

Agrippa, Henry Cornelius. *Three Books of Occult Philosophy,* London, 1651, New edition edited by Donald Tyson. Vol. I, book 1, chapter 57; book II, chapters 48, 51.

Agrippa, Cornelius (pseud.). *Oracle du Destin: or Ancient and Modern Ladies Oracle,* Evans, London, 1857.

Agrippa, Henry Cornelius (pseud.). *The Ladies Oracle,* Evelyn, London, 1962.

Aladin Ben Abdul Wahhâb (pseud.). *Nevestes grosses arabisches Punktierbuch. Nach den untrüglichsten orientalischen Quellen des Aladin ben Abdul Wahhâb ins Deutsche Übertragen,* Reutlingen, n.d.

Alfakinus. *See Fasciculus Geomanticus.*

Ambelain, Robert. *La Géomancie magique,* Niclaus, Paris, 1940, pp. 198-9. *

Anon. *Ausfürliches Punktierbuch. In neuer und gründlicher Weise ausgearbeitet und vervollständigt nach den Aufzeichnungen des weisen Arabers Harun al Raschid und der weltberühmten französischen Wahrsagerin Lenormand,* Reutlingen, 1920.

Anon. *Beliebtes Punktier-Buch mit einem belustigenden Frage und Antwortspeil...* Leipzig, n.d.

Anon. *Curieuse und ganz neue Art zu Punctiren. Aus dem Arabischen ins Deutsche übersetzet von einem Leibhaber dieser Kunst,* Darmstadt [c. 1970]. (Facsimile reprint of ed. published Weimar, S.H. Hoffman 1768).

Anon. *El Gran libro de los oraculos, arte de adivinar la suerte presente y futura de las personas, por el metodo ejipcio y por el de los astros. Manuscrito hallado en las catacumbas de Ejipto cuando la espedicion de los Franceses, y cuya propiedad fue esclusiva des Emperador, Napoleon... Contiene además la historia de los antiguos oraculos, la zodialogia ó sea la ciencia de pronosticar los tempos por medio de lost planetas,* Madrid, 1841.

Anon. *Géomancie où l'art de connaître les choses secrétes par points faits en terre,* Strasbourg, 1609.

Anon. *Geomantia Künstlicher und rechtschaffner gebrauch der alten kleynen Geomancey mit welcher durch hilff der Rechnung und des menschen Tauffnamens sampt der Planeten wirckung in iren stunden allen Adams kindern Künsstiger züfall des gütten bösen glücks eröffnet wirt...* Jordan, Mainz, 1534.

Anon. *Geomantia metrica seu ars punctandi nova, 1775.*

Anon. *Geomantia,* Jordan, Meintz, 1532.

Anon. *Geomantia. Künstlicher und rechtschaffner Gebrauch der alten kleynen Geomancey...* , Mainz, 1534.

Anon. *Neuestes Punktierbüchlein nebst Planeten für beide Geschlechter...,* Berlin, n.d.

Anon. *Neuvermehrtes, und mit einer mercklichen Anzahl wohl auszgeson-nener ungemeiner Staatsfragen verneuertes Oraculum, in Welchem allerhand verborgene Sachen menschlicher Zufälle künstiger Begebenheiten aus dem Grunde der bekandten Geomantie calculirt und artig entworffen... von Einem den die Unbekandten nicht Kennen,* Förster, Frankfurt, 1717.

Anon. *Punktierbuechlein nebst Blumen...,* Mulheim, n.d.

Anon. *Vollkommene Geomantia oder so genante Punctier-Kunst,* Freystadt, Jena, 1702.

Anon. *Vollkommene Punktierkunst oder...,* Vienna, n.d.

Aubier, Cathérine. *La Geomancia.* Signos/Granica, Barcelona, 1985.

Axon, W. E. 'Divination by Books,' in *Manchester Quarterly,* Vol. 26, Manchester, 1907.

Belot, Jean. *Les Œuvres de M. Jean Belot, curé de Mil Monts, Professeur aux Sciences Divines et Célestes. Contenant la Chiromence, Physiononie, l'Art de Memoyre de Raymond Lulle, Traicté des Divinations, Augures et Songes,* etc..., Rouen, 1640 & Lyon, 1654.

Bernardus Silvestris. *See* Savorelli *and see* Burnett.

Bolte, Johannes. 'Zur Geschichte der Losbücher,' in *Georg Wickram's Werke,* Tübingen, Stuttgart, 1903, Vol. IV, pp. 276-348 (especially pp. 288-9).

Bolte, Johannes. 'Zur geschichte der Punktier und Losbücher,' in *Jahrbuch für Historische Volkskunde,* ed. W. Franger, *Die Volkskunde und ihre Grenzgebiete,* Berlin, 1925.

Boncompagni, Prince. *Atti dell' Accademia dei Nuovi Lincei,* Vol. IV, Rome, 1851, pp. 100 *et seq.*

Braswell-Means, Laurel. 'The popular art of geomancy in the mediaeval West and contemporary Asia' in *Journal of Popular Culture,* Vol. 23 no. 4, Spring 1990. pp. 131-43. [This study completely confuses Chinese and Western geomancy, which are not at all the same thing. Amazingly academics who know about Western geomancy, but have no knowledge of feng shui, continue to mix these things up.]

[Breteau]. *Grand jeu de société. Pratiques secrètes de Mlle. Lenormand. Explication et application des cartes astro-mytho-hermétiques, avec... la manière de faire les talismans; suivi de la géomancie et d'un double dictionnaire des fleurs emblématiques,* 1st part, pp. XIV + 309, Chez l'Editeur, Paris, 1845.

Brett, Yvonne Margaret. 'Astronomical and Astrological Illustrations in printed books of the later Renaissance, with special reference to *Libri delle Sorti,*' M. Phil. Thesis, University of London, 1975, pp. 57-72.

Brewer, Derek. [ed.]. *Geoffrey Chaucer,* Bell, London, 1974.

Brini. *See* Savorelli.

Burnett, Charles S. F. 'What is the *Experimentarius* of Bernardus Silvestris? A preliminary survey of the material' in *Archives d'histoire doctrinale et littéraire du moyen age.* XLIV, 1977, pp. 79-125. [Reprinted in *Magic and Divination in the Middle Ages.* Variorum Collected Studies Series CS557, 1996.][Includes an edition of the *Experimentarius* of Bernardus Silvestris.]

Burnett, Charles. 'The *Sortes Regis Amalrici*: an Arabic Divinatory Work in the Latin Kingdom of Jerusalem?' in *Scripta Mediterranea,* 19-20, 1998-99. pp. 229-37.

Carey, Hilary M. *Courting Disaster: Astrology at the English court and university in the later Middle Ages*. St. Martin's Press, New York, 1992. [Sections on the geomantic books of Richard II of England and Charles V of France.]

Carreras y Candi, Francisco. 'Un libro de geomancia popular del segle XIII,' in *Miscelánea histórica catalana,* Series 1, Barcelona, 1905, pp. 161-74.

Case, John. *The Angelical Guide*. London: Isaac Dawkins, 1697.

Caslant, Eugène. *Traité Élémentaire de géomancie,* Editions Véga, Paris, 1935. [with bibliography by Dr Rouhier] *

Cattan, Christophe De. *La Géomance du Seigneur Christofe de Cattan, gentilhomme Genevois, livre non moins plaisant et récréatif, que d'ingénieuse invention, pour sçavoir toutes choses présentes, passées et advenir, avec la Roue de Pythagoras. Le tout corrigé, augmenté, & mis en lumiere par Gabriel du Preau...*, Gilles, Paris, 1558, pp. 178 ff. *

Cattan, Christophe de. *The Geomancie of Maister Christopher Cattan Gentleman... translated out of French into our English tongue* [by Francis Sparry], Wolfe, London, 1591 & 1608. *

Charmasson, Thérèse. 'Les premiers traités latins de géomancie' in *Cahiers de civilisation médiévale,* Vol. 21, 1978, pp. 121-36. [covers all the main mediaeval European MSS on geomancy.] *

Charmasson, Thérèse. *Recherches sur une technique divinatoire: la géomancie dans l'Occident médiéval*. Centre de Recherches d'Histoire de et de Philosophie de la IVe Section de l'École Pratique des Hautes Études, 44. Droz, Geneva, 1980. [Includes a list of manuscripts arranged by both author or incipit, and current location.] *

Chatterjee, Rushick Mohun. *Extracts from works on Astrology... containing genethlialogy, horary, mundane, atmospherical and medical astrology, to which are added extracts from geomancy, chiromancy, physiognomy and Napoleon Buonaparte's 'Book of Fate': with tables for calculating nativities,* 2 vols, Jyotish Prokash, Calcutta, 1880-3.

Cocles, Bartholomeo. *La Geomantia di Bartholomeo Cocle filosofo integerrimo; nuovissimamente tradotta e ancho datta in luce,* Venice, 1550. *

Colonna. *Le nouveau miroir de la Fortune, ou abrégé de la Géomance, pour la récréation des personnes curieuses de cette science,* Paris, 1726.

Contini, Gianfranco (ed.). *Maestre,* 'Un Poemetto provenzale di argomento geomantico' in *Collectanea Friburgensia,* fascicule 27, Fribourg, 1940.*

Craven, J. B. *Doctor Robert Fludd... Life and Writings,* London, 1902.

Crowley, Aleister. 'Geomancy' in *Equinox,* Vol. 1, no. 2, Simpkin Marshall, London, 1909.

Curtze, Max. *'Der Liber embadorum* des Savasorda in der Übersetzung des Plato von Tivoli,' in *Abhandl. zur Geschichte der Mathematik,* Vol. 12, Leipzig, 1902, pp. 3-183.

De Abano, Peter. [*Geomantia*] *Novamente dall' eccell.* MS. Musio da Capoa ricorsa, 2 parts, Venice, 1546-50.

De Abano, Peter. *Comincia la Geomantia di Pietro d'Abano* (in 2 parts), Venice, 1556, 1552.

De Abano, Peter. *Geomantia de Pietro d'Abano nuovamente tradotta di Latino in volgare per il Tricasso Mantuano,* Venice, 1542 & 1550. *

De Abano, Peter. *Œuvres Magiques... avec des secrètes occultes,* Liége, 1788.

Deacon, Richard. *The Book of Fate,* Muller, London, 1976.

Delatte, Armand & Louis. 'Un Traité Byzantin de Géomancie - codex Parisinus 2419' in *Melanges Franz Cumont, Annuaire de l'Institut de philologie et d'histoire orientales et slaves.* Université Libre de Bruxelles, Brussels 1936, Vol. 4, pp. 574-658. [Contains a Bibliography of European Geomancy]. *

Dubois, Philippe. *Geomancie.* Paris: Albin Michel, 1987.

Dubois, Philippe. *Geomancia: su práctica e interpretaciones adivinatorias.* Madrid: La Tabla de Esmeralda, 1988.

Ebneter, Theodor. *Poéme sur les signes géomantiques en ançien provençale,* Urs Graf-Verlag, Olten and Lausanne, 1955.

Fludd, de Pisis, *et al. Fasciculus Geomanticus: in quo varia variorum opera Geomantica continentur,* Verona, 1687 & 1704. Containing:

1) Robert Fludd. *De animae intellectualis scientiae... seu geomantia,* pp. 3-18.
2) Roberti Flud[d]. *Tractatus de Geomantia in Quatuor Libros Divisus,* pp. 19-160.
3) Robert Fludd. *De Geomantia Morborum,* pp. 161-70.
4) H[enri] de Pisis. *Opus Geomantiae Completum in Libros Tres divisum Quorum.* [reprinted Lyon, 1638 & 1625], pp. 171-523.
5) *Quaestiones Geomantiae Alfakini arabici filii a Platone. In latinus translatae ex Antiquo Manuscripto de Anno 1525. Nunc prima vice typis datae.*

[Translated originally from Arabic by Plato of Tivoli c. 1134-45], pp. 525-644.

6) *Tabulae geomanticae seu liber singularis de tribus ultimis,* 1693-1704.

Fludd, Robert. 'De Divinatiore Iatromathematica' in *Katholikon Medicorum Katoptron,* 1631.

Fludd, Robert. 'Tractatus Primi. Sectionis II. Portio II. De Animae intellectualis scientia seu Geomantia hominibus appropriata, quorum radii intellectuales extrinsecus, hoc est, circa negotia mundana versantes, & à centro dissipati in centrum recolliguntur,' in *Utriusque Cosmi…Historia,* Vol. II, part 2 (pp. 37-46), Oppenheim, 1619 [Chapters I to VI of this text reprinted with slight modifications in *Fasciculus Geomanticus* (q.v.).]

Fludd, Robert. 'Tractatus Secundi, Pars XI. De Geomantia in quatuor libros divisa,' in *Utriusque Cosmi Maioris scilicet et Minoris Metaphysica, Physica atque Technica Historia,* Vol. I, part 2 (pp. 715-83), Oppenheim, Frankfurt 1617-18. [Reprinted Verona 1687 and 1704 under the title: Roberti Flud 'Tractatus de Geomantia in Quatuor Libros Divisus,' in *Fasciculus Geomanticus* (q.v.)]

Fludd, Robert *see* Pierre Piobb.

Fränger, W. *See* Bolte, J.

G, Maestre. *See* Contini, G.

Gascon, Roger. *Pratique de la Geomancie.* De Vecchi, Paris, 1990.

Geber, Gio[v]anni. *De la Geomantia dell' eccel. Filosofo Gioanni Geber,* Venice, 1552.

Gerard Of Cremona. 'Of Astronomical Geomancy,' in *Fourth Book of Occult Philosophy,* London, 1655; reprinted Askin Publishers, London, 1978. Edited by Stephen Skinner, Ibis Press, Berwick, 2005. *

Gerardus Cremonensis. *Géomancie Astronomique...* traduite par le Sieur de Salerne, Salerne, Paris, 1669 & d'Hourg, Paris, 1697.

Godwin, Joscelyn. *Robert Fludd,* Thames & Hudson, London, 1979.

Greer, John Michael. *The Art and Practice of Geomancy, Divination, Magic, and Earth Wisdom of the Renaissance.* Weiser, York Beach, 2009.

Hali-ben-Omar, Abu. (pseud.) *Vollenkommene Geomantia, deren erster Theil die aufs neue revidirte... Punctier-Kunst in sich begreift... Arabers Abu-Hali--ben-Omar neimahls vorhin gedruckte astrologia terrestris oder Indische Stern-Kunde...* Leipzig, 1735. *

Hartmann, Franz. *The Principles of Astrological Geomancy,* Rider, London, 1913.

Herbert, Henry & Sidney, *see* Pembroke, Graf.

Heydon, John. *El Havareuna or the English Physitians Tutor in the Astrobolismes of Mettals Rosie Crucian... All Harmoniously united and operated by Astromancy and Geomancy...* London, 1665.

Heydon, John. *Theomagia, or the Temple of Wisdom,* 3 vols, London, 1662-4.*

Hofmann, Albert [Dr Berthof]. *Wie stelle ich ein Horoskop? Kurzer Schlüssel zur Geomantie (Punktierkunst) auf astrologischer Grundlage nach Agrippa von Nettesheim und Gerhard von Cremona,* Berlin, 1919.

Howe, Ellic. *Raphael, or the Royal Merlin,* Aborfield, London, 1964.

Jaulin, Robert. *La Géomancie. Analyse formelle* with *Notes Mathematiques* by Françoise Dejean and Robert Ferry, (Cahiers de I'Homme, N.S. IV.) La Haye, Paris, 1966. *

Josten, Conrad Hermann. 'Robert Fludd's Theory of Geomancy and his Experiences at Avignon in the Winter of 1601 to 1602' in *Journal of the Courtauld and Warburg Institutes,* Vol. XXVII, London, 1964. *

Khamballah, Hadji. *La Géomancie traditionelle...Traité pratique d'enseignement et dictionnaire d'interprétation géomantique,* Editions Véga, Paris, 1947.*

King, Francis & Skinner Stephen. *Techniques of High Magic,* C. W. Daniel, London, and Warner Destiny, New York, 1976.

King, Francis. *Astral Projection,* Neville Spearman, London, 1971.

Kirchenhoffer, Herman. *The Book of Fate,* London, 1826.

Láng, Benedek. *Unlocked Books: Manuscripts of Learned Magic in the Mediaeval Libraries of Central Europe,* Pennsylvania State University, Pennsylvania, 2008.

Layne, Meade. *The Art of Geomancy.* Borderland Sciences, Bayside, n. d.

Lemay, Richard. *See* Pomponazzi, P.

Lenormand, Mlle. *The Secret and Astro-Mythological Practices.* (Card pack with geomantic squeezer marks in the upper left corner), 19th century.

Lyndoe, Edward. *Everybody's Book of Fate and Fortune,* Odhams, London, 1935.

Martin of Spain *see* Means, L.

Maxwell, J. *La Divination,* Paris, 1927, pp. 135-7.

Means, Laurel. 'A translation of Martin of Spain's *De Geomancia*' in *Popular and Practical Science of Mediaeval England*, ed. Lister M. Matheson, Colleagues Press, East Lansing, 1994. pp. 61-121.

Ménéstrier, Françoise. *La Philosophie des Images,* 2 Vols, Paris, 1682-3 & Lyon, 1694.

Meyer, Paul. *La Géomance du Seigneur Christofe de Cattan...*, 1567.

Morbeca, Guglielmo Della. *Libro della geomantia fatto da frate.*

Morbeta, Gilles De (trans.). *Introduction à la Géomancie.*

Morbeta, Gilles De (trans.). *La Géomancie Plaine et Parfaicte.*

Néroman, Dom. *Grande Encyclopédie illustrée des sciences occultes.* 2 vols, Strasbourg, 1937. *See also* Rougie, Maurice.

North, John. *Chaucer's Universe.* Oxford: Clarendon Press, 1988. pp. 234-43.

Pedrazzi, Maino. 'Le Figure della Geomanzia: un Gruppo Finito Abeliano' in *Physis,* XIV, 1972, fasc. 2, pp. 146-161.

Pembroke, Graf and Gräfinn von [pseudonym for Henry and Sidney Herbert]. *Sämliche Werke der Punctirkunst nach welcher ein jeder sich selbst die Nativität stellen und wissen kan, ab er in die Welt glücklich oder unglücklich seyn, und ober jung oder alt sterben werde,* Lebrecht, Frankfurt and Leipzig, 1781.

Pembroke, Lady Emmy (pseud.). *Neues Punktierbüchlein oder die Kunst von dem Schicksal...*, Reutlingen, n.d.

Peruchio, Le Sieur De. *La Chiromance, la Physionomie et la Géomance, avec la signification des Nombres & l'usage de la Roüe de Pytagore,* Paris, 1657 & 1663.

Peucer, Gaspar. *Les Devins ou Commentaires des principales sortes de devinations,* Anvers, 1584.

Pingree, David, 'Hellenophilia Versus the History of Science' in *Isis* 83, 1992, pp. 554-563.

Piobb, Pierre, V. *Traité de Géomancie: étude du macrocosme,* Paris, 1947. [Translation of Robert Fludd's *De Geomantia,* q.v.].

Pisis, Henri De. *Opus geomantiae completum in libros III divisum,* Lyons, 1638 [reprinted in *Fasciculus Geomanticus* (q.v.)]. *

Placidus, Janus. *Jani Placidi a Ponte Albo med. cult. vanitas geomantiae detecta oder Bedencken über die vorjetzt so hochberühmte Punctir-Kunst,* Jena, 1703.

Poinsot, M. C. *The Book of Fate and Fortune,* Grant Richards, London, 1932.

Pomponazzi, Pietro. *Libri V de fato, de libero arbitrio et de praedestinatione* (ed. Richard Lemay), Lucano, 1957.

Popkin, Richard, *see* Agrippa, H.C.

Préau, Gabriel Du. *See* Cattan, C.

Raphael [Robert Cross Smith]. *The Philosophical Merlin,* London, 1822.

Raphael [Robert Cross Smith]. *The Straggling Astrologer,* or *The Astrologer of the Nineteenth Century or Compendium of Astrology, Geomancy and Occult Philosophy* (ed. for the Society of the Mercurii), London, 1825.

Raphael [Robert Cross Smith]. *Urania; or, the Astrologer's Chronicle,* London, 1825.

Raphael [Robert Cross Smith]. *The Royal Book of Fate,* London, 1828.

Raphael [Robert Cross Smith]. *The Royal Book of Dreams,* London, 1830.

Raphael [Robert Cross Smith]. *Raphael's Witch,* London, 1831.

Raphael [Robert Cross Smith]. *The Familiar Astrologer,* London, 1831.

Raphael [Robert Cross Smith]. *The Pythoness of the East,* London, 1894.

Raphael [Robert Cross Smith]. *The Prophetic Messenger,* London, 1927.

Raphael [Robert Cross Smith]. *The Book of Fate...,* London, n.d.

Regardie, Israel. *A Practical Guide to Geomantic Divination,* Aquarian, London, 1972.

Regardie, Israel. *The Golden Dawn,* Vol. 4, Llewellyn, St Paul, 1970.

Rougie, Maurice. *La Géomancie Retrouvée,* Paris, 1948. *See also* Néroman.

Rouhier, Dr. *See* Caslant, E.

Rowse, A. L. *Simon Forman,* Weidenfeld & Nicolson, London, 1974.

Sa[u]nders, Richard. *Physiognomie, and Chiromancie, Metoposcopie, The Symmetrical Proportions and Signal Moles of the Body, fully and accurately explained...,* London, 1671.

Sa[u]nders, Richard. *Physiognomie... divinative, Steganographical and Lullian sciences,* London, 1653.

Sarton, George. *Introduction to the History of Science,* vols. 1-3, (Carnegie Institution Pub. No. 376). Williams & Wilkins, Baltimore, 1927-47.

Savasorda *see* Curtze.

Savorelli, Mirella Brini [ed.]. 'Un manuale di geomanzia presentato da Bernardo Silvestre da Tours: (XII secolo): *l'Experimentarius,*' in *Rivista critica di storia della filosofia,* fascicule III, Florence, 1959, pp. 283-342.

Schwei, Priscilla, & Ralph Pestka. *The Complete Book of Astrological Geomancy.* Llewellyn, St Paul, 1990.

Sieur de Salerne, *see* Gerardus Cremonensis.

Silvestris, Bernardus *see* Savorelli *and see* Burnett.

Skeat, Theodore Cressy. 'An early Mediaeval "Book of Fate": the *Sortes XII Patriarchum* with a note on Books of Fate in general' in *Medieval and Renaissance Studies,* Vol. III, London, 1954.

Skinner, Stephen. *The Oracle of Geomancy,* Warner Destiny, New York, 1977, rpt Prism, Bridport, 1977. *See also* King, Francis *

Smith, Robert Cross. *See* Raphael.

Sparry, Francis, *see* Cattan.

Sylvester, Bernard. *See* Savorelli *and see* Burnett.

Taille, Jean de la. *La Géomance abrégée de Jean de la Taille de Bondaroy, gentilhomme de Beauce, pour sçavoir les choses passées, préséntes et futures...,* Breyer, Paris, 1574. *

Tannery, Paul. '*Geomantia nova.* Notice sur des fragments d'onomatomancie arthmétique' in *Notices et Extraits de mss. de la Bibliothèque Nationale,* Vol. XXXI, Paris, 1885, pp. 231-60.

Tannery, Paul. 'Practica Geometriae' in *Bulletin des sciences mathématiques,* Vol. 23, pp. 140-5, 1899. [the earliest Latin geomantic text]. *

Tannery, Paul. 'L'Introduction de la géomancie en Occident et le traducteur Hugo Sancelliensis' in *Mémoires Scientifiques,* 13 Vols, Gauthier Villars, Paris, 1920, Vol 4. pp. 318-353.

Tayssonnière, Seigneur de Chaneius, Guillaume La. *La Géomance, par laquelle on peut prévoir, deviner et prédire de toutes choses doubteuses et incertaines. Science repurgée des superfluitez qui l'offusquoyent, séparée de l'Astrologie et réduite à sa pure simplicité et vraye purité ancienne, pour les gens d'esprit, par tables briefves et familiéres,* Lyon, 1575. *

Thorndike, Lynn. *A History of Magic and Experimental Science,* vols. I-VIII, Columbia University Press, 1923-58. *

Thorndike, Lynn. *Michael Scot,* Nelson, London, 1965.

Treswell, Ralph. *See* Cattan, Christopher.

Turner, Robert, trans. 'Of Geomancy' in Henry Cornelius Agrippa, *Fourth Book of Occult Philosophy.* London, 1655, reprinted Askin, London, 1978. New edited by Stephen Skinner, Ibis Press, Berwick, 2005. *

Webster, Richard. *Geomancy for Beginners: Simple Techniques for Earth Divination.* Llewellyn, Wooddale, 2011.

Weisen, Meister. *Geomancj. Die viertzehen Weisen Mayster in der Geomancj,* Strasbourg, c. 1550.

Wietfeldt, Anna. *Neues Punktierbüchlein oder: Das Orakel in der Rocktasche...,* Muhlhausen, 1907.

Yates, Frances. *The Rosicrucian Enlightenment,* Routledge & Kegan Paul, London, 1972.

Ziegler, Aloysius K. *Histoire de la Géomancie latine du milieu de XIIe siécle au milieu de XVIIe siécle.* (Ecole Nationale des Chartes, Positions des Théses soutenues par les élèves de la promotion de 1934), Ecole Nationale des Chatres, Paris. pp. 159-170. *

Manuscripts

Manuscripts are designated by their place or collection and grouped geographically into London, Oxford, Cambridge, and then continental European manuscripts. I have tried to err on the side of completeness rather than risking the omission of a relevant manuscript, consequently some *libri delle sorti* and manuscripts of only peripheral interest to geomancy have crept into this list. More detail on the Latin manuscripts can be had in Charmasson (1980). Manuscript Arabic works are best documented in Savage-Smith (1980) and the *Encyclopaedia of Islam* (new edition article on *khatt)* should be consulted, while Paul Tannery provides the most extensive listing of relevant Greek manuscripts.

However this list contains every relevant manuscript mentioned by Charmasson, Sarton, Thorndike and Steinschneider, and is therefore very extensive in terms of manuscripts in European languages. There are additional interesting notes about Hebrew and Arabic manuscripts held in the Bibliothèque Nationale in Caslant (1935) although some of Caslant's and Rouhier's historical interpretations should be taken with a grain of salt.

UK

LONDON

British Library:

Additional 2472

Bernard Silvestris. *Experimentarius* (fifteenth century).

Additional 8790

La Geomantia del S. Christoforo Cattaneo, Genovese, l'inventore di detti Almadel Arabico.

Additional 9702

Bian Al Raml Turcice (Turkish geomancy ascribed to Daniel the prophet).

Additonal 10362

Bartholomaei de Parma, *Flores quaestionum et judiciorum Veritatis Geomanciae* (fourteenth century).

Additional 15236

ff. 95-112. *Prenosticon Socratis, Basilei* (Fortune telling by 'lots').

ff. 130-152r. *Libellus Alchandiandi de astrologia judiciali* (geomancy, late thirteenth or early fourteenth century), Bernard Silvestris.

Additional 21173

f. 97b Latin geomancy (twelfth-fourteenth century).

Additional 25881

f. 238b. Daniel, Prophet, *Oraculum et visio* (sixteenth century).

Additional 33788

Le Dodeche[d]ron de Maistre Jean Meung, qui est le livre des sorts et la fortune des nombres (sixteenth century *libro delle sorti* printed in Paris 1556 and later in London 1618, translated by Sir W.B. Knight).

Additional 33955

Lorenzo Spirito *Libro della Ventura* (sixteenth or seventeenth century Italian *libro delle sorti*, consulted by the cast of 3 dice).

Additional 40093

Libro de Goraloth (eighteenth-nineteenth century Ladino. A book of lots in Hebrew characters containing incantations).

Arundel 66

ff. 269-277b *'Incipit Liber scientie ar*[z]*ienalis de judiciis geomansie ab Alpharino filio Abrahe Judeo editus et a Platone* [Plato of Tivoli] *de Hebreico sermone in Latinum translatus sequitur nomina fisurariny [?] cum fisuris geomansie'* (Illuminated vellum MS of fourteenth-fifteenth century).

ff. 277b-287b *'Tabulae Humfridi Ducis Glowcestriae in Judiciis artis geomansie'* (fifteenth century).

Arundel 268

f. 75. Jacob Ben Isaac Alkhindi *de judiciis liber* (Latin, fourteenth century).

Cotton Appendix VI

f. 109. *Alkindi judicia* ['Alkindi's Judgements'] translated by Roberti de Ketene [Robert of Chester].

Harleian 671

ff. 2-168b. Tracts on Geomancy, Sections 3-22 (ranging from illuminated black letter on old vellum to sixteenth century paper: one of the best collections of MSS on geomancy covering such a wide range of centuries).

Harleian 2404

Codex... *in quo continentur Tractatus insequentes Geomantici*

ff. 1-19. *Indices Geomancie Indëane, 'Haec est Geomancia Indeana, que*

vocatur Filia Astronomie; quam fecit unus Sapientum Indie; et est facta per 7 Planetas.'
ff. 19-33. *Geomancia Indeana.*
ff. 33-58. Geomantic questions.

Harleian 3814
ff. 105-118v (art. 6). *Liber sortilegus, ad solvendas certas quaestiones accommodatus, cum tabulis, et responsis, versibus Leonis conceptis.* (A *libro delle sorti*, fourteenth century.)
ff. 119-139. Bernard Silvestris.

Harleian 3892
ff. 43-58v. Bernard Silvestris.

Harleian 4166
ff. 13-51v. *Artis Geomanticae & Astrologicae Tractatus quinq...* (fifteenth century).
ff. 52-65v, 67-70v. *Comprehensum Intus omnium figuram prima...*

Harleian 6482
A quarto, containing the Characters of the sixteen figures of Geomancy, expressed in the great & lesser Squares of [Dr John Dee's] *Tabula sancta;* together with an explication of the seven Tables of Enoch, which are charged with Spirits or Genii, both good and bad of several Orders & Hierarchies, which the wise King Solomon made use of. Collected from Dr [Thomas] Rudd's Papers by Peter Smart, M.A. It contains remarks on Sylphs, Salamanders, Gnomes, &c.

Royal 12.C. v
ff. 3v-202. *Presentum geomancie libellum. 'Prime omnium bonorum cause soli deo...'* (An elaborate astrological geomancy compiled for King Richard II in March 1391). *See* Plate I and Figure 23. *See also* CLM 1697.

Royal 12.C. xii
f. 94. Book of Sortes grouped under birds' names.
f. 98b. Book of Sortes grouped under planets' names.
ff. 98v-105v. *Par le Soliel...*
f. 108-123. Bernard Silvestris, *Liber Experimentarius* (fourteenth century: 3 libri delle sorti) *(See* Savorelli, M.B.).

Royal 12.C. xiv
ff. 2-17. Bernard Silvestris.

Royal 12.C. xvi
ff. 1-88. Roland Scriptoris. (Physician to the Duke of Bedford.)

'Compilatorium sive aggregatorium tocius artis geomanciae' (mid 15th cent.)

Royal 12.C. xviii

f. 26. Abraham Ben Meir Aben Ezra, Spanish Rabbi and astrologer (d. 1174). *Electiones Abraham,* Latin (fourteenth century). *Not* the same translation as that by Peter de Abano printed Venice 1507.

Royal 12.E. iv

Bernard Silvestris, *Liber Experimentarius* (fourteenth century). *(See also* Royal 12. C. xii, Harleian 3892 f. 43, and Sloane 2472.)

Royal 12.G. viii

Liber Novem Judicum - Jacobus Alkindus (fourteenth century Latin). (Printed with the omission of the first part at Venice 1509. *See also* Sloane 268 and Oxford Digby 149.)

Sloane 268

Ars judicatoria secundum novem judices (seventeenth century). (A *Libri delle sorti.*)

Sloane 309

Excerpta geomantica (fifteenth century).

Sloane 310

ff. 1-66. Gerardi Carmonensis *Geomantia. Praefigitur haec rubrica, 'In nomine illius, qui major est, incipit liber Geomancie magistri Girardi Crimonensis ab auditoribus via astronomic a composita'* (fifteenth century).

Sloane 312

ff. 252-255b, 215. Abraham ben Meir Aben Ezra. *'Perfectus est liber electionum laudabilium horarum ab Hali filio Hamethembram, translatus de Arabico in Latinum in civitate Barchinona* [Barcelona] *ab Abraam Judeo existente interprete, qui dicitur Salva Corda* [Savasorda?]*: perfecta est translatio.* (fifteenth century).

Sloane 314

ff. 2-65. *Et est Gremmgi Indyana, que vocatur filia astronomie quam fecit unus sapientum Indie.* ['This is the Indyana (i.e. geomancy) of Gremmgi which is called the daughter of astronomy and which one of the sages of India wrote.'] (fifteenth century).

Sloane 887

ff. 3-59b. *Liber Geomantie* (sixteenth century Italian).

ff. 68b-80. *Observationes quaedam astrologicae et geomanticae; cum figuris.* (sixteenth century).

Sloane 2186

ff. 1-97. Treatise on Geomancy (Probably a transcript from the Geomancy of Christopher Cattan). (seventeenth century).

Sloane 2472

ff. 3-30. Bernard Silvestris. *Experimentarius* (twelfth-century *libro delle sorti* - a copy of Bodleian MS. Ashmole 304).

Sloane 3487

ff. 1-193/233. Ro[landus] Scriptorici (physician to John Duke of Bedford). '*Compilatorium sive aggregatorum totius Artis Geomanciae.*' '*Explicit aggregatorium sive compilatorum geomancie editum per Ro[landus] Scriptoris...quantum possibile est ad astronomiam redacta. Et est scriptum per Martinum Carum auctoritatibus Apostolica et Imperiali notarium.*' (fifteenth century). *(See also* Royal 12.G. xii.)

Sloane 3554

ff. 14-31v. Bernard Silvestris.

Amalricus Physicus (Geomancy by wheel - fifteenth century).

Sloane 3810

ff. 1-79v. 'Treatise of Geomancy' by Nicholas Monnel (sixteenth century, French).

Sloane 3857

ff. 164-195b. Bernard Sylvestris. *Experimentarius.* (a Latin 'lots' book).

ff. 196-206. *Consideratio Socratica* (a book of 'lots' in Latin).

ff. 207-221. *Consideratio Pythagorae* (a book of 'lots' in Latin).

ff. 222-247v. Geomancy.

Montefiore Collection:

Hirschfeld No. 436[1]

f. 1. Geomancy

ff. 4-20v. *Mishpetei ha-Goral u-Ma'asehu* a lot book/geomancy by ibn Ezra.

ff. 20v-55. *Mishpat ha-Edim.*

ff. 55v-61. *Pesakim al Mishpetai ha-Goral*

ff. 66-73v. Another *Pesakim al Mishpetai ha-Goral*

[1] Or 432. Sold at Sotheby's in 2004. Current whereabouts unknown. See Figure 3, Plate XII and Plate XIII.

Warburg Institute:

Warburg FMH 2770

Morath, Johan Mathaeus von Creussen. MS containing astrological and geomantic tables, 1646.

Wellcome Institute:

MS 394

ff. 33-231. German geomancy of Knodus.

MS 531

ff. 1-30v. Gerard of Cremona.
ff. 35-36v. Geomantic notes.
ff. 38v-42v. *De stolio.*

MS 559

f. 46. Geomantic questions.

OXFORD

All Souls 96

ff. 1-15. Geomancy.
ff. 16-41. [Walter] Cato, Astrological geomancy in 125 chapters, c.1400. (Probably a translation from Arabic.)

Bodleian:

Ashmole 4

ff. 5-6. '*De 16 figuris Geomantiae, cum diversum notarum explicatione*'.
ff. 7-11. '*Hic incipiunt Flores quaestionem et judiciorum veritatis artis Geomantiae.*'
ff. 32-39v. *Tabula imaginum figurarum cum naturis et proprietatibus suis Ricardi Regis secundi*... King Richard II.
ff. 40-42. *Rosarium Regis Ricardi*...
ff. 44-47b. 'Gerardus Crimenensis *(sic)... variae quaestiones ex eo auctore deceptae.*'
ff. 47b-48b. '*Observationes ex libro Geomantiae compilato per magistrum Martinum Hispanum* [Martin of Spain] *Abbatem de Cernatis in ecclesia Burgen.*'
ff. 49-70. Various short geomantic questions (c. 1600. Includes a late recension of '*Estimaverunt Indi....*')

Ashmole 5

Art. 5: *16 figuris* (of geomancy) (fourteenth century).

Ashmole 304

ff. 2-30. '*Experimentarius Bernardini Silvestris...*' (a 'lot' book, not a geomancy. Thirteenth century, bound with other *libri delle sorti*).

Ashmole 342

ff. 2-22v. Bernard Silvestris.
ff. 30-34. Albedatus.

Ashmole 345

ff. 64-70. Bernard Silvestris.

Ashmole 354

ff. 5-170. 'S[imon] Forman *de Arte Geomantica*' 1589.
f. 198. '*Tabula... Geomantica.*'

Ashmole 360

ff. 15-44. English translation of Martin of Spain's *De Geomancia.*

Ashmole 392

ff. 46-254. '*Geomantiae liber per* [Simon] Forman' (a large practical treatise).

Ashmole 393

Art. 8. Geomantic tables (of the sixteenth century translated in Ashmole MS 417, art 33 (2)).

Ashmole 398

ff. 1-118b. William of Moerbeke. 'Ci comence la grand et la parfit [S]overaigne de Geomancie...' (fourteenth century).

Ashmole 399

ff. 54-58. Bernard Silvestris.

Ashmole 417

f. 124. 'How to know ye places... ' (geomancy).
ff. 126-141b. A treatise on geomancy in English.
ff. 169-176b. 'An introduction unto Geomancy. Nom yelkin Zyobrim.' [Nikolei Mirboys?]
ff. 177-180v. Abdallah in English.
ff. 181-183b. 'They that are desirous to give true judgement accordinge to... Geomancie.'

Ashmole 434

ff. 114-137, 36-41. Roland Scriptorius. '*Magna pars cujusdam tractatus, sive Summerum, de Geomantia....*' 'The [arte?] of geomancye by the worthie doctoure Parysiences [Parisiensis] in hys booke....'

Ashmole 1478

ff. 120-121v. 'To know ye intent of the querent' [by geomancy].

Ashmole 1488
II, f. 138-140. Questions resolved by geomancy, by Napier.

Bodley 581
ff. 9-89. *Liber Ricardi secundi.* Richard II.

Bodley 625
ff. 1-7v. *Acquisitio in Ariete continetur…*
ff. 8-13v. Rules about the intention and the querent.
Ff 14-54. Gerard of Cremona. *Si de statu…*
ff. 54-85. Hugh of Santalla.

Can. Misc. 46

Digby 46
ff. 1-39. *Experimentarius...* Bernard Silvestris (a 'lot' book not a geomancy. Two toothed divining wheels are inset into the cover).
ff. 93-106v. *Ars geomantiae.*
ff. 109b-110. *De geomantia Quaedam* (fourteenth century?).

Digby 50
ff. 1-92v. Hugh of Santalla.
ff. 93-106. *Notandum quod Leticia et Acquisitio…*

Digby 74
ff. 1-52v. Gerardi Cremonensis, sive Carmonensis, *Tractatus in Artem Geomantiae* (sixteenth century).

Digby 104
ff. 85v-89v. Geomancy.

Digby 127
ff. 56-66v. But of an old written boke of geomancie…
ff. 68-84. Out of the book of geomancye…

Digby 133
ff. 61-95v. *Geomancia e una scientia breve…*

Digby 134
ff. 1-128v. Bartholomew of Parma - *Summa* (complete version of 1288 CE), 128 fols. in an Italian hand, '*Ars Geomantie que docet hominem solvere omnes questiones de quibus vult certificari divina virtute per istam artem... Compositus quidem est iste presens liber a magistro Bartholomeo de Parma in Bononia* [?] *ad preces domini Tedesii de Flisco, qui erat tunc ellectus in episcopum civitatis Regii, curentibus annis Domini* MCCLXXXVIII.' (fifteenth century).

Rawlinson D 534

ff. 2-74. *Geomantia e una scienza breve…*

Rawlinson D 1227

ff. 35-38. Geomantic questions.

ff. 38v-40v. Plato of Tivoli.

Selden Supra 82. *Ein natürliche Kunst der Geomancia…*

Selden Supra 83. *Diss Buch, das ist ein Buech in Geomanici…*

Other Oxford Libraries:

Auct. F. 3-13, f. 104 et seq. Bernard Silvestris.

Hertford College 4, ff. 197-245v. *Incipit nobilis ars que geomancia nuncapata…*

Lyell 36, f. 34v-50v. Bernard Silvestris.

CAMBRIDGE

Clare College 15

ff. 145-169v. Alfadhol de Merengi.

ff. 174-184v. Latin geomancy.

Corpus Christi 190

ff. 11-52. Martin of Spain geomancy.

Emmanuel 70

Bartholomew of Parma - *Summa* (complete version) (fifteenth century), f. 80 gives the date as 1286 instead of 1288; '*Incipit breviloquium mag. bartholomei nacione parensis bononie compilatum et confirmatum per prudentes viros de fructis tocius astronomie ad preces domini Thedesii de fusco anno* 1286.'

Magdalene F. 4. 27

ff. 1-66. '*Ludus philosophorum qui apellatur filius* [? *filia*] *Astronomie. Rerum opifex deus qui sine exemplo nova condidit universa… Ego sanctelliensis geomantie interpretacionem ingredior et tibi mi domine tirasonensis antistes…*' Hugh of Santalla's *Ars Geomantiae* (late fourteenth century).

ff. 72-88. '*Hec est geomentia Indiana que vocatur filia Ast... quam fecit unius [sic] sapientum Indie....*'

ff. 120-125. Plato of Tivoli.

Magdalene Pepys 911

f. 59r. Socrates *Prognostica.* (Fortune telling by 'lots', not geomancy)

Trinity College 0. 7. 40

Last folio. Geomantic questions.

Trinity College 0. 8. 29 – II
ff. 2-16. Bernard Silvestris.

Trinity College 0. 9. 35
ff. 1-126v. William of Moerbeke geomancy (in French).

Trinity College 0. I. 46.
ff. 1-164. French geomancy.

Trinity College 1404 (II) (a book of 'lots' in Latin, not a geomancy).

Trinity College 1447

University Library Add. 1195
15th-16th century geomancy

University Library Add. 1705 (Ii. I. 13)
ff. 184-209. Latin geomancy.

EUROPE

AIX-EN-PROVENCE

Bibliothèque Municipale 1298 (1180)
ff. 1-96. *Estimaverunt Indi.*

BERLIN

Staatsbibliothek Lat. 965
ff. 64 et seq. Albedatus

BOLOGNE

Bibliothèque de l'Université Lat. 449 (760). Gerard of Cremona.

BRUGES

Bibliothèque Publique Lat. 524
ff. 47-74. Gerard of Cremona.

BRNO *Czech Republic*

Augustinian Monastery A 48
f. 71v-149r *Practica Geomantiae*

CASSEL

Landesbibliothek, Astronomy quarto 16
ff. 1-42. William of Moerbeke
ff. 43-75. Abdallah
ff. 75v-76v. Salio of Padua.

CHANTILLY

Musée Condé 322
ff. 37-48v. Latin geomancy (abridged Bartholomew of Parma) 1295.
ff. 49-61v. Latin geomancy.

DRESDEN

Sächsische Landesbibliothek Oc. 63
ff. 1-194. French translation of *Quoniam quamplures predecessorum…*

Sächsische Landesbibliothek N 100
f. 203r Geomantic treatise & *Sphera Pithagorae*

ERFURT

Bibliothèque Amplonius:

Quarto 345
ff. 47-50. Latin geomancy.

Quarto 361
ff. 62-68. Gerard of Cremona *De statu corporis.*
ff. 68v-69. *Acquisitio in Ariete continentur…*
ff. 69-70. *Tutela Exiens in prima domo…*
ff. 70v-74. *De significatione 12 domorum…*
ff. 74v-78. Hugh of Santalla.
ff. 78v-79. Geomantic questions.

Quarto 365
ff. 53-82. *Estimaverunt indi…*

Quarto 373
ff. 1-31v. Gerard of Cremona.
ff. 32-37. Note on Acquisitio.
ff. 39-118. William of Moerbeke.

Quarto 377
ff. 62-70v. William of Moerbeke.
ff. 70v-76. Hugh of Santalla.

ff. 76v-77v. *Tutela Intrans in prima domo...*

Quarto 380
ff. 1-47. Abdallah.

Quarto 384
ff. 1-82. William of Moerbeke.

Octavo 88
ff. 1-5. Albedatus.

Folio 389
ff. 56-99. Abdallah.

ERLANGEN

Universitätsbibliothek Papierhandschr. 666
ff. 1-104. William of Moerbeke.

FLORENCE

Bibliothèque Nationale:

Palat. 945
ff. 148-166. *Geomantia dicitur ex terra...*
ff. 239-252. *Estimaverund indi...*
ff. 253-258v. *In hujus operis principio...*
ff. 259-263. Gerard of Cremona, *Si de statu corporis...*

Magliabech XX, 13
ff. 1-60. Bartholomew of Parma - *Summa* (abbreviated version of 1294). *'Incomincia illibro dell' arte della geomancia nuovamente compilato da maestro Bartholomeo da Parma a contemplatione de' suoi scholari da Bologna anno Domini* MCCLXXXXIIII' (dated 1294 but fifteenth century).
ff. 61-97v. Gerard of Cremona (in Italian).
ff. 101-208v. William of Moerbeke (in Italian).
ff. 211-259v. Abdallah (in Italian).
Many other geomancies.

Bibliothèque Laurentian:

Laurentian, Plut. 29 cod. 4.
ff. 1-45. Alfadhol de Merengi.
Laurentian, Plut. 30 cod. 29.
ff. 1-25v. Hugh of Santalla's *Geomantia Nova 'Incipit liber geomantie nove magistri Ugonis Satiliensis, editus ab Alatrabuluci translatione...*

Estimaverunt indi... (thirteenth century?).

Laurentian, Plut. 89 sup. 34.

ff. 11-20. Ptolemy.
ff. 27-42. William of Moerbeke.
ff. 55-90. Latin geomancy.
ff. 90-177v. Gerard of Cremona *Si de statu corporis...*
ff. 188-274. *Libro quarto di geomantia...*
ff, 279-286. Geomantic consultations (1555-56).

Laurentian, Plut. 88. 58. (geomancies 15th-16th centuries)

Bibliothèque Riccard:

Lat. 829

ff. 43-76. *estimaverunt indi...*

KRACOW

Biblioteka Jagiellońska:

BJ 793

ff. 63v-73r *Sortilegium Geomanticum* [4 separate texts][1]
ff. 81r-85v Albedatus *Geomantia*

BJ 805

ff. 405-409 *Geomantia* (pre-1364)

BJ 838

Liber Geomantiae of Hugh of Santalla

LYON

Bibliothèque Municipale 1364

ff. 1-80. Gerard of Cremona (in Italian).

MUNICH

Staatsbibliothek:

CLM 192

f. 3-40v. Bartholomew of Parma - *Summa* (abbreviated version of 1294 and 1295). This copy 1544 CE.
ff. 41-139. Geomancy in Latin.

CLM 196

---

[1] See Plate XV and Plate XVII.

ff. 1-84v. Bartholomew of Parma - *Summa* (abbreviated version of 1294) (fifteenth -sixteenth century).

CLM 240

ff. 1-128. Bartholomew of Parma - *Summa* (abbreviated version of 1294 and 1295) (fifteenth century).

CLM 242

ff. 2-55v. *Hoc opus scientiae.*

ff. 56v-83. Acquisitio...

CLM 276

ff. 69-75. *Geomantia mag. Gerardi Cremonensis* (fourteenth century).

ff. 93-95v. *Geomancia est vaticinatio terrenorum...*

CLM 392

ff. 1-54v. *In nomine sia dedo...*

ff. 69-75v. *Desiderantibus...*

ff. 81-90. Petrus de Abano *Geomantia* (fifteenth century). Alkindi?

ff. 91-147v. *Geomantia dicitur a geos grece...*

CLM 398

ff. 1-105. Bartholomew of Parma - *Summa* (abbreviated versions of 1294 and 1295).

ff. 106-114. Albedatus.

ff. 116-138. Nativities.

CLM 436

ff. 1-45v. *Quoniam quamplures...*

f. 46-56. *Geomantia dicitur...* Bartholomew of Parma - *Summa* (complete version of 1288) (sixteenth century copy).

CLM 458

ff. 38-96v. *Archanum sublimis et magni Dei...*

ff. 105-116. Ptolemy.

ff. 142-153v. Gerard of Cremona.

CLM 483

ff. 1-109v. *Quoniam quamplures...*

ff. 110-114. *Omipotens opifex...*

CLM 489

(art. 1) ff. 1-60. Bartholomew of Parma - *Summa 'Incipit Prologus Libri Geomantiae editi a mgro Bartholomeo Parmensi Astrologo. Erba collecta de libro magno Geomantiae quae introducunt novum discipulum ut sciat sufficienter principia eiusdem artis per quae poterit cognoscere tot et tanta de arte Geomantia quod per se sciat universales regulas artis doctrinae ac questiones quaerentium generales iudicare absque errore si Deus voluerit. Hoc quidem opus est Bartholomaei astrologi Natione Parmensis Compilatum Anno Domini MCCLXXXXV Mense, Novembris Sole existente in primo gradu Sagittarii.'*

(art. 2) f. 61-110v. Bartholomew of Parma - *Summa* (abbreviated version of 1294) *'Incipit breviloquium artis Geomantiae noviter compilatae a mgro Bartholomeo de Parma, quod breviloquium extraxit de summa eius artis quam compilavit anno 1288 ad partes (preces) nobilis viri Theoderici de flisco. Et sic complevisse fatetur utrumque opus fideliter et verius quam scivit utilia scribens et superflua relinquens in hoc opusculo ad preces duorum suorum amicorum et discipulorum Johannes et Paulus Theutonicorum sub Anno Domini 1494* [1294] *de mense Octobris in Bononia'* (sixteenth century copy).

ff. 111-169v. *Populus e mediocre…*

(art. 3) ff. 174-206v. Michael Scot's *Geomantia. 'Incipit liber Geomantiae Michaelis Scoti. Geomantia dicitur ars judicandi per terram'* (sixteenth century).

(art. 4) ff. 207-221v. Alkindi's geomancy (sixteenth century).

(art. 5) Peter de Abano's *Geomantia* (sixteenth century).

CLM 541

ff. 1-70v. Gerard of Cremona.

ff. 74v-146. *Judicium temporum figurarum…*

CLM 547

ff. 2-85v. Bartholomew of Parma. 1295 version.

ff. 86-158. *Estimaverunt indi…*

(2) ff. 1-67v. *Geomantia dicitur a geos, quod est terra…*

CLM 588

ff. 6-55. William of Moerbeke.

ff. 56-57. *Acquisitio in Ariete continentur…*

ff. 62v-66v. Hugh of Santalla.

ff. 67v-78. *Superior pars firmamenti…*

ff. 78-79. *Capitulum de via puncti…*

CLM 595

ff. 1-6v. *Tabule continents…*

CLM 671

ff. 82v-84v. Notes of Conrad Buitzrosis.

ff. 89-98. Albedatus.

CLM 677

ff. 1-18 Bernard Silvestris.

ff. 19v-97. Gerard of Cremona.

CLM 905

ff. 1-64v. William of Moerbeke.

CLM 1697

f. 246. An elaborate astrological geomancy compiled for Richard II in 1391. *(See also* Royal 12. C. v.)

CLM 3216

ff. 18-113v. *Rerum opifex Deus...*
ff. 116-131v. *De iteratione omnium figurarum...*

CLM 11998

Fasciculus Geomanticus. Fludd, de Pisis, etc.

CLM 17711

Agrippa.

CLM 24940

ff. 1-25v. *Secundum precepta priorum inventorum...*
ff. 25v-30. *Dicitur in libro quod Estimaverunt indi...*
ff. 31-96. Geomantic questions.
ff. 98-106v. *In judicio geomancie, 9 sunt considerande...*
ff. 107-109. Notes on the points.
ff. 110-148. Gerard of Cremona.
ff. 155-162. *Quicumque vult habere artem...*
ff. 168-199v. *Igitur in revolutione firmamenti...*

CLM 26061

ff. 1-71v. *Antiqui philosophi considerantes...*

CLM 27032

ff. 23-24v. *Excerpta de geomancia...*

NUREMBERG

Bibliothèque Math.

2° 3, No. 11. *Methodus universalis Archani sublime et magni Dei...*

PARIS

Bibliothèque Arsenal:

MS 824

ff. 39v-75. Agrippa. *Remarques sur la Géomance.*

Bibliothèque Nationale:

BN Hebrew MS

Various rules relative to geomancy (c. 1320).

BN 8 (Arabico-Malgache collection).

BN 2406 (Greek geomancy).

BN 2419 (Greek geomancy).

BN 2424 (Greek geomancy).

BN Arabe 2631, 2632, 2697, 2699, 2716, 2725, 2727, 2730, 2731, 2732, 2734, 2758 (Arabic geomancies).

BN Fr. 2488
ff. 9 et seq. William of Moerbeke (in French).

BN Fr. 4066
ff. 71v-99. *La geomance, fille naturelle de l'astrologie est une science...*

BN Fr. 14777
Christopher Cattan (in French).

BN It. 449
ff. 2-14v. *Incomincia il numero delle figure...*

BN Lat. 7323
ff. 1 et seq. Alfadhol de Merengi.

BN Lat. 7348
ff. 3-6v. *Quoniam sapientes scientiam astrologie...*

BN Lat. 7349
ff. 106v-114. *Ail yes la manyera de far...*
ff. 130v-138. Hermes.
ff. 138v-141. Ptolemy.

BN Lat. 7353
ff. 1-65v. *Ad sciendum uti ac arte geomancie...*
ff. 66-68. *Scientia reperiendi ascendens questionis...*

BN Lat. 7354
ff. 2-55v. *Ars Geomantiae* of Hugh of Santalla (similar incipit to Cambridge Magdalene 27).

BN Lat. 7355
ff. 1-116. *Ingredientibus vel incipientibus...*
ff. 121-126. Art of geomancy.

BN Lat. 7378 A
f. 64. John de Morys.

BN Lat. 7420 A

ff. 109-112. Geomantic poem.
ff. 115-121. Geomantic poem.
f. 121v. *Si tu vis operare de geomancia...*
f. 126. Socrates *Prognostica.* (Fortune telling by 'lots', not geomancy)

BN Lat. 7457
ff. 1-64v. *Archanum magni et sublimis Dei...*
ff. 83-96. Ptolemy.

BN Lat. 7458
ff. 1-66. *In superioribus compendiis de astronomie...*
ff. 68-104. *Incipit libellus geomantiae ex hispano in latinum translatus...*

BN Lat. 7486
ff. 1-30 (?). *'Incipit liber alkardiani phylosophi. Cum omne quod experitur sit experiendum propter se vel propter aliud...'*
(fourteenth century). Alkardiani's geomancy.
ff. 30v-45v. Bernard Silvestris.
ff. 46-66. Albedatus.

BN Lat. 7487
ff. 1-132. *Pro intellectu artis geomantiae...*

BN Lat. 7488
ff. 5v-58. *Pro intellectu artis geomantiae...*

BN Lat. 10270
ff. 83-84. Salio de Padoue.

BN Lat. 14068
ff. 50-58v. Socrates *Prognostica.* (Fortune telling by 'lots', not geomancy)

BN Lat. 14070
ff. 131-141. Gerard of Cremona. *Si de statu corporis...*

BN Lat. 14778
Dictionnaire de Gèomance et des Rosecroix, 1778.

BN Lat. MS 15353
ff. 87-92. Ptolemy.

BN Lat. *Libellus geomantie juxta arabum semitas ex arabico in hispanum...*

PRAGUE

Bibliothèque Publique XIV.H.13

ff. 112-144. Gerard of Cremona. *Si de statu corporis…*

PNK XI C 2 (2027)

ff. 70-71 *Cursus fortunae (geomantia)*
ff. 72v-77 *Tractatus geomanticus*
ff. 78-85 *Tractatus geomanticus*

ST. PETERSBURG

National Library:

Yevr. I 262 (14th-15th centuries)

SEVILLE

Bibliothèque Colombine 5.2.27

ff. 1-68. *Libro de los juygios de Calatarama.*

UPSALA

MS C. 619

Geomancy.

VATICAN

Palat. Lat. 1392

ff. 144-154. *Die hebt sich an das buch…*

Palat. Lat. 1457

Hugh of Santalla.

Urbin. 262

ff. 2 et seq. Abdallah.

VENICE

S. Marco VIII, 44

ff. 64r-99r. Geomancy of Iohannis de Muris (fourteenth century), *'Compilatio magistri Iohannis de Muris in arte geome're (sic)… Sicut dicit Boetius in arismetica sua, omnia que a primeva rerum origne processerunt ratione numerorum formata sunt....'*
ff. 99v-102. *Et scias quod quando line lineantur…*
ff. 102-157. Gerald of Cremona.

VIENNA

Nationalbibliothek:

Lat. 2352

ff. 83-96. King Wenceslaus' geomancy dated 1392/3. [A very important geomancy unaccountably omitted by Charmasson]

Lat. 2469

ff. 1-40v. Bartholomew of Parma. 1288 version. (a later copy)
ff. 42-56v. *Prima domo querit de vita...*

Lat. 2804

ff. 22-101. Alfadhol de Merengi (in German).

Lat. 3059

ff. 73-92. Gerard of Cremona. *Si de statu corporis...*
ff. 93-105. William of Moerbeke.
ff. 136-172. William of Moerbeke.

Lat. 5327

ff. 59r-60v. *Operis de geomantia ad Tirasconensem anstitem prologus et caput primum* (fifteenth century). Hugh of Santalla's geomancy - prologue and first chapter only.
ff. 61-132. Hugh of Santalla (in German).

Lat. 5508

ff. 1-41v. *Omnipotens sempitern Deus...* William of Moerbeke.
ff. 41v-117. Gerard of Cremona.
ff. 117-123. *Sequitur in judicio geomancie, 9 sunt inquirenda...*
ff. 123v-137. *Ut scias intentionem querentis...*
ff. 137-141. *Punctis est punctus 15 signo...*
ff. 146v-157v, 209-218. Anthonius Majus.
ff. 182-200. Hugh Sacelliensis sive Saxaliensis, *Geomantia, 'Rerum opifex dues...sive mundus facie'* (fourteenth century). Hugh of Santalla's *Ars Geomantiae* (similar incipit of Cambridge Magdalene 27).

Lat. 5523

ff. 1-205v Bartholomew of Parma - *Summa* (complete version of 1288) (copy fifteenth - sixteenth century).

WOLFENBÜTTEL

Landesbibliothek 2725, ff. 95-205. William of Moerbeke.

WURZBURG

Universitätsbibliothek M ch. Ff. 167-214v. William of Moerbeke.

Index

Made in United States
Troutdale, OR
07/08/2023

11053762R00184